Canada: The State of the Federation 2005

Quebec and Canada in the New Century

New Dynamics, New Opportunities

Edited by

Michael Murphy

Institute of Intergovernmental Relations
School of Policy Studies, Queen's University
McGill-Queen's University Press
Montreal & Kingston • London • Ithaca

Canadian Cataloguing In Publication Data

Library and Archives Canada has catalogued this publication as follows:

Canada, the state of the federation

Annual.
1985-
Continues: Year in review (Kingston, Ont.), ISSN 0825-1207.
ISSN 0827-0708
ISBN 978-1-55339-017-6 (2005 edition ; bound).—ISBN 978-1-55339-018-3 (2005 edition ; pbk.)

1. Federal-provincial relations—Canada—Periodicals. 2. Federal government—Canada—Periodicals. I. Queen's University (Kingston, Ont.). Institute of Intergovernmental Relations II. Title: State of the federation.

JL27.F42 1985-   321.02'3'0971   C86-030713-1 rev

The Institute of Intergovernmental Relations

The Institute is the only organization in Canada whose mandate is solely to promote research and communication on the challenges facing the federal system.

Current research interests include fiscal federalism, health policy, the reform of federal political institutions and the machinery of federal-provincial relations, Canadian federalism and the global economy, and comparative federalism.

The Institute pursues these objectives through research conducted by its own staff and other scholars, through its publication program, and through seminars and conferences.

The Institute links academics and practitioners of federalism in federal and provincial governments and the private sector.

The Institute of Intergovernmental Relations receives ongoing financial support from the J.A. Corry Memorial Endowment Fund, the Royal Bank of Canada Endowment Fund, the Government of Canada, and the governments of Manitoba and Ontario. We are grateful for this support which enables the Institute to sustain its extensive program of research, publication, and related activities.

L'Institut des relations intergouvernementales

L'Institut est le seul organisme canadien à se consacrer exclusivement à la recherche et aux échanges sur les questions du fédéralisme.

Les priorités de recherche de l'Institut portent présentement sur le fédéralisme fiscal, la santé, la modification éventuelle des institutions politiques fédérales, les mécanismes de relations fédérales-provinciales, le fédéralisme canadien au regard de l'économie mondiale et le fédéralisme comparatif.

L'Institut réalise ses objectifs par le biais de recherches effectuées par son personnel et par des chercheurs de l'Université Queen's et d'ailleurs, de même que par des congrès et des colloques.

L'Institut sert comme lien entre les universitaires, les fonctionnaires fédéraux et provinciaux et le secteur privé.

L'Institut des relations intergouvernementales reçoit l'appui financier du J.A. Corry Memorial Endowment Fund, de la Fondation de la Banque Royale du Canada, du gouvernement du Canada et des gouvernements du Manitoba et de l'Ontario. Nous les remercions de cet appui qui permet à l'Institut de poursuivre son vaste programme de recherche et de publication ainsi que ses activités connexes.

CONTENTS

FOREWORD

In the period leading up to the Institute's annual conference in 2003, the decision was taken to revisit on an old but enduring theme in Canadian federalism – Quebec-Canada relations. Several factors influenced this decision. Following the 1995 referendum the country witnessed a steady decline in the intensity of the sovereignty debate. Public exhaustion with the issue and the apparent success of the *Clarity Act* in Quebec combined to deprive the Parti Québécois and Premier Lucien Bouchard of the winning conditions for a third and final referendum. Unable to advance the nationalist agenda, and weary of negotiating the fractious internal politics of his own party, Bouchard resigned from politics in 2001 and the sovereignty struggle had lost its most eloquent champion since René Lévesque. Succeeding Bouchard as leader of the Parti Québécois, Bernard Landry proved equally unsuccessful at reviving the sovereignty agenda. Quebecers were seemingly more concerned about health care, education, employment and economic development, security, and the environment – the same issues dominating the public agenda in the rest of the country. Completing the picture, in the 2003 election the Parti Québécois was replaced by a Liberal government committed to federalism and a more constructive relationship with the federal government.

Could it be that we were on the verge of a fundamental transformation of Quebec society and politics, and a critical realignment of Quebec's relationship with Canada and the rest of the world? Perhaps we were witnessing the rise of a new generation of Quebecers for whom the issue of sovereignty no longer constituted a viable or compelling challenge? Might the abatement of overt nationalist sentiment be attributed to the success of nationalist policies themselves, particularly those relating to the French language? Or perhaps fundamental change was not afoot in Quebec and it was only a matter of time before the right constellation of political circumstances once again fanned the flames of separatism? On 31 October 2003, the Institute of Intergovernmental Relations invited a group of established and emerging scholars to assess these new dynamics in Quebec society and politics, and to examine their implications in the context of intergovernmental relations in Canada. The conference attracted over 25 speakers, and an audience of close to 100 academics, students, government officials and interested members of the general public. The

Keynote Address was delivered by M. Benoît Pelletier, Quebec's Minister for Canadian Intergovernmental Affairs and Native Affairs.

Canada: The State of the Federation 2005 gathers together a selection of these conference papers which have been peer-reviewed and substantially revised for publication. If there is an overall message in the volume it is that the national question continues to be central to Quebec's internal politics and Quebec-Canada relations, but the tone and complexion of the nationalist debate is showing signs of change, and this may present fresh opportunities for constructive engagement between Quebec and the other members of the Canadian federation. Viewed in the context of recent events, the essays in this volume are more timely than ever. After an extended period of absence, the national question was abruptly, and unexpectedly, thrust onto the public stage during the 2006 federal Liberal leadership race, soon to find its way even more unexpectedly into Parliament in the Harper government's (ultimately successful) motion to recognize Quebec as a nation within a united Canada. With these events in tow, we now find ourselves on the eve of a Quebec Provincial election pitting the frequently embattled Liberal government of Jean Charest against Parti Québécois newcomer André Boisclair, and ADQ leader Mario Dumont – still searching for a breakthrough with a new generation of Quebecers. Quebec will also be a key battlefield in the looming federal election. Under new leader Stéphane Dion, the federal Liberals will strive to rebuild their support base after the debacle of the sponsorship scandal, but will face a freshly invigorated Conservative party that seems increasingly within striking distance of an elusive majority government. With both parties looking to pick up seats in Quebec, the depth of support enjoyed by the Bloc Québécois and its sovereignty message will also be on trial. For those with an interest in the future of Quebec and its place in the Canadian federation, this volume should prove to be stimulating and informative reading.

Credit is due to a number of individuals and organizations, without whom the conference and the book would not have been possible. First and foremost a warm thank you to our generous sponsors for their financial and logistical support: the Privy Council of Canada the Social Sciences and Humanities Research Council of Canada, the Government of Quebec, and the Canadian Network of Federalism Studies. A very special thanks to Harvey Lazar for his work in developing the thematic architecture of the conference and for hosting the event with such skill and good humor. Thanks also to Daniel Salée for his contribution to the intellectual development of the project, for his editorial assistance, and for an excellent job as a rapporteur on the final day of the conference. As ever, Mary Kennedy and Patti Candido carried the weight of the conference organization on their shoulders, and played a vital role in seeing the volume through to publication. Thanks also to Katrina Candido and Adele Mugford for their part in running a successful conference.

Thanks must also go out to a number of other individuals who helped along the way. To Richard Simeon, Martin Papillon and Marc Hanvelt for helpful suggestions on conference themes, and to Aron Seal, James Nicholson, Stéphanie Quesnelle, and Ying Feng for preparing the chronology of events. To Michael Munroe and Steve Sarik for audio taping the conference and preparing an excellent summary report of the proceedings for the Privy Council Office. A very special thanks for the excellent work of our panel discussants and chairs: Robert Young, David Cameron, Patrick Fafard, Peter Meekison, Richard Simeon, Ted Morton, Marc Levine, Alain Gagnon, Nelson Michaud, Alain Noël, Michel Venne, Claire Durand, and to Benoît Pelletier for taking the time out of a very busy schedule to deliver the keynote address. Thanks to our blind referees for donating their time and expertise, and to our authors for their valuable contributions and patient indulgence in waiting for a volume that was far too long in the making. To our desktop publishing team of Valerie Jarus and Mark Howes, to our copy editor Carla Douglas, and to Kingston Language Services, thanks once again for your excellent work. Last, but not least, thanks to Tom Courchene for preparing the introductory chapter on such short notice, and for helping guide the volume through the final stages of publication.

Michael Murphy
January, 2007

CONTRIBUTORS

Michael Murphy is Assistant Professor and Canada Research Chair in Comparative Indigenous State Relations at the University of Northern British Columbia.

Thomas J. Courchene is the Jarislowsky-Deutsch Professor of Economic and Financial Policy in Queen's School of Policy Studies and is senior scholar of the Institute for Research on Public Policy (Montreal). For the academic year 2006-2007 he is acting director of the Institute of Intergovernmental Relations.

Pascale Dufour is Assistant Professor in the Department of Political Science, Université de Montréal.

Peter Graefe is an Assistant Professor in the Department of Political Science, McMaster University, and a member of the Centre de recherche sur les politiques et le développement social, Université de Montréal.

Guy Laforest is Full Professor and teaches Political Science at Université Laval. His most recent book is Pour la liberté d'une société distincte: Parcours d'un intellectuel engagé, Québec: Presses de l'Université Laval, 2004.

Rachel Laforest is Assistant Professor and Head of the Public Policy and Third Sector Initiative at the School of Policy Studies, Queen's University. She is also senior research associate at the Centre for Voluntary Sector Research and Development, Carleton University.

Matthew Mendelsohn is Deputy Minister of Intergovernmental Affairs and Democratic Renewal for the Government of Ontario. He is on leave from the Department of Political Studies, where he is an Associate Professor.

Éric Montpetit is Associate Professor in the Department of Political Science, Université de Montréal. He is the author of *Misplaced Distrust*, winner of the 2006 American Political Science Association's Lynton Keith Caldwell Prize for the best book on environmental politics and policy.

Andrew Parkin is the Director of Research and Program Development at the Canada Millennium Scholarship Foundation. From 2000 to 2004, he served as research director and subsequently co-director at the Centre of Research and Information on Canada (CRIC).

Maurice Pinard is Professor Emeritus in the Department of Sociology at McGill University. He continues to follow closely the developments in Quebec politics.

John Richards teaches in Simon Fraser University's Graduate Public Policy School and is a fellow-in-residence at the C.D. Howe Institute.

Aron Seal served as a research assistant at the Institute of Intergovernmental Relations from March 2004 to July 2006. He graduated from Queen's University with a Master of Arts degree in Economics in September 2006; he is currently employed by SECOR Consulting as a business strategy analyst.

Brian Tanguay is Professor and Chair of the Department of Political Science at Wilfrid Laurier University. He is also Acting Coordinator of the Canadian Studies program.

I

Introduction

1

Introduction and Overview

Thomas J. Courchene

Le rôle principal de cette introduction est de présenter les articles des différents auteurs du volume Quebec and Canada in the New Century; New Dynamics, New Opportunities (Le Québec et le Canada en ce début de siècle : de nouvelles dynamiques et de nouvelles possibilités). Puisque plusieurs chapitres portent sur différents aspects du « modèle québécois », dans la dernière partie de cette introduction, on compare ce qu'on appelle désormais « le capitalisme individualiste » de la variété américaine et « le capitalisme communautarien » de la variété européenne continentale. Le modèle québécois se situe du côté du capitalisme communautarien, ce qui, entre autres, rend compte du leadership québécois sur le plan des mesures progressistes prises en matière de politique sociale. Tel que démontré par plusieurs auteurs, le débat et les préoccupations concernant l'avenir du modèle québécois, qui ont également cours dans d'autres sociétés pratiquant le capitalisme communautarien, ont joué un rôle dans les élections de 2003, et ils joueront sans doute un rôle encore plus important au cours des prochaines (au moment de la rédaction) élections en 2007.

INTRODUCTION

In the fall of 2003, Queen's University's Institute of Intergovernmental Relations hosted *Quebec and Canada in the New Century: New Dynamics, New Opportunities*, a conference held under the aegis of the Institute's Director, Harvey Lazar, and organized by Michael Murphy and Daniel Salée. As it turned out, and as reflected in the analyses of many of the chapters, the early years of the new century represented an eventful period in Quebec. Lucien Bouchard had recently resigned as Premier of Quebec and was replaced by Bernard Landry. The ensuing April 2003 election saw the defeat of the PQ at the hands of Jean Charest's Liberals. At the pan-provincial level, this led to the creation, under Charest's guidance, of the Council of the Federation (COF) and, again with Quebec's urging, the first priority of the COF was the restoration of vertical fiscal balance in the federation. While the rest of Canada (ROC) presumably took some comfort in the defeat of the PQ, almost immediately the support in Quebec for the Charest Liberals dropped dramatically, and equally dramatically the support for sovereignty rose above the 50 percent mark. One proximate cause of this collapse in Liberal support was their commitment to roll back some key aspects of the "Quebec model." Indeed, so sure was the PQ of regaining power at the next election that word was out that there would be yet another referendum by decade's end. This was the political environment in Quebec that prevailed as the conference participants prepared their contributions.

However, the current (January 2007) political environment in Quebec is markedly different – the Harper Conservatives are in power federally, replete with a political breakthrough in Quebec; Harper has embraced "open federalism" and is committed to redress vertical fiscal imbalance; and parliamentary legislation has recognized that the Québécois form a nation within a united Canada. Beyond this there is a widespread presumption that the 2007 federal budget will cater to Quebec and will be a direct lead-in to the Quebec election, an election that the Quebec Liberal Party (PLQ) may well win since they are now neck-and-neck with the PQ in the polls, a dramatic turnabout from the reality at conference time. Given this remarkable shift in the underlying political environment, it is important to again remind readers that the authors drafted their papers in the earlier time frame and that virtually all of the final drafts were completed before the appearance of the Harper Conservative minority government.

Because the events surrounding the forthcoming Quebec election are bound to be subjected to an intense research effort, this arguably makes the contributions in this volume all the more valuable since the period in question – from the election of the Charest government in 2003 to the events culminating with the Bouchard *et al* manifesto *Pour une Québec lucide* (2006) – will likely end up being relatively under-researched. And this is in spite of the fact that this was the very period in which Quebec's *concertation* or consensus model became the centre of much of the societal debate, as evidenced by the fact that the Quebec model is the focus of several of the ensuing papers. Morever, there are many aspects of the papers that provide insight or understanding to the recent turn of political events in Quebec.

With this backdrop, this introduction to the Institute's 2005 version of its *State of the Federation* series proceeds, first, by summarizing (often in the authors' words) the main thrust of each of the ensuing nine chapters and, then, by embarking on a brief interpretative commentary on the relationship between the Quebec model and the typical Anglo-American model, or between communitarian capitalism and individualist capitalism.

OVERVIEW OF THE AUTHORS' CONTRIBUTIONS

CHANGING ATTITUDES: 1996–2003

In Chapter 2 (*A New Chapter on the Same Old Story? Public Opinion in Quebec from 1996-2003)*, Matthew Mendelsohn, Andrew Parkin and Maurice Pinard assess the evolution of polling results on a range of Quebec/Rest-of-Canada socio-political issues. Drawing from the polling results, the authors advance six observations that have had an impact on the evolution of the province over the 1996–2003 period, and that capture the current state of play within Quebec and between Quebec and ROC. The first is a "demobilization" around the national question (*la question nationale*) as well as a "depolitization" of the Quebec electorate on issues relating to Quebec's place within Canada, albeit with a caution not to interpret this as a rejection of sovereignty. Second, Ottawa's focus on rules, processes and terms of future referendums and possible secession (including the 2000 Clarity Act) has helped federal forces in Quebec. Nonetheless, and their third point, some traditional grievances remain, justifying the above cautionary note. Fourth, the consensus around Quebec's distinct economic and social model is being contested, an issue that will be addressed in much more detail in several of the following chapters. Fifth, in addition to making French the working language of the province, Bill 101 has also succeeded in facilitating the integration of newcomers into Quebec society. Finally, Premier Charest's model of more cooperative intergovernmental relations with ROC (e.g., the Council of the Federation) has polling support. These conclusions lead the authors to argue that "the public opinion environment has undergone a shift, featuring a comfort with a multicultural and pluriethnic French-speaking Quebec, a questioning of the consensus around the Quebec social and economic model, and a decline of salience of and interest in the national question as it has been defined since 1970."

These broad generalizations mask a wealth of relevant detail relating to the attitudes of Quebecers. For example, even "[b]y 1999, Quebecers were overwhelmingly likely to believe that following a referendum victory for the 'Yes' side, secession would be quite difficult, even with a large and clear majority." Or, "Quebecers were more likely than Canadians in any other province to support more privatization in the health care field." And beyond these and many other implications, the authors append a lengthy data appendix which treats readers to much more detailed polling information presented in ways that can track changes over time.

This synthesis of Quebecers' attitudes over 1996–2003 is the appropriate underlying context for the later papers dealing with the internal social, political and institutional patterns of representation in Quebec. In order to provide similar backdrop to the final two papers dealing with Quebec/Canada relations, we need a broader sweep of the evolution of the national unity issue, to which we now turn.

REFLECTIONS ON *LA QUESTION NATIONALE*

In *One Never Knows ... Sait-on-jamais*? Guy Laforest appraises the long sweep of Canada/Quebec relations and particularly the lessons deriving from the sovereignty referendums. His initial point is that while the *Constitution Act 1982* marked the end of all forms of subordination of Ottawa to London, it left in place much of the former imperial remnants in the form of the Ottawa/Quebec relationship (and more generally the Ottawa/provinces relationship). In particular, it did not and still does not embrace the shared-rule, self-rule vision of federalism, in part because there is no provincial input at all in the governing institutions at the centre and also because the 1982 constitution has served to promote "a logic inimical to the political freedom and the distinct identity of Quebec" and, relatedly, has served to defederalize "the political culture of the country." In this context, it is only "natural" that many Quebecers, deeming the degree of political/constitutional recognition with Canada to be inadequate, would look toward the option of independence which, as Laforest notes, is "the highest, most advanced level of political fulfilment." This perceived failure of the federal idea led to the 1980 and 1995 "rebellions." This reference to "rebellions" is appropriate, Laforest asserts, since, in the sociology of political behaviour, "rationally and logically a referendum is a democratic political rebellion."

Laforest's second theme is that failed referendums have quite dramatic consequences: the sequence tends to be "rebellion, failure, tightening of the system, negative consequences for the losers." The negative consequences for Quebec of the 1980 referendum included the *Constitution Act, 1982*, and of the 1995 referendum included the *Clarity Act*. Additionally, in both cases Quebec and the sovereignty movement suffered setbacks, including for 1995 the demise of Parizeau and later, arguably, of Bouchard as well.

In terms of the immediate future, Laforest takes some comfort from the emergence of the Council of the Federation and from Harper's embracing "open federalism," recognizing fiscal imbalance and enlarging the role of Quebec in the international arena. At the same time, he suggests that Quebecers ought to become pro-active as well: "we should first recognize ourselves as Québécois, strengthening the backbone of our political community by placing some of our key laws (*Chartre des droits et libertés de la personne, Loi sur les consultations populaires, Loi 101*) in a fundamental document that would have its own amending formula and could possibly be ratified by the population in a referendum." By way of a concluding comment, Laforest notes that it is clearly possible that there will be a third referendum in the foreseeable future which, depending on the question, he may well support. His parting comment, how-ever, is a cautionary one: "we Québécois should integrate better in our public sphere my basic historical point [that] there are drastically negative conse-quences for a political community whenever those who organize a referendum happen to lose it."

Meanwhile, the political landscape within Quebec may well be undergoing a significant alteration, which could have implications for the likelihood of another referendum, as Tanguay informs us in Chapter 4.

REALIGNING QUEBEC'S PARTY SYSTEM

In *The Stalled Realignment: Quebec's Party System After the 2003 Provincial Election*, A. Brian Tanguay addresses two questions. The first is whether the 2003 Quebec election results imply that the anticipated surge of Mario Dumont's *Action démocratique du Québec* (ADQ) and the predictions of a "great realignment" of political parties have simply been postponed for an-other election cycle or were somehow grossly overestimated. The second part of Tanguay's contribution focuses on the prospects for the PQ and the sover-eignty movement in the aftermath of the 2003 election.

In terms of the likelihood that the ADQ would achieve a breakthrough in the 2003 election, Tanguay lists the following favourable factors that were in play in the election run-up: "[c]onstitutional fatigue and depolarization of the sovereignty issue; Mario Dumont's personal popularity as [ADQ] party leader; widespread dissatisfaction with the incumbent PQ government; deepening cynicism among voters about traditional political institutions [including as-pects of *concertation* or the Quebec model]; [the ADQ's] neo-liberal ideology that had a distinct appeal for certain segments of the francophone population; and disproportionate strength among the most politically engaged and aware sections of the electorate, those between the ages of 45 and 64." These factors are in addition to the four ADQ by-election wins in 2002, all previously held by the PQ. While the ADQ did increase its popular vote in the 2003 election from 12 percent to 18 percent and its number of seats from one to four, this was not the realignment predicted by Pinard and others. Tanguay concludes the "Quebec's two-and-a-half party system is likely to consign the ADQ to the margins of power in the province."

In terms of the fortunes of the PQ and the national question, Tanguay notes that support for sovereignty in May 2005 registered 54 percent, compared to only 40 percent at the time of the 2003 election, much of this resurgence due to the fact that "the Charest government has seen its popularity plummet as it has haltingly embarked on its project of 're-engineering' the provincial state." Since this may be attributable to voter unhappiness with the Liberals rather than an embrace of sovereignty, Tanguay then turns to addressing the set of challenges that have to be addressed if the sovereignty movement is to recapture its former dynamism. Among these is the challenge of holding the sovereignty coalition together:

> This party has always been a coalition of forces – social democrats, *bleus*, dysfunctional Liberals – held together by the glue of charismatic leadership (Lévesque, Parizeau, Bouchard) and by a common commitment to some notion of independence for Quebec ... Increasingly, unhappy social democrats in the province are opting out of the PQ, and they continue to attempt to create new, more progressive parties.

Related, but more succinctly, "the Parti Québécois itself is showing signs of its age, and party elitists are finding it increasingly difficult to hold together the centrifugal forces within the sovereignist coalition." This is a prescient observation since in February of 2006 (after Tanguay had completed his paper) a new left-wing party, *Quebec Solidaire*, came into being. More to the point, the PQ have tumbled in the polls.

The next four chapters address the various ways in which external (principally globalization) and internal forces have been brought to bear on the nature and role of what has come to be called the Quebec Model, beginning with Éric Montpetit's interpretation of the essence of this model.

THE QUEBEC MODEL

The Quebec model, and especially its industrial policy variant, often referred to as Quebec Inc., has come under criticism from a variety of quarters. In *A Policy Network Perspective on the Quebec Model*, Éric Montpetit draws on a wide range of relevant literature to distill the essence of what he perceives as the Quebec model and he then mounts a defence of this vision against all critics. This essence, writes Montpetit, is a *policy network perspective*: "a pattern of interconnection between organized civil society and state actors during the development and the implementation of a specific policy." In more detail:

> From a policy network perspective, interest groups are not blamed for carrying specific policy interests, but are valued for this contribution ... the public interest is not conceived as being somewhere out there waiting to be discovered by technical expertise, statistics or social movements. Rather, the public interest results from deliberation over interests brought into the policy process, notably but not exclusively, from interest groups.

Montpetit goes on to argue that among the various models of policy networks, the corporatist version ("[r]elatively closed to new actors; anchors relatively cohesive policy ideas; state and civil society actors are closely interconnected; policy capacities are evenly distributed between state and civil society actors") is the preferable perspective. This is so because corporatist networks are best at organizing deliberations which engage a manageable set of actors holding a diverse range of ideas. These deliberations are likely to deliver outcomes which represent a balance between cohesion and efficiency and are also likely to be deemed to be in the public interest, i.e. the corporatist model achieves "output-oriented legitimacy." Montpetit does recognize, however, that it does not fare all that well in terms of "input-oriented legitimacy" because, relative to other types of policy networks, it is closed to new actors. Indeed, he notes that "several of the attacks on the Quebec model ... have their origin in the exclusionary nature of corporatist policy networks."

Finally, with respect to industrial policy, Montpetit argues that, once implemented, industrial strategies then tend to generate corporatist policy networks and not the reverse. Specifically, corporatist policy networks did not generate the new strategy of clusters, but the implication would seem to be that these industrial clusters will now lead to new corporatist policy networks.

GLOBALIZATION AND NATIONAL QUESTION

Pascale Dufour's contribution, *Globalization as a New Political Space: The End of the Quebec-Quebec Debate?* assesses the impact of globalization from the perspective of a force that is serving to create a new political space which has "challenged the relationships between social forces (including the state) and has altered the framework of the nationalist debate in Quebec." Specifically, from the middle of the 1990s, globalization has progressively become a distinct political space, indeed a "field of political action, particularly for social actors who protest against globalization." One sees this coalition of progressive social forces in Quebec's 1996 economic and social summits, in the Quebec Peoples' Summit associated with the FTAA meetings in Quebec City, and also in support of Bill 112 (the law against poverty and social exclusion). Thus in this globalization playing field "[n]ew enemies are identified, new battlefields are designed, new actions take place, and new relationships are built between the various actors involved, including the state." A key conclusion from this perspective is that this rallying of social movements around the poverty, exclusion and anti-globalization nexus of issues has led to the situation where the internal debate in Quebec (i.e., the "Quebec-Quebec debate" alluded to in the title of the paper) is today "more accurately depicted in terms of a right-left problematic than in terms of a federalism-sovereignty problematic."

By way of elaborating on this point, the PQ government adopted two positions with respect to globalization: first, Quebec would gain from and, therefore, the PQ supports globalization and the opening of markets; second, if Quebec wants a voice in this globalization, it needs independence. In contrast, the social movements (at least those referred to by Dufour as the "progressive activists") view globalization and free markets as threats to their social agenda, whether Quebec is part of Canada or not. As a result it is increasingly difficult for social actors to be on side with the PQ since their support of free markets represents a "constraint" that prevents the [PQ] government from responding to social claims." Therefore, the development of globalization as a political space in Quebec has influenced the reappearance of the division between left and right, and the delegitimization (at least partially) of the traditional federalist-sovereignist debate.

Along similar lines, Dufour concludes that for the *Union des force Progressistes* and for the movement *Option citoyenne* (which united in February of 2006 to form a new political party, *Québec Solidaire*) "the question of the political status of Quebec is at best a secondary objective to the project of forging a more just and progressive society," and this, Dufour continues, "explains why today the PQ sovereignty platform looks like a political project with a very low probability of success.".

We now turn to the two generic groups – civil society and labour – that are integral players, alongside the state, in the Quebec model.

LABOUR AND THE QUEBEC MODEL

State Restructuring and the Failure of Competitive Nationalism: Trying Times for Quebec Labour is Peter Graefe's contribution of the recent evolution of the Quebec labour movement. His analysis begins by situating labour in relation to the state:

> [T]his essay will argue that [the unions (FTQ and CSN)] did manage to articulate a new strategic agenda in the late 1980s and early 1990s, which provided a means of renewing their intervention in a variety of spaces of economic and political governance, including the national question. The unions adopted a "progressive-competitive" political economy that argued for social partnerships or forms of "conflictual concertation" in the workplace and in forums of economic and social governance, on the grounds that this could lead to positive-sum class compromises. This led into an embrace of "competitive nationalism," wherein the nation [Quebec] could provide additional cultural resources and social solidarity to ease and reinforce such positive-sum compromises ...

While this strategy did bring initial successes, the paper goes on to highlight how competitive nationalism has handcuffed the labour federations, as the national imperative of competitiveness was taken up by firms and by the state to justify one-sided deals or inaction that served to hobble the transformative potential of the unions' project. With labour thus having cast its voice with the government, the women's and community movements have started to take on the mantle of articulating an alternative left-wing project.

By way of more detail, in a highly competitive environment a "progressive competitiveness" strategy offers capital a deal that is hard to refuse: unions can "agree to cooperate in enhancing productivity in return for employment guarantees, workplace democratization, and the maintenance of high wages and working conditions." The approach enabled a rapprochement with the PQ (i.e., the "competitive nationalism" alluded to earlier). And in the 1995 referendum, the federalist/sovereignist split closely mapped the right/left split, suggesting that a sovereign Quebec would be a more inclusive Quebec. Post referendum, however, this competitive-nationalist strategy pulled the unions in the Quebec government's direction of concluding that competitiveness required a significant reduction in public spending and government services: "competitiveness went from a shared objective that allowed for a renewal of the labour agenda around themes of democratization and participation, to a binding consensus that attacked the interests of their members." And of course, matters got considerably worse for the unions with the election in 2003 of the Charest Liberals and their intention to review aspects of the institutions inherited from the Quiet Revolution, especially the corporatist elements:

> Important changes in late 2003 included changes to the labour code facilitating contracting out, a partial reduction of the scope of the training tax ... and the reduction in the number of bargaining units in the health sector. More generally, the government has studiously bypassed existing mechanisms of shared governance and consultation.

Graefe concludes by noting that the unions' buying into the PQ's national competitiveness agenda made the union federations' projects look old and tired, and offside vis-à-vis the Quebec left. As a result, they are engaged in a rebuilding mode, such that over the medium term the challenge of "redefining the articulation of a mainstream nationalist project with progressive demands may nevertheless reduce conflict along the Quebec-Canada cleavage by reducing the salience of the sovereignty issue."

By way of a bridge to the civil society paper, Graefe notes that another result of the unions' embracing of competitive nationalism is that they came to "lose some of their dominance in setting the program for the Quebec left." The result was that civil society (the women's movement and the community movement) "overtook them as the leaders in articulating ideological alternatives to the government's restructuring policies." But even civil society was falling on hard times, as Rachel Laforest elaborates in her chapter.

CIVIL SOCIETY AND THE STRUCTURE OF REPRESENTATION

In *The Politics of State/Civil Society Relations in Quebec*, Rachel Laforest focuses first on the pivotal role that civil society has come to play in Quebec politics and policy making, and second on the dramatic transformation that this civil-society model is undergoing at the hands of the Jean Charest Liberal government. In terms of the first of these, Laforest argues that the "structure of representation" is the key to assessing the place of these community organizations within the broader society:

> [The structure of representation] directly affects the terms of access to policy making, the routes of political representation, the forms of political expression through which claims are made, and perhaps more importantly, it affects the legitimacy and credibility of the actors involved in the policy process.

Laforest argues that this web of civil society associations has championed a vision of society that recognized community participation as a fundamental exercise in citizenship and democracy and as a means of empowering citizens, often with the aim of developing "a *projet de societé* to shape values, to develop a vision for society and to bring about social change." The capstone of this civil society role came with the creation of the Secretariat for Autonomous Community Action which, among other things, assured civil society organizations of core funding "to support their original mission, to cover basic infrastructure needs (rent, staff, and equipment), and to cover the expenses for activities of consultation, representation, education and advocacy." What is particularly unique about this is that advocacy organizations will not have to rely on the ministry in their policy field in order to receive this funding. In other words, the "autonomy of the sector is protected by this distance between organizations and their lead departments."

The second part of Laforest's chapter ("The Dawn of a New Era") focuses on the reforms introduced by the Charest Liberals early in their mandate. Her views here are as straightforward as they are forceful and merit quotation in full:

> Since becoming premier, Jean Charest has publicly called into question the Quebec model of interest representation and consensus building which has come to symbolize the distinctive character of Quebec politics. Plans announced by QLP to re-engineer and modernize Quebec government call for a reconfiguration of the prevailing structure of representation and a reformulation of the forms of legitimate representation. These reforms have the potential to profoundly transform the internal political dynamic in Quebec by closing off access to the political arena for community organizations, by undermining their credibility and legitimacy, and by rendering them more dependent on contracting and partnership. These are real and significant changes, which may affect the very nature of the

relationship between state and society that has contributed to Quebec's distinct social and economic development.

Laforest then reviews the implications of the Liberals' agenda for negatively influencing the traditional roles for cross-sectoral concertation and consensus building, for aggregating collective interests, for citizen engagement and for advocacy. This too is a Quebec/Quebec debate. Laforest's parting caution is: "[w]ith the polls showing a rise in the support for the sovereignty option, placing it at the highest level since 1998, and the historical link between the community movement and the nationalist movement, Charest may have taken on more than he had bargained for."

The final two chapters take leave of the Quebec/Quebec debate and direct attention to the old chestnut – Quebec/Canada relations.

QUEBEC AS A NATION

In *Quebec and the Canadian Federation: From the 1980 Referendum to the Summit of the Canadas*, Thomas J. Courchene highlights the political and institutional developments that are progressively allowing Quebec to become a nation within the Canadian state. The two major external forces driving this evolution are a) the shift toward cross-border economic regions operating in NAFTA economic space (which implies policy asymmetry across the regions and, hence, more tolerance for Quebec to also march to its own policy drummer) and b) the knowledge/information era which serves to make provincial powers (education, health, day care, training) the essence of 21st century nationhood. This sets up an intriguing jurisdictional tug-of-war – Ottawa attempting to infiltrate provincial jurisdiction (via what Courchene calls "hourglass federalism) in order to access these nation-building provincial powers on the one hand, and Quebec eschewing further powers, (except on the international front) but pursuing, along with other provinces, access to revenues sufficient to implement these same nation-building provincial powers. Along the way, Courchene addresses and assesses the many interprovincial and federal/provincial signposts of this evolution – among others, AIT, SUFA, the APCs, the Calgary Declaration, and the Council of the Federation (COF).

The endpoint of the analysis is what the author refers to as the Summit of the Canadas – the June 2004 COF meeting and the First Ministers' Conferences on health and equalization in the fall of 2004. The important symbolism emanating from the COF was the proposal for Ottawa to take over pharmacare, with the formal recognition by all ROC provinces that Quebec would maintain its existing program with federal compensation. Likewise, the First Ministers' 2004 Health Accord recognized Quebec's distinctiveness in the form of a signed Canada/Quebec addendum that recognized Quebec's jurisdiction in this area. The bottom line is that these and other federal/provincial and interprovincial initiatives are pointing in the direction of ROC allowing Quebec to become its own nation in the Canadian state. In this sense, the 2006 Parliamentary confirmation that the Québécois form a nation within a united Canada is but the latest step in Quebec's evolution toward formal if not constitutional recognition.

LANGUAGE AND CANADA/QUEBEC RELATIONS

John Richards' contribution, *Breaking the "Vicious Cycle:" A Retrospective and Prospective Examination of Quebec-Canada Relations*, begins by addressing an omitted feature of the Courchene paper, namely the linguistic dimension of the evolution of Quebec. Richards takes readers through the rationale for, and passage of, *La Charte de la langue française* (Bill 101, as it has come to be known), with emphasis on the role of French as a language of work, instruction, communication, commerce, and business on the one hand and its associated attempt to ensure respect for ethnic minorities on the other. (Note that the contribution by Mendelsohn and his associates emphasised that Bill 101 has indeed played a role in making Montreal a pluralistic, multilingual community). Among the implications arising from Quebec's language policy was the 1988 *Ford v. Quebec* (sign law) decision rendered by the Supreme Court. This triggered Quebec's resorting to the notwithstanding clause, which in turn arguably played a role in the demise of the Meech Lake Accord. Richards' intriguing argument here is that the "patriation of the constitution in 1982, with minority language rights provisions of the Charter as drafted, unnecessarily exacerbated Quebec/Canada relations." The problem here, continues Richards, is that "Bill 101, an innovation of iconic importance to contemporary Quebec, received no constitutional sanction [in the Charter]."

In the context of his overview of more recent Quebec history, Richards highlights the "manifesto" *Pour un Québec lucide* signed by several high profile Quebecers (including Lucien Bouchard, André Pratte, Pierre Fortin ...) drawn from all walks of Quebec life. The signatories recognized that the Quiet Revolution allowed Quebec to close much of the income gap with ROC, but that this catch-up has now stalled. Beyond singling out public sector unions, Richards summarizes their concerns as follows: "Quebec must embrace efficiency enhancing changes to public policy, such as higher university fees, combined with income-contingent loans, ... reforms that shift taxation from income to consumption, and an end to cheap electricity so as to raise public revenue and lower the provincial debt."

All of this analysis is sandwiched between an opening and closing quotation from an impressive set of articles by Alain Dubuc of *La Presse*, the essence of which is that Quebec's next national project must be to succeed in education, culture, and in the new economy, with Montreal the crucible for this knowledge-based society. For this to happen, Dubuc suggests that this requires (as Richard's title indicates) "breaking the vicious cycle" that for too long now has constrained Quebec.

COMMUNITARIAN VS INDIVIDUALIST CAPITALISM

What is presumably new for many ROC readers in these papers is the prominent role played by the "Quebec model." Yet in international context, Quebec is hardly unique. Much of continental Europe as well as Japan embraces some version of this "communitarian" approach to capitalism, where the comparison is with the Anglo-American or "individualist" capitalism. Given that communitarian capitalism achieved its full blossoming in the post-war Federal Republic of Germany, Michel Albert in his 1993 book *Capitalism vs Capitalism* labels this as the "Rhine model" so named because Bonn, the then capital of Germany, is situated along the Rhine. In terms of the contrast between the Rhine model and the Anglo-American model, or between communitarian and individualist capitalism, Lester Thurow (1992, 2-3) reflects as follows:

> In the Anglo-Saxon [individualist] variant of capitalism ... since shareholders want income to maximize their lifetime consumption ... firms must be profit maximizers. For profit-maximizing firms, customer and employee relationships are merely a means to the end of higher profits for the shareholders. Wages are to be beaten down where possible and, when not needed, employees are to be laid off ... Job switching, voluntary or involuntary, is almost a synonym for efficiency.

> The communitarian business firm has a very different set of stakeholders who must be consulted when its strategies are being set. In Japanese business firms employees are seen as the number one stakeholder, customers number two, and the shareholders a distant number three. Since the employee is the prime stakeholder, higher employee wages are a central goal of the firm in Japan. Profits will be sacrificed to maintain either wages or employment. Dividend payouts to the shareholders are low.

> Communitarian societies expect companies to invest in the skills of their work forces. In the United States and Great Britain, skills are an individual responsibility ... Labour is not a member of the team. It is just another factor of production to be rented when it is needed, and laid off when it is not.

Beyond this, communitarian societies tend to have their companies financed by credit markets whereas in individualist capitalist societies companies tend to focus on equity finance. Relatedly, communitarian societies tend to have

universal banking systems that operate in all of the traditional pillars (banking, insurance, trusts and securities markets) whereas, until recently at least,
Canada's chartered banks were restricted to banking. Moreover, by the very
nature of credit-based finance, communitarian systems tended to be characterized by complex webs of cross-ownership of firms, replete with the mixing
of finance and commerce. This makes it very difficult for outsiders to take
over dominant firms in communitarian societies. For example, to attempt to
takeover a major German firm in the heyday of the Rhine model, one would
first need to take over most of the big German banks.

There is an analytical reason, beyond mere protectionism, why
communitarian societies are not fond of company takeovers, namely that companies are part of the "organic" nature of these societies:

> ... communities to which a person belongs – whether company, town, trade un-
> ion or charitable organization – are regarded as crucial; they are the structures
> that protect the individual and provide stability for the whole society (Albert,
> 1993, 124).

and

> That the company should enjoy its exalted status in Rhine countries is a logical
> outgrowth of the economy culture. Unlike the neo-American view of the com-
> pany as, at best, a collection of the contractual arrangements between temporarily
> convergent interests or, at worst, as a 'cash flow machine', the Rhine model sees
> the company as a social institution and an enduring community deserving of the
> loyalty and affection of its members, who can expect a measure of company
> care and protection in return (Albert, 1993, 146).

The best exemplars here are the Japanese Keiretsus and their policies of lifetime employment which at their zenith effectively became an integral, albeit
unofficial, component of the Japanese social security system.

By way of a final, and personal, reflection on these two types of capitalism,
not enough attention is paid to the fact that individualist capitalist countries
tend to be underpinned by English common law while communitarian societies are governed by civil law. Actually, if there is a causation here it presumably
runs in the other direction. The very process of codifying civil law necessi-
tates an ongoing dialogue and relationship between the state and civil society,
a dialogue that is not required in the precedent-driven evolution of the common law. The presumption would be that it becomes more natural in civil law
than in common law regimes to carry this enhanced role of the state over to
the socio-economic spheres. Indeed, one might take this comparison further
by noting that it is in individualist-capitalist and common-law countries that
one tends to still find first-past-the-post electoral systems. The prevalence of

coalition governments in proportional representation systems would seem to accord better with civil-law philosophy than common-law philosophy. What readers should take from these speculative comments is that this common-law/civil-law comparison and the implications that flow from it have not received the research attention that they merit.

This caveat aside, it is important that readers be apprised that the above comparisons between individualist capitalism and communitarian capitalism have been couched in rather stark terms. It is not so much that they are misleading; rather it is that these contrasts have been eroding over time. For example, continental Europe is rapidly trying to develop equity markets to compete with London, while America has now done away with its Glass-Steagall Act which prohibited commercial banks from owning securities firms. At a much deeper level both communitarian and individualist capitalism are under strain. The broad shift toward "socialist" regimes in South America represents a turning away from the Anglo-American model. And under the pressures of advancing globalization, the traditional communitarian economies are facing challenges:

> The social consensus characteristic of the Rhine model is also in jeopardy. One by one, the priorities that underpin this consensus – the primacy of collective over individual interests, the power of trade unions and the voluntary sector, co-responsibility in company management – are proving vulnerable to new and destructive forces. (Albert, 1993, 172)

These "destructive" forces are, of course, globalization and the heightened mobility of capital.

With this comparison of communitarian and individualist capitalism as backdrop, the remainder of this introductory chapter focuses on how all of this relates to the Quebec model in the Canadian context.

CANADA AND THE QUEBEC MODEL

Beyond restoring to the Province of Quebec the right to maintain its religion, the 1774 *Quebec Act* also granted "his Majesty's Canadian Subjects within the Province of Quebec... [the right to] hold and enjoy their Property and Possessions, together with all Customs and Usages relative thereto, and all their other Civil Rights," where such property and civil rights were to be determined by the then laws of Canada (i.e., by pre-revolutionary French law). Indeed, the *Quebec Act* phrase, "property and civil rights," found its way into the *Constitution Act, 1867* as s.92(13) and also in s.94. That "property and civil rights" would assume the role as the most effective source of residual power in the Constitution is less surprising when one considers its expansive sweep under the *Quebec Act*.

Irrespective of whether Quebec became a more communitarian society because of a desire to preserve and promote its linguistic and cultural identity within a North American "sea of Anglos," as it were, or because of the collective nature of its civil-law legal framework need not detain us here. All that is required in what follows is that Quebec falls, relative to the rest of North America, into the communitarian capitalism camp. The issue then becomes: What effect have Quebec and the Quebec model had on the evolution of Canada?

Elsewhere (1995) I identified a potential range of such influences. Given that this was written in the time frame leading up to the second Quebec Referendum, the analysis comes at this issue from the opposite perspective: were Quebec to exit the federation, what would be the implications for ROC? My conclusions were along the following lines:

- Quebec brings legal and institutional pluralism to Canada. The former relates primarily to the civil law tradition, while one aspect of the latter related to Quebec's "opting out" of various policy areas. Thus, absent Quebec, at the margin ROC becomes much less legally and institutionally pluralistic or, in the way that we are used to expressing this, Canada becomes more symmetric. This may not be good news for the First Nations. How much of our apparent willingness to accommodate alternative institutional/constitutional arrangements for the First Nations is a reflection of the existing degree of pluralism? With Quebec gone, will ROC remain as accommodating?
- The taste for regional redistribution is likely to erode. The argument here is that the magnitude of interpersonal and interregional transfers has been influenced in no small way because Quebec, one of the "founding nations," is also a "have-not" province.
- ROC will probably become more centralized. Quebec is the clear leader in terms of decentralization, whether in terms of revenues (with its own separate personal income tax system) or expenditures (with its continuing requests for greater powers). It is true that there are other decentralist provinces in the federation. With oil at $60 US per barrel, Alberta is obviously tilting in a decentralist direction. But while Quebecers are decentralist, Albertans (as distinct from Alberta) are not, or at least not yet.
- With Quebec in the family, the tensions in the federation revolve around federal/provincial or territorial axes. With Quebec gone, these may become eclipsed by pan-ROC and non-territorial cleavages – that is, the tensions will relate more to Charter interests vs vested interests. While this is related to the issue addressed in the previous bullet, it is conceptually distinct.
- Canada's embracing of multiculturalism is, in part at least, a response to "official bilingualism." This support for multiculturalism will presumably erode were Quebec to exit.
- More to the core of communitarian capitalism, Quebec is a bastion of "collective rights." With Quebec out of the federation, the focus will tilt toward

individual rights. I recognize that the collective rights in the Charter may appear to contradict this, but I agree with the conclusion of Seymour Martin Lipset (an eminent US commentator on things Canadian) that the Charter is inherently a "republicanizing" document.

- Relatedly, Quebec has distinguished itself as a member of the communitarian capitalist camp. Apart from the West's experimentation with cooperative capitalism (consumer and producer co-ops), from the Antigonish Movement, and from Canada's earlier enchantment with Crown Corporations, Quebec is the leading exponent of communitarian capitalism. In particular, the Quebec state is a much more important economic player in its economy than is the case for other provinces (or US states).
- Only Quebec fully engages its civil society institutions – labour and the third sector – in interest-group representation and social consensus mechanisms toward the end of developing and implementing public policy. This is an integral part of the essence of communitarian capitalism. While Saskatchewan was an early pioneer in terms of creative innovations in the social envelope (e.g., Medicare), the mantle of social policy innovator has clearly shifted to Quebec –the CLSCs, universal day care and, very recently, parental leave, to mention just a few examples. This is the Quebec model in action.

What is striking about these influences is that each of them has moved Canada away from the dictates of the American Creed, i.e., away from "Life, Liberty and the Pursuit of Happiness" and toward "Peace, Order and Good Government," (or, in the words of the *Quebec Act*, toward "Peace, Welfare and Good Government").

Intriguing, perhaps, while Canadians have embraced, and largely taken for granted, these defining features of Canada, several of the authors in the chapters that follow express concern that the Quebec model in the early years of the 21st century appears to be falling on hard times. As John Richards notes in his paper the most dramatic instance of this questioning has taken the form of the 2006 "manifesto" *For a Clear-eyed vision of Quebec* (*Pour un Québec lucide*) issued by a dozen prominent Quebecers from all parties and all walks of life (Lucien Bouchard, Pierre Fortin, André Pratte, Guy Saint-Pierre ...). Among their concerns would appear to be the very interest-group representation and consensus building that is part of the essence of the Quebec model:

> Social discourse in Quebec today is dominated by pressure groups of all kinds, including the big unions, which have monopolized the label "progressive" to better resist any changes imposed by the new order...

and

> Unfortunately, at the very moment when we should be radically changing the way we view ourselves and the world around us, the slightest change to the way

government functions, a bold project, the most timid call to responsibility or the smallest change to our comfortable habits is met with an angry outcry and objections or, at best, indifference. This outright rejection of change hurts Quebec, because it runs the risk of turning us into the republic of the status quo, a fossil from the twentieth century.

This is not that different from the concerns aired above with respect to the operations of the Rhine model. Yet the challenge from the manifesto's perspective is not to do away with the Quebec model. Rather it is to introduce some degree of flexibility into the operations of Quebec's version of communitarian capitalism in order that the province can accommodate the dictates of the new global order.

If there is a message in all this, it is that while Bay Street tends to take a dim view of the operations of the commercial variant of the Quebec model (i.e., Quebec Inc), it is nonetheless the case that the civil society operations of the Quebec model have left their imprints on Canada and Canadians in myriads of ways and places. And some of these qualify as *les acquis* of 21st century Canada. For this reason alone, the ensuing papers and their grappling with the future of the Quebec model are of importance well beyond the borders of Quebec.

By way of some concluding comments, it is instructive to view aspects of the forthcoming Quebec election from the perspective of the conference papers. The earlier-noted formation of a new party on the left – Québec Solidaire – would not surprise Pascale Dufour because the "progressive activists" are more interested in a social agenda than they are in the PQ agenda (which from the author's perspective adheres to a sovereignty agenda in a free trade context), and because Québec Solidaire embraces a social justice agenda for Quebec. Indeed, the looming four-party contest is especially interesting. As if responding to Rachel Laforest's warning that the Liberals were losing support because of their hard line on the Quebec model, Charest and company have pulled back on their earlier efforts to unwind selected aspects of the Quebec model. As already noted, Québec Solidaire on the left would like to deepen the communitarian aspects of the Quebec model whereas Mario Dumont and the ADQ on the right now have the individualist capitalism platform to themselves (unlike the 2003 election where the platform of the Liberals contained planks that embraced aspects of Anglo-American capitalism). What remains the same is that the sovereignty issue still divides the PLQ and the PQ. But even here there is an important new factor – the Harper Conservatives adoption of "open federalism" and the commitment to redress the federal-provincial fiscal imbalance. Other things equal, this has to favour the Charest Liberals. Finally, given the apparent revival of the ADQ, Brian Tanguay's paper will merit a second round, as it were, to again assess whether the ADQ achieves the "great realignment" of Quebec parties or gets squeezed out in yet another election fought around *la question nationale*.

Stay tuned.

NOTE

I wish to thank Marc-Antoine Adam for valuable comments on an earlier draft. However, full responsibility for the views that follow rests with me.

REFERENCES

Albert, M. 1993. *Capitalism vs. Capitalism.* New York: Four Wall Eight Windows.

Courchene, T.J. 1995. "Staatsation vs. Kulturnation: The Future of the ROC." In *Beyond Quebec: Taking Stock of Canada*, ed. Kenneth McRoberts. Montreal and Kingston: McGill-Queen's University Press, 388–399.

Pour un Quebec lucide (For a Clear-Eyed Vision of Quebec). 2006. 222.pourunquebeclucide.com.

Thurow, L. 1992. *Head to Head: The Coming Economic Battle Among Japan, Europe and America.* New York: William Morrow and Company Inc.

II

Setting the Stage: Quebec Society and Politics

2

A New Chapter or the Same Old Story?
Public Opinion in Quebec from 1996–2003

Matthew Mendelsohn, Andrew Parkin and Maurice Pinard

En se basant sur des données recueillies lors des scrutins entre 1996 et 2003, cet article évalue l'opinion publique au Québec en ce qui a trait aux questions relatives à l'unité nationale. Cet article pose six constats. Premièrement, on peut parler de démobilisation en ce qui touchait à la question de l'unité nationale et de dépolitisation chez l'électorat québécois en ce qui concernait les questions relatives à la place du Québec au sein du Canada, en particulier chez les jeunes. Ceci ne s'est pas reflété dans les scrutins comme un rejet catégorique de la souveraineté tel que ça avait été le cas lors des élections qui eurent lieu entre 1982 et 1987. Au cours de la période étudiée, plusieurs Québécois affirmaient qu'ils étaient en faveur de la souveraineté, mais ils étaient peu enclins à rouvrir le débat. Les termes « dépolitisation » et « démobilisation » sont donc appropriés. Deuxièmement, la stratégie du gouvernement fédéral de mettre l'accent sur les règles, les processus et les conditions des futurs référendums et d'une sécession possible a eu un impact sur le plan tactique en faveur des forces fédéralistes et correspondait davantage à l'opinion publique au Québec que plusieurs leaders d'opinion au Québec ne l'avaient cru. Troisièmement, plusieurs des préoccupations (parfois appelées doléances) traditionnelles des Québécois demeuraient, faute d'y avoir trouvé des solutions, si bien que, l'opinion publique n'avait guère chargée depuis 1996 au sujet des facteurs sous-jacents en faveur de la souveraineté, ce qui laissait croire qu'elle pouvait encore être mobilisée a-dvenant une crise. Quatrièmement, le consensus social et démocratique de la Révolution tranquille en ce qui avait trait au modèle social et économique distinct du Québec était remis en question. Cinquièmement, la loi 101 qui avait fait en sorte que les immigrants soient davantage intégrés à la communauté de langue française avait été un succès sur le plan des relations sociales puisque les jeunes Québécois se sentaient très à l'aise avec la diversité sociale et ethnique. Et sixièmement, le nouveau modèle de relations intergouvernementales du premier ministre libéral, Jean Charest, misant sur la coopération, avait l'appui de l'opinion publique au Québec.

INTRODUCTION

There is little doubt that the election of the Liberal Party of Quebec in the 2003 provincial election signalled an important change in the dynamic of inter-governmental relations. A federalist rather than a sovereignist government in Quebec City has far-reaching consequences for Canadian politics. Some have extrapolated from this obvious fact and presumed that public opinion in Quebec has also undergone a major shift, but this may not be accurate: we know that governing parties are often defeated for a variety of reasons having little to do with fundamental shifts in underlying public attitudes. Has public opinion in fact shifted in Quebec on issues related to the national question?

This essay will address the period from the aftermath of the 1995 referendum to the aftermath of the 2003 provincial election. We know that Quebec public opinion underwent major shifts in the late 1980s and early 1990s due to the rejection of the Meech Lake Accord, along with the highly politicized events associated with this period. We also know that the intensity of nationalist feeling, which had peaked in late 1990 in the aftermath of the defeat of the Meech Lake Accord, declined thereafter, but was still strong at the time of the 1995 referendum. The "Yes" side was narrowly defeated, and within six months of that defeat the sovereignist option entered a new phase of decline in mid-1996. This pre-1996 story is well known and we will not retell it here (see, for example, Pinard 2002; Pinard, Bernier and Lemieux 1997).

Instead, we will weigh in at the beginning of Quebec's next chapter, which began in mid-1996, and we will end in 2003. This chapter featured a number of important events: the federal government adopted a new confrontational strategy towards the Quebec sovereignist movement; an apparent demobilization of the Quebec sovereignist movement; the meteoric rise and fall of a new nationalist but non-sovereignist party in Quebec; and the election of a federalist government in Quebec, featuring unarguably the most federalist and Canadian premier elected in Quebec since 1962. We will examine public opinion in Quebec for insights into how and why these developments occurred.

We advance six arguments. First, there has been a demobilization around the national question and a depoliticization of the Quebec electorate on issues related to Quebec's place within Canada, particularly among the young. This does not appear in polls as a firm rejection of sovereignty, as it appeared in polls in the 1982–1987 period; today, many Quebecers continue to say they support sovereignty, but they have little interest in re-opening this debate, and thus "depoliticization" and "demobilization" are the appropriate terms. Second, the federal government's strategy to focus on the rules, processes, and terms of future referendums and possible secession had a tactical impact in favour of federalist forces and was more consistent with latent public opinion in Quebec than many Quebec opinion leaders expected. Third, many of the traditional concerns of Quebecers, sometimes referred to as grievances (see, for example, Pinard and Hamilton 1986), remain unresolved, and opinion on the underlying factors that motivate support for sovereignty (see Mendelsohn 2003a for a discussion of these factors) have not evolved much since 1996, suggesting they could again be mobilized during a time of crisis. Fourth, the social democratic Quiet Revolution consensus around Quebec's distinct economic and social model is today contested. Although Quebecers' values remain more to the left than the values of other Canadians, Quebecers have less confidence in the state, taxation, and unionization as pathways to attain their goals of greater social equality. Fifth, Bill 101's insistence that new immigrants integrate more fully into the French-speaking community has been a success in terms of social relations, as young Quebecers and young Canadians outside Quebec demonstrate equally high levels of comfort with ethnic and social diversity. And sixth, the new model of more cooperative intergovernmental relations endorsed by Quebec's new Liberal premier, Jean Charest, is largely consistent with Quebec public opinion, and is in fact consistent with where the Quebec public has been for some time.

Taken together, these six conclusions lead us to argue more broadly that the public opinion environment has undergone a shift, featuring a comfort with a multicultural and pluriethnic French-speaking Quebec, a questioning of the consensus around the Quebec social and economic model, and a decline of salience of and interest in the national question as it has been defined since 1970. However, unlike in the early 1980s, Quebecers have not turned against sovereignty, but today express little interest in the question.

Data in this paper are taken overwhelmingly from three sources. First, the Privy Council Office commissioned CROP to conduct major surveys in Quebec in 1996, 1997, and 1999. The first two of these focused largely on traditional issues related to the national question, while the 1999 survey focused largely on issues related to the rules, terms, and processes of future referendums and secession. The first author was the architect of these surveys, along with officials in the federal government. Second, the Centre for Research and Information on Canada (CRIC) began major surveys in Quebec in early 1998, conducted by CROP. They include their annual fall survey, *Portraits of Canada*, but also occasional ad hoc surveys in addition to *Portraits*. All three authors, along with the management staff at CRIC, including Joan Fraser, Pierre O'Neil, and Marie-Josée Gariepy have been responsible for the design of these surveys. Third, the CRIC-*Globe and Mail* survey on the New Canada, designed in collaboration with the Canadian Opinion Research Archive, was conducted by Ipsos-Reid in the spring of 2003. It was designed by the first two authors, along with journalists from the *Globe and Mail*, including Edward Greenspon, Michael Valpy, Catherine Wallace, Catherine Bradbury, and Erin Anderssen. (Survey data is compiled in the appendix.)

DEPOLITICIZATION AROUND THE NATIONAL QUESTION

The defining feature of Quebec public opinion since the 1970s (but with a very important interlude from 1981 to around 1987) has been polarization on the national question (Pinard and Hamilton 1977). That polarization was much stronger among elites, especially political elites, but by the options they offered the population, they forced the public to take sides. "Normal" politics took a back seat to the more existential questions of national identity and constitutional status. The strong polarization around Quebec's place within Canada began to take shape in the 1970 provincial election, culminating first in the 1980 referendum, but remained the defining feature of the Quebec party system for three decades. The major electoral battles of the 1990s in the aftermath of the collapse of the Meech Lake Accord – including the 1992 Charlottetown referendum, the 1995 sovereignty referendum, the 1993, 1997, and 2000 federal elections, and the 1994 and 1998 provincial elections – all demonstrated that federalist and sovereignist forces were each able to consistently mobilize about half the Quebec electorate.

The polarization and mobilization around the national question as the defining feature of Quebec politics may have run its course. We are now witnessing a return to the normal debates of politics – including the size of the state, social values, and levels of taxation – as we saw briefly in the period after 1982. One of the most important features of Quebec mass opinion in the early 21st century is the depoliticization on the national question, particularly amongst young Quebecers and new Quebecers. It has been widely reported in the media that Quebecers are tired of the national question and have little appetite for a new referendum or for re-opening constitutional negotiations. Since 1998, that fatigue has remained fairly constant (figure 1). The debates of the late 1980s and early 1990s hold little appeal to younger Quebecers. In 1999, an overwhelming majority of Quebecers did not wish for another referendum, and those who did support holding another referendum were far less intense in their opinion than opponents of another referendum. A desire to avoid ongoing constitutional disputes, and a desire to avoid reliving debates that already seemed dated in the 1990s, in part explains both the success of the Parti Libéral du Québec (PLQ) and the shorter-lived success of the Action démocratique du Québec (ADQ). While a lack of interest in the national question has often been a feature of Quebec mass opinion, the feeling is more intense today. Those who do not desire another referendum are far less likely to hold this view intensely, and most say that they would not be upset if there was no referendum (appendix, number 1).

We asked Quebecers in 2002 whether they thought of themselves primarily as sovereignists, federalists, somewhere in between, or neither. While 40 percent of francophone Quebecers embraced one of the first two labels, 58 percent embraced neither label (appendix, number 2). It is amongst the young, however, where one notes the most extreme rejection of both of these labels. Fully

Figure 1: Support for Another Sovereignty Referendum?

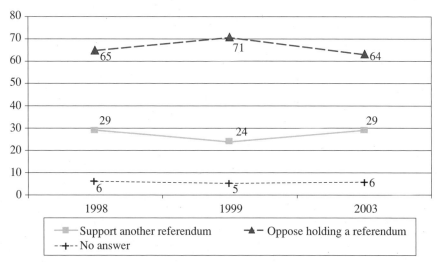

Are you personally very favourable, somewhat favourable, somewhat opposed or very much opposed to the Parti Québécois government holding a referendum on sovereignty during its current mandate? (some small modifications to questions)

Source: CRIC

67 percent of young Quebecers identify with neither of these two labels. Additional analyses (not reported) showed that the young are more likely to say "neither" (rather than "in between the two") and that this response is heavily correlated with a general lack of interest in politics. One should also note that it was supporters of the ADQ who were by far more likely to say that they identified with neither of these two labels, and although the ADQ failed to make significant gains in the 2003 provincial election, its positioning on the national question – nationalist but neither sovereignist nor federalist – is nonetheless shared by a large majority of Quebecers, particularly young Quebecers. Other recent findings highlight this depoliticization: only 36 percent of Quebecers wish to return to the constitutional question (appendix, number 3); 75 percent say they no longer believe Quebec will ever be sovereign (figure 2); and 56 percent agree with the statement that "sovereignty is an idea of the past" (appendix, number 4).

None of this is to suggest that many Quebecers do not continue to support Quebec sovereignty on some level. Despite a decline in support during the late 1990s, support never dropped below 40 percent on the sovereignty/partnership question (figure 3), although support for "independence" and other "harder" questions is significantly lower, usually hovering at about one third of the electorate. Following the provincial Liberals' election victory in 2003, sup-

Figure 2: Will Quebec Become Independent? (1998–2002)

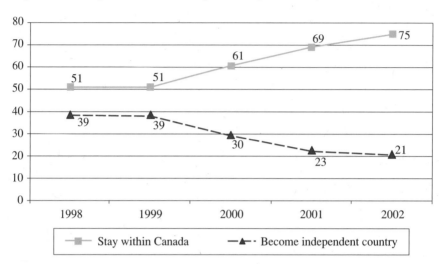

Do you think Quebec will probably become an independent country one day, or do you think it will probably stay in Canada?

Source: CRIC

port for sovereignty/partnership jumped to the mid-40s. This jump confirms a well established pattern that rhetorical support for sovereignty often jumps when a federalist government is in power in Quebec City and sovereignty is less likely. The conclusion to emerge from these data is that about half of francophone Quebecers continue to embrace sovereignty at some ideological and rhetorical level, while at the same time, the overwhelming majority of Quebecers are willing to expend little energy to pursue sovereignty and support removing the issue from the agenda. Whether the current mood is long-term or only short-term remains to be seen. What is different between now and the period between 1981–1987, when we also witnessed a demoblization of sovereignist forces, is that in the earlier period few Quebecers said they supported sovereignty. Following the 1980 referendum, there was a substantial drop in sovereignist support, but no large drop following the 1995 referendum. Today, large numbers continue to support sovereignty, even if they do not wish to pursue the project. This is a categorical change. These numbers suggest a general disengagement from the national question rather than a rejection of the sovereignist option, and suggest opinion could be again mobilized in Quebec in favour of sovereignty.

**Figure 3: Support for "Sovereignty Partnership" and "Independence,"
1996–2003 (Undecided respondents distributed prorata)**

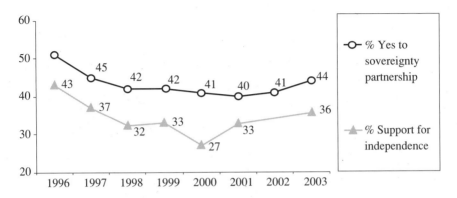

Source: CROP polls, yearly averages

THE TACTICAL SUCCESS OF THE FEDERAL GOVERNMENT'S
POST-REFERENDUM STRATEGY

There were many substantive arguments offered by federalists during the 1980 referendum, but they can be broken into three general categories: 1) Canada is a good place to live and belongs to all Quebecers; 2) the economic damage of a "Yes" vote will be serious; and 3) there are a variety of practical issues that have not been addressed, such as the fact that there is no one with whom to negotiate a new association (we will ignore the major strategic argument, namely that a "No" vote rather than a "Yes" vote would lead to renewal of the federation). These first two substantive categories remained relatively consistent through the 1980s and into the 1995 referendum, but the third category, the one which focused on practical considerations and asked whether sovereignty was actually possible in any kind of straightforward manner, largely disappeared. It reappeared in the federal government strategy following the 1995 referendum, in part due to the consistent finding that many "Yes" voters to a question on sovereignty/partnership would not vote in favour of independence. For example, while nearly half of francophone voters say they would vote "Yes" to the 1995 referendum question on sovereignty/partnership, far fewer would vote "Yes" to a question on independence (figure 4). In fact, many of these voters who would vote "Yes" to sovereignty/partnership and "No" to independence believed Quebec would remain in Canada following a "Yes" vote in the 1995 referendum, and believed that a "Yes" vote to sovereignty/partnership was a good way to renew the federation (see Mendelsohn 2003a, appendix).

Figure 4: Support for Various Secessionist Options (Francophones only)

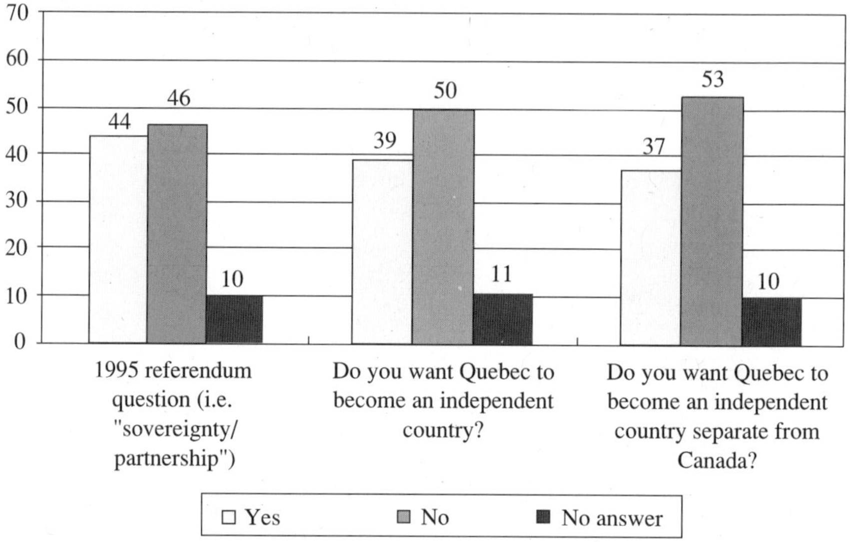

| | 1995 referendum question (i.e. "sovereignty/ partnership") | Do you want Quebec to become an independent country? | Do you want Quebec to become an independent country separate from Canada? |

Yes: 44, 39, 37
No: 46, 50, 53
No answer: 10, 11, 10

☐ Yes   ▨ No   ■ No answer

Source: PCO Surveys, 1999

A widely shared misconception following the 1995 referendum was that the arguments used by the federal government were bundled into two categories: Plan A ("positive" arguments for Canada) and Plan B ("negative" arguments about sovereignty). This conceptualization misses an important part of the reality of post-1995 federal government strategy. While making arguments in favour of a federal Canada and underlining the costs and risks of sovereignty continued to play an important role in initiatives and discourse, the Supreme Court reference and the Clarity Bill were in fact designed to address the practicalities of the PQ approach. In 1980, Prime Minister Trudeau was quite prepared to state that there was no one with whom Quebec could negotiate following a "Yes" vote; such practical considerations were reintroduced into the debate by federalists after 1995.

This strategy has been a tactical success in weakening support for sovereignty. The most dramatic changes of opinion in Quebec since 1996 relate to the practicalities of secession. Quebecers are less sanguine about the ease with which it could be accomplished. Following the 1995 referendum, the federal government was concerned that the practicalities of the PQ proposal for secession had been subjected to far too little scrutiny. The Supreme Court reference, the Clarity Bill, and the general change in discourse – one which was more prepared to directly challenge the conventional wisdoms of nationalist discourse – all played a role in this.

The data suggest that on issues related to the practicalities of the PQ project, mass opinion in Quebec has been consistently more open to federalist arguments than suggested by the Quebec media and some elements of the Quebec elite. The political culture of Quebec – and we define "political culture" as the conventional wisdom that sets the boundaries of political activity – underwent a real shift in the late 1990s. A direct questioning of the assumptions of the PQ approach to secession became much more acceptable parts of the political discourse. Facile and misleading arguments, such as "the people will decide, not the courts," gave way to more thoughtful deliberation on how secession could actually take place in an established liberal democracy. The Supreme Court decision set an appropriate and reasonable tone by acknowledging that Quebec had a right to secede, that the rest of the country would have to negotiate such a secession, but that those negotiations would only begin after it had become apparent that a clear majority of Quebecers wished to secede from Canada.

The political conversation has thus changed. In both the 1980 and 1995 referendums, two debates were actually taking place. One asked Quebecers whether they wished to be sovereign, and a consistent majority of Quebecers have always opposed independence. But a second asked Quebecers whether a "Yes" or a "No" vote would be more likely to lead to a renewal of the federation; in both referendums, the sovereignist and federalist leaderships offered up their option as the one best able to reform the Canadian federation in a manner consistent with the majority preference of Quebecers in favour of more autonomy within Canada and a recognition of Quebec's national existence within Canada. A large part of the rationale for the federal government's strategy beginning in 1996 was to ensure that, in the future, the second debate could not take place under the guise of the first. A referendum on secession is serious, and it should focus on just that. Seeking more autonomy for Quebec within Canada is legitimate, and pursuing secession through a referendum is legitimate, but using the referendum or the threat of a referendum as a knife at the throat of the rest of Canada is unlikely to be a viable option in the future.

A clear majority of Quebecers found the 1995 referendum question to be unclear (appendix, number 5). When asked directly whether a question on sovereignty/partnership or independence was a clearer question, 49 percent of francophones said a question on independence was clearer, while only 38 percent said a question on sovereignty/partnership was clearer. However, when forced to choose between "secession" and "sovereignty/partnership," only 25 percent found the secession question clearer, suggesting that the word perplexed many respondents (figure 5). A strong majority agreed that the question should be set jointly by the government and the opposition in the National

Figure 5: Which Question is Clearer? (Francophones only)

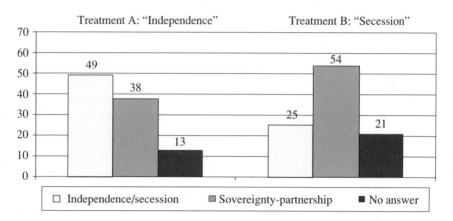

Treatment A: Which question is a clearer referendum question: One on sovereignty/partnership or one on independence? (Split sample)

Treatment B: Which question is a clearer referendum question: One on sovereignty/partnership or one on secession? (Split sample)

Source: PCO Surveys, July 1999

Assembly, and a majority was even open to the idea of federal government participation in setting the question (appendix, number 6). This is not surprising. In focus group testing conducted by the PCO from 1996–1998, "Yes" and "No" voters alike complained about the question and an inherent sense of fairness pervaded the conversations: there was a perception that if we are going to undertake something as serious as secession, all the players should agree to the rules.

A majority of Quebecers believed that "50 percent plus 1" did not constitute a clear majority, though 70 percent believed that 60 percent did constitute a clear majority (appendix, number 7). By 1999, Quebecers were overwhelmingly likely to believe that following a referendum victory for the "Yes" side, secession would be quite difficult, even with a large and clear majority (appendix, number 8). Another important change since 1995 was the sense that after a "Yes" vote, Quebecers would be more divided rather than more united (appendix, number 9). It is unfortunate that we don't have data on these questions from earlier periods and thus we cannot be as explicit as we would like on the extent of the change in public opinion. However, we do know that in the 1995 referendum, the "Yes" side invoked with much success a mythical Québécois people freed from the ugly world of political divisions getting along merrily with one another for the purposes of building a new country in a post-"Yes" environment. This belief was plainly absent in 1999. The evolution towards a more skeptical stance in regards to Lucien Bouchard's invoked magic wand is one piece of the story that explains the depoliticization around the national question and a decline in support for sovereignty.

In the PCO panel study, when survey respondents from 1997 were re-interviewed in 1999, a trend emerged: those voters who had moved from the sovereignist to the federalist camp had changed their view on issues related to the rules and processes of a referendum and secession. For example, those Quebecers who had been "Yes" voters in 1997 but had become "No" voters in 1999 were significantly more likely to say that a "Yes" vote could lead to a crisis (figure 6). Likewise, they were significantly more likely to say that a "Yes" vote was not the best way to end bickering between the federal and provincial governments (figure 7). In short, by 1999, the Quebec public was more likely to see practical problems with the PQ's plan for a quick and seam-less transition to sovereignty.

Figure 6: Could a "Yes" Vote Lead to a Serious Crisis?
(Percent agreeing with the statement)

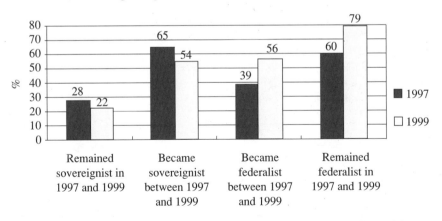

Question: Agree/Disagree: "A YES vote on sovereignty could lead to a serious crisis in Quebec."

Source: PCO Surveys

Figure 7: Is a "Yes" Vote the Best Way to End the Constitutional Debate? (Percent agreeing with the statement)

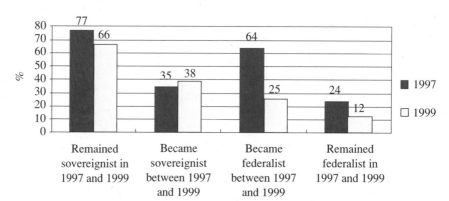

Question: Agree/Disagree: "The best way to end the bickering between the Governments of Canada and Quebec is for Quebec to become a sovereign country."

Source: PCO Surveys

CONTINUING GRIEVANCES AND UNRESOLVED ISSUES

Despite the depoliticization around the national question and the progress made by the federal government on issues related to the practicalities of the PQ project, the distribution of opinion on traditional issues has changed little. Despite the obvious successes in regards to language preservation and economic progress amongst French speakers in Quebec, many francophone Quebecers continue to voice many of the same complaints about the federation as they did in the 1970s and 1980s.

About 60 percent of Quebecers believe that the French language is threatened in Quebec, and this has not changed significantly in recent years (figure 8) (for earlier data, see Pinard, Bernier and Lemieux 1997, 320). A significant minority of Quebecers believe that they contribute more to confederation than they take out, and only Albertans are more likely than Quebecers to believe that their own province contributes more than it takes out of confederation (appendix, number 10). Only 37 percent of Quebecers believed in 2003 that the federal and provincial governments were working well together (appendix, number 11). Almost 60 percent of Quebecers supported a greater devolution of

**Figure 8: Is the French Language Threatened in Quebec?
(Francophones only)**

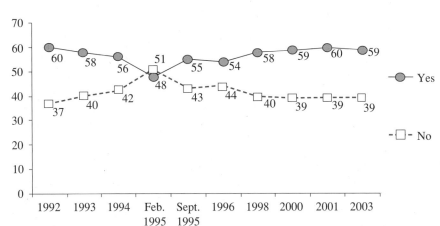

In your opinion, is the French language threatened in Quebec?

Source: 1992–1996, *Un combat inachevé*; 1998–2003, CRIC

power to the provinces in 2003 (appendix, number 12). This represents a significant increase from recent years, as only 43 percent of Quebecers supported a greater devolution of powers as recently as 2001 (not reported).

The number of Quebecers who say that their province is not treated with the respect it deserves in Canada has not changed much over the past six years, with about only four in ten saying that it is treated with respect (appendix, number 13). The fact that there has been no evolution on these numbers in Quebec since 1998 is itself significant: despite predictions to the contrary about a nationalist backlash, the Supreme Court reference and Clarity Bill produced no change in Quebec on these measures. There is also no evidence to suggest that the basic pattern of self-identification – greater attachment to Quebec than Canada and identification first as Quebecer but also as Canadian – has changed much in recent years (appendix, number 14) (for more documentation on this, see Mendelsohn 2003b). As Pinard has argued in earlier work, the presence of these continued grievances, coupled with an external crisis and a sense that sovereignty is possible, could lead to a resurgence of sovereignist mobilization.

END OF THE QUIET REVOLUTION CONSENSUS?

When Jean Charest left federal politics to take over the leadership of the PLQ in early 1998, his opponents mocked him as an *arriviste* outsider who did not understand the realities of Quebec society. The 1998 Quebec election featured muscular attacks against him by then-premier Lucien Bouchard. The general thrust of these attacks was that Charest was a *parvenu* who would undermine the Quebec economic and social model and destroy 40 years of progress that had begun in 1960. The "Quebec economic model" and the "Quiet Revolution consensus" were invoked as sacred mantra, and Charest was depicted as a neo-conservative import from English-speaking Canada who would undermine the consensus.

This depiction was unfair at the time, and was not consistent with Quebec mass opinion. Beginning during the mid-1990s, when Bouchard and Landry both focused on deficit reduction, the consensus around the Quebec economic model had begun to fray. Quebec society had evolved, and while the Quiet Revolution consensus may have existed as an incantation in the late 1990s, it no longer had the same significance. Quebec mass opinion had shifted towards a greater willingness to question some of the conventional understandings of Quebec political culture. In the 1998 election, the PLQ directly challenged the size of the state and the Quiet Revolution mythology and ended up taking more votes than the PQ. Moreover, the ADQ, running a campaign that was even more explicit in its attack on the size of the state, and more explicit in its attack on the deficiencies of Quebec's neo-corporatist model, took an additional 12 percent of the vote. The shift crystallized in the election of 2003, where the Liberals and the ADQ combined took 64 percent of the vote. Their challenge of the Quiet Revolution consensus explains at least in part why some Quebecers voted for these parties, and supporters of the PLQ, and even more so the ADQ, were more supportive of privatization in the health care system (figure 9).

As the most heavily taxed province in Canada, over the last five years Quebecers have been consistently more supportive of tax relief than Canadians elsewhere. When asked to choose between three priorities for a potential budgetary surplus – tax cuts, more social spending, or debt repayment – Quebecers were more likely to choose tax cuts (37 percent) and were no more likely than Canadians outside Quebec to choose more social spending (33 percent) (appendix, number 15). In surveys from 2000–2002, using two different questions, Quebecers were more likely than Canadians in any other province to support more privatization in the health care field (appendix, numbers 16–17). This may in part be explained by the fact that "Canadian public health care" is a more important symbol of Canadian citizenship outside Quebec than it is inside Quebec, but nonetheless, that almost half of Quebecers

Figure 9: Support for Health Care Privatization by Vote

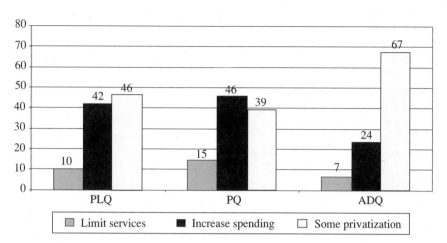

Health care costs are expected to rise in the future because of our aging population and because of the costs of new treatments and medications. Which of the following statements comes closest to your view? Would you say (a) governments should significantly INCREASE THEIR SPENDING on health care to cover these rising costs; (b) governments should LIMIT THE AVAILABILITY of some treatments or medications; or (c) governments should allow THE PRIVATE SECTOR to provide some health care services to those people who can afford to pay for them.

Source: CRIC, 2002

support more privatization in the health care field is striking. This shift in Quebec in attitudes toward the state and the Quiet Revolution social democratic consensus is important, but it should not be taken to mean that Quebecers' fundamental social values have changed. Quebecers continue to demonstrate values more to the left than Canadians in other provinces; for example, they are more likely to believe in equality over liberty and more likely to believe that the state has a responsibility to reduce income inequality (appendix, number 18). The sense of solidarity that animated the Quebec economic model is still present. However, the size of the state, its accompanying bureaucratization, and the comparatively high tax burden have all taken their toll. The fact that support for the provincial Liberals declined in 2004 does not detract from the 'fact that the Quiet Revolution consensus has become contested.

BILL 101 AND THE "NEW QUEBEC"

The evidence is increasingly incontestable that Bill 101 succeeded in making Quebec a more multicultural, integrated society along linguistic and ethnic lines. While older Quebecers lived in far more homogenous social networks than their counterparts in the "rest of Canada" (ROC) (figure 10), younger Quebecers and their ROC counterparts live in virtually identical worlds in terms of social diversity, and demonstrate virtually indistinguishable attitudes on questions related to ethnic diversity. While older Quebecers stand out as being less comfortable with religious and ethnic diversity, younger Quebecers and younger Canadians outside Quebec demonstrate no discernible attitudinal differences on these questions (figure 11). While one of the projects of Bill 101 was to facilitate the integration of immigrants in the French-speaking community, particularly through the school system, the data clearly show that the integration has been a two-way street. Young Quebecers have developed a sense of identity based on an acceptance of cultural diversity. In particular, young francophone Montreal has evolved into a pluralistic, multilingual community (for additional data on this phenomenon, see Parkin and Mendelsohn 2003).

Figure 10: The Changing Social Circle (Non-visible minorities only)

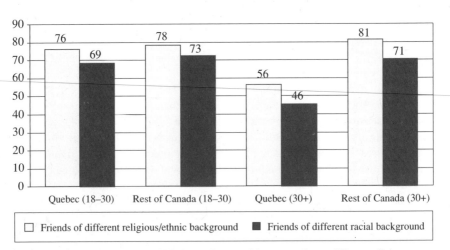

Please think about your few closest friends. (a) Do any of them come from a different religious or ethnic background than you do? (b) Do any of them come from a different racial background than you do?

*Source: Globe & Mail/*CRIC survey, 2003

Figure 11: Levels of Comfort with Different Groups

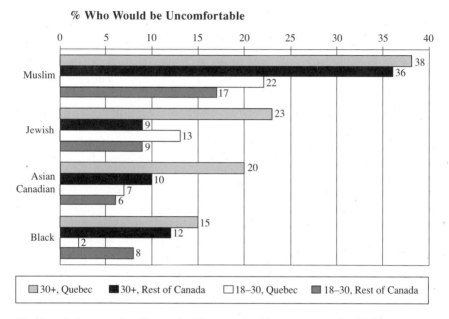

% Who Would be Uncomfortable

Would you feel very comfortable, comfortable, uncomfortable or very uncomfortable if …
a close relative, like your sister or daughter, was going to marry someone who is:

*Source: Globe & Mail/*CRIC survey, 2003

A NEW MODEL OF INTERGOVERNMENTAL RELATIONS

One of the single animating features of the Canadian federation since 1960 has been the drive of Quebec to secure more autonomy within Canada, and this has been true for federalist and sovereignist governments alike. During many periods this support for devolution co-existed with active participation in the federation; at other times – the period following patriation with the PQ in government and then again following the rejection of the Meech Lake Accord with the Liberals in government – Quebec governments have boycotted or abstained from many federation activities. During the 2003 election campaign, the PLQ argued that Quebec was hurting itself by boycotting many federation activities and made commitments to participate more actively in the federation for the benefit of Quebecers. At the same time, the PLQ also focused on securing greater autonomy for Quebec, and the focus on rectifying the fiscal imbalance is one such overture. By focusing both on more coopera-tive engagement with other Canadian governments while also suggesting a need for more provincial resources, the PLQ has attempted to appeal to both of the animating spirits of Quebec public opinion: a desire for greater au-tonomy for Quebec, as well as a desire to participate in a larger Canadian project that is respectful of French Canada.

The first thing to note is that Quebecers generally respond favourably to the idea of participating actively in the federation (appendix, number 19). Over the past two decades, the Quebec government has often refused to go along with arrangements agreed to by the federal and other provincial gov-ernments. Alain Noël coined the apt phrase "federalism with a footnote" to describe the pattern whereby press releases would announce that the prov-inces and federal government had reached an agreement "not counting Quebec." However, at a general level, Quebecers would usually like to have the foot-note moved into the body of the text. Of course the nature of the text sometimes prevents this from happening, and Quebecers or the Quebec government may decide that they cannot accept a particular agreement, but the point remains that Quebecers' instinctive preference is for participation and engagement rather than non-participation. Having an "empty chair" in Quebec's place at the bargaining table is rarely the preference of a majority of Quebecers.

The next thing to note in the public opinion data is that Quebecers are far more likely to believe today that a provincial Liberal government strengthens Quebec's position vis-a-vis other provinces than they were to believe in 1999 that the PQ did (appendix, number 20). This is quite significant. The PQ has certainly argued that a Liberal government in Quebec City would weaken Quebec in its relations with the rest of Canada, but the Quebec public does not share this concern. This may be consistent with other changes in the pub-lic opinion environment in the late 1990s regarding the success of the PQ at extracting concessions from the ROC. Quebecers may have come to believe that a PQ government, threatening another referendum, was not the best way to secure Quebecers' primary goal: a better relationship with the rest of Canada based on more provincial autonomy and recognition of Quebec's national sta-tus within Canada. By a margin of 57–26 percent, Quebecers stated that a PLQ government strengthens Quebec. Quebecers are also not nearly as tied to the federal principle as one might expect, with most Quebecers preferring a codecisional model of federalism rather than a watertight jurisdictional model of federalism (appendix, number 21). Much like Canadians outside Quebec (see Cutler and Mendelsohn 2004), Quebecers are not particularly tied to the division of powers as laid out in Sections 91 and 92 of the BNA Act.

Quebecers do not believe that governments have been getting along particu-larly well (see appendix, number 11), but blame both orders of government equally, and this has not changed since 1997 (appendix, number 22). In sum, these data paint a portrait of a public that values cooperative intergovernmentalism. On the other hand, Quebecers also believe that a fiscal imbalance exists: only 14 per-cent of Quebecers think the federal government has too little revenue to fulfill its responsibilities, while 43 percent believe that the provincial government has too little revenue (appendix, number 23). But Quebecers are not signifi-cantly more likely than other Canadians to believe a fiscal imbalance exists, and hence, these data provide further evidence of potential common cause between the various provincial governments. These latter findings should be looked at in the context of the earlier finding which showed that a majority of Quebecers support devolution of powers to Quebec.

Quebecers today simultaneously support greater provincial autonomy and an improved federal/provincial relationship. They simultaneously support greater respect for provincial jurisdictions, but also support having a strong say in federal institutions and enjoy participating alongside other provincial governments to make Canada work. This is nothing new, but in 2004, Quebecers have a government that shares this dual vision, rather than one that highlights only the first aspect of Quebecers' attitudes.

CONCLUSION

If one were to simply look at public opinion on traditional issues, such as threats to the French language and the fairness of the federation, one would think that the public opinion environment in Quebec had changed little be-tween 1996 and 2003. This would be a mistake. Although Quebecers do have many of the same concerns and unresolved issues that they had during the 1995 referendum, there has been a change in Quebecers' desire to pursue sov-ereignty or even talk about sovereignty as a way of addressing these unresolved issues. This, then, is the public opinion environment in Quebec in 2003: 1) a continuation of unresolved issues; 2) a new found belief that secession is not a particularly feasible path for dealing with these issues; and hence 3) a desire to avoid issues of national status and identity entirely. In sum, the agenda has changed and there is a real lack of appetite for another national discussion on Quebec's place in Canada, but this should not be mistaken for a renewed sense of attachment to and support for Quebec's current status within Canada. Ac-quiescence rather than support is the appropriate way to describe Quebecers' current vision of their place within Canada.

A final conclusion might also be offered. As we know, the state and gov-ernment are not viewed as pathways to political change as much as they once were. The terms of the debate were formulated in the 1960s, long before we felt the effects of the most recent wave of globalization. We may have failed to fully appreciate the importance this has for the Quebec nationalist move-ment. To political scientists, it is natural that the state will be uppermost in our consciousness when we think about the development of a national community. To citizens of the advanced information democracies, this is not nearly as apparent. The protection and development of the Quebec national community can take place at an interpersonal, social, and economic level on a daily basis. To most citizens, that which takes place in the formal political world is only one small part of the effort to strengthen Quebec. Which government does what and who has formal sovereignty are of course important political issues, but they are not at the core of most citizens' preoccupations when they ponder the protection, definition, and development of their community and identity.

Although "the national question" has clearly not been resolved for governments and political scientists, many Quebec citizens may have resolved it for themselves. Quebecers will continue to create and recreate a national community regardless of what governments do, and they will use their Canadian and global identities when these are convenient. Whether Quebec is in a federal Canada or is a sovereign country is a far less important agenda item; instead, what is important is the kind of society Quebec chooses to build within Canada, and whether it has the tools – in terms of powers and money – to do it.

NOTE

This paper was completed in December 2004.

REFERENCES

Breton, R. 1998. "Ethnicity and Race in Social Organization: Recent Developments in Canadian Society." In *The Vertical Mosaic Revisited*, eds. R. Helmes-Hayes and J. Curtis. Toronto: University of Toronto Press.

Cutler, F. and M. Mendelsohn. 2004. "Unnatural Loyalties? The Governments and Citizens of Canadian Federalism." In *Insiders and Outsiders: Alan Cairns and the Reshaping of Canadian Citizenship*, eds. G. Kernerman and P. Resnick. Vancouver: UBC Press.

Mendelsohn, M. 2003a. "Competing Approaches to Explaining Support for Sovereignty in Quebec." *Canadian Journal of Political Science* 36(3): 511–37.

– 2003b. "Measuring National Identity and Patterns of Attachment: The Case of Quebec and Nationalist Mobilization." *Nationalism and Ethnic Politics* 8(3): 72–94.

Noël, A. 2002. "Without Quebec: Collaborative Federalism with a Footnote?" In *Building the Social Union: Perspectives, Directions and Challenges*, ed. T. McIntosh. Regina: Saskatchewan Institute of Public Policy.

Parkin, A. and M. Mendelsohn. 2003. "A New Canada: An Identity Shaped by Diversity." The CRIC Papers, Centre for Research and Information on Canada.

Pinard, M. 2002. "The Quebec Independence Movement: From its Emergence to the 1995 Referendum." In *Political Sociology: Canadian Perspectives*, ed. D. Baer. Don Mills: Oxford University Press.

Pinard, M. and R. Hamilton. 1977. "The Independence Issue and the Polarization of the Electorate: The 1973 Quebec Election." *Canadian Journal of Political Science* 10: 215–59.

– 1986. "Motivational Dimensions in the Quebec Independence Movement: A Test of a New Model." *Research in Social Movements, Conflicts and Change* 9: 225–80.

Pinard, M., R. Bernier and V. Lemieux. 1977. *Un combat inachevé*. Sainte-Foy: Presses de l'Université du Québec.

APPENDIX: Survey Questions and Results

Question number	Questions and results		Date	Source
1	Those opposed to another referendum only:		1999	CRIC
	Would be upset if a referendum was held:	70%		
	Would not be upset:	30%		
	Those in favour of another referendum only:			
	Would be upset if a referendum was NOT held:	24%		
	Would not be upset:	74%		

Question 2: Do you consider yourself to be mainly a federalist, mainly a sovereignist, someone who is in between the two, or someone who is neither one nor the other? (Francophones only) — 2002 — CRIC

	Sovereignist %	In between/neither %	Federalist %
Total	21	58	19
18–34 yrs	23	67	9
35–54 yrs	21	63	15
55 + yrs	18	45	35

Question 3: In order to improve the way the federation works, some people say we should make changes to Canada's constitution. Others disagree. In your opinion, is this the right time to return to the constitutional question, or should governments leave the issue alone? (All Quebecers) — 2003 — CRIC

Return to question:	36%
Leave issue alone:	52%
No answer:	12%

Question 4: Do you strongly agree, somewhat agree, somewhat disagree or strongly disagree with the following statement: "Quebec sovereignty is an idea whose time has passed"? — CRIC

	2000	2002
Agree	51%	56%
Disagree	44%	38%

Question 5: During the last referendum in October 1995, the Government of Quebec asked the following question: "Do you agree that Quebec should become sovereign, after having made a formal offer to Canada for a new economic and political partnership, within the scope of the bill respecting the future of Quebec and of the agreement signed on June 12, 1995?" In your opinion, is this referendum question… — 1999 — PCO

Question number	Questions and results	Date	Source
	Very clear 15%		
	Somewhat clear 24%		
	Not very clear 40%		
	Not at all clear 20%		
6	In the 1980 and 1995 referendums, the Quebec Government decided on the wording of the questions. If another referendum was to take place...	1999	PCO Survey

Treatment A: Do you think that the Quebec Government should decide the wording of the question on its own, as it has done in the past or that the Government and the opposition parties in the National Assembly should agree to the wording of the referendum question together?

Treatment B: Do you think that the Quebec Government should decide the wording of the question on its own, as it has done in the past or that the Governments of Quebec and Canada should agree to the wording of the referendum question together?

Treatment C: Do you think that the Quebec Government should decide the wording of the question on its own, as it has done in the past, or that Quebec and the rest of Canada should agree to the wording of the referendum question together?

Treatment:	A	B	C
Gov't of Quebec should set the question alone:	29%	43%	44%
Question should be set jointly:	68%	56%	53%
No answer	3%	1%	3%

7	Agree/Disagree statements:	1999	PCO Survey

"50% + 1 of votes in favour of sovereignty represents a clear majority."
"60% of votes in favour of sovereignty represents a clear majority."

	50% + 1	60%
Agree – represents clear majority	40%	70%
Disagree – does not represent clear majority	56%	25%
No answer	4%	5%

... continued

APPENDIX (Continued)

Question number	Questions and results	Date	Source
8	If the "Yes" side in a future referendum receives 50% + 1 of the vote, will it be very easy, somewhat easy, somewhat difficult, or very difficult for Quebec to become independent?	1999	PCO Survey

If the "Yes" side in a future referendum receives 60% of the vote, will it be very easy, somewhat easy, somewhat difficult, or very difficult for Quebec to become independent?

	With 50% + 1	With 60%
Very easy	2%	8%
Somewhat easy	10%	28%
Somewhat difficult	46%	41%
Very difficult	39%	19%

Question number	Questions and results	Date	Source
9	Question: Which of the two following statements more closely reflects your own view: After a "Yes" victory in a referendum, Quebecers will be more united than ever OR after a "Yes" victory in a referendum, Quebecers will be more divided than ever?	1999	PCO Survey

More united than ever	33%
More divided than ever	57%
No answer	11%

Question number	Questions and results	Source
10	Overall, including money and other considerations, does your province/territory put more into Confederation than it takes out, does it take out more than it puts in or does it take out about as much as it puts in?	CRIC

	Puts more in	Takes more out	About even
	%	%	%
NF	25	31	32
PEI	8	33	47
NS	9	39	32
NB	6	33	40
QC	37	15	34
ON	32	22	27
MB	10	23	46
SK	10	27	44
AB	55	8	26
BC	36	22	30

Question number	Questions and results	Date	Source
11	In recent years, do you think the federal and provincial governments have:	2002	CRIC

worked very well together	1%
worked somewhat well together	36%

Question number	Questions and results	Date	Source
	worked not very well together 46%		
	not worked at all well together 15%		
12	In your opinion, in the future, should the provincial govern- ments have more power, the federal government have more power, or should things stay as they are?	2003	CRIC

	Provincial gov't	Federal gov't	No change
	58%	9%	28%

| 13 | In your opinion, is your province treated with the respect it deserves in Canada or not? (percentage saying "Yes") | | CRIC |

1998	1999	2000	2001	2002	2003
41	39	43	45	42	42

| 14 | People have different ways of defining themselves. Do you consider yourself to be a Canadian only, a Canadian first but also a Quebecer, equally a Canadian and a Quebecer, a Quebecer first but also a Canadian, or a Quebecer only? | | CRIC |

	Cdn. only %	Cdn. first %	Both equally %	Que. first %	Que. only %
1999	8	16	25	31	17
2003	6	20	25	31	15

| 15 | If governments have budgetary surpluses, which of the following three things should be the HIGHEST priority: cutting taxes, paying down the debt or putting more money into social programs? | 2000 | CRIC |

	Cutting taxes %	Debt repayment %	Social progs. %
Atlantic	21	32	44
Quebec	37	28	33
Ontario	23	47	30
Man/Sask	27	42	31
Alberta	27	50	24
BC	30	34	35

| 16 | Health care costs are expected to rise in the future because of our aging population and because of the costs of new treatments and medications. Which of the following statements comes closest to your view? Would you say (a) governments should significantly INCREASE THEIR SPENDING on health care to cover these rising costs; (b) governments should LIMIT THE AVAILABILITY of | 2002 | CRIC |

... continued

APPENDIX (Continued)

Question number	Questions and results	Date	Source

some treatments or medications; or (c) governments should allow THE PRIVATE SECTOR to provide some health care services to those people who can afford to pay for them.

	Private services %	Limit services %	Increase spending %
Atlantic	29	8	62
Quebec	46	10	44
Ontario	30	7	63
Man/Sask	39	8	53
Alberta	36	11	53
BC	40	10	51

17 In your opinion, should Canada allow privately owned companies to deliver some health care services in Canada, or should the health care system be operated entirely as a public program?   2000   CRIC

	Allow private %	Entirely public %
Atlantic	24	74
Quebec	47	44
Ontario	29	66
Man/Sask	45	51
Alberta	39	58
BC	41	57

18 Question 1: Do you strongly agree, agree, disagree or strongly disagree with the following statement? It is the responsibility of the government to reduce the differences in income between people with high incomes and those with low incomes.   2002   CRIC

Question 2: Which of these two statements comes closest to your own opinion? (a) Both freedom and equality are important, but I consider personal freedom to be more important, that is, everyone can live in freedom and develop without hindrance; (b) Both freedom and equality are important, but I consider equality to be more important, that is, nobody is underprivileged and social class differences are not so strong.

	Quebec %	ROC %
Agree: Government responsibility to reduce income inequality	68	42
Equality more important than than freedom	59	43

Question number	Questions and results	Date	Source
19	The current Quebec Government wants to play a very active role in making the Canadian federation work. Do you strongly support, support, oppose, or strongly oppose this position?	2003	CRIC

	Support %	Oppose %
All respondents	74	20
"Yes" voters	64	30
"No" voters	86	10

Question number	Questions and results	Date	Source
20	Which of the following statements is closest to your opinion? 1999: The fact that the Parti Québécois is in power weakens Quebec's position in relations with the rest of Canada, or the fact that the Parti Québécois is in power strengthens Quebec's position in relations with the rest of Canada? 2003: The fact that the Liberal Party is in power in Quebec weakens Quebec's position in relations with the rest of Canada, or the fact that the Liberal Party is in power in Quebec strengthens Quebec's position in relations with the rest of Canada?	1999, 2003	1999: CROP/PCO; 2003: CRIC

	Weakens Quebec %	Strengthens Quebec %
PQ, 1999	40	42
PLQ, 2003	26	57

Question number	Questions and results	Date	Source
21	Thinking about how governments make decisions, which of the following do you think would be best for Canada? Is it: (a) the federal government should have the final say on some things, the provincial governments on others, and they should both stay out of each other's way; or (b) both levels of government should work most things out together?	2000	Cutler/ Mendelsohn CRIC

	Stay out of each other's way %	Work most things out together %
Atlantic	6	94
Quebec	31	65
Ontario	16	82
Manitoba	14	85
Saskatchewan	8	91
Alberta	17	82
BC	13	86

... continued

APPENDIX (Continued)

Question number	Questions and results	Date	Source
22	When there is a conflict between the federal government and your government, which one do you think is usually to blame: the federal government, your government or that both are usually equally to blame?		PCO 1997; CRIC 2003

	1997 %	2003 %
Federal government	9	12
Provincial government	3	3
Both equally	83	79
No answer	5	5

Question number	Questions and results	Date	Source
23	Do you feel that the federal government has enough, too much or too little revenue to fulfill its responsibilities? Do you feel that your provincial [territorial] government has enough, too much or too little revenue to fulfill its responsibilities? Do you feel that local or municipal governments have enough, too much or too little revenue to fulfill their responsibilities?	2003	CRIC

	Federal gov't too little revenue %	Provincial gov't too little revenue %	Local gov't too little revenue %
NF	58	87	70
PEI	31	59	59
NS	31	68	73
NB	32	58	58
QUE	14	43	48
ONT	24	40	58
MA	26	48	58
SA	35	65	62
AB	23	20	52
BC	27	48	46
YK	40	47	46
NWT	27	71	26

Refusals and the undecided have sometimes been excluded from the reporting to ease presentation.

3

One never knows… Sait-on jamais?[1]

Guy Laforest

Ce chapitre porte sur les particularités de l'expérience canadienne en ce qui a trait à cette institution politique moderne qu'est la nation-état. Ce chapitre compare divers éléments de l'identité du Canada et de celle du Québec. Ensuite, une interprétation des dynamiques derrière le mouvement souverainiste du Québec y est donnée. Ce chapitre essaie de répondre aux trois questions suivantes : pourquoi est-ce qu'un mouvement d'indépendance est apparu au Québec au cours de la deuxième moitié du vingtième siècle; pourquoi ce mouvement a-t-il échoué, du moins jusqu'à maintenant, et finalement; comment quatre décennies de pression exercée par le Québec et par le mouvement souverainiste depuis la Révolution tranquille ont-elles transformé la nature de l'État canadien et des politiques canadiennes ? Ce chapitre étudie aussi les conséquences des référendums de 1980 et de 1995 selon la logique géo-politique, mais en s'intéressant plus précisément aux tendances à long terme sur le plan de l'évolution historique. On peut considérer ces référendums comme étant les rébellions, manquées, de l'âge démocratique alors que les rébellions de 1837-1838, qui ont aussi échoué, furent celles de l'âge impérial. Ce chapitre se termine sur l'analyse des politiques québécoises et canadiennes compte tenu des arguments apportés dans cette étude.

INTRODUCTION

I borrow the French part of this title – modifying it slightly based on my own experiences – from the conclusion of a text written by one of my colleagues in sociology at Université Laval, Jean-Jacques Simard, for the 2000 edition of the *Annuaire du Québec* published by Fides (Simard 1999). Summarizing the evolution of Quebec in the last century, during which it emerged to the world with the clear conscience of a collective political identity, Simard proposes a synthesis while opening wide a path to the future by recalling license plate slogans. In the course of the 20th century, Quebec went from "La Belle Province" to "Je me souviens," carrying all the connotations that each of these expressions holds. And for the future? Simard leaves it open-ended with the suggestion of a new slogan for the contemporary era – "On sait jamais."

We have been gathered here at Queen's to share reflections and perspectives on the current state of Canada/Quebec relations, *grosso modo* a decade after the failed referendums on the Charlottetown Accord in Canada and on the sovereignty/partnership project in Quebec. Our common primary focus has to do with the relationships between state and society in Quebec, leading to some analysis and forecast concerning relationships between Quebec and Ottawa.

Much has indeed changed since the fall of 1995, and more so since the first months following the October 30 referendum. In both Quebec and in the rest of the country, the atmosphere between federalists and sovereignists is no longer characterized by aggressive rhetoric and the demonization of key personalities in the opposite camp. The path of dialogue has come full circle, even though, in elite establishments as well as in public opinion, a perceived mutual disloyalty has not completely disappeared (Laforest 1998, 414–15). A climate of deep bitterness and resentment characterized the years between 1996 and 1998. The following years leading to the election of Jean Charest's Liberal government in Quebec in 2003 were marked by the diffusion of anger and annoyance and, on both sides of the Outaouais river, a sort of overwhelming indifference. Much has changed, but much has nevertheless remained the same! It would be a grave mistake to merely seek to outline a hypothesis delineating a new Quebec, the kind one would find in the "new Canada" which was the subject of a series of articles in *The Globe and Mail* in June/July 2003.[2]

To avoid such pitfalls, this essay will proceed, first, with an attempt to identify some invariants in Canada/Quebec relations in the 19th and 20th centuries. I will thereafter discuss three questions concerning Quebec's sovereignty movement: what explains its birth; why has it failed so far; and how have its misfortunes contributed to the reshaping of Canada? Finally, I will briefly discuss some key transformations of the past decades in Canada and Quebec, attempting to show linkages between these changes and the forms of movement we have witnessed in our political environment between 1998 and 2006.

UNDERSTANDING CANADA

For some years, along with Stéphane Kelly, I have been quite interested in the parliamentary debates that took place in Britain's North American colonies in the 19th century, and which led to Canada's foundation as a federal Dominion in 1867. Many will recall that Stoddart's millennial project was a reference work edited by Janet Ajzenstat, Paul Romney, Ian Gentles and William Gairdner (Ajzenstat et al. 1999). A French-language edition was subsequently published by Presses de l'Université Laval, supervised by Kelly and myself. We added a new introduction and proposed a bibliographic synthesis skimming through the evolution in the interpretation of our founding debates in the French-speaking political and intellectual classes of the country. Kelly and I believe that these debates help us understand Canada's unique place in the historical journey of that key institution known as the "modern state." In his recent theoretical work, British philosopher Bhikhu Parekh presents and defines the characteristic principles of the modern state:

First, it should be territorially distinct, possess a single source of sovereignty and enjoy legally unlimited authority within its boundaries.

Second, it should rest on a single set of constitutional principles and exhibit a singular and unambiguous identity.

Third, citizens of the state should enjoy equal rights. And since their social, cultural and other differences are abstracted away, equal rights generally mean identical or uniform rights.

Fourth, citizenship is a unitary, unmediated and homogeneous relationship between the individual and the state.

Fifth, members of the state constitute a single and united people.

Finally, if the state is federally constituted, its component units should enjoy broadly the same rights and powers, as otherwise citizens in different parts of the country would possess different rights, thereby detracting from the principles of equal citizenship and homogeneous legal space. (Parekh 2000, 182–3)

In this definition, Parekh describes the dominant traits of what passes for a "normal nation-state" in our modern era. It is the model that emerged in the aftermath of the treaty of Westphalia in 1648. This model roughly corresponds to the historical experiences of France and of the United States of America. Both Germany and Spain were developed from a looser version of this model, stemming both from a more diffused understanding of sovereignty and from an acceptance of substantial asymmetrical forms. However, for my own purposes here, the essential lies elsewhere. As is well known, the founders of the Canadian federation wished for the new Dominion a constitution based on the British inheritance. Great Britain was – and remains – substantially at odds with the hegemonic approach towards the nation-state. In a regime where predominant authority lies with the "King or Queen in Parliament," sovereignty is not clearly rooted with either the "people" or with the "nation." The idea of a transparent, single national political identity is moreover lacking in Great Britain. In the 19th century, the general configuration of the Empire further complicated this portrait, tossing in a good dose of asymmetry in the general identity of the whole structure: the United Kingdom of Great Britain and Ireland, the Dominions, India, the colonies which cherished the principle of responsible government, the colonies of the Crown, and other dependent entities. Perhaps Great Britain was not as diverse as the Holy Roman German Empire before the era of Napoleonic simplifications, but it was certainly not a concrete example of Parekh's model.

In the context of this theoretical development, how should we perceive the political identity of the Dominion of Canada in 1867? That year, the colonies of United Canada, New Brunswick and Nova Scotia obtained from London the creation of a new power, a Dominion comprising a federal union of four provinces, including Quebec. A quarter of a century after the Act of Union, Lower Canada – Quebec – had rediscovered an autonomous political existence. The question of self-government occupied a crucial place in the debates of the time. In my opinion, however, to understand the equilibrium and nature of the Dominion's entire political configuration, we must look, once more, to the words of John A. Macdonald:

> As this is to be one united province, with the local governments and legislature subordinate to the general government and legislature, it is obvious that the chief executive officer in each of the provinces must be subordinate as well. The general government assumes towards the local government precisely the same position as the imperial government holds with respect to each of the colonies now... (Ajzenstat 1999, 284)

Understanding Canada in 1867 means noting the development of a three-tiered hierarchical structure. The British government and the Parliament of Westminster were vital to the Empire's grandeur. In the face of these powers, the government of the Dominion and Ottawa's parliament enjoyed a substantial degree of autonomy while still remaining, in various domains, subject to their authority. Between central authorities on one side, and their equals in the Canadian provinces on the other, there was a seemingly prevailing relationship, except that, for the Dominion and Ottawa, there was a variation in the position. It was the Dominion and Canadian parliament that found themselves in the dominating role, and often in the same spheres of activity.

In the history of the modern state, France and the United States have been characterized by a taste for radical ruptures and doctrinaire spirits. By contrast, Great Britain has developed a political culture adhering to an unmistakable quest – think of Burke – for moderation, evolution and a pragmatic attitude. In the search towards its own identity as a nation-state, Canada has for the most part respected the constitutional and political morality of the British Motherland. From 1867 to 1982, gradually, moderately, and without much radical conflict, Canada has achieved legal and political modernization, thus becoming a clearly recognizable independent nation-state. This is the story of the quiet decolonization of Canada, that of a progressive elimination, completed in 1982, of all forms of subordination of Ottawa to London. The main stages of this history are well known: the Imperial Conferences of 1897 and 1902, where Laurier opposed the recentralization of the Empire as desired by the then Secretary of the Colonies, Joseph Chamberlain; the statute of Westminster in 1931; the abolition in 1949 of the procedure of appeal to the Judicial Committee of the Privy Council; the repatriating of the Constitution in 1982, carrying with it a Charter of Rights and Canadian control for the newly-minted amending formula. Since April 17, 1982, there has been no trace of the umbilical cord linking Canada to London. But what of the relationship between Ottawa and the provinces?

To formulate my opinion on this matter, I begin with two logically related definitions of federalism, borrowed respectively from André Burelle and Réjean Pelletier:

> The genius of federalism is to allow fruitful cohabitation within one large political entity comprising two orders of sovereign government: one known as master of local matters, to ensure the privacy of culture and political autonomy for its federated communities, and the other, declared master of all that is managed at the central level, to enable the realization of common economic, social and political goals necessary to regulate the problems that are beyond the limited means of action and jurisdiction shared by the diverse partners of the federation. (Burelle 1994, 127)[3]

Considered from this angle, federalism must respect two principles:

> [A] principle of autonomy in which each state member of the federation, including the central authority, can act freely within its sphere of competence, and can make decisions that will not be revised by another level of government;

> [A] principle of participation in which the federated communities are implicated in decision-making at the central level by their presence, for example, in political institutions (House of Commons, Senate, Executive Council) where decisions concerning the federation as a whole are made. (Pelletier 2005, 44)

Of course, many other definitions of federalism can be found in academic literature. Possibly the most famous one has come out of the very precise mind of Ronald Watts: federalism is a combination of self-rule and shared rule. The definitions provided by Burelle and Pelletier seem to me quite representative of the dominant vision of federalism in post-Quiet Revolution Quebec. I am not saying that such a contemporary understanding perfectly renders the way in which our founders, including Cartier, saw this doctrine. Burelle certainly in my mind comes close to Cartier's vision when he insists on the desire for the federated communities, beginning with Quebec, to manage, in an autonomous fashion, all that has to do with their local cultures. Furthermore, recent work has clearly established that, in the Maritimes but also in Ontario, a strong autonomist tradition actively sustained the federalization of the British North American domain in 1867, struggling as they were to develop their own approach to the principle of self government.[4] Customary mechanical repetitions of Macdonald's centralist vision substantially impoverish anglophone political thought at the time of Confederation. However, from the perspective of comparative analysis of federal regimes, we also neglect something important in the historical and political culture of Canada when we lose sight of the unavoidable role of the imperial principle in the institutions and mentalities of the Dominion of Canada in 1867. There remains even today something of this latter principle at work in the relationships between the Dominion and the provinces.

There will of course be an air of familiarity, to anyone who has perused introductory textbooks on Canadian politics or on Canadian constitutional law, in the list of elements establishing the subordination of the provinces to the Dominion Parliament and governments after 1867: the preamble of Article 91 of the then *B.N.A. Act* (the "peace, order and good government" doctrine), the powers of reservation and disallowance of provincial legislation, the extreme centralization of the judiciary branch in general including judicial appointments, the process of appointments to the Senate, the capacity of Ottawa to introduce remedial legislation in the field of education, residuary authority on all general matters, declaratory power, the privileges of the centre related to the creation of new provinces, the power to nominate Lieutenant-Governors in provinces. Let there be no misunderstanding: my premises here are in no way deterministic. All these elements could have disappeared after 1867, and it remains possible, although quite difficult for those matters related to the Crown such as the appointments of Lieutenant-Governors, subject to the unanimity side of the 1982 amending formula, that they could become null and void during the span of the 21st century. We miss, however, something crucial in the assessment of the nature and role of the federal principle in the relationship between Ottawa and the provinces, when we neglect both the power of the imperial principle and the presence of the three-tiered hierarchical structure (Westminster/Dominion/provinces) alluded to by Macdonald in the aforementioned passage. These elements form part of what political scientists call the institutional logic ("the principles that make it tick and give a sense of order and purpose to the actors within it") of the structure in 1867 and they are still necessary to understand the institutions and the political context of contemporary Canada (Archer et al. 1999, 6).

Imagine, for the sake of argument, that in 1867 there was a creative tension between the imperial and federal principles in Canada's political system.[5] In the decades following 1867, numerous factors combined to widen the area devoted to the federal principle, thus bridging the power and sovereignty gaps between Ottawa and the provinces. Many historical and theoretical dimensions related to the doctrine of federalism combined their efforts to produce such a result: the judicial doctrine of coordination without subordination, the philosophical approach insisting on the need, jointly, to preserve the autonomy of federated entities and to foster their participation in central institutions, the originally neglected relevance of provincial constitutional powers to address key aspects of the evolution of 20th century modern societies, the transformations of nationalism in Quebec, province-building elsewhere in Canada, the depth of federalist convictions of numerous political leaders of the country from Laurier to Pearson.

I would go as far as claiming that at least twice Canada came remarkably close to setting into motion a dynamic that could have led to perfecting the federal modernization of its political regime: between 1965 and 1968, under the political leadership of Pearson and the intellectual inspiration of Laurendeau, and then between 1987 and 1992 during the Meech Lake–Charlottetown era. Both attempts failed, not without consequences, as we shall see later on in this chapter on the future of our political life. This story was further complicated by the fact that Quebec tried twice to break free from the country founded in 1867. This dimension has to be integrated, if we are to understand correctly the current predicaments of Canada and Quebec. To repeat the point, one must identify the rapport, the logic between the 1980 and 1995 referendums on one side, and the spirit of the foundation on the other.

The previous development was premised on historical reason. Without abandoning history altogether I now turn to strategic reason, of the kind we learn about in realist schools of thought in international relations (going back at least as far as the famous Greek historian, Thucydides). From this perspective, the 1980 and 1995 referendums hold the value of rebellions. According to the sociology of political action, sovereignty referendums are the second highest level in the scale of opposition political behaviour, immediately below the seizing of arms in a guerrilla, revolution or civil war.[6] Rationally and logically, a referendum is a democratic political rebellion. Whenever we rebel, we do it on the premise that we will be stronger if we win; thus, we should accept that we will be weaker if we happen to lose. Notwithstanding the remarkably close results of the 1995 referendum, there were clearly three categories of losers: Quebec as a geo-political entity, the sovereignty movement, and the dominant political leaders within it. I have come to believe on this issue exactly the contrary of what I wrote in the pages of *Le Devoir* in the immediate aftermath of the referendum. Since 1995, I believe that not only Parti Québécois governments and leaders, from Jacques Parizeau to Lucien Bouchard, Bernard Landry and André Boisclair, but also the vast majority of sovereignist intellectuals, have neglected the strategic task of analyzing without complacency the referendum saga and its consequences.[7] I offer here, as well as in the next section, some preliminary reflections in the hope of contributing to such a task.

In the 19th century, the failed and armed rebellions of the imperial era in 1837 and in 1838 led to the Durham Report and the Act of Union. The act of rebelling, and failing, led to negative consequences for the rebels, their leaders, their cause and their colonial society. In the matter at hand, it seems to me both logical and fair to distinguish the issue of the evaluation of the rebels' motives from the judgment of the tactical opportunity of the very act of rebelling. This caused dreadful dilemmas for the principal political players of the time, notably Etienne Parent and Louis-Joseph Papineau from Lower Canada (Lamonde 2000, 238ff). The failure of the rebellions at the time led to a tightening of the system, to a reinforcement of its imperial dimension. Scarcely two years after the rebellions were subdued, London imposed a new constitution. Durham's great design, as we all know, was neither completely applied nor permanently executed: he sought complete amalgamation of the colonies, assimilation and responsible government. He got the first two, but only for a short time, and did not live long enough to witness the conventional granting of responsible government in 1848. In large part thanks to the actions of Lafontaine and Robert Baldwin, the status of the French language in parliament was rather quickly re-established. As I just wrote, responsible government was next in 1848, and Lower Canada rediscovered a substantial kind of political autonomy under the name of the Province of Quebec in 1867. This flow of events, however, takes nothing away from the logical sequence in my argument: rebellion, failure, tightening of the system, negative consequences for the losers, at least for a certain time.

In the structure of my argument, the 1980 and 1995 referendums represent the failed rebellions of the democratic era. The first referendum led directly to the constitutional reform of 1981–1982, achieved without the consent of either the government or the National Assembly of Quebec. This goes along with the evaluation that the referendum led to the weakening not only of the sovereignist movement, but also of Quebec as a whole in the forum of Canadian politics. Much has been written and said about the existence of a veto right for Quebec in our federal system. The key point remains that the referendum and its result changed everything. The second referendum on sovereignty/partnership in 1995 led a few years later to the Supreme Court's reference case concerning the secession of Quebec and to the Clarity Act in 1999. Feeble public reactions in Quebec to the latter initiative of the Chrétien government left the premier of Quebec, Lucien Bouchard, completely stupefied. This event, coupled with the progression of the Chrétien Liberals during the November 2000 federal elections were the real causes provoking Bouchard's retreat from the public sphere. The Trudeau regime and the recently completed Chrétien era have both been characterized by legislative initiatives made possible by two Quebec referendums organized and ultimately lost by sovereignist governments.

In Canada's modern political history, there remains a shared logic, not-withstanding huge differences, in the failed rebellions of our democratic era and the failed rebellions of the 19th century. The transition from the first era to the second one has of course been characterized by substantial liberalization and democratization of our institutions and political culture. I nevertheless claim that there are still some imperial remnants in our political system, notably regarding the relationships between Ottawa and the provinces, and singularly in the relations between the Canadian state and Quebec. Paradoxically, in twice trying to escape the system or change it, Quebec has perhaps reinforced these elements, making it even more difficult to eliminate them. Whatever the case, and with all the necessary caveats involved in comparing different historical periods, the logical chain of events would be the same in the 20th century as that which prevailed in the previous one: rebellions, failures, hardening of the system and negative consequences for the losers (individual actors, the cause they defended and their self-proclaimed political community or "patria").

I have argued in this section that in order to understand contemporary Canada as a federal political community, it is necessary to consider at length the historical and strategic importance of Quebec in its evolution. The following excerpts from a book on Canadian federalism, published over 50 years ago by the late Senator Maurice Lamontagne, then Professor of Economics in the Faculté des sciences sociales at Université Laval, will help me make the transition to a section devoted to understanding Quebec, the dynamics of the sovereignty movement and their consequences for the Canadian state:

> Quebec's actual position is hybrid and ambiguous and cannot last. One member of a federation cannot cling indefinitely to a bygone phase of federalism while all other members desire to evolve to new forms. The way in which Quebec currently participates in the life of the Canadian federation is that of a province submitting to the drawbacks of the federation without benefiting from all its advantages, while the rest of Canada is in a hurry to attain new objectives... The province of Quebec must therefore become conscious of this reality and make a choice. She is currently in a dilemma: either she accepts the new Canadian federalism and integrates, or she refuses it and disassociates. What should she do? By and large, this is the question the population poses. (Lamontagne 1954, 284 and 286)

Lamontagne wrote this passage at the beginning of the 1950s, during the era of the Tremblay Commission (Commission of Inquiry on Constitutional Problems), put into motion by Maurice Duplessis' government to respond to a

phase of recentralization in Canada brought about by the conclusions of the
Report of the Rowell-Sirois Commission, as well as by the necessities of ad-
ministering the land in the time of war and reconstruction. Yet, this passage
remains pertinent in reflecting on Quebec's situation since the advent of the
first Parti Québécois government in 1976 and until today. It remains a hybrid
and ambiguous situation – Quebec doesn't leave the federation, yet doesn't
participate in it to its full advantage. Contrary to what Lamontagne believed,
this situation can last. I would add that, on a political horizon expanded by the
October 30 1995 referendum, this situation could get worse. To see this more
clearly, I now turn to the genesis of Quebec's sovereignist movement, to search
its motivations and the reasons for its failures, and finally to establish the
consequences of all of this on the Canadian state.

UNDERSTANDING QUEBEC, THE SOVEREIGNTY MOVEMENT AND THE CONSEQUENCES OF THE 1980 AND 1995 REFERENDUMS

To provide the kind of understanding I have in mind in this section, it will be
necessary to answer the following three questions: What are the principal
motives explaining the birth and later on the development of a strong independence movement in Quebec in the second half of the 20th century? What
are the key factors that have accounted at least until now for the inability of
this movement, led by the Parti Québécois in the political sphere, to secure its
primary objective? How have the Quiet Revolution and four decades of for-
midable political pressures exerted by Quebec and the independence movement
transformed Canada? Each of these questions deserves a specific and ad-
equately elaborate study. I will be satisfied in this essay to sketch the main
outlines of my answers, without delving too deeply into the debate with exhaustive scholarly references. To better see the future paths of Quebec and
Canada, it seems to me one must seriously consider such questions, rather
than dodging them.

We shall start by looking again at the definition of the nation-state which I
presented in the previous section, borrowing it from Bhikhu Parekh. An independence movement was first born in the second half of the 20th century to
perfect, within the boundaries of Quebec, the plan for a modern nation-state.
Frequently employed by sovereignist leaders from René Lévesque to Jacques
Parizeau, the logic of historical and political standardization, or normalization, was well summarized by Gérard Bergeron:

> It is the call to independence. The idea trickled, timid at first, over a couple
> centuries, then ran strong for 20-odd years. And aside from Séguin's idea, this
> "nation annexée" (annexed nation) is in possession of a state, a federated state
> in a federal state: moreover, its territory is vast and rich, its population strong

and developed, its homogeneous culture dominant and capable of expanding. Can you find amidst a hundred new independent states since the war, more than five or six whose society can boast such clear titles of independence and international sovereignty as ours?

For the believer in independence, it's only natural. It is the first sacred duty of our fraternity, a requirement of our dignity before history to reach the end of this process of progressive freedom. This independence should have been achieved long ago, as it is inscribed in our destiny, we possess all of its elements, and we have the means to realize it , including the technical and economic means, etc. In brief, it is absurd to think otherwise, or to accept a lesser destiny. (Blouin and Bergeron 1982, 21–22)[8]

The decolonization of the Americas was an important chapter in the plan to universalize the modern nation-state born in Western Europe. The British, Spanish and Portuguese empires left over 20 sovereign states in the Americas. That Quebec, the most important settlement colony of France – in other words the son or daughter of the mother of all nations to use an expression dear to Christian Dufour – was tempted in the course of its political modernization by the movement of standardization associated with the idea of the nation-state, should not surprise anybody. It's the opposite that would have been surprising! It's also evident that the sovereignist movement was sustained in the 1960s by theories and practices linked to the ideology of decolonization that accompanied the new independences, notably in Africa.

To this design of political normalization we must add the reasons and interpretations proposed by nationalist thought in its diverse incarnations. Some wanted independence to achieve republican self-rule, others to erase the traces of the Conquest and thus cure a deep wound in the collective unconscious of the community, others to attain for Quebec the full political autonomy needed to preserve the security of its identity in America, while others came to believe in the necessity of independence from a weariness with a Canada refusing to carry out its transformation into a true modern federation. Others, such as Fernand Dumont and Marcel Rioux, were stirred by a deep and genuine thirst for social justice.[9]

The desire for recognition played equally in all these reasonings. In modernity, independence is the highest, most advanced level of political fulfillment. Consequently, it guarantees recognition in and from the international community. This quest for acknowledgment took on particular traits in the unfolding of the aspiration towards Quebec sovereignty. The political and intellectual classes of Quebec had, since Henri Bourassa to the era of André Laurendeau, strongly viewed Canada in dualistic categories (two founding peoples, two nations, two distinct societies). For those who start with such intellectual background, achieving independence has the additional merit of securing the

recognition by English-speaking Canada, viewed, to borrow from Charles
Taylor's conceptual apparatus as the "Significant Other," precisely the kind
of recognition that is seen as having eluded French Canada and Quebec in the
history of the country.

At its last plenary congress in June 2005, the Parti Québécois adopted a
new program entitled "Un projet de pays," which attempts to clarify for our
times the various motivations that animate the sovereignty movement. The
first two categories of reasons are deemed to be fundamental. The first one
pertains to identity matters: Quebec is seen as a nation, belonging to this nation is a reality, the people of Quebec are linked by a common history, a
language, a culture that have fashioned a distinct national identity in the Americas. The fact that the nation exists and the reality of this sense of belonging
form the basis of the will to transform this nation into a country. The second
reason has to do with political freedom: the nation of Quebec should have the
ability to make its own choices, to foster its own institutions, to control its
own resources and to speak in its own name in the concert of nations. The new
program identifies three additional categories of motivations, seen as essential and complementary to the fundamental ones: these reasons cover the issues
of global governance (sovereignty seen as necessary in the context of the
emergence of new international decision-making centres), tackle the perspective of increased resources (repatriating sources of revenue that are in Ottawa,
greater control of Maritime resources and infrastructures), and they insist finally on the requirements of democratic modernization (republican self-rule,
decentralization and transparency) (Parti Québécois 2005, 10–23).

How to explain that Quebec, in these first years of the new millennium, has
not yet been able to obtain the much-cherished status of a modern, normal
nation-state? The first answer springs from the evidence: because, at two intervals, citizens who were democratically invited to join a political movement
nourished by this goal simply refused to lend it their majority support. If he
were still with us, Gérard Bergeron would give the same answer. So why,
then, didn't it work? The following list of reasons opens debate on the subject:

- The sovereignist campaign, particularly in 1995, failed because of misfor-
  tune. Luck simply didn't attend the rendez-vous. 30,000 votes more and it
  would have been in the bag. This argument fails to convince me. Canada
  and Quebec barely escaped a very serious political crisis in 1995, in part
  because in Ottawa Mr. Chrétien and his government were ill-prepared, while
  in Quebec City Mr. Parizeau and his own government misunderstood the
  complexity of the situation. A triumph for the "Yes" side could have changed
  the system, but it remains improbable that sovereignty would have come
  about.
- The sovereignists failed, especially in 1980, because of the presence in Ottawa of an exceptional Québécois political leader in the person of Pierre

Elliott Trudeau. More generally, their project was rejected in 1980 but also to a certain extent in 1995 because Canadians, during the strategically most important periods of democratic discussion on sovereignty, were given a great number of quality federal rulers originating in Quebec.

- What happened was quite predictable, because secessions are rare events in a democracy. This argument has been put forward by Stéphane Dion in his academic career. It goes back to the sharp mind of John Locke, who famously suggested in the 17th century that it is not as simple as many believe to motivate people to fix unjust institutions, even when everyone sees that the time is right and favourable. According to this argument, criticisms of the shortcomings of the Canadian federation were not strong or decisive enough to persuade the Québécois people to vote in favour of sovereignty. The greatest strength of a political regime is the simple fact that it exists. This is the law of inertia. Why, one could ask, take significant political risks when people have a fair dose of economic prosperity, of personal comfort and enjoy fundamental rights and institutional stability? At a micro level, I would claim that this argument sheds some light on the fact that in the region where I live, largely francophone greater Quebec City, the "Yes" side only got 53 percent in 1995.

- The 1980 and 1995 referendum results are explicable in part because sovereignists paid no heed to the pan-Canadian loyalty of a substantial sector of the francophone population, that which directly benefited from socialization and schooling experiences outside the institutional network produced by the Quiet Revolution. My explanation here is possibly too complex. Older Québécois, but not only they, can in no way whatsoever bring themselves to abandon the country that many see as having been founded by their ancestors.

- The vast majority of anglophones and allophones in Quebec were against sovereignty. Their unconditional allegiance to Canada is the cornerstone of their political identity. As long as this remains so, it will prove difficult for sovereignists to come close to the kind of qualified majority necessary not only to win a referendum, but mostly to sustain through time the realization of independence.

- Sovereignty failed, in both 1980 and 1995, because in a variety of ways the federal government failed to comply with Quebec's referendum legislation. Many episodes linked to the recent inquiry by Judge Gomery have heightened the popularity of this explanation in Quebec's sovereignist circles.

- Quebec's accession to sovereignty was blocked by the inadequacies of the principal political vehicle of its cause, the Parti Québécois. The model of nationalism endorsed by the PQ remained too unanimous (even the very name of the party appeared to monopolize the national identity), too close to French-Canadian cultural homogeneity to draw a sufficient proportion of anglophone and allophone voters, and ultimately too close to the old ethnic

French-Canadian nationalism passed on from the ultramontane clergy of the 19th century to the Alliance Laurentienne in the 1950s, and which made its way into the founding of the Parti Québécois with the contribution of the Ralliement national in the 1960s. These motives suggest that between the drive to protect a distinct identity and the broadening – in classic republican style – of collective and political liberties, the Parti Québécois chose to make the first their priority, as seen in the party's first big legislative initiative, the Charter of the French Language (which ultimately became Bill 101). The PQ has thus failed, to the present day, on the side of political freedom, because it has concentrated instead on identity issues. By the way, the logic of identity remains, as we just saw the first one mentioned by the PQ in the most recent edition of its program.[10]

- The misfortunes of the sovereignist movement are also attributable to a series of strategic errors: the 1974 adoption of gradualism (étapisme), forcing the PQ to concentrate on the day-to-day management of a provincial state and depriving party rhetoric of much of the symbolical power and logical coherence associated with the aspiration to independence; the decision in 1980 to go forward with the referendum after the dramatic return of Pierre Trudeau on the federal scene; finally, Jacques Parizeau's decision in 1994–1995 not to precede the vote on sovereignty with a referendum attempting to contest the legitimacy of the 1982 Canadian constitution in Quebec.

- A different approach to the latter aspect of the previous argument is possible. We can argue that, until now, Quebec sovereignists have been by and large "state sovereignists." They have always been very hesitant to put the people first. It is for this reason that they became gradualists in the mid-seventies, that they did not hold immediately a referendum in the early eighties to contest the legitimacy of a Canadian constitution that had never been directly submitted to the people, either throughout Canada or in Quebec. Thus, they may be seen as having failed for lack of nerve and coherence vis-à-vis their primary ground, the logic of sovereignty.

- Quebec's sovereignty movement was also slowed by its inability to round up a critical support system in the international community. On this issue, one could take time to reconstruct the positions and strategic calculations of the United States, France, Great Britain, India, Russia, China, the European Union, and finally the Commonwealth and Organisation de la francophonie. A full examination of this dimension would require considering the role of the Canadian state on both bilateral and multilateral levels. The late Gérard Bergeron has always maintained that the international dimension (mostly the interests or "reason of state" of France, the U.K. and the United States) was the Achilles heel in the drive towards independence for Quebec.

- Still on the international front, and in particular at the time of the 1995 referendum, analysts paid too little attention to the importance of aboriginal issues. 1994–2004 was considered by the United Nations as the International Decade of the World's Indigenous Peoples. The Oka crisis in 1990, the situation in Mexican Chiapas in 1994, and the ceremonies surrounding the 500th anniversary of the arrival of Columbus in America are just some of the markers that, combined, provoked a resurgence of the aboriginal issue in the international conscience during the course of the last decade. The question surrounding the rights of the Cree and Inuit peoples in Northern Quebec was an important complicating factor in 1995 for advocates of Quebec sovereignty.

- In transforming not only Canada's legal environment but also its political culture, and notably by reinforcing the unconditional allegiance of important segments of the Quebec population to Canadian national symbols and institutions, including the Charter of Rights and Freedoms, the constitutional reform of 1982 played a significant role in the outcome of the 1995 referendum.

- The aforementioned factors stem from various schools of thought. Further arguments could be added. To conclude this list without exhausting the subject, I quote an excerpt from an article by my colleague, Daniel Jacques, who has described the disillusionment of first generation sovereignists who had given greater importance to social justice as a catalyst for independence: "In truth, this nationalism can no longer fool anyone; its drought, its poverty on the symbolic level, its insignificance, are all manifest. If the priority is really on individual well-being, if this apparently collective plan is at the service of the economy and thus if sovereignty is nothing but an economic lever, then call things by their name, and at best a hypertrophied form of regionalism will emerge" (Jacques 1995, 222).[11]

Whatever the causes for the failure of Quebec's march towards sovereignty, it seems evident to me that for as long as they were in power between 1995 and 2003, PQ leaders have lacked the kind of cold rationality that is needed to assess the strategic situation of one's political community. For a long time, they assumed that victory had been close at hand. They preferred to see the 1995 results as a quasi-victory rather than a harsh defeat carrying with it bleak consequences. I shall now attempt to consider the numerous transformations of the Canadian political system that can be mostly related to the dynamism of Quebec society and to the sovereignty movement born with the advent of the Quiet Revolution. The consequences of the failed referendums will be once again integrated in my remarks.

It begs repetition that Quebec has put intense pressure on the Canadian political system since 1960. Canadian institutions and political culture were altered either to incite a better integration of Quebec's realities, or to respond directly to Quebec's demands, or to prevent Quebec's grievances from threatening the very integrity of Canada. The linguistic alienation in Montreal at the end of the fifties, elevated to poetic universality by Gaston Miron and the Hexagone generation, led ultimately to the adoption in 1969 of a pan-Canadian politics of symmetric bilingualism. The cohort of demands in favour of cultural and national dualism, carried by Daniel Johnson (Sr.), André Laurendeau and Léon Dion, prepared the ground for a pan-Canadian politics of multiculturalism. The considerable energy devoted to the struggle for constitutional changes increasing provincial powers in general and those of Quebec in particular were the object, to borrow an expression from Hegel, of a remarkable "Aufhebung" (the act of transforming, of surmounting something to one's own advantage); a new constitution was indeed ratified in 1982, but without a new division of powers, without the consent of the government and National Assembly of Quebec, and finally with reduced powers for Quebec. This logic has also had its international dimension: the rationale and passion behind the quest for sovereignty were largely fed by a desire for greater international recognition. Paradoxically, Quebec didn't achieve this desired state of international recognition, but Canada did gain substantial international acknowledgment with the fact that, since 1999, it can claim to be perhaps the only state on the planet to specify in constitutional language the democratic conditions for a legitimate secession attempt by one of the members of its federation.

Since the advent to power of Pierre Trudeau in 1968, the federal government has gradually moved to higher degrees of determination in its will to use all means to battle Quebec sovereignty, not only in Quebec but also all over Canada and across the world. It seems to me that this determination was augmented with the first victory of a PQ government in 1976, and that it achieved strongly effective means with the adoption of the new constitutional law in 1982. With regards to Pierre Trudeau, whom I regard as the last and probably the greatest of the founders of modern Canada, it is clear that he has coherently believed that it was necessary to transform the country into what I have called in this essay a "normal nation-state" to counter the aims of Quebec sovereignists. The following passages were respectively published in 1967 and 1987:

One way to counterbalance the lure of separatism is to invest time, energy and massive funds in federal nationalism. We must create an image of the national reality that is so enticing, the sovereigntist movement dulls in comparison. We must commit a part of our resources to things like the Canadian flag, the national anthem, education, the council of the arts, radio and television societies, film bureaus... In brief, we must make all our citizens feel that in the setting of the federal state, their language, culture, institutions, their most sacred traditions and their quality of life are shielded from all exterior assaults and all interior conflicts. (Trudeau 1967, 204–5)

But once again, it's the all-important tendency, the weight on the scale on the side of provincialism at the expense of a federal institution, or legislation that, until now, gives to Canadians a sense of national belonging, a bit like how the *Charter of Rights and Freedoms* was important for Canadian unity, a bit like the repatriation of the Constitution, a bit like the Canadian flag. All this is important in the sense that it helps Canadians understand that they share with all Canadians from all corners of the nation the same fundamental values. (Trudeau and Johnson 1988, 41)

One of the first effects of the October 1995 referendum was to intensify, even more than during the Trudeau era, the determination of key federal leaders in Ottawa to resort to all the symbolic and financial means of Canadian "nation-building" to save the country and protect it from all new threats coming from the sovereignist camp in Quebec. We find examples of this in the diverse programs of Heritage Canada under the stewardship of Sheila Copps on both the citizenship and educational fronts. With the sponsorship scandal of the past couple of years, all kinds of new evidence was parlayed through the daily workings of the Gomery Commission. This affair, our sponsorship scandal, had political consequences in the January 2006 federal election, and it has led to a report suggesting all kinds of institutional reforms. I will discuss current politics in the last section of this essay. Although there is no need to belabour the point, it seems clear to me that revelations made to Judge Gomery confirmed my hypothesis: after 1995, literally all means, including breaking laws and bribing people, were deemed appropriate at the highest level of the state in order to save Canada. With all the emphasis on the doubtful ethical practices behind all this, we run the risk of forgetting that there were immediate and harsh consequences in the fiscal domain after the 1995 referendum. Since 1996, in the context of its efforts to reduce both deficit and debt, Ottawa chose to sharply diminish the level of its transfers to all provinces; that this policy came with the additional advantage of weakening the financial base of a sovereignist government in Quebec had to play a significant role in the rationale for it. In view of the immense fear felt by Chrétien and by the entire country the night of October 30, 1995, and in view of the ferociousness of the arguments against Chrétien in the anglophone media after that fateful evening, is it not logical to think that the Prime Minister and his colleagues did all they could, including in the economic realm, to complicate the Parti Québécois' task of creating winning conditions? In my opinion, the contemporary problem widely known as the fiscal imbalance is in direct line with the referendum fear of 1995.

The structural effects of the 1995 referendum and, more generally, the consequences of the pressures exerted by the sovereignist movement, have been numerous and lasting. This explains, at least partially, the enormous concentration of power in the hands of the Prime Minister, as analyzed by Donald Savoie.[17] This has also explained the post-Meech and post-Charlottetown fragmentation of political parties at the federal level with a paradox that is nothing short of cruel: Mr. Chrétien and his allies in the federal Liberal Party contributed to the demise of the Meech Lake Accord, and they were thereafter "punished" by three majority governments that enabled them to rule Canada without much opposition for more than a decade. I add that the fear instilled by the 1995 referendum was of such great scope that it profoundly diminished the taste for critical reflection in media and academic circles, and in the enlightened public of English-speaking Canada. To be loyal Canadian patriots, after 1995, it was preferable not to dwell too much on the deficiencies and problems of our political system. The federation worked and, for the vast majority of observers, that's all that mattered. At a deeper lever, it is fully possible that the fears of 1995 contributed to a heightened and genuine sense of patriotism and Canadian nationalism throughout the land.

In support of the pioneering work of Alan Cairns, I have tried to show in research done in the 1990s that the 1982 reform concealed a defederalizing potential for Canada's political culture and constitutional evolution. This defederalizing logic was reinforced by the 1995 referendum and by the nature of its results. Over the last decade, there has been precious little talk advocating the modernization of Canadian federal institutions (the Senate, Supreme Court, coordinating mechanisms such as the First Ministers Conference, elimination of quasi-federal or quasi-imperial elements listed earlier in this essay). Until quite recently, provincial governments have chosen to listen to their public and they have retreated and left to the central government the essential of the initiative in the battle to "preserve the integrity of the nation." Ever since 1995, the existing gap between Quebec and the rest of Canada has widened with regards to reciprocal perceptions (I take this to be relevant for media and government elites, but also for public opinion on both sides). In Quebec, most people believe that the 1982 constitution was imposed on us in a disloyal fashion (to give an example, it will never be possible to do to any province, in the future, according to the 1982 amending formula, what was done to Quebec at the time). On the other side, most Canadians reproach the Quebec sovereignist governments for having acted in a disloyal manner in its referendum initiatives (one camp chooses the question, the timing, the organizational parameters, and benefits from a potentially infinite multiplication of referendums until the "Yes" wins). Political authorities and the people of Quebec are also blamed for putting the very existence of the country in peril.

The re-election in 1998 of a sovereignist government in Quebec guaranteed for several years the durability of the circumstances described for an earlier period by Maurice Lamontagne: a hybrid and equivocal situation, wherein Quebec is an actor on the legal and political stages of Canadian federalism, while its government considers that it has a mandate to secure a referendum on sovereignty whenever winning conditions will exist. This situation lasted through the kind of rather despairing political climate that prevailed in the relations between the country, Ottawa and Quebec between 1995 and 2003.

The dynamism of the Quiet Revolution and the colossal efforts of Quebec sovereignists have unmistakably changed the country, strengthening the will to transform Canada into a modern, normal nation-state. This ultimately led to a weakening of the federal principle in the system and much lesser sympathy for asymmetric arrangements crafted to appease Quebec. All in all, these dynamic factors leading to the referendums of 1980 and 1995 have made the elimination of quasi-federal or quasi-imperial remnants even more difficult than before. In a way, this looks paradoxical, somewhat contradictory. But although these remnants seem endowed with doubtful usefulness seen from the perspective of federal modernity, they can be regarded as immensely precious instruments whenever a country faces exceptional circumstances threatening its very survival. It is here that we tap into the nervous system of that which is called the "raison d'etat" (reason of state or national interest). The least we can say is that this phenomenon took on important proportions in Canada in the aftermath of the great fear of October 30, 1995.

I have proposed in this section and the previous one some developments, concepts, historical interpretations that I deem appropriate to foster an appropriate understanding of Canada, Quebec, and the way their states and national identities are related to one another.

TRULY RENEWED FEDERALISM, SOVEREIGNTY AT LAST OR JUST THE PLAINLY EVOLVING STATUS QUO? REFLECTIONS ON OUR FUTURE

I regard the constitutional reform of 1982 and the establishment of the *Canadian Charter of Rights and Freedoms* as the most significant change of the last quarter century in Canada. Born of centralist and nationalist inspiration, this reform increased the legitimacy of the central government and of its officials and transformed the understanding of the political community in the political classes, the population at large as well as in the media and the academic establishments. Coupled with the immense fear of October 1995 and the profound disgust with Jacques Parizeau's infamous speech on that occasion, the Charter has strengthened the idealistic dimension at the heart of Canadian nationalism: the country must preserve its integrity and its distinctiveness vis-à-vis the United States, in part because it represents the model of a state tolerant of minorities, capable of edifying humankind as a whole. If this vision has penetrated the political culture of the whole country, it is nowhere more present than in the Liberal Party of Canada. We have seen this at work in the acts and speeches of Stéphane Dion leading to the Clarity Act, and in the contributions of Michael Ignatieff to the preliminary reflections leading to Paul Martin's minority government's new statement on Canadian foreign policy. The presence of these two politicians and thinkers as leading candidates for the leadership of the Liberal Party will make this whole exercise fascinating to watch. To repeat the point, it is also my claim that the 1982 constitution has contributed to defederalizing the political culture of the country. Once again, this is most obvious when one examines the performance of the Liberal Party in power over the last decade. What is most striking here is the continuity between Jean Chrétien and Paul Martin. All in all, when one examines Mr. Martin's most important speeches and key pronouncements of the Canadian government under his two-year stewardship, the principle of coherence at work is the involvement, and often the unilateral action, of the central government in many social issues that fall squarely or substantially within the confines of provincial jurisdiction: national control over health policy, key involvement in higher education (scholarships, research foundations, innovation policy), a national day-care program and new initiatives vis-à-vis municipalities and communities. Mr. Martin went one step further during the federal campaigns of 2004 and 2006 by coming out clearly in favour of the primacy of judiciary constitutional interpretation over the principle of parliamentary sovereignty. This made him the champion of the "Spirit of 1982," marching in the footsteps of his predecessors, Pierre Trudeau and Jean Chrétien. In contrast, the current Prime Minister and leader of the Conservative Party of Canada, Stephen Harper, stood firmly during the last electoral campaign for the idea of an equilibrium between these two pillars of our regime, the sovereignty of the constitution (the "Spirit of 1982") and Parliamentary supremacy (the "Spirit of 1867"). There is an unmistakable tension between these two principles in our system; it will be interesting to watch our upcoming federal electoral contests from this perspective.

During the last twenty-five years, Canada has substantially consolidated its economic relationship with the United States. The Free Trade Agreement with the US in 1988 and the enlargement of the integration to include Mexico with the passing of NAFTA in 1994 caused deep changes in the domains of exports and employment, but also in our value system. Canada now sends over 85 percent of its exports to the US – a level of concentration that is pretty much unique in the world. This situation provokes strong reactions concerning identity, particularly in anglophone Canada and singularly in the intellectual establishment of Toronto and Ottawa. In these elite circles and beyond, many people worry about the effects of too large an economic and strategic dependence on the US. Their inflexibility concerning the maintenance of strict Canadian health laws is not solely explained by virtue of a centralist vision, inimical to federalism. It answers also to deep identity and nationalist motives. Stephen Harper's political accomplishments have been nothing short of extraordinary in the last five years: securing the leadership of the Canadian Alliance, becoming a competent party boss and Leader of the Opposition in Parliament, driving the efforts to create a new, unified Conservative Party and becoming its first leader, conducting an able campaign in 2004 and then surviving tough challenges during Mr. Martin's minority government, to finally become Prime Minister of Canada following the election of January 2006. On the scale of these exceptional performances, Mr. Harper's ability to assuage the fears of Canadians over the identity-related minefields of health policy ranks very high. In a moment, I will make a similar remark concerning his approach with regards to federalism and Quebec.

Beyond constitutional changes and those associated with greater North American integration, some of the major transformations of the past twenty-five years in Canada have to do with the demographic and economic evolution of the West, particularly Alberta and British Columbia. In less than two decades, these provinces will have 75 representatives in the House of Commons, just like Quebec. Oil-rich Alberta remains the top fortress of conservatism and with the end of the Klein regime, all eyes will focus on this province. Now debt-free and swimming in escalating surpluses, Alberta has the financial means and the ideological disposition to dare a full-scale confrontation with Ottawa regarding Canadian healthcare legislation and the role of the private sector within this environment. The next conservative leader of Alberta and Mr. Harper will have to manage a tough balancing act on this issue. In British Columbia, Gordon Campbell's government has moved forward many elements on the populist agenda of democratic reform: fixed-date elections, a Citizens' Assembly and a failed referendum on a new electoral system. These initiatives, in whole or in part, are in the process of being replicated in many provinces, including Ontario and Quebec.

How will the Western provinces play their cards in the new dynamics surrounding federalism coming first from the consolidation of the Council of the Federation and then broadened by Stephen Harper's new language of openness concerning both respect of provincial jurisdictions and flexible approach towards the reformist agenda promoted by the government of Jean Charest in Quebec? I have no clear answer to this question, but I do not doubt for one second that the West, with its considerable new weight, will count mightily in the calculations of official Ottawa.

The political resurgence of aboriginal peoples also profoundly changed Canada over the course of the last two decades. This renaissance found a constitutional anchor in the clauses of the 1982 fundamental law that acknowledged the collective and national ancestral rights of native Canadians, while defining a process of negotiations regarding their self-government. The publication in 1996 of the Report of the Royal Commission on Aboriginal Peoples augmented the intellectual and administrative legitimacy of this resurgence, through the formulation of a grandiose program of national and linguistic reengineering for aboriginal peoples. Since the publication of this report, there has been more progress on this front through judiciary decisions than through political negotiations, with some exceptions like the agreement with the Nisga'a in British Columbia and the Paix des Braves (Peace of the Braves) with the Cree in Quebec. Symbolically, it was the Oka Crisis following in the immediate aftermath of the failure of the Meech Lake Accord in 1990 that inaugurated the era of this new Canada, characterized by an unavoidable national dialogue with the native peoples. That such a crisis emerged in Quebec at a time of heightened concerns over the integrity of Canada was probably not a mere coincidence. As the events of 1995 clearly established, any major fracture in the tectonic plates linking Canada and Quebec is bound to be affected by the demands of native peoples and to have consequences on their fate.

If indeed there is a new Canada making a larger place for native peoples, there is surely another one that requires that similar attention be given to immigrants and to the discourses (laws, policies, ideologies, doctrines) of multiculturalism. More than a third of the Canadian population is made up of those (and their subsequent children) who arrived in Canada after 1945. In a study published in October 2003, Andrew Parkin and Matthew Mendelsohn noted an increase in tolerance and appreciation of the multicultural diversity of the Canadian population (Parkin and Mendelsohn 2003, 11). This is particularly true for those under 30 years old. On this issue, there is no distinct Quebec society. Québécois under 30 seem to have the same attitudes and values as other Canadians.

In the last two federal elections, the Liberal Party performed much better than elsewhere in the country's large cities – Toronto, Montreal and Vancouver – where we find the strongest contingents of the immigrant population. Liberals also received support from various native leaders and continued to be successful in communities where linguistic minorities form an important part of the population, such as New Brunswick and anglophone Montreal. Moreover, Liberal publicity implored Canadian women to believe that the Conservative agenda represented a threat to their rights, notably in the area of health and regarding the issue of abortion. If we add to this the question of gay marriage and equality rights, it becomes even clearer that Paul Martin's Liberals had firmly maintained Trudeau's legacy, that of collective rights embedded in the Charter (for all minorities except for Quebec). The role of women, the general issue of equality, bilingualism, multiculturalism and the recognition of national rights for native peoples have all become in 20 years the determining aspects of the Canadian political identity. In this landscape, the question worth asking is this: once Canadians will have begun to forget the association between the Liberal Party on one side, the sponsorship scandal and the issue of corruption on the other, how will Stephen Harper's Conservatives be able to maintain their standing as the dominant party at the helm of a minority government, and furthermore possibly extend it to form a majority? To answer this question, I need to go back to the issue of Quebec.

In the course of the last 25 years, both sovereignists and federalists in Quebec have met setbacks on political and constitutional fronts. The former tried unsuccessfully, at two intervals in 1980 and 1995, to leave Canada. The latter tried twice with the Meech Lake and Charlottetown Accords to shift Canada in the direction of Quebec's interests. They also failed. It seems at first sight that to look for success stories in Quebec over the last two decades, one needs to look beyond politics, for instance at economic and cultural matters. A closer look reveals that three referendums in fifteen years, including two rather existential ones, have demonstrated on the whole the strength and depth of democratic civility in Quebec. This is not a meager accomplishment. Most people are very proud of this. It is perhaps what explains the loss of affection Quebec citizens have expressed for the federal Liberal Party, whose disloyalty towards Quebec democracy was revealed through the sponsorship scandal, in 2004 and even more dramatically in 2006. Within the framework of a systematic strategy, planned at the highest level of the state, Mr. Chrétien's government and the Liberal Party tried to sell Canadian allegiance in Quebec with posters, flags and all kinds of other gimmicks. It was profoundly distasteful and Mr. Martin's Liberals ended up paying the ultimate political price for this. They were thrown out of power and have been relegated to third-party status in Quebec.

Although it has rather lamentably failed with regards to its fundamental objective – securing independence or at least much greater political freedom for Quebec – the political party founded by René Lévesque can take pride in the fact that the language policies it has promoted have been remarkably successful. When 95 percent of the people in a society claim to know one language sufficiently for use in everyday life (the figure was about 83 percent in the 1960s), how can we not acknowledge that this language has indeed become the common public idiom of this society? At a time when English imposes itself as the *lingua franca* in America and in the world, Quebec today is more French than at any other time since the early decades of the 19th century. In this area, as in others, according to André Laurendeau's famous formula, we Québécois are "condemned" to excellence in America and our tasks for the future remain plentiful.

More democratic, more French, Quebec is also older than it was 20 years ago. In all likelihood, this is not going to improve anytime soon. In 2020, people aged 65 and older will represent more than a quarter of the population. The combination of this factor with the considerable weight (close to 120 billion dollars) of the public debt carried by the government of Quebec is seen more and more as a cause of concern for the future prospects of our society. A group led by former Premier Lucien Bouchard, with the participation as well of *La Presse* editorialist André Pratte and UQAM economist Pierre Fortin, published in the fall of 2005 a manifesto inviting Québécois to a greater lucidity vis-à-vis these problems, calling urgently on our political leaders to act responsibly to move our society beyond a certain political culture of immobility.[13] On these issues, contemporary Quebec seems to be the theatre of a sharper polarization than before. The call from Bouchard and others for a politics of greater lucidity and responsibility was answered forcefully by political and social forces on the left. Merely two weeks after the publication of "Pour un Québec lucide," this first manifesto was answered point for point by a second one, "Pour un Québec solidaire." expressing the views of the left on the future of Quebec. Clearly, there is a kind of momentum at the left in Quebec politics: after three years in power, the Charest government is facing unprecedented levels of dissatisfaction; Mario Dumont's ADQ appears to be stagnating, both at the polls and organizationally; the Bouchard-led manifesto, "Pour un Québec lucide," has provoked all kinds of comments but not the slightest realignment of political forces. Whereas on the left, there have been major developments: Option citoyenne, the group led by Françoise David, has merged in February 2006 with Union des forces progressistes to form a brand new political party, Québec solidaire. Social issues are the mainstay of the new party, although it suggests that sovereignty is a means to transform its ideas into reality. Québec solidaire says that it will fight for the environment, participatory democracy, feminism, social justice, equality and solidarity. The candidate of Québec solidaire garnered 20 percent of popular support in a recent by-election in the Montreal riding of Ste-Marie-St-Jacques.

Two tasks at hand seem to me priorities for the broadening of political freedom in Quebec. The first, which for 30 years has belonged to all the large political parties, from the PQ to the Liberals to the ADQ, aims for the unification of our political and legal identity through the adoption of an internal constitution, just like the Catalans did in Spain in 1980 and are about to repeat in 2006. At the time of the Meech Lake and Charlottetown Accords, Quebec sought to have its collective identity recognized by the rest of Canada. Instead of trying to repeat this process, I think we should first recognize ourselves as Québécois, strengthening the backbone of our political community by placing some of our key laws (*Charte des droits et libertés de la personne, Loi sur les consultations populaires, Loi 101*) in a fundamental document that would have its own amending formula and could possibly be ratified by the population in a referendum.[14]

The second task is more closely tied to the new political configuration that emerged following the January 2006 federal elections, in the wake as well of the installation of a federalist government in April 2003 in Quebec. This second task consists of federating, or refederating to be more precise, the Canadian state. Jean Charest's Liberal government gained points on this front by piloting the project that led to the creation in December 2003 of the Council of the

Federation, to foster greater cooperation and greater efficiency in the relationships between provinces and territories as member-states in the Canadian
political system.

In less than three years, the Council of the Federation has obtained a measure of success on at least three fronts: an agreement with Mr. Martin's
government on the nature, principles and financing of the healthcare system
in September 2004, along with the signing of an asymmetrical accord with
Quebec; a much better coordination between provinces and territories on their
requirements concerning the role of the federal government in higher education and the financial engagements that should correspond to this role; the
establishment of a common front concerning the existence of a vertical fiscal
imbalance between Ottawa and the partners of the federation, an efficient
public-relations job on this issue during the Canadian elections of 2004 and
2006, highlighted by the recognition during the campaign and afterwards, of
the existence of such a problem by Conservative leader Stephen Harper and
by his government in its first Throne Speech, and finally the sponsoring and
the publication of a major study on this multidimensional phenomenon in
Canadian politics along with detailed recommendations to solve it.[15] As matters currently stand, the political planets seem to be aligned for an agreement
between Ottawa and its provincial partners, including Quebec, on two fronts:
a significant measure of progress on redressing the fiscal imbalance, and the
enlargement of Quebec's international role in spheres relating to culture, language and identity, for instance through formalizing the principle of its
participation in the activities of UNESCO. Mr. Harper seems to be calculat-
ing that the avenue leading to the formation of a majority Conservative
government passes through Quebec, whereas Mr. Charest desperately needs
good news from Ottawa prior to his own next electoral campaign.

Beyond the vexing issue of the fiscal imbalance and the difficulties associated with broadening in international affairs a Quebec-based principle of
asymmetry, Mr. Harper's will for a more open federalism could be seriously
challenged by the administrative elite in Ottawa. For various reasons (imperial origins of our political system, the tradition of competence and the
self-definition of the members of the upper echelons of the civil service, dis-
proportion in financial resources between Ottawa and the provinces, pressures
of globalization, problems of many provincial civil services to shore up sufficient expert knowledge in their own areas of jurisdiction, contempt of the rule
of law and public ethics that was shown in the war against Quebec sovereignty, and finally the legitimate worries of Canadian nationalists concerning
our position vis-à-vis the United States), it appears to me that the administrative elite of the central state has become the main stumbling block in the
struggle to deepen the institutions and political culture of federalism in Canada.
If indeed he is serious about reinforcing the federal principle in the political
culture of Ottawa and in the machinery of the central state, Mr. Harper will

have to speak clearly and persuasively to the administrative elite, convincing its members that such a move would be in the superior interests of the country, and he will have to be consequential in his actions. This should start with concrete gestures. I believe, marching in the footsteps of Richard Simeon and Martin Papillon, that this should start with a substantial transformation of the workings of the First Ministers Conference (Papillon and Simeon 2004, 132–34). As Simeon and Papillon have argued, such conferences should take place regularly, on an annual basis, they should be better prepared and a well-defined public dimension should be integrated in their operations to insure greater transparency. I would go some steps further than my colleagues. Future conferences should be co-presided by the Prime Minister and the Premier at the helm at that time of the Council of the Federation, and the order of the day should be jointly prepared as well. I am enough of a realist to believe that the implementation of such a reform remains improbable in the political circumstances of 2006. Improbable, but not impossible! Sait-on jamais? One never knows… Who would have predicted, in the summer of 2005, that Mr. Harper's Conservatives would get 25 percent of the vote in Quebec in the upcoming federal election, collecting 10 new members of parliament?

I have always thought, in accordance with the teachings of the great German sociologist Max Weber, that the fate of peoples, states and societies remains open. I cannot predict with any certainty what the future has in store for Canada and Quebec. I am still clinging to my conviction that the constitutional reform of 1982 promoted a logic inimical to the political freedom and the distinct identity of Quebec. Transforming Canada into a true, fully modern federation would be difficult, because it would require making neither victors nor vanquished between those who support the idea of Canada as an autonomous, distinct national community in the Americas, with those who have similar hopes for Quebec. At some point in time, this would require radically amending the constitutional heritage of Pierre Elliott Trudeau. I have not completely abandoned the idea of seeing this during my lifetime. As matters stand, this hypothesis, although quite unlikely, still seems less improbable to me than the scenario of a winning referendum on Quebec sovereignty. In this realm of our political sphere, there have been many elements of novelty in 2005 and 2006. In the person of André Boisclair, the PQ has elected a savvy, media-conscious, new young leader, who will be seriously tested in our next provincial election. Mr. Boisclair has inherited a political formation that has just adopted in June 2005 a new program that is clearly more radical, both on the axis of political independence (decoupling sovereignty from the need to negotiate and obtain a form of partnership with Canada), and with its vision concerning the role of the state and social justice in Quebec. In the span of one year, the PQ has lost with Bernard Landry and Pauline Marois two of its most experienced and prominent political figures. Meanwhile, the disappointing – at least compared to what was anticipated some months prior to the election – performance of the Bloc Québécois in the Canadian elections of January 2006 (the Bloc got 42 percent of the vote whereas many people had expected 50 percent), has done much to deflate the hopes of the repetition for our times of the three-period scenario of the mid-nineties: great performance by the Bloc federally in 1993, triumph of the PQ in 1994 followed by a too-close-to-call referendum contest in 1995. This being said, it remains possible that the PQ could win the next election, only to face the hardships of realizing that many factors combine, if I am not too mistaken in my analysis in this chapter, to make the attainment of sovereignty highly unlikely. Could the people of Quebec be consulted once more in an existential referendum in the foreseeable future? I cannot exclude it. Having voted "Yes" twice in the past, how would I vote in a future referendum? Like all citizens, I would have to see the question. Human beings, and peoples, always maintain their faculty to judge according to circumstances. Sait-on jamais? One never knows. To the repetition of my title I add one cautionary remark. We Québécois should integrate better in our public sphere my basic historical point: there are drastically negative consequences for a political community whenever those who organize a referendum happen to lose it.

NOTES

1 Jean-Jacques Simard, "Ce siècle où le Québec est venu au monde," in Roch Côté (ed.), *Québec 2000: rétrospective du XXe siècle*, Montreal: Fides, 1999.

2 See for example Matthew Mendelsohn, *The Globe and Mail*, July 2, 2003, p. 1 and 18.

3 Burelle has recently reformulated his understanding of federalism, steeped in the political philosophy of Emmanuel Mounier and Jacques Maritain. See André Burelle, *Pierre Elliott Trudeau: l'intellectuel et le politique*, Montreal: Fides, 2005, p.41–44.

4 See for instance Paul Romney, *Getting it Wrong: How Canadians Forgot their Past and Imperilled Confederation*, Toronto: University of Toronto Press, 1999, p.87.

5 Other principles were clearly at work in our founding, as the Supreme Court reminded us in its reference case concerning the secession of Quebec in 1998. I am not trying to be exhaustive here.

6 See Gérard Bergeron, *La gouverne politique*, Paris: Mouton, 1977.

7 One such exception is Christian Dufour, Lettre aux souverainistes québécois et aux fédéralistes canadiens qui sont restés fidèles au Québec, Montreal: Stanké, 2000.

8 It should be noted that Bergeron's personal position was complex. Here he is summarizing the logic of independence, not necessarily propounding it. The following formula renders well his approach: Quebec's independence should not fail, if it has to happen.

9 For an anthology showing the logic of sovereignty in all the variety of its ideological colors and motivations, see Andrée Ferretti and Gaston Miron (eds.), *Les grands
   textes indépendantistes; écrits, discours et manifestes québécois 1774–1992*, Montreal: L'Hexagone, 1992.

10 This point is made in an illuminating way by Denis Monière in his recent essay on
   Quebec nationalism. The fundamental problem, or vice, of Canadian federalism,
   according to Monière, is that it maintains French Canadians, in Quebec, in the
   institutional shackles and psychologically debilitating situation of minority status. His arguments are made all the more instructive by the fact that they dovetail
   very closely with the rationale proposed by the PQ in its new program. See Denis
   Monière, *Pour comprendre le nationalisme au Québec et ailleurs*, Montreal: Presses
   de l'Université de Montréal, 2001, p.138–139.

11 In April 2006 two world-class Quebec artists, Michel Tremblay and Robert Lepage,
   echoed this judgment by Jacques and distanced themselves from the PQ and from
   the project of sovereignty.

12 Donald Savoie, *Governing from the Centre: The Concentration of Power in Canadian Politics*, Toronto: University of Toronto Press, 1999. Savoie has recently put
   his very capable mind at work in the efforts of Judge Gomery to bring some equilibrium back in our political system.

13 Manifeste pour un Québec lucide, La Presse, October 20, 2005, p. A25. Two weeks
   later a group of people on the left of the political spectrum, led by Françoise David
   published a second manifesto, *Pour un Québec solidaire*, defending the institutions of the welfare state and the values associated with it. See *Manifeste pour un
   Québec solidaire*, La Presse, November 1, 2005, p.A-23.

14 See Guy Laforest, *Pour la liberté d'une société distincte*, Quebec: Presses de
   l'Université Laval, 2004, p.256. See also Guy Rocher, "Postface: des intellectuels
   à la recherche d'une nation québécoise," in Michel Venne (ed.), *Penser la nation
   québécoise*, Montreal: Québec/Amérique, 2000, p. 296.

15 Guy Laforest and Eric Montigny, " Le fédéralisme exécutif: problèmes et
   actualités ," in Réjean Pelletier and Manon Tremblay (eds.), *Le parlementarisme
   canadien*, 3rd edition revised and enlarged, Quebec: Presses de l'Université Laval,
   2005, p.366. See also "Reconciling the Irreconcilable: Addressing Canada's Fiscal Imbalance." Report of the Advisory Panel on Fiscal Imbalance of The Council
   of the Federation, March 31, 2006. The report is available online at
   www.councilofthefederation.ca/pdfs/report.fiscalim_mar3106.pdf, accessed April
   19, 2006. Concerning this report, the voice of the Council has not been unanimous. Ontario has distanced itself from the approach of the report and of the Council
   concerning equalization payments.

REFERENCES

Ajzenstat, J., Romney, P., Gentles, I. & Gairdner, W. (Eds.). 1999. *Canada's Founding Debates*. Toronto: Stoddart.

Archer, K., Gibbins, R., Knopff, R. & Pal, L. 1999. *Parameters of Power: Canada's Political Institutions*, 2nd Edition. Toronto: Nelson Canada.

Blouin, J. & Bergeron, G. 1982. *De l'autre côté de l'action*. Montreal: Nouvelle optique.

Burelle, A.1994. *Le mal canadien*. Montreal: Fides.

Jacques, D. 1995. "La mort annoncée d'un projet insignifiant." *Possibles*, XIX (1-2).

Laforest, G. 1998. "The Need for Dialogue and How to Achieve It." In R. Gibbins and G. Laforest, *Beyond the Impasse: Toward Reconciliation*. Montreal and Kingston: IRPP.

Laforest, G. & Montigny, E. 2005. "Le fédéralisme exécutif: problèmes et actualités." In *Le parlementarisme canadien*, 3rd Edition Revised and Enlarged, R. Pelletier and M. Tremblay, eds. Quebec: Presses de l'Université Laval.

Lamonde, Y. 2000. *Histoire sociale des idées au Québec (1760–1896)*. Montreal: Fides.

Lamontagne, M. 1954. *Le fédéralisme canadien. Évolution et problèmes*. Sainte-Foy: Presses de l'Université Laval.

Papillon, M. & Simeon, R. 2004. "The Weakest Link? First Ministers Conferences in Canadian Intergovernmental Relations." In *Canada: The State of the Federation 2002: Reconsidering the Institutions of Canadian Federalism*. P. Meekison, H. Telford and H. Lazar, eds. Kingston and Montreal: McGill-Queen's University Press.

Parekh, B. 2000. *Rethinking Multiculturalism: Cultural Diversity and Political Theory*. London: Macmillan Press Ltd.

Parkin, A. & Mendelsohn, M. October 2003. "Un nouveau Canada: le temps de la diversité." *Les Cahiers du Cric*. Montreal: Centre de recherche et d'information sur le Canada.

Parti Québécois. *2005. Un projet de pays*. Montreal: Parti Québécois.

Pelletier, R. 2005. "Constitution et fédéralisme." In R. Pelletier and M. Tremblay, eds. *Le parlementarisme canadien*, 3rd Edition. Quebec: Presses de l'Université Laval.

Simard, J-J. 1999. "Ce siècle où le Québec est venu au monde." In *Québec 2000: rétrospective du XXe siècle*, R. Côté, ed. Montreal: Fides.

Trudeau, P.E. 1967. Le fédéralisme et la société canadienne-française. Montreal: Editions HMH.

Trudeau, P.E. and Johnston, D. 1988. *Lac Meech Trudeau parle*. Montreal: Hurtubise HMH.

4

The Stalled Realignment: Quebec's Party System After the 2003 Provincial Election

A. Brian Tanguay

Dans les mois qui précédaient l'élection provinciale en avril 2003, certains analystes, tels Maurice Pinard et d'autres, ont affirmé que la province était sur le seuil d'un grand réalignement des partis politiques. L'Action démocratique du Québec (ADQ) de Mario Dumont venait de remporter quatre victoires dans des élections partielles en 2002; dans les sondages à cette époque, l'ADQ devançait le Parti québécois (PQ) et le Parti libéral du Québec (PLQ) par une marge confortable. Pour à peu près 60 pourcent des électeurs au Québec qui refusaient de se classer soit comme fédéraliste soit comme souverainiste, l'ADQ semblait une option partisane séduisante. Mais malgré tous ces indices d'un réalignement possible des partis politiques au Québec, dans l'élection en avril 2003, l'ADQ ne récoltait que quatre sièges et 18 pourcent du vote. Ce chapitre examine le système des partis au Québec à la lumière de l'élection provinciale de 2003. Il tente d'esquisser une explication des résultats, pour déterminer si la prédiction de Pinard d'un grand réalignement des partis politiques dans la province était simplement fausse ou prématurée. Après avoir déterminé les bases sociales et idéologiques de l'ADQ, et après un survol des défis qui confrontent le mouvement souverainiste au Québec actuellement, le chapitre conclut que l'ADQ sera probablement marginalisé dans le système des partis au Québec pour l'avenir prévisible.

INTRODUCTION

In the year or so leading up to the provincial election of 14 April 2003, a number of signs pointed to the possibility of a "great realignment of political parties" in Quebec (Pinard, 2003; Tu Thanh Ha 2002). A series of public opinion polls in the summer and fall of 2002 indicated that a solid majority of francophones in Quebec wanted Mario Dumont's Action démocratique du Québec (ADQ) to form the next government. Dumont himself was the overwhelming favourite among francophones as the best premier of the province, well ahead of both the PQ's Bernard Landry and Jean Charest of the Quebec Liberal Party. These favourable survey results came on the heels of surprising by-election victories for the ADQ in four ridings formerly held by the PQ, including the nationalist stronghold of Saguenay (renamed René-Lévesque for the 2003 provincial election) and Joliette, which had been represented by the PQ since 1981. Three of the four successful ADQ candidates were relatively young, like party leader Mario Dumont, giving the impression that a generational shift in Quebec politics might be in the making.

Some observers believed that the meteoric rise in the ADQ's popularity was more than the simple by-product of voters turning away from the two parties that had dominated provincial politics since the 1970s – the PQ and the PLQ – and saying "a pox on both their houses." Nor could the surge in support for "Mario Dumont's team" be explained merely as a symptom of widespread unhappiness with Bernard Landry's government – although to be sure there was considerable dissatisfaction with the incumbent PQ.[1] According to Maurice Pinard and others, the shifting bases of support for the various political parties in 2001–2002 reflected the waning interest in constitutional questions among Québécois of all language groups. In a separate survey conducted by the Centre for Research and Information on Canada (CRIC 2002), almost 60 percent of francophones refused to label themselves either as sovereignists or federalists, preferring instead to say that they stood between the two camps or belonged to neither. The ADQ was ideally positioned to benefit from this widespread constitutional fatigue, since one of its main pledges was to impose a moratorium on any future referendum. The ADQ electoral program promised that an ADQ government would not "initiate major constitutional moves in the next mandate since it will be busily occupied in laying the foundations of a Quebec that is free to choose." Another referendum campaign would serve only to further divide an already divided population, in the ADQ's estimation: "We need to put aside old labels, unite the forces for change and rally Quebecers behind other challenges that unite them" (ADQ 2003, 63).

Predictions of a critical realignment of Quebec's party system, along with the ADQ's hopes for a breakthrough to major party status, were dashed in the 2003 provincial election. Although Mario Dumont managed to retain the riding of Rivière-du-Loup, and three other candidates were elected in predominantly francophone ridings south of Quebec City, all of the star candidates who had won by-elections a year earlier went down to defeat. The party failed to make any inroads into urban Quebec. As table 1 indicates, the election seemed to mark a return to something resembling the norm in Quebec politics – competition between two dominant parties, the federalist and free market Liberals versus the sovereignist and social democratic PQ.

Or did it? Certainly the magic of the first-past-the-post electoral system played a role in producing this result. The Liberals, with 46 percent of the vote (up only marginally from 44 percent in 1998), took 76 seats in the National

Assembly (61 percent of the total). The PQ won 45 seats (36 percent of the total) with 33 percent of the vote (down considerably from 43 percent in 1998). For its part, the ADQ won a disappointing 4 seats (3 percent of the total) with just over 18 percent of the vote (up from 12 percent in 1998).[2] Do these statistics indicate that the predicted realignment of Quebec party politics has merely been stalled for one more election cycle, or that Pinard and others overestimated the strength and durability of the ADQ?

Table 1: Provincial Election Results in Quebec, 1970–2003[1]

	Election year								
Party	*1970*	*1973*	*1976*	*1981*	*1985*	*1989*	*1994*	*1998*	*2003*
Liberal	45 (72)	55 (102)	34 (26)	46 (42)	56 (99)	50 (92)	44 (47)	44 (48)	46 (76)
PQ	23 (7)	30 (6)	41 (71)	49 (80)	39 (23)	40 (29)	45 (77)	43 (76)	33 (45)
UN	20 (17)	5 –	18 (11)	4 –	– –				
Créditiste	11 (12)	10 (2)	5 (1)	– –					
ADQ							6 (1)	12 (1)	18 (4)
Equality						5 (4)	– –		
Other	– –	– –	2 (1)	1 –	5 –	5 –	4 –	1 –	3 –
Turnout	84	80	85	82	76	75	82	78	70

[1]Figures represent percentage of popular vote; figures in parenthesis are seat totals won by each party; column percentages may not add up to 100 due to rounding.

This essay provides an assessment of Quebec's party system in the wake of the 2003 provincial election. It addresses, in turn, two sets of questions: First, what were the factors that led Pinard to conclude that Quebec's two-party system was evolving, "at least in the short term, into a relatively well balanced three-party system such as Quebec has never seen before" (Pinard 2003, 7)? Was his prediction of a great partisan realignment in Quebec simply premature or fundamentally wrong? Secondly, what is the status of the sovereignty movement in Quebec? Is it in irreversible decline, or will it benefit from its time in opposition and re-emerge with greater vitality in the near future, once the Liberals in Quebec City are inevitably disappointed or rebuffed by their brethren in Ottawa? What factors will determine the future health of the sovereignty movement?

PINARD'S THEORY OF THIRD PARTY EMERGENCE AND THE RISE OF THE ADQ

Maurice Pinard's classic study of the Créditiste breakthrough in Quebec in the 1962 federal election, when the party emerged virtually from nowhere to capture over a third of the province's seats, is one of the most innovative and important attempts to construct a general theory of minor party development in Canadian political science. Pinard hypothesized that two variables – one-party dominance and economic strain – combined to create the conditions for the emergence and success of minor parties of protest. Pinard defined one-party dominance as a situation in which the principal opposition party receives less than one-third of the votes over a series of elections. Strain was defined as a sharp economic reversal after a period of prosperity, and was measured by such indicators as climbing rates of unemployment and lowered economic expectations among the population. In such a situation, according to Pinard, unhappy voters rally behind a new protest party or movement, rather than channelling their anger and frustration through a weak opposition party.

Pinard's theory generated a great deal of discussion and was revised in light of criticisms made by Blais (1973), White (1973) and others.[3] In particular, Pinard reduced the explanatory weight of one-party dominance, which he argued was only one possible manifestation of a larger structural problem – the nonrepresentation of interests and social groups by the major parties. In their seminal study of the rise of third parties in the United States, Rosenstone, Behr and Lazarus (1996, 129) also cite "issue unresponsiveness," or the "distance between the positions of the voter and the major party candidates" on salient issues as a key factor in the rise of a third party.

This background discussion is important for understanding Pinard's explanation of the rise in voter support for the ADQ in 2002, along with his prediction of an imminent realignment of the province's party system. Figure 1 shows that in the summer and fall of 2002 approximately 40 percent of decided voters in Quebec said that they would have cast ballots for the ADQ if an election were held at that time. Although this high level of support for the ADQ might have been in part an artifact of the way in which Léger Marketing redistributed undecided voters, other public opinion polls at the time also revealed surprisingly strong support for the ADQ. Political surveys undertaken by CROP, for instance, indicated that 23 percent of decided voters supported the ADQ in February 2002, and that this increased to 38 percent in November of that year. Comparable figures for the other two parties were (February figures first, followed by November data in parentheses): Liberals 39 percent (30 percent), PQ 37 percent (32 percent).[4]

This period of ADQ growth – when it won by-elections in the very diverse ridings of Saguenay, Berthier, Joliette and Vimont (which includes some of the Montreal bedroom community of Laval) – could hardly be characterized as one of notable economic strain in Quebec, if we measure this variable by annual percentage changes in unemployment rates.[5] By 2002, unemployment had been dropping steadily in Quebec: from a high of 13.3 percent (seasonally adjusted) in 1993, the unemployment rate declined each succeeding year (with the exception of 1996 and 2001) to 8.6 percent in 2002. More importantly,

Figure 1: Provincial Voting Intentions in Quebec

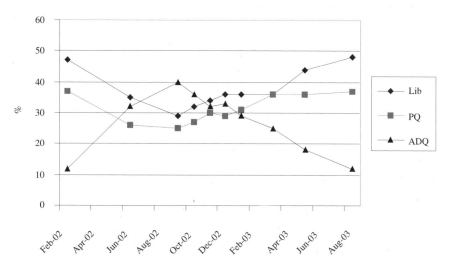

Source: Data taken from Leger Marketing <http://www.legermarketing.com/eng/intprov.asp?prov=QC&1>

the area in which the ADQ exhibits its greatest electoral strength – the Chaudières–Appalaches administrative region, where it won three ridings in the 2003 election (Beauce-Nord, Lotbinière and Chutes-de-la-Chaudière) – is the one with the lowest unemployment rate in the province.[6]

Pinard does not mention one-party dominance at all in his study of the rise of the ADQ, presumably because Quebec politics has been characterized by healthy two-party competition for most of the period since 1960. Each of the major parties has won at least 40 percent of the vote in the elections held between 1976 and 1998, with the exception of the Liberals in 1976 (when they won 34 percent of the vote) and the PQ in 1985 (39 percent). Moreover, even if one-party dominance is defined at the riding level, it does not seem to help us understand the rise in support for the ADQ in 2002. Of the four ridings won by the ADQ in by-elections in 2002, only Joliette had experienced a lengthy period of domination by a single party – in this case, the PQ.[7] The others had alternated fairly regularly between Liberal and PQ victories since the early 1980s.

This is not to say that there is *no* relationship at all between the strength of the two major parties and ADQ success, only that Pinard assigns no explanatory weight to one-party dominance in his analysis of the new party. Instead, he emphasizes five factors that in his view have fuelled the rise of the new party. First among these is the depolarization of opinion on the issue of Quebec sovereignty. As mentioned in the introduction, a majority of francophones in Quebec – about 60 percent – refuse to identify themselves as either sovereignists or federalists. It is precisely among this group of francophone voters who refuse to label themselves on the constitutional question that the ADQ receives its strongest support: 48 percent of these voters supported the ADQ, whereas only 34 percent of those who identified themselves as federalists and 26 percent of sovereignists did so (Pinard 2003, 2).

Pinard also cites Mario Dumont's considerable personal popularity, widespread dissatisfaction with the incumbent PQ government (both of which were mentioned in the introduction), and deepening political disaffection among Quebec's voters as three additional factors contributing to the spectacular growth in support for the ADQ in the summer and fall of 2002. According to Pinard, "voters who expressed their disaffection with politics constituted a majority [in Quebec] and it is within this majority that the ADQ got its largest support" (2003, 4).

The fifth factor contributing to the growth of the ADQ is its neo-liberal ideology. Pinard notes that there is a strong streak of economic conservatism among francophones in Quebec, and the ADQ's program, which includes such articles of right-wing faith as school vouchers, a flat tax and a greater role for the private sector in the delivery of health care, appeals to this segment of the population. Pinard points out that while the ADQ is to the right of the median voter on economic issues, it does not embrace social conservatism. In fact, its electoral program is silent on such deeply divisive questions as the right to abortion, same-sex marriage, the definition of the family, the right to die, and so on, which have mobilized the religious right elsewhere in this country and in the United States. The party's overriding objective is to liberate individual autonomy from what it calls an invasive and "paternalistic" state apparatus, and to inculcate in these autonomous individuals an understanding of their responsibility both for their own actions and for their fellow citizens (ADQ 2003, 5).

Table 2 draws on data from a CROP survey conducted in November 2002 in order to shed some additional light on the nature of the ADQ's neo-liberal ideology (CROP 2002b). Respondents were asked whether they agreed with four policies that are key elements of neo-liberal ideology: reducing the size of the civil service in the province, allowing more room for the private sector in health care, school vouchers,[8] and a flat tax. A majority of voters agreed with these policies: 59 percent supported both reducing the size of the civil service and allowing a greater role for the private sector in the delivery of health care, and 55 percent supported school vouchers. The only exception was the flat tax: 36 percent agreed with this proposal while 56 percent disagreed; another 8 percent either did not know or refused to answer.[9]

As the data in table 2 show, neo-liberal voters – those who agree with each of the four proposals – are much more likely to support the ADQ (about half of them in each of the four cases) than either of the two major parties. The

Table 2: Party Support by Neo-liberal Attitudes, 2002

Party preference	Reduce size of civil service %	Increase private-sector role in health %	School vouchers %	Flat tax %
ADQ	48	48	48	50
LIB	26	27	27	23
PQ	26	25	25	27
(N)	(267)	(266)	(260)	(183)

Note: Each column shows only those voters who either *agree* or *agree strongly* with each of the items in question; their party preferences, in percentages, are included in each cell of the table.
Source: CROP 2002b

differences in neo-liberal attitudes among the various party supporters are, moreover, statistically significant. We can construct a neo-liberalism scale by taking the arithmetic mean of the four items included in table 2. The resultant variable would range from a low of 1 to a high of 4, with the higher values indicating greater neo-liberalism. The average score on this neo-liberalism scale for the entire population is 2.6. For ADQ supporters it is 3.0, for Liberal supporters 2.5, and for PQ supporters 2.3.[10] These findings tend to reinforce Pinard's conclusion that the ADQ could benefit "from the traditional economic conservatism of a majority of francophone voters" (2003, 4).

Age is another important variable that affects support for the ADQ. As I noted in the introduction, the nature of the ADQ's by-election wins in 2002, which brought to the National Assembly a handful of noticeably young representatives, made it appear as though the party might be the political vehicle for a younger generation skeptical of traditional, old-line parties. But the party has not consistently appealed to this category of the population, nor has it really succeeded in drawing them into the traditional arena of politics. Indeed, as the data in table 3 indicate, the ADQ appeals disproportionately to *older* voters, those in the 45 to 64 age cohorts. These voters tend to be the most politically engaged and knowledgeable, and can therefore be among the most attuned to new political movements. Voting turnout is significantly higher in these older cohorts than it is among the young, and this also stands to benefit the ADQ. The youngest voters (18–24) are most likely to support the PQ (39 percent, as opposed to 33 percent for the Liberals and only 28 percent for the ADQ), while the oldest voters (those 65 years of age and up) prefer the Liberal party (41 percent, versus 35 percent for the ADQ and 24 percent for the PQ).

Table 3: Party Support in Quebec by Age Cohort, 2002

Party preference	18–24yrs %	25–34yrs %	35–44yrs %	45–54yrs %	55–64yrs %	65+yrs %
ADQ	28	38	33	48	52	35
LIB	33	35	27	19	23	41
PQ	39	28	40	32	25	24
(N)	(46)	(69)	(106)	(103)	(52)	(63)

Note: Cramer's V = .154 (p < .05); column percentages may not total 100 due to rounding.
Source: CROP 2002b

Constitutional fatigue and depolarization on the sovereignty question; Mario Dumont's personal popularity as party leader; widespread dissatisfaction with the incumbent PQ government; deepening cynicism among voters about traditional political institutions; a neo-liberal ideology that had a distinct appeal for certain segments of the francophone population; and disproportionate strength among the most politically engaged and aware sections of the electorate, those between the ages of 45 and 64 – with all of these factors apparently working in favour of the ADQ in mid-2002, how do we explain what happened to the party between November of that year and the election on 14 April 2003? A glance at figure 1 shows that the party's fortunes declined steadily after the fall of 2002, as the date of the provincial election approached. The party's 18 percent of the popular vote in the election represented a modest gain over its results in 1998, when it won 12 percent, but it was not nearly the breakthrough for which most party activists had hoped. Nor did the outcome represent the critical realignment predicted by Pinard.

The ADQ's declining fortunes after November 2002 were partly attributable to self-inflicted wounds, and partly the result of the two main parties' ability to right their own ships. As noted previously in the discussion of the survey results in table 2, a majority of Québécois appear willing to accept a greater role for the private sector in the delivery of health care. Despite this, when the ADQ released a document in the fall of 2002 that openly endorsed a two-tier medical system, serious questions were raised in the media about the party's health care program. This document was released just weeks before the Romanow Commission report on the Future of Health Care in Canada provided a ringing endorsement of the fundamental principles of the Canada Health Act.[11] Even more harmful, however, were the comments of Marcel Dutil, president of the successful manufacturing firm, Canam-Manac, and a high-profile recruit to the ADQ cause. At the ADQ convention held in

Drummondville in September 2002, Dutil publicly voiced his opposition to the flat tax, which he said would benefit only the wealthiest citizens in society (David 2003, 584). This prompted some waffling on Dumont's part, and fuelled doubts among voters about his leadership qualities.

At the same time that Dumont and his party were encountering serious turbulence in public opinion, both Jean Charest and Bernard Landry seemed to hit their stride. In the early months of 2003, the looming election was shaping up to be a contest between the managerial competence of Landry and the PQ, on the one hand, and Jean Charest's Liberals as the embodiment of the electorate's desire for change, on the other. The ADQ and its leader floundered to find their own niche with voters, and never really succeeded. In the end, Dumont and his advisers simply ran a disorganized and ineffective election campaign, frittering away the lead in public opinion that they had enjoyed only six months earlier.

It would not be accurate to lay the blame for the ADQ's disappointing election results in 2003 entirely on the party's poorly run campaign or on Dumont's missteps as leader. The issue of sovereignty did flare back into prominence towards the end of the campaign, despite the efforts of Bernard Landry to bury it. In the leaders' debate, Jean Charest seized on a campaign speech made by Jacques Parizeau in which he repeated his infamous assertion that the "Yes" side lost the 1995 referendum because of "money and some ethnic votes." Charest skilfully put Landry on the defensive during the debate, asking whether the PQ placed greater emphasis on sovereignty than on health care (Moore 2003). The Quebec Liberal Party's take-off during the campaign began shortly after the leaders' debates, and so Charest may have tapped into widespread fear among voters that a PQ victory would guarantee an unwanted third referendum.[12] The ADQ may have simply been squeezed between the federalist and sovereignist parties over the course of the campaign, losing votes to both camps. Whether or not this constituted a "re-polarization" of the sovereignty debate is difficult to say at this point. It is clear that the moderate constitutional position of the ADQ still appeals to a sizeable number of Quebec voters. To cite just one example, a recent poll conducted by Léger Marketing (2005) found that 58 percent of respondents described themselves as "autonomists" – precisely the term utilized by the ADQ in its most recent program (ADQ 2004). Léger Marketing found that "astonishingly" it is the supporters of the PQ who are the most willing to describe themselves as autonomist (65 percent, as opposed to 57 percent of ADQ supporters and 49 percent of Liberals). This suggests that there is still considerable partisan space on the constitutional question within which the ADQ can manoeuvre to mobilize voters who do not identify with either federalism or sovereignty.

One of the most interesting features of the 2003 provincial election results is that the ADQ vote was concentrated in specific regions of Quebec. The party won 25 percent or more of the vote in 24 different ridings, and most of this in two administrative regions: Chaudières–Appalaches, which consists of the Beauce and other districts directly south of Quebec City and near the U.S. border, and the Quebec City region (not including the capital itself). These ridings, especially those in the Chaudières–Appalaches region, are overwhelmingly francophone, rural, with lower than average household income and an undereducated workforce (see table 4). This was the region where the Créditistes derived much of their strength in the 1970s; the Union Nationale also did well here.[13]

Table 4: Comparison of ADQ Strongholds* with Province as a Whole, Selected Characteristics (2003 Election)

Indicator	ADQ "strongholds"*	Provincial average
Turnout (%)	74.4	70.4
Household Income (2000$)	40,492	42,581
French Mother Tongue 2001† (%)	97.7	82.9
French Home Language 2001† (%)	97.7	83.4
University degrees 1996 (%)	8.0	11.5
Population 60 years+ (2001)	18.0	18.0

*Ridings in which the ADQ won 25 percent of the popular vote or more in the 2003 provincial election (24 in total)

†Single and multiple responses, i.e. those who indicated speaking more than one language in the home or having more than one mother tongue – whose parents came from two different linguistic groups, for example – have been included in the calculations. If, for example, 120 respondents indicated that they spoke English, French and a third language in the home, 40 would be placed in each category (francophone, anglophone, allophone).

Source: Québec, Directeur-général des elections 2003a and 2003b. The author would like to thank François Simard in the office of the Directeur-général des elections du Québec for supplying 2003 election results, census data, and transposed election results from 1998 using the 2003 electoral map, all in machine-readable format. The DGE bears no responsibility for the interpretations of the data made here, nor for any errors that might have been made.

Pierre Drouilly (2003, 615–18) has somewhat tendentiously labelled the regions of ADQ strength as *le Québec tranquille* or *le Québec mou*.[14] In economic terminology, *les secteurs mous* are those that lag behind the rest of the Quebec economy in terms of wages, technological development, value added and so on – woodworking, textiles, and furniture-making are some examples. These are labour-intensive sectors of the economy with smaller than average sized firms; they may be in decline, but they are also politically sensitive industries, since they employ so many workers. By analogy, Drouilly defines certain regions of the province as lagging behind the others; voters in these areas are, according to Drouilly, "plus *craintives* idéologiquement devant le projet souverainiste" (2003, 617; my emphasis).[15] The clear implication of his reasoning is that if the areas were less *backward*, they would embrace the sovereignty project with greater enthusiasm. As it is, these overwhelmingly francophone ridings voted "Yes" in the 1995 referendum at an average of 53–54 percent, compared to 60 percent among francophones as a whole.

If we set aside the overtly teleological basis of Drouilly's argument, we can derive an important strategic lesson that the ADQ must learn if it is to enjoy greater electoral success and perhaps precipitate the "great realignment" predicted by Maurice Pinard. If the party is to appeal to more than this relatively small slice of Quebec society, then it must promote ideas that can mobilize a broad coalition of voters, including the young. One policy championed by Dumont and the ADQ that might have had the potential to link up with young voters was its campaign against so-called "clauses orphelins." This term refers to the practice of "grandfathering" in industrial relations – creating two (or more) tiers of workers by assigning lower wages and differential working conditions to newly hired employees in a bargaining unit. The policy is rightly seen as discriminatory toward the young and non-unionized, and although it is a somewhat technical issue, it has the potential to highlight some of the drawbacks of the neo-corporatist bargains that underpin the Quebec Model. The ADQ needs to focus on issues like this one (as opposed to the flat tax and school vouchers) if it hopes to grow in Quebec.

However, simply to argue that the ADQ's policies are at odds with Quebec's core values, as so many self-styled progressive critics of the party do, misses the point that there is considerable variation and tension within these core values. The data in table 2 show that a surprisingly high number of Quebec voters are at least receptive to some neo-liberal ideas. Other polls have shown Quebecers to be quite open to the idea of "queue-jumping" in health care. Blais et al. (2002, tables 7.1 and 10.4) demonstrate that Quebecers are among the most favourable toward free enterprise of all Canadians and the least committed to the public health care system. Thus the ADQ still has room to grow in the Quebec party system, and its fortunes would obviously be helped by any reform of the electoral system that introduced a measure of proportional representation.

More than anything else, however, the future health of the ADQ is linked to the fate of the sovereignty movement: if public opinion on the constitutional question continues to be depolarized, and if a majority of francophone voters continue to express their fatigue with the issue of independence, then the ADQ will possibly find the necessary partisan space in which to mobilize francophone voters around its neo-liberal vision of individual autonomy and a pared-down provincial state. But is the ADQ ever going to displace one of the two major parties in the province – as the PQ did with the Union Nationale in the 1970s – or is it more likely to evolve into a kind of "half-party," similar to the NDP in Ontario? To answer this question, we need to examine the key factors that will shape the future of Quebec's sovereignty movement and its most important political vehicle, the Parti Québécois.

OPPORTUNITIES AND CONSTRAINTS FOR THE SOVEREIGNTY MOVEMENT IN QUEBEC

On 11 January 2001, Lucien Bouchard announced that he was resigning as both provincial premier and leader of the Parti Québécois. Bouchard cited his inability to capitalize on the close referendum result in 1995 as one of the principal reasons he was stepping down. Admitting that his efforts to create the "winning conditions" for a third and final referendum on Quebec sovereignty had failed, Bouchard voiced the hope that his resignation would clear the path for a new leader who might finally succeed in strengthening the Parti Québécois's militancy and revitalizing the sovereignty project.

In his two years as party leader and provincial premier, Bernard Landry failed to re-energize the slumbering sovereignty movement. By the time the provincial election was held in April 2003, support for sovereignty had drifted down to its lowest level since the mid-1980s, with only 40 percent of voters indicating that they would vote "Yes" if a referendum were held on the question of sovereignty-association.[16] After an election campaign in which the issue of sovereignty was intentionally placed on the back burner by the PQ, the party won only 33 percent of the popular vote, its worst result since 1973 – although it did manage to win substantially more seats than it had in the elections of 1985 and 1989 (see table 1).

No one should start drafting an epitaph for Quebec's sovereignty movement just yet, however, since it recovered quite nicely from a similar near-death experience in the mid-1980s. Moreover, in the past year, the sponsorship scandal has tainted the federal Liberal Party and the Charest government has seen its popularity plummet as it has haltingly embarked on its project of "re-engineering" the provincial state. Not surprisingly, then, support for sovereignty has rebounded in the polls: in May 2005, a poll conducted by Léger Marketing indicated that 54 percent of voters in the province (after the undecideds have been redistributed) would vote "Yes" in a referendum on sovereignty-association.[17]

It will take some time before we can determine whether this uptick in support for the "Yes" option truly represents the emergence of a revitalized sovereignty movement or whether it is simply attributable to contingent factors, the natural by-product of voters unhappy with the Liberal-dominated status quo and endorsing the most viable partisan alternative. If the sovereignty movement is to recapture its former dynamism, which it appears to have dissipated in the years following the 1995 referendum, then it will have to confront four fundamental challenges.

First among these is the generation gap that is increasingly apparent in Quebec politics (and politics in the rest of the country as well). Bernard Landry has recently called for the creation of a grand alliance between generations (baby boomers and those now under the age of 24) in order to achieve sovereignty within 2000 days – the earlier goal of 1000 days having been set back by the PQ's defeat in the 2003 election (Dutrisac 2003). On the face of it, the prospects for such an intergenerational coalition in favour of sovereignty within the PQ appear to be quite good. Drawing on data from the two most recent national election studies in Canada,[18] we find an important relationship between age group and support for sovereignty. Following the example of the election study team, I have grouped respondents in the survey into four different age categories: those born before 1945 (pre-boomers), the boomers (born between 1945 and 1959), Generation X (born between 1960 and 1969) and Generation Y (born after 1969).[19]

Blais et al. (2002, 48) find that voter participation has dropped off sharply among Generation Y, and that this is not simply a life-cycle effect. Turnout among Generation Y voters is ten percentage points lower "than it was among generation X at the same age." Milner (2004, 28) also notes that this phenomenon extends beyond Canada: in western Europe, "[w]hile young people have, on balance, historically voted less than their elders, by the early 1990s the gap between average turnout for citizens 18 to 29 and those over 30 had grown to 12 percent." This generation of voters, the most populous since the baby boom of the post-war years, is disengaged from politics, though not necessarily disaffected – they are tuned out, but not yet turned off (Gidengil et al. 2003). It is the youngest age cohort that provides the strongest support for sovereignty in Quebec: 56 percent of Gen-Y in 1997 supported sovereignty, 49 percent in 2000 (within the margin of error, see Figure 2). No other age cohort, in either of the two surveys, provided majority support for the idea of Quebec sovereignty. Gen-X and the boomers were equally supportive of sovereignty in both surveys (49 percent in 1997, 43 percent in 2000). It is the pre-boomer generation, born before the end of World War II, that is the most skeptical of sovereignty: only about 3 in 10 members of this age group endorsed the idea of sovereignty in 1997 and 2000. Support for sovereignty among francophone members of Generation Y (data not shown here) was highest among all age/home language categories – 64 percent in 1997 and 58 percent in 2000.

These high levels of support for sovereignty among Generation Y voters (especially the francophones among them) do not necessarily mean that the independence project is bound to receive a boost once these voters replace older generations. Bernard Landry recently boasted that "mathematics plays in our [the PQ's] favour" (cited in Dutrisac 2003). However, Generation Y in Quebec has a much higher rate of non-voting than any of the other age cohorts:

Figure 2: Support for Sovereignty by Age Cohort

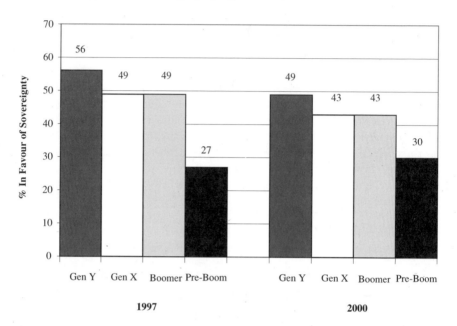

just over 30 percent did not vote in the 2000 federal election, as opposed to 20 percent of Generation X, 16 percent of boomers, and a mere 7 percent of pre-boomers (data not shown).[20] Even if the members of Generation Y do become more politically engaged as they get older, their levels of participation will likely never come close to those of the baby boomer and pre-war generations.

In addition, Durand points out that Landry's hope that the "mathematics" of generational replacement will inevitably lead to the realization of the sovereignist dream is based on the assumption that young voters do not change their attitudes as they age (Durand 2001, 5). Although there is as yet insufficient data to test this hypothesis satisfactorily in Quebec, evidence from other jurisdictions does seem to point to a less "experimental" attitude among citizens as they age.

There is another impediment to Landry's dream of an alliance of generations in favour of sovereignty: the baby boomers who increasingly dominate the Parti Québécois have very distinct economic interests which do not entirely intersect with those of the younger generation. In their dissection of the contemporary sovereignty movement, Gagné and Langlois (2002, 135) note that

Après un séjour de vingt-cinq ans dans les institutions du pouvoir, dans ses appareils de contrôle et dans les organizations économiques qui en sont les "partenaires," l'élite politique du PQ appartient à plein titre au groupement social qui a le plus profité des transformations de la société québécoise depuis 1960.[21]

The technobureaucratic elite at the core of the PQ organization is overwhelmingly concerned with defending the welfare state apparatus – the principal source of its economic and political power. This technostructure is viewed with some skepticism by some members of the younger generation, especially since many of the better-paying and more rewarding jobs appear well out of their reach until the baby boomer generation retires. Generational conflicts like these are evident in Quebec, in Ontario, and undoubtedly throughout the developed world. They militate against any easy coalition of young and old in the sovereignty project, at least in the short term.

The second challenge facing the sovereignty movement is to be found in the linguistic composition of the province. Together, anglophones and allophones constitute just over 17 percent of the province's population.[22] Neither of these groups is especially receptive to the PQ's sovereignty project. As Gagné and Langlois (2002, 104) point out, allophones have quite rational reasons for opposing Quebec independence: "Les immigrants n'émigrent pas dans un nouveau pays pour en transformer le statut constitutionnel, ils y viennent d'abord pour refaire leur vie, y vivre et y travailler."[23] Since a significant number of allophones have fled countries that were in the throes of civil wars or ethnic violence, they are also quite naturally suspicious of most forms of nationalism. Anglophones, because they are caught in the contradictory position of being members of the national *majority* at the same time that they are a provincial *minority*, are also rationally opposed to Quebec sovereignty. Gagné and Langlois (2002, 96, 107) estimate that only 6 percent of anglophones and 14 percent of allophones voted "Yes" in the 1995 referendum.

Is this situation likely to change fundamentally in the near future? One factor working in favour of the sovereignty movement is the continuing exodus of anglophones from Quebec: in the space of a mere five years, the proportion of anglophones (measured by mother tongue) in the province declined from 8.4 percent to 7.9 percent, and there is very little reason to believe that this decline will be either halted or reversed in the immediate future.

As for allophones in Quebec, recent studies of younger (18 to 34 years of age) members of this group in Quebec – the so-called "children of Bill 101" – may give some hope to sovereignists. Beaulieu (2003, 263–64) demonstrates that 40 percent of these young Allophones in early 2003 would have voted "Yes" in a referendum on sovereignty-association. However, only 16 percent of this group labeled themselves sovereignists, and the majority of them remained uninterested in traditional party politics (Beaulieu 2003, 261, 265). It remains an open question just how salient the issue of sovereignty is for young allophones: for many of the children of Bill 101, "the sovereignist/federalist debate is no longer *the* main issue. For twentysomethings, these labels are often meaningless" (Elkouri 2003).

The third challenge confronting the sovereignty movement in Quebec centers on the status of the French language in the province. Historically, support for sovereignty has gone up as the perception that the French language is under attack has increased. In 2000, nearly 60 percent of Québécois believed that the French language was threatened. This was up marginally from levels recorded in the 1997 national election study, and the biggest increases in the perception of threat appeared to occur among anglophones (who are obviously not likely to lend significant support to the cause of sovereignty) and allophones. For this latter group, the key question remains whether they believe that only sovereignty will provide the Quebec government with the necessary tools to protect the French language against the forces of globalization. At this stage we simply do not have sufficient data to answer this question.

It could be argued that the prevailing view that French is threatened in Quebec is at odds with reality, and that this places some limits on the long-term capacity of the sovereignty movement to mobilize support. As a recent Quebec government report has implicitly acknowledged, in terms of the principal objectives of René Lévesque's government in 1977 when it passed Bill 101 – making French the dominant, "normal" language of the workplace and the private sector, increasing the occupational space for francophone managers, and compelling immigrants to integrate into the French-language school system – the existing *Charter of the French Language* has been a resounding success (Québec, Ministère de la Culture et des Communications 1996).[24] Nationalists are currently focusing their attention on violations of the sign law (or technical loopholes exploited by companies such as Second Cup in order to display their corporate English name on their signs) and on the issue of allophones attending English-language CEGEPs. Developments since the implementation of Bill 101 show, however, that allophones have been able to adapt to the new language regime with minimal difficulty and could probably deal with any new restrictions on their choice of CEGEP with relative equanimity.[25] Despite the assiduous efforts of some nationalists to stoke the fires of linguistic tension in the province, in many respects the system is working remarkably well to ensure the predominance of French in Quebec.

This linguistic peace could well be shattered, however, as the government of Jean Charest plunges ahead with its policy of municipal de-mergers. On the island of Montreal, this issue concerns more than simply the make-up of the local government: it is also about relations between anglophones and francophones in Quebec's largest city. Some of the more zealous proponents of de-merger in the west-island communities of Montreal evoke images of partitionists among the francophone community. It will require considerable skill on the part of Charest and his cabinet to negotiate this particular dossier.

This is one of the main reasons that the PQ's election loss in 2003 could, in some respects, prove beneficial for the party, by giving it an issue that it might use to mobilize its supporters in the run-up to the next provincial election.

The fourth and final obstacle confronting the contemporary sovereignty movement in Quebec is to be found within the most important political expression of this movement, the Parti Québécois. This party has always been a coalition of forces – social democrats, *bleus*, disaffected Liberals – held together by the glue of charismatic leadership (Lévesque, Parizeau, Bouchard) and by a common commitment to some notion of independence for Quebec (whether hyphenated or not). In a sense, the elites within the PQ have practised a "politics of permanent postponement" in trying to keep the coalition together. They have offered the hope to those militants on the left that once the issue of sovereignty has been dealt with, then the more radical or progressive elements in the party program can be implemented. But not before. And pressing too hard on economic claims is represented by party elites as rocking the boat, endangering the *projet de société*. At times grudgingly (especially in the late 1970s, when the labour movement in Quebec was much more radical than it currently is), at times more willingly, the progressive faction in the PQ has gone along with this two-stage strategy: it has accepted the postponement of key elements of its own economic and social agenda. Even as late as the 1995 referendum, this strategy "worked:" trade unions and progressive community groups provided the PQ of Jacques Parizeau with key political support during the campaign.

In the nearly ten years that have elapsed since the referendum, the willingness of the progressive elements within the PQ to acquiesce to the strategy of postponement has slowly evaporated. Social democrats in Quebec, who really have no other credible political option at election time but the PQ – the Union des forces progressistes captured about 40,000 votes in the last election, or one percent of the total – have found it increasingly difficult to support a party that they feel has demonstrated a disturbing willingness to subordinate the principle of democratic equality to the dictates of the international capitalist economy. Increasingly, unhappy social democrats in the province are opting out of the PQ, and they continue to attempt to create new, more progressive parties. For example, Françoise David, former president of the Fédération des femmes du Québec, recently helped found a new feminist, progressive organization called Option citoyenne.

This suggests that the PQ may not derive long-term benefits from the Charest government's thus far ham-handed attempts at re-engineering the provincial state and its plummeting popularity. Certainly, the PQ has rebounded in public opinion polls since the 2003 election: in May 2005, 47 percent of voters (after redistribution of undecideds) indicated that they would vote for the PQ if a provincial election were held, as opposed to 25 percent each for the governing Liberal Party and the ADQ.[26] Nevertheless, the growing disillusionment of the PQ's left-wing activists – which will only be strengthened if François Legault manages to win the party leadership instead of Pauline Marois (assuming Landry does indeed stand down) – may mean that the party will encounter difficulties mobilizing its voters in a future election. This is especially true if the planned merger of the UFP and Option citoyenne takes place, creating a new party to the left of the PQ (Option citoyenne 2005).

In summary, the sovereignty movement in Quebec must successfully confront a number of key challenges if it is to recapture its former dynamism and create the conditions for a third referendum on independence. First of all, the growing disengagement of young voters – the strongest supporters of the sovereignty project – in Quebec and elsewhere may mean that the PQ, as the only credible political vehicle of the sovereignty project, will not benefit automatically from the mathematics of generational replacement. Moreover, there is no guarantee that today's young sovereignists will not become tomorrow's federalists. Secondly, although young allophones appear more receptive to the idea of sovereignty-association than their parents, there is little to suggest that the sovereignty project is as salient for this increasingly important group of voters as it was for young francophones in the 1970s. Thirdly, as the political scientist Jean-Herman Guay (2003) has pointed out, the PQ project has in many ways been realized, even if Quebec does not yet have a seat at the UN:

> Le projet souverainiste n'a pas abouti, mais il a néanmoins provoqué des changements importants dans la structure économique de la société….Les raisons de la colère ont disparu. L'insécurité linguistique n'habite plus le milieu du travail ou celui du commerce et le sentiment d'infériorité est rentré dans les livres d'histoire.[27]

Finally, the Parti Québécois itself is showing signs of its age, and party elites are finding it increasingly difficult to hold together the centrifugal forces within the sovereignist coalition.

None of this is to suggest that the PQ is moribund. But if it is to survive as a dominant party, it is likely to do so as an increasingly and moderate pragmatic party that continually postpones the final referendum on sovereignty because it has failed to create the winning conditions for such a vote.

CONCLUSION

This essay began by asking whether the "great realignment" of parties predicted by Pinard has simply been postponed for another electoral cycle, or whether Pinard and others may have overestimated the strength and staying power of the ADQ. In their analysis of the 2003 Quebec election, Allen and Vengroff (2004, 19) write that "[w]e could be seeing the second stage in the twilight of the PQ and its replacement by the next generational party, the ADQ as the leading opposition party and contender for power." They base this conclusion on the fact that the ADQ drew most of its support in the 2003 election from the PQ, the party it would likely displace in the provincial party system if a realignment were to occur.[28] On the basis of the evidence presented in this essay, however, this conclusion appears to be premature. Despite the serious difficulties confronting the PQ as a party, and despite the growing fatigue of many of the province's voters with the never-ending debate over sovereignty, there are significant obstacles to the growth of the ADQ. Its inability to attract young voters, or to make inroads in urban, industrialized parts of the province, or to gain significant support among allophones all indicate that for the time being, the ADQ is not likely to displace the PQ in a critical realignment of the partisan order. Of course, a year is a long time in politics and a number of unanticipated events might combine to jeopardize the PQ's long-term electoral prospects. For now, though, Quebec's two-and-a-half party system is likely to consign the ADQ to the margins of power in the province.

NOTES

1 According to a Léger Marketing poll conducted in late May, 2002, "[s]atisfaction with the Landry government is down to 40 percent, a loss of 8 points compared to February 2002. This is the lowest score ever obtained by this Government" (Léger Marketing 2002). By comparison, satisfaction with the Charest government in the first half of 2005 was in the low 20s.
2 Figures taken from the website of the Directeur-général des elections du Québec, http://www.dgeq.qc.ca/generales/resultats/sommaire_prov_soir_vote_f.html.
3 See Gagnon and Tanguay (1996, 123–26) for a discussion of Pinard and his critics.
4 Undecided voters, who constituted 15 percent of the sample in February and 20 percent in November, have been redistributed evenly among all three parties. Each polling firm follows its own decision rules when redistributing undecided voters, and this has an important effect on levels of support registered for each of the parties. The point here, however, is that both Léger Marketing and CROP indicated roughly similar levels of support for the ADQ in the summer and fall of 2002 – between 35 and 40 percent. See CROP (2002a, 2002b), in addition to the Léger Marketing surveys cited in figure 1.
5 In his reassessment of the Pinard model, Bélanger (2000, 5) operationalized economic strain as the "average difference, over the 12 months immediately preceding the election, between the rate of unemployment in a given month and the average rate of unemployment in the previous five years." In the revised version of his article, Bélanger (2004, 587–88) operationalizes economic strain "on the basis of the respondents' personal financial situation" – that is, whether or not they believed that their personal financial situation had deteriorated in the year prior to an

election. I do not have access to survey data for the different regions of Quebec and therefore cannot test this revised version of Pinard's model.

6 Unemployment in the Chaudières–Appalaches region (one of seventeen in the province) averaged between 6.1 and 6.6 percent between 1998 and 2002; comparable figures for the province as a whole during the same period were 8.4 and 10.3. All data are from Québec, Institut de la statistique (2004). This region does lag behind much of Quebec in terms of technological development and innovation, a point that will be discussed in greater detail later in the paper. It should be noted that the apparent absence of any relationship between unemployment rates and support for the ADQ does not rule out the utility of "strain" as an explanatory variable in accounting for the rise of minor parties. As Bélanger (2004, 585–88) points out, strain can encompass a variety of economic and non-economic factors such as perceptions of one's personal economic situation, regional grievances, and so on.

7 Guy Chevrette, who held various cabinet portfolios in a number of PQ governments, won the riding of Joliette-Montcalm in 1976, and represented the new riding of Joliette from 1981 until his resignation in 2002.

8 The exact question wording is as follows: Do you agree or disagree with the following point in the ADQ program, namely to "give directly to the parents their share of the subsidies provided for their children's education to enable them to afford the school of their choice, whether public or private." There were four response categories for this and the three other questions – strongly agree, agree, disagree, and strongly disagree. These were recoded into two categories, agree/disagree. Those who refused to answer or replied that they "did not know" averaged between 6 and 13 percent on the four questions. Sample size of the survey was 601. See CROP (2002b). It should be noted that these survey questions are somewhat biased, since they ask respondents whether or not they agree with specific elements of the ADQ platform, and not whether they hold neo-liberal values per se. They are therefore subject to strong projection effects. The author is grateful to an anonymous reviewer for pointing this out.

9 There were too few anglophones (42) and allophones (10) included in the survey to make generalizations about differences in neo-liberal attitudes among the dominant linguistic groups in the province.

10 Analysis of variance shows that the differences in neoliberalism scores between the three groups of party supporters are significant ($p < .000$; $F = 41.1$).

11 According to David (2003, 583), the ADQ's health care plan, entitled *En santé autrement*, envisaged, "pour ceux qui en avaient les moyens, la location des installations publiques sous-utilisées, en flagrante contradiction des dispositions de la loi canadienne sur la santé [for those who have the means, the rental of under-utilized public facilities, in flagrant violation of the provisions of the Canada Health Care Act]."

12 The author is grateful to an anonymous reviewer for pointing this out.

13 Lotbinière, one of the ridings won by the ADQ in 2003, was held by Rodrigue Biron from 1976 to 1981. He was briefly leader of the UN, and later switched to

the PQ, eventually becoming a cabinet minister in the second Lévesque government. Another riding won by the ADQ, Chutes-de-la-Chaudière, was held by Jean Garon, a conservative Minister of Agriculture in the Lévesque government, from 1976 to 1989.

14 "Quiet" or "soft" Quebec.

15 The phrase translates as "ideologically more timid in the face of the sovereignty project."

16 Among decided voters, 38 percent would have voted "Yes," 57 percent "No;" 3 percent were undecided. The survey was conducted by Léger Marketing in January 2003; sample size was 955. Referendum voting intentions from 1995 to the present are available on the Léger Marketing website: <http://www.legermarketing .com/fr/intref.asp?prov=QC&l=1>

17 Sample size was 2008. The percentages among francophones were 62 percent for "Yes," 38 percent for "No" (Léger Marketing 2005). These data should be interpreted with caution, however, since another poll conducted by CROP at around the same time placed support for sovereignty-association at 47 percent (CRIC 2005).

18 Principal investigators for the two national election studies are André Blais, Elisabeth Gidengil, Richard Nadeau and Neil Nevitte. They in no way bear any responsibility for the use of the data in this paper, or for my interpretations of the data.

19 These categories correspond very roughly to those outlined in David Foot's well-known study of Canadian demographics, *Boom, Bust and Echo* (1996). Generation Y is the popular label applied to the baby boom echo, the current generation of teenagers and young adults. The question on attitudes towards sovereignty in the National Election studies simply asks respondents whether they are favourable to Quebec sovereignty, "that is, that Quebec is no longer a part of Canada." Given that there is no mention of a possible economic partnership between an independent Quebec and the ROC (rest of Canada), this undoubtedly understates support for some notion of qualified sovereignty, or sovereignty-association.

20 Actual levels of non-voting are probably somewhat higher, since non-voters are typically under-represented in survey samples.

21 "After a 25-year stay in the institutions of power, in the state's administrative apparatus and in the economic organizations that are its 'partners,' the political elite within the PQ qualifies as the social group that has benefited the most from the changes in Quebec society since 1960."

22 Anglophones – those whose mother tongue is English – constituted 7.9 percent of the provincial population in 2001, down from 13.8 percent in 1951. Allophones constituted 9.2 percent of the population in 2001, up from 3.7 percent in 1951. All figures are based on both single and multiple responses to the language question. Calculated from Québec, Directeur-général des elections (2003a).

23 "Immigrants do not emigrate to a new country in order to change its constitutional status; they come above all to remake their lives, to live and work there."

24 See Tanguay (2002) for an examination of language policy in Quebec.

25 Even if this issue is not strictly about language of schooling at the post-secondary level. It also involves the quality of programs offered by each type of institution; French-language CEGEPs may have to improve the quality and range of their programs if they are to succeed in attracting more allophones and anglophones without higher levels of state coercion.

26 Léger Marketing (2005). Sample size was 2008. Among francophones, 53 percent supported the PQ, 18 percent the Liberals, and 26 percent the ADQ. Among allophones, the figures were: 24 percent PQ, 48 percent Liberals, and 21 percent ADQ.

27 "The sovereignty project has not yet succeeded, but it has nevertheless produced important changes in the economic structure of society...The reasons for anger have disappeared. Linguistic insecurity is no longer a feature of the workplace or of business, and the feeling of inferiority has been relegated to the history books."

28 The authors also note that "election-specific" factors such as the drop in voter turnout contributed to the ADQ's success in certain parts of the province. As well, short term policy issues such as the municipal mergers engineered by the government bled support away from the PQ (Allen and Vengroff 2004, 5).

REFERENCES

Action démocratique du Québec [ADQ]. 2003. *For a Responsible Government: Action Plan for the ADQ's First Mandate*. Pre-electoral Council. Quebec City, 1 March.

– 2004. *Voir grand pour le Québec*. Vᵉ Congrès des membres. Cahier du participant. Drummondville, 25–26 September.

Allen, J.P. and R. Vengroff. 2004. "The Changing Party System in Quebec: The 2003 Elections and Beyond." *Québec Studies* 37 (Spring/Summer): 3–22.

Beaulieu, I. 2003. "Le premier portrait des enfants de la loi 101." In *L'annuaire du Québec 2004*, ed. M. Venne. Saint-Laurent, QB: Fides.

Bélanger, É. 2000. "Third Parties in Canada: The Pinard Theory Revisited." Paper presented to the annual meeting of the Canadian Political Science Association, Quebec City, 29 July–1 August.

– 2004. "The Rise of Third Parties in the 1993 Canadian Federal Election: Pinard Revisited." *Canadian Journal of Political Science* 37(3): 581–94.

Blais, A. 1973. "Third Parties in Canadian Provincial Politics." *Canadian Journal of Political Science* 6(3): 422–38.

Blais, A., E. Gidengil, R. Nadeau and N. Nevitte. 2002. *Anatomy of a Liberal Victory*. Peterborough, ON: Broadview Press.

CRIC. 2002. "Constitutionally Fatigued Quebecers Reject Labels." Accessed online at http://www.cric.ca/pdf/cric_poll/portraits/portraits_2002/portraits02_quebec_const_eng.pdf

– 2005. "Referendum Voting Intentions." Accessed online at http://www.cric.ca/en_html/sondages /issues /sovereignty.html

CROP. 2002a. Political Survey [CR0202]. CROP, Inc. Montreal QB [producer]. Canadian Opinion Research Archive, Queen's University. Kingston ON [distributor] (February).

- 2002b. Image ADQ [CR0211]. CROP, Inc. Montreal QB [producer]. Canadian Opinion Research Archive, Queen's University. Kingston ON [distributor] (November).

David, M. 2003. "La fin d'un cycle: l'année politique au Québec." In *L'annuaire du Québec 2004*, ed. M. Venne. Saint-Laurent, QB: Fides.

Drouilly, P. 2003. "Qui a voté quoi, où et pourquoi?" In *L'annuaire du Québec 2004*, ed. M. Venne. Saint-Laurent, QB: Fides.

Durand, C. 2001. "The Evolution of Support for Sovereignty – Myths and Realities." *Working Paper no. 8*. Kingston, ON: Institute of Intergovernmental Relations, Queen's University.

Dutrisac, R. 2003. "Conseil national du PQ – Landry mise sur une alliance entre générations pour réaliser la souveraineté." *Le Devoir*, 20 October [online edition]. Accessed online at http://www.ledevoir.com/2003/10/20/38663.html

Elkouri, R. 2003. "Bonjour, ethno-sovereigntists." *The Globe and Mail*, 30 June.

Foot, D. 1996. *Boom, Bust and Echo*. Toronto: Macfarlane Walter & Ross.

Gagné, G. and S. Langlois. 2002. *Les raisons fortes: Nature et signification de l'appui à la souveraineté du Québec*. Montreal: Presses de l'Université de Montréal.

Gagnon, A.-G., and A.B. Tanguay. 1996. "Minor Parties in the Canadian Political System: Origins, Functions, Impact." In *Canadian Parties in Transition*, 2nd ed., eds. A.B. Tanguay and A.-G. Gagnon. Scarborough: Nelson.

Gidengil, E., A. Blais, N. Nevitte and R. Nadeau. 2003. "Turned Off or Tuned Out? Youth Participation in Politics." *Electoral Insight* 5(2): 9–14.

Guay, J.-H. 2003. "Le Parti Québécois, un parti rendu à maturité: Allocution pour le Conseil national du PQ du 18 octobre 2003." Accessed online at http://www.vigile.net/ds-actu/docs3a/03-10-20-1.html

Léger Marketing. 2002. "Liberal[s] and ADQ are neck and neck." *Press Release*. 31 May–1 June. Accessed online at http://www.legermarketing.com/eng /home.asp

- 2005. "Communiqué de Presse." Accessed online at http://legermarketing.com/documents/spclm/050516ENG.pdf

Milner, H. 2004. "Political Drop-Outs and Electoral System Reform." In *Steps Toward Making Every Vote Count*, ed. H. Milner. Peterborough, ON: Broadview Press.

Moore, P. 2003. "Leaders' Debate Unleashes Sovereignty." *CBC News Online*. Accessed online at http://www.cbc.ca/quebecvotes2003/features/feature9.html

Option citoyenne. 2005. *Congrès de la vision fondatrice*. 22–24 April. Accessed online at http://www.optioncitoyenne.ca/pdf/rn2005/rn2005_textes_conjoints_oc-ufp.pdf

Pinard, M. 2003. "A Great Realignment of Political Parties in Quebec." *The CRIC Papers, Special Edition*. Montreal: Centre for Research and Information on Canada.

- 1975 [1971]. *The Rise of a Third Party: A Study in Crisis Politics*, enlarged ed. Montreal and London: McGill-Queen's University Press.

Québec, Directeur-général des elections. 2003a. *Dossier Socio-économique: Le Québec*.

– 2003b. *Résultats officiels des élections générales, 14 avril 2003, 20 mai 2003 (Champlain)*.

Québec. Institut de la statistique 2004. *Principaux indicateurs économiques conjoncturels*. Accessed online at http://www.stat.gouv.qc.ca/princ_indic/default.htm#text

Québec. Ministère de la Culture et des Communnications. 1996. *Le Français, langue commune: enjeu de la société québécoise*. Rapport du Comité interministériel sur la situation de la langue française.

Rosenstone, S.J., R.L. Behr and E.H. Lazarus. 1996. *Third Parties in America,* 2nd ed. Princeton, NJ: Princeton University Press.

Séguin, R. 2003. "Charest Letter About Bias Stings Labour." *The Globe and Mail*, 15 October, A5.

Simpson, J. 2003. "Puttin' on the Grits – Again." *The Globe and Mail*, 4 October, A21.

Tanguay, A.B. 2002. "The Politics of Language in Quebec: Keeping the Conflict Alive." In *The Challenge of Cultural Pluralism*, ed. S. Brooks. Westport, CT: Praeger.

Tu Thanh Ha. 2002. "ADQ's Rise Shows Shift in Quebec, Pollster Says." *The Globe and Mail*, 9 November, A10.

White, G. 1973. "One-Party Dominance and Third Parties." *Canadian Journal of Political Science* 6(3): 399–421.

Yakabuski, K. 2003. "Quebec Winter Going to Be Steamy." *The Globe and Mail*, 24 October, B2.

III

Challenging the Quebec Model

5

A Policy Network Perspective on the Quebec Model: Moving Beyond Simple Causation and Fights over Numbers

Éric Montpetit

Ce chapitre propose de jeter un nouveau regard sur le modèle québécois qui se situe à mi-chemin entre les perspectives conventionnelles lesquelles sont, soit très pessimistes, soit très optimistes. En utilisant la notion de réseaux de politiques publiques, ce chapitre tente de réorienter le débat entourant le modèle québécois dans une nouvelle direction. Suite à une revue de la littérature, on constate que la politique industrielle interventionniste du Québec et la concertation macro-économique sont à la base des perspectives conventionnelles sur le modèle québécois. Ces éléments constituants ont mené à des généralisations et surtout à une guerre de chiffres improductive concernant la performance économique du modèle québécois. Le chapitre explique comment une analyse du modèle québécois en termes de réseaux de politiques publiques permet de sortir des débats interminables associés aux perspectives conventionnelles.

INTRODUCTION

In his 1986 film, the *Decline of the American Empire*, Denys Arcand presents a depressing picture of Quebec's intellectual elite. One of the characters in the film makes it clear: "The signs of decline are everywhere" and among them are the "loss of control over public spending and the invasion of bureaucrats." Although Arcand meant to send a message of general relevance with this movie, one might view it as no coincidence that the action took place in Quebec, a province that underwent rapid modernization during its Quiet Revolution and which, by the 1980s, had built a disproportionately large state by North American standards.

2003's main cinematographic event in Quebec was the release of a new Arcand movie, *The Barbarian Invasions*. Meant as a follow-up to *Decline*, the film updates viewers on how depressing Quebec's situation has become since the 1980s. In the background of a crumbling hospital, Arcand depicts bureaucrats, along with unions, as invasive and disgustingly corrupted. Although a work of fiction, Arcand's most recent movie has contributed to the political debate on the Quebec model – a contribution Arcand himself reaffirmed during several interviews. Nevertheless, although widely acclaimed for its artistic quality, the political contribution of the movie was never examined closely. For example, no one noticed that several of the signs of decline identified by Arcand in his earlier film had vanished. Quebec's budgetary situation at the end of the 1990s had significantly improved in comparison with the early 1990s, an achievement attributed by some observers to civil servants who accepted "a freeze or limited increases in hiring and salary levels" (Gagnon 2001, 69). After steady increases in the 1980s and early 1990s, the total number of provincial civil servants in 1993 reached 71,395, of which 22.2 percent were casual employees rather than permanent or career public servants. The effort to balance the budget led to a reduction of 12.9 percent in the number of civil servants between 1993 and 1998, a period of just five years. Indeed, in 1998, the total number of civil servant reached a low of 62,212. Moreover, in 1998, the proportion of casual employees reached 33.4 percent, indicating a sharp decline in the working conditions of provincial civil servants in this context of severe budgetary strain (Secrétariat du Conseil du trésor 2003; Gouvernement du Québec 1995). Furthermore, quoting the Institut de recherche et d'information sur les rémunérations, Gow (2000, 305) claims that the salary of provincial civil servants had fallen 12.9 percent behind that of unionized private sector employees by the end of the 1990s. Quebec's civil servants today earn 4.7% percent less than the Canadian average for public sector employees (Fortier and Hébert 2003, 671). Far from being self-centered and invasive, Quebec civil servants deserve to be credited for the rapid improvement in the provincial budgetary situation at the end of the 1990s.

Unfortunately, caricatures similar to those Arcand projected on movie screens increasingly inform political positions against the so-called Quebec model. Several political actors, including the Action démocratique du Québec (ADQ), depict Quebec's public institutions in a manner that can inspire nothing but support for their dismantlement. The objective of this essay is to present an alternative image of the Quebec model. This image is primarily informed by a policy network perspective. A policy network is a pattern of interconnection between organized civil society and state actors during the development and the implementation of a specific policy. In contrast to competing perspectives, notably rational choice models, the policy network perspective acknowledges possible differences in the functioning of public institutions from policy sector to policy sector. Documenting the development of social relationships, and thereby patterns of actor inclusion and exclusion from policy making in different sectors, is a key contribution of the policy network perspective.

From the policy network perspective, I cannot claim that the performance of the Quebec model is indisputably superior to that of other models. However, the perspective should inspire more optimism about Quebec's public institutions than Arcand's movies, but perhaps a little less optimism than conventional perspectives supporting the Quebec model (e.g. Bourque 2000; Lisée 2000). Unlike conventional perspectives, which emphasize industrial policy and concerted action for macro-economic coordination, the policy network perspective hypothesizes variations in the type of actors involved in policy making, in the nature of the relationships they have constructed and in the performance of policy from sector to sector. Naturally, conducting a study to fully document these variations and to assemble some aggregate measure of performance would command a large budget, which no researcher has yet assembled. However, the limited empirical evidence currently available suggests that policy networks in Quebec adopt a form conducive to satisfying policy-making performance in several sectors.

The essay begins with a presentation of the key elements of what I refer to as the conventional perspectives on the Quebec model, followed by a description of my alternative policy network perspective. Next, I move on to an assessment of the dynamics and performance of the Quebec model provided by conventional perspectives. In this section, I insist on the difficulties encountered by conventional perspectives when it comes to imputing performance, measured quantitatively, to industrial policy or macro-economic coordination. I end the essay with a discussion of the level of policy-making performance that could be expected of the Quebec model from a policy network perspective.

CONVENTIONAL PERSPECTIVES ON THE QUEBEC MODEL

Over the years, various expressions have been used to describe the Quebec model. Some people speak of the inheritance of the Quiet Revolution. In brief, the Quiet Revolution relieved the Catholic Church of important public responsibilities, notably in the fields of education and social services, transferring them to a modern state newly constructed along the Weberian bureaucratic principles of hierarchy, merit and impersonal ruling (Montpetit and Rouillard 2001, 123). In the 1980s, the expression "Quebec Inc." appeared to signify a spill-over of the Quebec model into the private sector. The central aims of Quebec Inc. were to accelerate the province's economic growth and to foster the development of a francophone elite to catch up to anglophones in business leadership (Smith 1994, 92; Paquet 1994). The chief instrument of Quebec Inc. was an industrial policy championing a number of businesses through advantages supplied by state-owned enterprises such as Hydro-Québec, la Caisse de dépôt et placement du Québec (CDP) and la Société générale de financement (SGF).

Quebec Inc. has apparently succeeded in encouraging the emergence of a francophone economic elite (Smith 1994, 93), so much so that giving priority to francophones in business ownership and leadership has even become an untenable policy objective since the 1990s. When the CDP supported Québécor in the purchase of Vidéotron, the president of the CDP had to defend himself by claiming the transaction was purely financial, and the Parti Québécois premier had to reassure the population that he had not intervened in favour of the francophone bidder. Moreover, the earlier sale of Provigo, a francophone food distribution chain championed by Quebec Inc. in the 1980s, to Loblaws, an Ontario-based business, was achieved without any significant political intervention and debate. Before the end of the 2004 parliamentary session, the Liberal government passed a bill placing profit before any other objective the CDP might have, thereby preventing any political intervention in the organization's business. Distancing itself from the 1980s, the conventional perspective suggests that the Quebec model eschews nationalist objectives in favour of economic growth.

Conventional observers of the Quebec model would agree, however, that the idea of having an interventionist industrial policy to achieve economic objectives for the province has survived throughout the 1990s and early 2000s. Take, for example, those government initiatives that encourage clusters of knowledge economy businesses in so-called *cités*. Such cités exist in the areas of multi-media, e-commerce and biotechnology, to name just three. The CDP, the SGF and Hydro-Québec also remain key players in the province's industrial policy, providing capital and energy at low cost. Even if the Parti libéral du Québec (PLQ) expressed worries about the economic role of these actors during the 2003 electoral campaign, it has done very little to dismantle the province's industrial policy since the election.

Conventional observers would also agree that concerted action – the negotiation of key policies between economic, social and state actors – is another enduring element of the Quebec model. Although often neglected in analyses of the Quiet Revolution, concerted action, institutionalized in the Conseil d'orientation économique, was an important innovation in 1960s Quebec (Gow 1986, 306). Indeed, Michael Smith (1994, 100) places concerted action between labour, capital and the state next to the province's industrial policy as the constitutive elements of Québec Inc. The summits organized by the Parti Québécois after it came to power in 1994 were often viewed as evidence that Quebec continued to value concerted action. So much so that even the Liberal government, which adopted a confrontational approach to interest groups immediately after the 2003 election, organized such a summit in the fall of

2004. In any case, most analysts still treat concerted action as a corporatist way of achieving macro-economic coordination between labour, capital and the state (see Smith 1994; Paquet 1994; Noël 1994; Tanguay 1984). Concerted action, according to this conventional perspective, became an official component of the Quebec model after the Parti Québécois attempted, in the 1970s, to emulate the Swedish model (Milner 1989). Although the presence of representatives of the social economy at summits signals the economic relevance of new actors, concerted action is still primarily understood by proponents and many analysts as consisting of a corporatist method of macro-economic coordination.

In summary, according to conventional views, the Quebec model has two constitutive elements:

1. an interventionist industrial policy; and
2. economic coordination among relevant actors through concerted action.

Furthermore, from this perspective, in contrast with the 1980s, the Quebec model is no longer oriented toward nationalist objectives and seeks only to encourage economic performance. Although I agree that nationalist objectives have been replaced by economic objectives, I argue that the focus of the conventional perspectives on concerted action and industrial policy is unsatisfactory, particularly when considering developments since the 1990s. In contrast to the image of a homogenous Quebec projected by these conventional perspectives, the network perspective presented in the next section provides analytic tools to understand the specific features of distinct policy sectors. These tools facilitate an examination of the Quebec model that transcends a narrow focus on industrial and economic policy. Viewed through the lens of the policy network perspective, the Quebec model is far more complex than has been suggested by its critics.

A POLICY NETWORK PERSPECTIVE ON THE QUEBEC MODEL

One of the key criticisms of the Quebec model is that economic coordination through concerted action is not actually taking place. Tanguay (1984, 378) argues that Quebec business groups and unions, not to mention all the other groups invited to summits, are too divided to enable effective concerted action (see also Paquet 1994, 71–73). Moreover, the state has played too dominant of a role in the organization of summits to approximate corporatism of the Scandinavian type in Quebec (Tanguay 1984, 378). Smith (1994, 102) agrees, pointing to the inadequacy of any provincial corporatism in a federation where the most influential macro-economic policy tools are controlled by the federal government.

Although the very idea of a Quebec model invites macro-level generalizations about governance of the type just presented, such generalizations are always vulnerable to criticism. Anecdotal evidence of dysfunction or of failure to abide by the logic prescribed by the model can too easily be identified. Therefore, although I argue that a Quebec model exists, and that the province's governance in several sectors is relatively unique in the North American context, I do not believe that the model explains all the province's policies or even its most important policies. In fact, I even acknowledge, along with Tanguay (1984) and Smith (1994), that there is probably nothing very unique about macro-economic coordination in Quebec, in spite of the corporatist projects of the Parti Québécois government in the 1970s.

Concerted action in Quebec, in my view, should be studied at the meso rather than the macro level. The meso level is the level of relations between state actors and organized civil society *in specific policy sectors*. The policy network perspective, popularized in Canada by Coleman and Skogstad (1990), is particularly well suited to such studies. As explained above, a policy network regulates interactions between interest groups and state actors in given policy sectors. Policy networks vary from sector to sector along the following interdependent dimensions:

1. openness to new actors;
2. cohesion around policy ideas; and
3. interconnectedness between the state and civil society; and
4. policy capacity (or expertise) distribution between the state and civil society (Montpetit 2003b).

Several types of policy networks have been identified as operating along these dimensions (see Rhodes 1997; van Waarden 1992). Coleman (1997), for example, identifies the six types which are most commonly observed. These are presented in table 1.

At the meso level, concerted action normally occurs in corporatist policy networks. Corporatist policy networks have been identified more frequently in more sectors in Quebec than elsewhere in North America, hence the idea of a distinctive Quebec model. For example, corporatist networks have been identified in the agricultural policy sector by Skogstad (1990), the construction sector by Coleman (1988), the manpower training sector by Haddow (1998), and the environmental sector by Montpetit (1999). Coleman (1995) has also argued that interests in a range of policy areas from health, the condition of women, and labour are all organized to operate in corporatist networks. To my knowledge, however, no empirical study has attempted to provide an exhaustive picture of policy networks in Quebec. Documenting their frequency with precision would require tremendous resources and the research could rapidly become outdated as networks change over time (Marsh and Smith

Table 1: Types of Policy Networks

Network type	Main network features
Corporatist networks	Relatively closed to new actors; anchors relatively cohesive policy ideas; state and civil society actors are closely interconnected; policy capacities are evenly distributed between state and civil society actors.
State-corporatist networks	Closed to new actors; policy ideas of state actors prevail; state and civil society actors are closely interconnected; policy capacities are distributed in a manner that favours state actors.
Clientelist networks	Closed to new actors; policy ideas of a single civil society actor prevail; state and civil society actors are closely interconnected; policy capacities are distributed in a manner that favours civil society actors.
Pressure pluralist networks	Open to new actors; fragmentation among actors along policy ideas; state and civil society actors are loosely interconnected; policy capacities are evenly distributed, but the state essentially acts as a broker or a referee between competing ideas.
State-directed networks	Open to new actors; fragmentation among actors along policy ideas; state and civil society actors are loosely interconnected; policy capacities are distributed in a manner that elevate the ideas of state actors above the competing ideas in civil society.
Issue networks	Open to new actors; fragmentation among actors along policy ideas; state and civil society are loosely interconnected; policy capacities are distributed in a manner that favours fragmented civil society actors and that reduce the efficacy of state actors as decision-makers.

2000). Nevertheless, while it is difficult to form an exact picture of the level of corporatist networking in Quebec, existing theoretical research, in concert with the limited empirical evidence cited above, suggest strongly that it is extensive.

For example, interest groups in the province are often structured, for historical reasons, as peak associations – hierarchical organizations whose members are groups rather than individuals. As Archibald (1983) argues, the Catholic Church's metaphor of the mystic body, which values a hierarchical society composed of complementary rather than competing groups, has encouraged the unification of most sectors of society through peak associations.

Although Quebec has since become a secular society, it has inherited the organizations of its Catholic past. For example, the Union des producteurs agricoles, structurally speaking, remains close to its ancestor, the Union des cultivateurs catholiques. Such peak associations, which can legitimately claim to represent all or at least a large majority of the constituents of a particular policy sector, enable the functioning of corporatist policy networks (Coleman 1988). The most obvious reason for this is the fact that the discussion or the negotiation of policy is far more difficult when a large number of groups compete for influence within a single sector.

A second reason for expecting more corporatist networks in Quebec is that the state, although closely interconnected with peak associations in corporatist policy networks, has to maintain some independent policy capacity. Streeck (1992) argues that such capacity is often essential for the very maintenance of peak associations themselves, which may require state support to fend off challenges from alternative constituency groups emerging in their particular policy sectors. To this I would add that policy capacity, when understood as expertise, is a necessary asset for meaningful participation since policy making is essentially about arguing and policy arguments have increasingly become technical (Majone 1989). Deprived of expertise and therefore of a capacity to argue, government bureaucracies could easily be rendered subservient to peak associations in clientelist type networks (see table 1). To counteract this possibility, Quebec has mobilized more resources to shore up its bureaucracies than governments elsewhere in North America, and this has correspondingly increased its capacity to maintain extensive corporatist networks in several sectors.

To sum up, peak associations and capable state agencies, two key elements of corporatist policy networks, are more common in Quebec than in the rest of North America. Taking these observations together with the limited empirical evidence presented above suggests that corporatist policy networks are likely to be much more extensive in Quebec than in the rest of America, supporting the idea of a distinctive Quebec model of socio-economic development.

REVISITING INDUSTRIAL POLICY

The conventional perspective holds that Quebec's industrial policy is a key feature of the Quebec model. With the foregoing arguments in mind, one might ask if the province's industrial policy is a product of a corporatist policy network. Not only do I claim that the province's industrial policy cannot be attributed to a corporatist policy network, I also claim that the conventional perspective has accorded too much importance to industrial policy.

Paquet (1994, 75–76) argues that corporatist networks emerge and play their full role only once policy makers have put in place an industrial policy that defines broad economic goals for the country. In other words, corporatist policy networks do not explain industrial policy, but are often explained *by* industrial policy. As mentioned above, since the Quebec Inc. period, the province's industrial policy has shifted away from championing francophone businesses and toward encouraging the clustering of knowledge economy firms into the so-called cités. The press (see Castonguay 2003, B1) typically attributes the creation of the first and most important cité, the Cité du multimédia, to a policy entrepreneur, Sylvain Vaugeois, who elaborated a scheme that became known as the *Plan Mercure*, designed to attract knowledge economy firms in a given area through tax credits attached to job creation. Vaugeois happened to be close to Bernard Landry, then the minister responsible for industry, who was impressed with the idea and used it to lay the foundation of the Cité du multimédia. Since then, similar cités have been created in various areas and sectors of the knowledge economy.

Behind the concept of the cité is the belief that clusters of firms are sources of innovation. Naturally, such clusters can also be fertile ground for the organization of firms into policy-relevant actors, if only to protect the benefits they receive from the province's industrial policy. That the firms in the cités and their workers have had sufficient time since the end of the 1990s to organize effectively enough to participate in corporatist policy networks is, however, doubtful. For example, no more than a few fragmented voices from this sector greeted the Charest government's announcement of the reduction of subsidies and tax credits going to knowledge economy firms. In short, if the idea of the cités is an innovative one, it is neither associated with a corporatist network nor has it encouraged, thus far, the formation of such networks, which I view as the key feature of the Quebec model.

Be that as it may, the conventional perspective on the Quebec model has accorded far too much attention to industrial policy. Emphasizing industrial policy has served only the critics who believe the Quebec model should be abandoned. Notably, it has allowed attacks on the model using Hayek's old argument about the waste of resources that follows any attempt at central planning for a complex economy (Migué 1998, 45–58; Paquet 1999). A central agency's economic reasoning, the argument goes, cannot reliably provide the basis for an optimal distribution of subsidies or tax credits. Instead, its interventions obey political pressures, which arguably are best exercised by the least productive industries. The proof supporting this argument, critics claim, rests in Quebec's relatively poor economic performance (Boyer 2001). Naturally, I do not share this view of Quebec's economic performance, but I leave the discussion of this question to the next section.

I will not rehearse the debates surrounding Hayek's argument. All I want to argue at this time is that a single policy, whether industrial or of another type, no matter how defective it might be, is unlikely to have the disastrous consequences critics attribute to Quebec's industrial policy. The effects of policies are rarely so self-evident. First, because every single policy, besides those relating to the provision of health and education, represent only a small proportion of the budget of the provincial government and most of these policies are subjected to frequent re-evaluation. The provision of education and health make provincial budgets globally stable, but smaller expenditures change. Therefore, if a policy relating to a field outside health and education were to misallocate resources, it follows that it could have only a small economic impact in the short term.

Second, evaluating a misallocation of resources engendered by policy poses significant difficulties. A first difficulty rests in the definition of a misallocation. Allocating money, even when it seeks to achieve a specified end (although policy makers rarely specify ends clearly), always has unexpected effects. And these unexpected effects are rarely unilaterally negative. As Stone (1997) argues, policies are an incredible source of paradox and can have several different, often opposing, effects at once. An environmental policy, for example, can simultaneously be a source of non-productive and productive investments. Such a policy may require investments by polluting industries in green technologies which appear non-productive. An evaluation may even show that the investments required by the environmental policy do not reduce releases of contaminants into the environment as much as expected. However, this same policy may encourage environmental industries to invest more in research and development to supply the polluting industries more efficiently. In the longer term, and in unexpected manners, polluting industries may benefit from this technological development, which at first appeared non-productive, granting them access to markets that value green products. Returning to the case in question, some of the money channelled through Quebec's industrial policy may not have produced its intended effects (Bélanger 1994); however, it is doubtful that the policy had the wholly negative effects critics insist upon. In short, it is rarely entirely accurate to deduce a misallocation of resources on the basis of nothing else besides an assessment of the end for which the allocation was designed.

Be that as it may, a second difficulty rests precisely with the establishment of a causal relationship between allocated resources and a given outcome. Indeed, so many factors normally influence the results policies seek to achieve that statistical linkages between a single policy and an outcome are rarely satisfying (Putnam 1993, 65–66; Vogel 1986). Investment decisions in the multimedia in Montreal were certainly influenced by tax credits, but also by the presence of four universities, bilingualism, a multicultural environment, the city's geographical location, the cost of living, the personal contacts of decision makers and several other government policies. Any change in one factor can affect the outcome or cancel out the effect of change in another factor. Tracing all these changes and interactions, often among variables for which no statistical data exist, is nearly impossible. Moreover, statisticians seeking to measure the effect of a policy relative to that of other factors often do not have a sufficient number of cases (degrees of freedom) to test the effect of such a large number of independent variables. But assessing a misallocation of resources requires more than just knowledge of the effect of an existing policy on a desired outcome. It also requires knowledge of the potential effect of a policy that might have been adopted if the resources had not been spent by the adopted policy. Economists call this the opportunity cost of a policy, whose calculation demands a prospective evaluation. Naturally, if evaluating the effect of a real policy on a real outcome poses difficulties, prospective evaluations can produce, at best, only speculative conclusions. One should therefore be aware that any judgment about misallocation of resources rests on such speculative conclusions.

These arguments naturally invite conventional analysts of the Quebec model to avoid limiting their observations to industrial policy. Environmental policy, social policy, family policy, leisure policy, cultural policy, etc., also matter, even if the analyst's objective is simply to explain economic performance. If the goal is a comprehensive assessment of the value of the Quebec model, all policies produced by corporatist policy networks must be taken into account. Moreover, analysts must be prepared to accept the limited relevance of industrial policy, for as I explained above, it is not clear at all that the province's industrial policy results from discussions in corporatist networks or that it encourages their formation. To put the problem differently, if Quebec's allegedly poor economic performance cannot be linked straightforwardly to its industrial policy it could, in theory, be linked to the cumulative effect of policies produced by the relatively numerous corporatist networks in other policy sectors. In the last section of this essay, I examine this hypothesis closely. For the moment, I turn to conventional analyses of the performance of the Quebec model.

STATISTICAL ANALYSES OF QUEBEC'S PERFORMANCE

Corporatism in Quebec has received plenty of bad press. In an open letter to Québécois, Premier Jean Charest asked "interest groups who benefit from the status quo ... to demonstrate their openness, avoiding placing their corporatist interests above the historical interests of Quebec and of all Québécois" (Charest 2003, A7). Unions were particularly upset that the Premier dared using the word "corporatist" to characterize their interests. In this context, my claim that the prominence of corporatist networks is the key feature of the Quebec model may not surprise critics who view the province's economic performance as poor. In response, I would insist on the fact that my understanding of corporatism is informed by a policy networks perspective, which is anchored in academic analysis rather than a pejorative view of corporatism. I would also insist that it is far from clear that the province's economic performance is poor. This is the matter to which I now turn.

Statistics on the province's economic performance are numerous. They are collected by different organizations, they are aggregated, crossed, lagged, or compared in different manners. In the absence of broad agreement on an appropriate method to measure Quebec's economic performance, analysts tend to use statistics to support their preferred but frequently conflicting stories. To illustrate this point, I compare two prominent economists who sit on opposite sides in the debate over the value of the Quebec model: Pierre Fortin and Marcel Boyer.

For Fortin, the model put in place during the Quiet Revolution in Quebec in the 1960s has made Québécois wealthier, slowly closing the gap the province has historically sustained with Ontario. To support this story, Fortin (2000, A7; 2001) uses data from Statistics Canada. He argues that in 1960 the difference in the GDP per capita between Quebec and Ontario was 26 percentage points; in 1999, the difference was reduced to 14 points. Boyer's story significantly differs for he believes Quebec's policies make Québécois poorer. Also relying on data from Statistics Canada, Boyer (2001, 3) argues that far from closing a gap in wealth, Quebec's annual average real growth between 1990 and 1999 was 2 percent, while it reached 2.6 percent in the rest of Canada.

Fortin (2000; 2002) further argues that Québécois are not only wealthier on average, but more of them work today in comparison with the period immediately preceding the Quiet Revolution. In 1982, he argues, the difference between Ontario and Québec in the employment rate for the adult population was 15 points. In 1999, it was reduced to 8 points. Between Toronto and Montreal, he adds, the difference is only of 4 points. Boyer (2001, 3) disagrees, claiming that between 1981 and 1999, Quebec's economy created 568,000 new jobs, making total employment grow by only 20.4 percent. In comparison, the rest of Canada created 2,666,000 new jobs, an increase of 31.3 percent.

For Fortin (2000; 2002), the investments the Quiet Revolution enabled in education, infrastructure and research and development have made the province more productive. In 1960, global productivity by worker represented 86 percent of that of Ontario. In 1999, the gap was reduced to 93 percent. Again, Boyer is not convinced. Economic performance, he suggests, is more accurately assessed when looking at data on high technology industries. Quebec exports in medium to high technologies, he shows, represent only 15 percent of Canadian exports in these sectors (Boyer 2001, 5–6).

I should underline that I use Fortin and Boyer for the sake of illustration; they are only two among several authors who participate in the debate over the Quebec model using statistics as an argumentative tool (see also Lisée 2000; Boucher and Palda 2003; Guay and Marceau 2004). Fortin and Boyer clearly disagree on which data provide an accurate picture of the province's economy. And this difficulty in measuring the province's economic performance is matched by the additional difficulty of assessing the importance of each and every contributing factor (see the above discussion on policy evaluation). The central point of the illustration is that several years of debates on the Quebec model using statistics have failed to produce an agreement on its economic impact.

Numbers measuring social phenomena, Stone (1997) suggests, should not be viewed, when used in policy debates, as revealing an incontestable reality in a politically neutral manner. Rather, statistical arguments are constructed and therefore work in a manner similar to metaphors. Stone writes: "To categorize in counting or to analogize in metaphors is to select one feature of something, assert a likeness on the basis of that feature, and ignore all the other features" (1997, 165). Assuredly, statistical arguments can make a useful contribution to political debates, but they should not exert any more authority than logically rigorous metaphoric arguments. In some cases, political actors may agree on the numbers providing a plausible picture of a situation just as they may agree on an image that increases understanding in a particular situation, and in both cases the search for a policy solution may thereby be facilitated. In many cases, however, agreements on numbers, just like agreements over a proper image to describe a situation, simply do not emerge, stalling the debate and endangering policy-making progress. As the statistical analyses of Fortin and Boyer reveal, numbers used in the debate over the value of the Quebec model provide little certainty on whether policy makers should consider reforming the model or leaving it largely unchanged. When this occurs, Stone suggests, actors should turn to alternative argumentative tools. In the next section, I suggest the metaphor of policy networks as an argumentative tool for advancing the debate over the performance of the Quebec model.

POLICY NETWORKS AND PERFORMANCE

The policy network perspective, I suggest, sheds a relatively positive light on the Quebec model. While the arguments underlying this perspective may become controversial in the longer term, as statistical arguments have become, it has the benefit of bringing analysts of the Quebec model into unexplored territory. In this territory, I hope, analysts will engage in a dialogue that statistical approaches are incapable of encouraging.

Statistical analyses focus on expected outcomes, that is, the impacts of policy on the economy or society. The perspective on performance that fits best with the policy networks perspective focuses on policy outputs or policy designs, which is to say the combination of goals, instruments and implementation arrangements contained in policy designs. Any assessment of the performance of a policy, therefore, has to rest on the substance of the reasoning that justifies the particular combination of elements that it contains. Note that such reasoning is not limited to contributions of policy makers, but can emerge from communities of experts supporting particular policy choices. These communities are known as epistemic communities (Haas, 1989). High performance policy making, then, is observed when a policy is anchored in powerful justifications and oriented toward the public interest. Even if powerfully justified policy is expected to yield the anticipated outcome, the measurement difficulties discussed in the previous section suggest it is wiser to focus on the substance of policy designs. Moreover, anticipated outcomes may provide too narrow a focus on performance, neglecting policy effects unexpected by policy makers but which may nevertheless contribute to the public interest. In short, the perspective I suggest on policy-making performance in this chapter requires detailed analyses of particular policy designs (see Montpetit, 2003a). Focusing on particular sectors facilitates the conduct of such analyses, hence its appropriateness for the policy network perspective.

The network perspective incorporates a positive treatment of the contribution of interest groups to policy making. This may appear unusual because the prevailing political discourse portrays interest groups as bearers of subjective interests (the term "special interest" is commonly used in English) that differ from the objective interest of the public, if not from their own objective interests. It follows that when they participate in policy processes, interest groups inhibit the realization of the objective interest of all citizens (Stone 1997, chapter 9). This sort of reasoning about interest groups appears in the clearest of terms in Jean Charest's open letter to Québécois, quoted at the beginning of the previous section. But politicians are not alone in demeaning the contribution of interest groups to policy making. Many academics, for example, argue that social movements make a more valuable contribution to governance than interest groups, because their motivations are taken to be altruistic rather than self-centered. This type of reasoning, popular among members of the Parti Québécois government, has encouraged the development of the so-called social economy (Lévesque and Mendell 1998). As the expression social economy suggests, altruistic ideas cannot be detached so easily from interests.

From a policy network perspective, interest groups are not blamed for carrying specific policy interests, but are actually valued for this contribution. This perspective in fact refuses to engage in the *a priori* ranking of the ideas of given actors, be they social movements, experts, government agencies or interest groups (Rhodes 1997, 20). Policy network authors tend not to assume that an objective public interest pre-exists deliberations among actors who are the bearers of various particular interests. In other words, the public interest is not conceived as being somewhere out there waiting to be discovered by technical expertise, statistics or social movements. Rather, the public interest results from deliberations over interests brought into the policy process, notably but not exclusively, by interest groups. Policy network analysts are largely indebted to theories of communicative action and deliberation for providing most of the reflection on this matter (Risse 2000; Öberg 2002).

If actors cannot be blamed for carrying interests, even specific interests, policy networks can be responsible for failing to encourage a deliberation over interests capable of generating decisions that serve the community well. Among all of the network types identified in table 1, corporatist networks, I argue, are those least likely to be victims of such a failure. I base this argument on two ideas: Scharpf's (1997) notion of "problem solving" and Weiss' (1998) concept of "governed interdependence."

Scharpf (1997, 130–132) calls problem solving a deliberation in which actors direct their attention toward the "joint creation of better projects or objects." He adds that the "power of problem solving is the power of joint action." For problem solving to occur, policy networks need to be consistent with two potentially conflicting principles. First, the joining of actors into a common endeavour requires a minimum of cohesion in actors' policy ideas. As Scharpf argues, "Problem solving is most likely to succeed if the participants are able to engage one another in truth-oriented 'arguing' about the best possible solution and the best way of achieving it." A common worldview or paradigm, it has been argued, normally binds together the actors of corporatist networks and provides the necessary cohesion for effective communicative action and eventually decision-making (Coleman, Skogstad and Atkinson 1997). Second, the power of joint action requires the presence of sufficiently diverse actors within policy networks to ensure complementary resources are brought into the policy-making process (e.g. information, skills, administrative capacity). If a network is too cohesive, communicative action should be achieved easily, but actors will not have much to learn from each other.

Incidentally, corporatist networks, among all the network types presented in table 1, offer the best balance between diversity and cohesion. Unlike pressure pluralist networks, corporatist networks are not open to everyone with an opinion on policies relevant to a sector. Deliberation among actors who can trust each other from personal experience (Offe 1999) is therefore easier in relatively closed corporatist networks than in pluralist networks (Öberg 2002). Decisions in corporatist networks can hardly be anything other than a derivation from deliberation or negotiation. In pressure pluralist networks, where inconclusive deliberations are common, politicians tend to decide by brokerage or arbitration (Sabatier and Jenkins-Smith 1999). At the same time, corporatist networks are not as dominated by a single actor as clientelist networks are. I have argued elsewhere that policy issues in modern states most of the time cut across several sectors. Consequently, even agricultural corporatist policy networks in Quebec, often portrayed as dominated by a single powerful group, the Union des producteurs agricoles, have included a diverse range of actors (Montpetit 2003c). Among these actors are environmentalists who are more frequently associated with social movements than with corporatist networks (Montpetit 1999).

Governed interdependence "refers to a negotiated relationship in which public and private participants maintain their autonomy, but which is nevertheless governed by broader goals set and monitored by the state" (Weiss 1998, 38). Governed interdependence requires strong civil society actors who can participate in policy making and strong state actors who can exercise leadership. According to Weiss, this type of governance offers the best guarantee for maintaining the necessary transformative capacity needed in the current context of globalization. Transformation occurs through governed interdependence when state agencies are capable of proposing mobilizing projects and when specific action is informed by civil society actors. Corporatist networks, among all types presented in table 1, again appear most favourable to governed interdependence. In state-directed or state-corporatist networks, state agencies can exercise leadership, but civil society actors are too weak to inform specific action. In such network conditions, policy transformations are likely to be common; they are also likely to be ineffective. In pressure pluralist networks, state agencies can only act as policy brokers or referees and can therefore hardly exercise leadership. Under such network conditions, policy transformations originate from a fragmented civil society and therefore are likely to suffer severe inconsistencies. In corporatist networks, state agencies have the capacity to exercise leadership; participating civil society groups possess sufficient policy expertise to inform policy development; and the level of interconnection between state agencies and participating groups facilitates the flow of information about projects and policies (for further elaboration on this idea see Montpetit 2003a).

Corporatist policy networks do not always succeed in producing problem solving and governed interdependence. Scharpf (1997), in fact, argues that problem solving is a rare occurrence because distributive conflicts among network participants are often too salient. Distributive conflicts encourage negotiation and compromise rather than problem solving. However, the perspective presented above suggests that corporatist policy networks possess attributes enabling them to make policies that serve the community well, or at least better than other network types. In short, Quebec citizens should not fear that the main feature of the Quebec model, namely corporatist policy networks, harms their province's performance. On the contrary, the arguments presented in this essay suggest that corporatist networks make a positive contribution, albeit possibly a modest one, to the province's governance.

CONCLUSION

Leaving behind the unresolved debates generated by the conventional perspectives on the Quebec model is assuredly the main benefit of adopting the policy network perspective. It is not worth spending energy on industrial and macro-economic policy debates, in which both sides assume simple policy causation. If one moves beyond simple causation and adopts the policy network perspective, it becomes clear that the province's industrial policy simply does not deserve to be placed above other policies, even when the analyst's objective is to assess the economic performance of the Quebec model. Analysts who adopt a network perspective, however, should not delude themselves into thinking that they will establish easy statistical proofs of the economic superiority or inferiority of the Quebec model, if only because collecting data for all the relevant policy sectors would amount to an enormous task. In any case, moving beyond statistical analysis has the benefit of bringing an end to senseless fights over numbers on the Quebec model, which has contributed to a perpetually stalled dialogue among analysts.

The lessons of this paper are not only relevant to analysts; they may also enlighten movie-goers around the world. Opposing Denys Arcand, I argue that Quebec does not epitomize the *Decline of the American Empire*, nor was it invaded by barbarians. In this essay, I have suggested that corporatist policy networks, the main feature of the Quebec model, in all likelihood, contribute positively to the province's governance. The argument rests on the idea that corporatist networks, among several types of possible networks, are best at organizing deliberations which engage a manageable set of actors holding a diverse range of ideas. One cannot hope for anything better to serve the public interest than such deliberations.

This is not to say, however, that everything goes well in Quebec. First, several sectors may not benefit from the presence of corporatist networks, including the sector of industrial policy. Second, corporatist networks do not always result in deliberations conducive to problem solving or governed interdependence. As Scharpf (1997) argues, negotiations are more common than problem solving, although he also acknowledges that negotiations can also serve the public interest (Montpetit 2003a). Following Scharpf (1999), one might add that corporatist networks are also better at providing output-oriented legitimacy than input-oriented legitimacy. As explained above, corporatist networks are effective at problem solving, as well as negotiations, partly because they exclude from policy participation actors whose ideas appear too distant from those of key participants. The ideas of participating actors have to be sufficiently cohesive to enable communicative action in search of the best possible solutions. When this occurs, some legitimacy is derived from these solutions. This is what Scharpf (1999) calls output-oriented legitimacy. However, participation, or the provision of input, is also a source of legitimacy in a democracy. Participation in democratic systems is in fact valued for its own sake, independently of its effect on policy results. This is input-oriented legitimacy. Therefore, the exclusion inherent to corporatist networks will always generate important criticisms. Several of the attacks on the Quebec model, in fact, have their origin in the exclusionary nature of corporatist policy networks.

It is important to underline, however, that input- and output-oriented forms of legitimacies are not mutually exclusive. As I have argued above, networks that exclude too many actors should do rather poorly at producing output-oriented legitimacy. It is equally important to underline that some exclusion from policy participation in modern complex states remains unavoidable. Assuredly, maintaining citizens' trust in policy-making arrangements in such a context is a serious challenge (Offe 1999). In fact, maintaining citizens' trust in the Quebec model is a challenging endeavour. Unfortunately, movies such as *Barbarian Invasions* pull us misleadingly in the other direction.

NOTE

The author wishes to thank Charles Blattberg, Mike Murphy, Alain Noël and Christian Rouillard for useful comments.

REFERENCES

Archibald, C. 1983. *Un Québec corporatiste?* Hull: éditions asticou.

Bélanger, Y. 1994. "Québec Inc.: la dérive d'un modèle?" In *Québec État et Société*, ed. A.-G. Gagnon. Montreal: Québec/Amérique.

Boucher, M. and F. Palda. 2003. "Le rapport de l'Institut Fraser: La prospérité ou la stagnation." *Le Devoir*, 19 December, A8.

Bourque, G.L. 2000. *Le modèle québécois de développement: de l'émergence au renouvellement*. Quebec: Presses de l'Université du Québec.

Boyer, M. 2001. "La performance économique du Québec: Constats et défis." Rapport bourgogne du Centre interuniversitaire de recherche en analyse des organisations, Montréal.

Castonguay, A. 2003. "Sylvain Vaugeois n'a pas eu le temps de réaliser son dernier projet." *Le Devoir*, 26 August, B1.

Charest, J. 2003. "Lettre ouverte aux Québécois: Le Québec a fait un pas en avant depuis six mois." *Le Devoir*, A7.

Coleman, W.D. 1988. *Business and Politics: A Study of Collective Action*. Kingston and Montreal: McGill-Queen's University Press.

– 1995. "Le nationalisme, les intermédiairies et l'intégration canadienne." *Politique et sociétés* 28: 31–32.

– 1997. "Policy Communities and Policy Networks: Some Issues of Methods." Paper prepared for a presentation to the System of Government Conference, University of Pittsburgh.

Coleman, W.D. and G. Skogstad, eds. 1990. *Policy Communities and Policy Networks in Canada: A Structural Approach*. Mississauga: Copp Clark Pitman.

Coleman, W.D., G. Skogstad and M. Atkinson. 1997. "Paradigm Shifts and Policy Networks: Cumulative Change in Agriculture." *Journal of Public Policy* 16(3): 273–301.

Desrosier, É. 2003. "Sous-traitance: Jacques Ménard appuie les réforme de Charest." *Le Devoir*, B1.

Detlef, J. 1998. "Environmental Performance and Policy Regimes." *Policy Science* 31(2): 107–31.

Fortier, I. and K. Hébert. 2003. "Les enjeux de la réingénierie: choix générationnels ou collectifs." In *L'annuaire du Québec 2004*, ed. M. Venne. Montreal: Fidès.

Fortin, P. 2000. "Le Québec a comblé la moitié de son retard sur l'Ontario." *Le Devoir*, A7.

– 2001. "Has Quebec's Standard of Living Been Catching Up?" In *Regional Innovation Systems: The Role of Governance in a Globalized World*, eds. H.-J. Braczyk, P. Cook and M. Heidenreich. London: UCL Press.

– 2002. *Abaisser le taux de chîmage au Québec: L'objectif, les contraintes et les moyens*. Quebec: étude réalisée pour le ministère des Finances, de l'Économie et de la Recherche.

Gagnon, B. 2001. "La situation économique." In *Portrait social du Québec: Données et analyse*. Quebec: Institut de la statistique du Québec.

Gouvernement du Quebec. 1995. *Portrait statistique des effectifs régulier et occasionnel de la fonction publique du Québec*. Quebec: Office des ressources humaines.

Gow, J.I. 1986. *Histoire de l'administration publique québécoise 1867–1970*. Montreal: Presses de l'Université de Montréal et Institut d'administration publique du Canada.

– 2000. "The Career Public Service in Quebec: How to Reinvigorate the Closed Shop." In *Government Restructuring and Career Public Services*, ed. E. Lindquist. Toronto: The Institute of Public Administration of Canada.

Guay, A. and N. Marceau. 2004. "Réponses aux détracteurs du modèle québécois: Le Québec n'est pas le cancre économique qu'on dit." In *L'annuaire du Québec 2005*, ed. M. Venne. Montreal: Fidès.

Haas, P. 1989. "Do Regimes Matter? Epistemic Communities and Mediterranean Pollution Control." *International Organization* 43(3): 377–403.

Haddow, R. 1998. "Reforming Labour-Market Policy Governance: The Quebec Experience." *Canadian Public Administration* 41(3): 343–68.

Institut économique de Montréal. 2003. "Le fardeau fiscal et réglementaire des Québécois." Notes économique de l'Institut économique de Montréal.

Kingdon, J.W. 1995. *Agendas, Alternatives and Public Policies*. New York: HarperCollins College Publishers.

Lévesque, B. and M. Mendell. 1998. "Les fonds régionaux et locaux de développement au Québec: des institutions financières relevant principalement de l'économie sociale." In *Territoires et développement économique*, ed. M.-U. Proulx. Paris: L'Harmattan.

Lisée, J.-F. 2000. *Sortie de secours: Comment échapper au déclin du Québec*. Montreal: Éditions du Boréal.

Majone, G. 1989. *Evidence, Argument, and Persuasion in the Policy Process.* New Haven: Yale University Press.

Marsh, D. and M. Smith. 2000. "Understanding Policy Networks: Towards a Dialectical Approach." *Political Studies* 48(1): 4–21.

Migué, J.-L. 1998. *Étatisme et Déclin du Québec: Bilan de la Révolution tranquille.* Montreal: Les éditions varia.

Milner, H. 1989. *Sweden: Social Democracy in Practice.* Oxford: Oxford University Press.

Montpetit, É. 1999. "Corporatisme québécois et performance des gouvernants: analyse comparative des politiques environnementales en agriculture." *Politique et Sociétés* 18: 79–98.

– 2003a. *Misplaced Distrust: Policy Networks and the Environment in France, the United States and Canada.* Vancouver: UBC Press.

– 2003b. "Biotechnology, Life Sciences and Policy Networks in the European Union." *Swiss Political Science Review* 9(2): 127–35.

– 2003c. "Le néo-corporatisme québécois à l'épreuve du fédéralisme canadien et de l'internationalisation." In *Québec: État et Société*, deuxième édition, ed. A.-G. Gagnon. Montreal: Québec/Amérique.

Montpetit, É. and C. Rouillard. 2001. "La Révolution tranquille et le réformisme institutionnel: pour un dépassement des discours réactionnaires sur l'étatisme québécois." *Globe: Revue internationale d'études québécoises* 4(1): 119–39.

Noël, A. 1994. "Le chômage en héritage." In *Québec État et Société*, ed. A.-G. Gagnon. Montreal: Québec/Amérique.

Öberg, P. 2002. "Does Administrative Corporatism Promote Trust and Deliberation?" *Governance* 15(4): 455–75.

Offe, C. 1999. "How Can We Trust Our Fellow Citizens?" In *Democracy and Trust*, ed. M. Warren. Cambridge: Cambridge University Press.

Paquet, G. 1994. "Québec Inc.: Mythes et réalités." In *L'État interventionniste: le gouvernement provincial et l'économie du Québec*, ed. F. Palda. Vancouver: Fraser Institute.

– 1999. *Oublier la Révolution tranquille: pour une nouvelle socialité.* Montreal: Liber.

Putnam, R. 1993. *Making Democracy Work: Civic Tradition in Modern Italy.* Princeton: Princeton University Press.

Risse, T. 2000. "'Let's Argue!': Communicative Action in World Politics." *International Organization* 54(1): 1–39.

Rhodes, R.A.W. 1997. *Understanding Governance: Policy Networks, Governance, Reflexivity and Accountability.* Buckingham: Open University Press.

Sabatier, P.A. and H.C. Jenkins-Smith. 1999. "The Advocacy Coalition Framework: An Assessment." In *Theories of the Policy Process*, ed. P.A. Sabatier, 117–66. Boulder: Westview Press.

Scharpf, F.W. 1997. *Games Real Actors Play: Actor-Centered Institutionalism in Policy Research.* Boulder: Westview Press.

– 1999. *Governing in Europe: Effective and Democratic*. Oxford: Oxford University Press.

Secrétariat du Conseil du trésor. 2003. *L'effectif de la fonction publique du Québec 2002*. Quebec: Conseil du trésor.

Skogstad, G. 1990. "The Farm Policy Community in Ontario and in Quebec." In *Policy Communities and Policy Networks in Canada: A Structural Approach*, eds. W.D. Coleman and G. Skogstad. Mississauga: Copp Clark Pitman.

Smith, M.R. 1994. "L'impact de *Québec Inc.*, répartition des revenus et efficacité économique." *Sociologie et sociétés* 26(2): 91–110.

Stone, D. 1997. Policy Paradox: *The Art of Political Decision Making*. New York: W.W. Norton and Company.

Streeck, W. 1992. "From National Corporatism to Transnational Pluralism: European Interest Politics and the Single Market." In *Participation and Public Policy-Making: The Role of Trade Unions and Employers' Associations*, ed. T. Treu, 97–126. Berlin: Walter de Gruyter.

Tanguay, B.A. 1984. "Concerted Action in Quebec, 1976–1983: Dialogue of the Death." In *Quebec: State and Society*, ed. A.-G. Gagnon. Agincourt: Methuen Publications.

Van Waarden, F.V. 1992. "Dimensions and Types of Policy Networks." *European Journal of Political Research* 21: 29–52.

Vogel, D. 1986. *National Styles of Regulation: Environmental Policy in Great Britain and the United States*. Ithaca: Cornell University Press.

Weiss, L. 1998. *The Myth of the Powerless State*. Ithaca: Cornell University Press.

6

Globalization as a New Political Space: The End of the Quebec-Quebec Debate?

Pascale Dufour

Ce chapitre traite de la mondialisation comme enjeux sociétal québécois qui contribue à modifier les frontières du débat politique et a un impact direct sur la façon dont est posée la question nationale au Québec. Après avoir posé la mondialisation comme un enjeu politique (première partie), nous montrons comment cet enjeu a profondément modifié les relations entre les forces sociales en présence de même que le cadre des débats publics. La dernière partie tente de lier deux enjeux politiques en transformation : celui du nationalisme et celui de la mondialisation.

INTRODUCTION

Although in these times it could be considered a good "marketing" strategy to speak about globalization, it is increasingly difficult to choose how to address it, given the abundance of literature that has been produced on the subject. My own discussion of globalization is unique in several ways. First, I do not seek to address economic globalization or the objective trends of globalization that occur in the economic sphere. Secondly, I am analyzing globalization neither as an external factor that can contribute to the national economic development of Quebec, nor as an hegemonic economic force preventing Quebec society from developing itself. I propose instead to show how globalization has contributed to a shift in the contours of political debates on the "national question" in Quebec.[1]

The essay is divided into three sections. In the first section, I develop the concept of globalization that informs the empirical part of the research. In the second section, I demonstrate how globalization, as a new political space, has radically challenged the relationships between social forces[2] (including the state) and has altered the framework of the nationalist debate in Quebec. The third section attempts to link these two shifting political spaces – nationalism and globalization – in the context of Quebec politics.

CONCEPTUALIZING GLOBALIZATION AS A POLITICAL SPACE

Within social protest literature, two prominent means of addressing globalization are evident. The first, following Tarrow's work, examines the transnational effects of globalization on social actors, analyzing the meaning, capacity, and potential of transnational movements (Tarrow 2000; Ayers 2001) or global counter-projects (Waterman 2001). The second addresses globalization at the national level, conceptualizing it as a new opportunity structure for national and local social movements (Guidry, Kennedy and Zald 2000) or as a new object provoking different reactions depending on the national context considered (Ancelovici 2002).

In this essay, I adopt the second perspective in analyzing globalization in Quebec society. Nonetheless, I do not consider globalization to be a force that originates purely externally to Quebec society. Instead, I view globalization as a complex process that is linked equally with local, national and global actors. In other words, my interest is focused not on the reaction of Quebec's social actors to globalization as an external factor, but instead on the development of a new political arena that accompanies the problematic of globalization. In order to further formalize this point of departure, I propose a conceptualization of globalization as a space (and in this sense, globalization is simultaneously local, national and global)[3] which is political in two ways: first, in the sense that there is a lack of consensus among political actors concerning the nature of contemporary globalization, and second, in the sense that there is a lack of agreement concerning the desirability of its various forms. Thus, globalization is a political issue and an important source of debates and claims. Moreover, it is a field of political action, particularly for social actors who protest against globalization.

From the point of view of collective social actors, from Seattle to Porto Alegre, something significant has happened in the world's streets (Ayres 2001). Social forces everywhere have generated numerous discourses concerning globalization: some relating to its negative effects (the anti-globalization perspective), others to its status as the last chance of defeating capitalist hegemony (the counter-globalization perspective), and yet others which seek an alternative to it (the alternative-globalization perspective). Globalization, as an issue, is implicated in a multiplicity of discourses (Hay and Rosamund 2002), which means that a large variety of actors are working to define what globalization is or is not. These actors, although sharing a common opposition to neo-liberal globalization, disagree on other issues. In this sense, globalization is an issue through which multiple oppositional discourses are constructed.

These discursive differences between social actors concerning globalization are evident at the global scale, as several studies of Seattle and the World Social Forum have demonstrated.[4] These differences, however, also have specific significance on the national scale. In a recent article, Ancelovici argues that in the case of France, although the discourses of the movements opposed to globalization were framed in a manner determined in large part by previous contentious episodes, the new interpretative processes surrounding the globalization issue make possible the formation of new coalitions between actors that previously did not work together (Ancelovici 2002, 431). These issues are taken up in the second part of the essay, which focuses on the manner in which globalization has been progressively framed in political discourses within Quebec from the middle of 1995 until 2002.[5]

Globalization is, however, also a new field of action. New enemies are identified, new battlefields are designed, new actions take place, and new relationships are built between the various actors involved, including the state. An increasing amount of academic work has demonstrated how social protests against globalization (or for an alternative to globalization) utilize a new repertoire of collective actions and are characterized by distinctive elements that are sufficient to qualify those protests as "new" (Sommier 2001). In particular, the internal organization of the new groups is more horizontal than the hierarchical approach of more traditional groups (such as unions), and together function as networks of protest. Direct democracy, understood as "consensus building" (rather than rule by majority vote), nomination of spokesmen (instead of elected chiefs or leaders), informal structures and revocable delegates are the main tools that these new groups claim to use in their decision-making processes. In addition, new actors seem to prefer pragmatic over ideological positions, and concrete actions, even if modest, if they can bring about tangible results (Hamel et al. 2000). Finally, even if these new groups continue to use the 19th century modern repertoire of collective action, as described by Tilly, such as demonstration, strikes and petitions (Tilly 1986), they also add three elements:

1. The idea that each action should be a "happening" (as in the tradition of the 1968 social movements, a festive event that allows some place for spontaneous actions);
2. the use of expertise (counter-reports, alternative media, organization of conferences and meetings) (Offerlé 1994); and
3. actions that are easily promoted through the media, including civil disobedience (Pedretti 2001).

Does this mean that for a group to be part of the globalization space, it needs to have all of these organizational characteristics? Not necessarily, for as I demonstrate in the second part of the essay, in the case of Quebec, social actors progressively involved in the globalization field of action were not only "new" actors but also unions and political parties. In other words, to be part of the globalization space an actor does not need to be "new" or to be organized along certain fixed dimensions. Potentially any actor could be part of this space if it develops a discourse on or a position towards globalization and if it acts in this field of protest at certain key moments in time.[6] In the case of Quebec, the Quebec Summit of the Americas in April 2001 was such a key moment.

However, beyond these sociological considerations, new forms of social protest are not free from all predetermined structures. They exist in a context in which the history of state/society relationships poses specific constraints on actors and offers specific opportunities for actions. In other words, not everything is possible in a given society; all social actors involved in protest must take account of and act within a given structural milieu. In order to analyze relationships between social actors and the state, I modify Mahon's conception of the "unequal structure of representation" that reflects the inequality of social forces (Mahon 1977) in relation to access to the state. According to Mahon, "inside the state, the structure of representation is unequal with one hegemonic class and subordinate class that have a 'room' inside the state but a pre-defined room." The concept of structures of representation developed by Mahon designates the totality of relations that are produced and reproduced according to largely stable (though not unchanging) relations between selected central political actors situated within the State. I adopt an expanded and more flexible perspective that considers the structures of representation of the totality of society, rather than only those of actors within the State. My conception is also more flexible in the sense that it considers the structure of representation to be in constant transformation. In other words, even if structural effects have a tendency to attempt to identically reproduce relations between actors, one time period is always different from the next, and therefore, the question of the relations between actors and structures in each period must be addressed empirically. Within this perspective, the state is not only influenced by collective action but also influences it. In part three I demonstrate that in the case of Quebec during the period considered, complex relationships were established between the state and social actors. On one hand, it can be concluded that social actors in Quebec have slowly altered the "unequal structure of representation" in their favour. On the other hand, new divisions have emerged. In particular, I conclude that the debate concerning the field of globalization is today more accurately depicted in terms of a right/left problematic than in terms of a federalism/sovereignty problematic, that the target of protest has shifted, and that the image of the enemy is no longer the same for social actors.

GLOBALIZATION AS A POLITICAL SPACE IN QUEBEC: WHAT'S NEW?

GLOBALIZATION AS A NEW ISSUE OF PROTEST

From the middle of the 1990s, globalization has progressively become a distinct political space for social actors, and took on a concrete form with the Quebec Summit of 2001. The history of the community of social actors in Quebec is characterized mainly by its specific capacity to work with unions and its strength as an agent of social and political transformation. Thus, to mention only a few examples, community actors were a central piece of the Centres locaux de services communautaires project and of the (mostly) public daycares network (Shragge 1999). During the 1990s, community actors were also very active on the public scene, becoming a "full partner" of the state during the two Quebec summits in 1996 and successfully forcing the adoption of a law against poverty in 2002. Beyond these unquestionable successes, I propose a rereading of the main events concerning social protest in Quebec between 1995 and 2002, in light of the previously outlined globalization problematic.

From 1995 to 2002, two trends became evident. First, there was a growing integrated movement against poverty in Quebec, unified around a specific task; and second, it is possible to detect a progressive globalization of issues, claims and actors around, but also beyond, issues of poverty. In 1995, the women's movement built a mass mobilization around the 1995 women's Bread and Roses march against women's poverty. The march was designed to highlight nine demands, including six measures to correct specific inequalities and three more general measures – including a revalorization of the minimum wage, pay equity, and the creation of an efficient and affordable network of daycares (Graefe 2002; Graveline 1995). The result of the march is generally considered to be highly positive. Indeed, the march was followed by the creation of a consultative committee on the social economy, an increase in the minimum wage (Lévesque and Mendell 1999), and it also became the point of departure for the creation of a low cost public daycare program (Jenson 1998). Even if the success of the march was in large part due to circumstances (a pre-referendum context in Quebec, during which the Fédération des Femmes du Québec (FFQ), the principal leader of the march, had taken a clear position on the "Yes" side of the referendum), it also marked the first step towards what would be known as the World March of Women in 2000. As Isabelle Giraud has argued, in the

1995 march, women from Quebec, for the first time, joined their claims to those of women from other parts of the world, particularly those from the global South (Giraud 2001). The collective action that took place around the march allowed feminists from Quebec to identify the world economic system as a level of political and economic regulation that limited the capacity of their state. For the first time, the idea that women's poverty and women's problems were directly linked with economic decisions at the global level that promoted deregulation of markets, privatization of public services and fiscal conservatism emerged from the feminist movement. In the years following the march, these analyses also found a place in the advisory council on the Status of Women, the Conseil du Statut de la femme (Harvey 1998).

After losing the referendum, the new premier, Lucien Bouchard, called two summits in which economic and social actors negotiated with the government over the future of Quebec society. The first Socio-Economic Summit, in March 1996, took social actors (excluding unions) by surprise (it was the first time that they were invited to the table) and they did not come to the negotiation table with a clear plan in mind (Interview Saillant, 2002). In that respect, Lucien Bouchard easily took the lead of this first summit and imposed the main theme of the meeting: the need for Quebec society to reach a situation of "zero deficit." During the second summit, the Summit on Economy and Work in October, which was later labelled the Summit of Decisions, social actors (including unions) came with a counter proposal of "zero poverty" that was only partially adopted. Thereafter, a large coalition of actors was convinced of the necessity of working together on the issue of poverty. In 1998, the Collectif pour une loi sur l'élimination de la pauvreté was created, and in 2002, Bill 112, Loi visant à lutter contre la pauvreté et l'exclusion sociale was adopted (Noël 2003).

With the exception of these more nationally oriented protests, the protest against free trade altered its scope and form, especially during the second half of the 1990s. In Quebec, protests against free trade began as early as 1986, shortly before the adoption of the first free trade agreement with the US. The Coalition québécoise d'opposition au libre-échange, composed mainly of unions, did not have much success at the national level before the mid-1990s (Brunelle and Deblock, 2000). Confronted with a consensus of the elite on the subject of free trade, and with an absence of clear allies on the political Left, the coalition developed differently from its Canadian counterpart (the Action Canada Network), which was formed mainly around the left nationalist movement. During its first ten years, the Quebec coalition (which became the Réseau québécois sur l'intégration continentale (RQIC) in 1994), adopted a position in favour of free trade but was concerned about the social consequences for Quebec society (and not with the consequences for other regions). Moreover, the question of free trade was first addressed by unions, with few other social actors involved.

This first period was marked by the use of protectionist discourse and a relatively limited scope of protest. In the second period, the scope was enlarged and discourses became increasingly global. As Lemire (2003) notes, in 1998 a new type of protest emerged against the Multilateral Agreement on Investments (MAI). Beginning in 1995, the MAI discussions were first conducted in secret between the OECD members. The agreement proposed "to establish a broad multilateral framework for international investment with high standards for the liberalization of investment regimes and investment protection and with effective dispute settlement procedures" (MAI 1997). Early in 1998, the text of the agreement was published on the Internet by the Public Citizen movement of Ralph Nader and then by the monthly French magazine *Le Monde diplomatique*. The MAI mobilization was followed by the first step in the process of the globalization of protest in Quebec. From this point on, all actors, including unions, adopted positions on this issue. For example, in line with what was occurring elsewhere (particularly in France), the Front des Travailleurs du Québec (FTQ) adopted a resolution supporting the implementation of a Tobin tax, an international tax on foreign currency exchange in 1998 (FTQ 1998; Harvey 2000).[7] This new awareness of globalization as a highly political issue was solidified during 2000, with the organization of the World March of Women against Poverty and Violence by the Fédération des femmes du Québec. Although this World March could be considered a success at the global level, it was declared a failure by participants as a result of its inability to produce a direct impact on the Quebec government (Interviews Barbot and Paquette, 2002). Meanwhile, during the World March (and its preparation) new alliances were created with new actors involved in the anti-globalization field (such as Opération Salami), and also with other women's organizations in English Canada. Progressively, the claims of Quebec women joined with those of English-Canadian women and those of women from all over the world. The organization of this worldwide event represents a turning point in the way social protest is embedded in Quebec. The World March had an impact not only on the women's movement itself (Maillé 2003), but it also demonstrated to all social actors that similar claims could exist from one country to another, and that the target of protest is not solely the national or provincial state but also international institutions. By the year 2000, social actors in Quebec had occupied the globalization space and had contributed to its construction as a political space, which was not the case five years earlier. In 2001, the globalization of protest was even more evident in the Quebec People's Summit, which coincided with the negotiation of the Free Trade Agreements of the Americas.

GLOBALIZATION AS A NEW FIELD OF ACTION

In addition to the penetration of globalization into the activities of existing social actors in Quebec, it is necessary to mention that since 1998, several new social actors have emerged that are specifically oriented towards the fight against globalization (or for a different form of globalization). To mention only the most well known, Opération Salami was created in 1998; Attac-Quebec and the Convergence des luttes anti-capitalistes (CLAC) became officially active in 2000 (for more details see Lemire 2003). Beyond differences in terms of their degrees of radicalism, it is important to highlight the common ground between these groups. Each fights for global social justice, wants people to recover control over their lives, denounces economic and financial hegemonic powers, and has some alternative propositions. What is at stake for most opponents of globalization is not simply jobs and north-south relations, but also labour conditions, social and environmental norms, food quality, and so forth. The Quebec Summit of 2001 was a moment of crystallization for these claims and an instance where the partial unity of the fight against globalization was realized.

If we focus our attention on the debates around the summit, we can outline a spectrum from the less radical to the most radical actors. At the centre, we find those groups working inside large coalitions, more or less institutionalized, and prepared to enter into a process of negotiations. In Quebec, such groups were involved in the organization of the People's Summit, namely the Regroupement Québécois sur l'Intégration Continentale (RQIC) and the Coalition Common Frontiers, both members of the Hemispheric Social Alliance.[8] These groups believe that it is possible to reach an "agreed Free Trade Agreement of the Americas" (FTAA), an agreement that takes into account democratic and environmental clauses and that could be accepted by the majority of social actors. Their first aim is to become "insiders," playing the negotiation game, even if they are disappointed by the consultation process (Cornellier 2001, A1; Harvey 2001, E3). They have been successful in the promotion of two ideas: one is "responsible business" and the other is "globalization with a human face." The first idea is to render business entrepreneurs more socially and environmentally responsible for their actions and decisions while the second idea is to promote the need to politically regulate economic globalization in order to restore human rights and dignity. These terms are now promoted by the dominant discourses of most international organizations and governments, and could be considered part of the dominant discursive framework used by moderate social actors. But, of course, their meanings are variable, depending on who is speaking.

Around this core group are located other groups who believe that the FTAA is not a process that can be constructively changed. In the name of social justice they accept non-violent strategies of protest, including civil disobedience. In

Quebec City, this included those groups meeting in the Opération Québec Printemps 2001, members of the Table de Convergence 2001, who promoted the Popular Forum (including, from the province of Québec, Opération Salami, ATTAC-Québec, the Fédération des Femmes du Québec, the Syndicat de la fonction publique du Québec and, for the English speaking provinces, the Council of Canadians and most of the groups involved in the Solidarity Network[9]). These groups do not necessarily want to be insiders in the sense that they do not necessarily want to be at the negotiating table. They prefer to create a dynamic of conflict in order to allow public expression of opposition. During the Quebec Summit, they succeeded in obtaining the publication of the FTAA treaties. Their target of protest was to prevent such agreement from happening.

Both types of coalitions are fighting against the lack of democracy and transparency in the globalization process. Each supports alternative media (such as the Centre des média alternatifs de Québec 2001) and popular education as the main instruments with which to build a constructive protest. Despite their divisions concerning which strategic choices to adopt (to work with institutional actors on the inside, or to work with them while remaining outside of the system), and their different conclusions regarding the process of globalization itself (one that is definitely a severe limitation on the potential of the overall movement), the two types of coalitions share sufficient values to be able to work together if necessary, and therefore, it is more appropriate to speak of a division of tasks between the two rather than about implacable divergences.

With regard to a third position, there exist more radical groups who do not condemn violence, even if they themselves do not participate in it. In Quebec City, an example of such a group was the Comité d'accueil du Sommet des Amériques (which included, as one of its more popular animators, CLAC), who prepared the Carnival Against Capitalism. Beyond the difference regarding the acceptability of violence (which is a major battle line between groups), there is also a profound divergence concerning the appropriate behaviour to adopt in front of the "enemies" (who can be specific international organizations, business groups, or the state). In this third type of protest, militants do not make claims in order to gain marginal ameliorations; rather, they favour direct actions that destabilize the entire system. The final aim is not to negotiate or to obtain a "formal" voice in the decision-making process, but instead to prevent the success of meetings such as the Quebec Summit or to push more traditional actors such as unions in a more radical direction (oblige them to take positions on certain issues that they otherwise would not adopt). The target of protest is not the state, as with the first two categories of groups, but other social actors. Nevertheless, these more radical groups are able to work with (or beside) the first two sets of groups that we have identified. They share common enemies and a will to provide education regarding global issues.

Finally, in the fourth category we find smaller groups – often linked to anarchist movements – who promote violence, and include the small membership of the Black Bloc, an organization infamous to both journalists and police forces. These groups do not have specific demands addressed to specific central actors. Their objectives are both more diffused and more concrete. Their first concrete objective is to disturb the progress of the event (here the summit) as much as possible and to confront all actors involved, not just the mainstream participants. Longer-term objectives vary from group to group. For some, it might be to disturb the capitalist system as a whole or to prepare a revolution, but it might also serve to promote the group and its philosophy or way of life (Dupuis-Déri 2003).

In considering the first two categories of actors – the main players in the game – we see a new frame of protest emerging.[10] This frame can first be characterized by a clear change in the scale of social protest. As we have seen with the World March of Women, social actors throughout Canada (and increasingly throughout the world) have common claims. This has previously not been the case. For the first time in the recent history of Canada, we see pan-Canadian coalitions of actors fighting for the same purpose. We can also analyze this phenomenon as a politicization of protest. Collective actors generally agree on the main goal: the return of political control over economic forces. Some of them are concerned with access for all citizens to political rights and the deepening of democratic structures (at the global and national levels), while other actors propose the creation of international political organizations that could regulate social, cultural, political and economic relationships at the global level. In Quebec, this politicization of protest is highly visible on the left side of the political spectrum, where new links have been built between some "new left" groups (the Rassemblement pour l'alternative politique, followed by the creation of the Union des forces progressistes) and some social actors, such as eminent members of the FFQ, the Conseil central de montréal de la Confédération des syndicats nationaux (CSN), and some anti-poverty advocacy groups.

According to all the leaders I met, greater political commitment for their organization was a new issue, as traditionally they were "neutral" as community actors, or at least not directly implicated in politics. Thus, during the last Quebec provincial election, the Collectif D'abord solidaires proposed a detailed analysis of each party's program in order to inform "the public." If it is true that the presence of the Action Démocratique du Quebec (ADQ) and its radical program on certain issues was implicated in the process of the politicization of social actors, it is also true that the emerging political space of globalization is also integral to the explanation. In particular, the events of 2001 have intensified the involvement of most social groups in debates around economic globalization, and have produced new coalitions between groups both within Quebec and from outside the province.

Finally, new bases of protest have been built. Social actors generally agree on the main analysis of the situation: that the globalization of markets accompanies the globalization of poverty and social exclusion, as social inequalities are rising. As a consequence, most of the claims are framed in terms of "global social justice," the redistribution of wealth, and greater equality. The less radical groups fight for capitalism with a "human face," promoting a redistribution of resources between the rich and the poor in each country (through an end to both fiscal conservatism and dramatic cuts in public spending), but also between countries (proposals for a Tobin tax and the cancellation of the debt of the poorest countries). The main targets of claims are those that are seen as responsible for these negative social developments: those international organizations that wield significant economic and financial powers (Lemire 2000, 4), and also national states if they are seen to be actively participating in the construction of this neo-liberal order.

In order to grasp the true significance of this new form of social protest, we must consider the specific context in which it emerged. In the final part of the essay I consider the changing relationships between the Quebec state and social movements during the 1995–2002 period, and the impacts of this shifting "unequal structure of representation" on the national question.

IMPACT ON THE QUEBEC-QUEBEC DEBATE

THE CHANGING STRUCTURE OF REPRESENTATION

Two types of stories coexisted in Quebec society during the period under consideration (1995–2002). On one side, we note some remarkable progress for the community sector. It has become a new partner for the state and a legitimate and valorized interlocutor. Additionally, it is a carrier of alternative projects, particularly in the field of social economy. From this perspective, one might conclude that community actors worked in a relative symbiosis with the state, actively participating in the design of welfare policy (Graefe 2003, Noël 2003). This story has some plausibility. It corresponds to the dominant discourse regarding the "Quebec model," which concludes that elements of neo-corporatism can be found in the Quebec mode of governance (Gagnon 2000, Piotte 1998). Not only have unions always been privileged partners in the decision process, but increasingly community actors are involved (Lévesque 1993, Vaillancourt et al. 2000), especially the women's movements, which has been particularly dynamic (Lamoureux 2001, Maillé 2003). Moreover, when the Parti Québécois is in power, the relationship of social actors with the state is embedded in "the national question." Since the beginning of the 1970s, unions have progressively adopted the sovereignty cause, becoming concurrently the guardians of two societal projects: one social and one national

(Gagnon 2000). In reference to the 1995 referendum, most of the unions – as well as some key social actors such as the FTQ – took a clear position in the "Yes" camp. For this reason, it is reasonable to highlight the state's openness to the claims of social actors and a degree of co-operation or complicity between the two.

However, it is possible to tell another story, focusing more on the ruptures between social actors and the Quebec state. During the first summit in 1996, the main social actors (excluding unions) believed that the government used them as an instrument in creating a "false consensus" around the public deficit question (Interviews Labrie, Saillant, Desgagné 2002; Lamoureux 2001, 152). During the second summit, the common front of unions and other social actors on the "zero poverty" proposal did not succeed, and three actors (as well as student representatives) left the table[11] (Interview Barbot 2002; Labrie, 1996). Later, in 1997, the reform of the social assistance system was considered a clear failure by social actors (Dufour 2003), as was the Quebec section of the World March of Women in 2000 (Interview Barbot 2002; Leduc 2000). None of the twenty proposals were granted and the minimum wage was raised by only ten cents, which was perceived as an affront to women. Finally, during the Quebec Summit in 2001, the rupture between social actors and the Quebec state seemed to deepen, with a radicalization of the actors involved in the protest.

From this perspective, during the period from 1995 and onward, the distance between the Quebec state and social actors grew. Why have two different pictures of this relationship emerged? Part of the answer likely rests on the type of events emphasized. Should we focus on the adoption of *Bill 112*, the Quebec law against poverty and social exclusion, or on the figures showing that between 1993 and 2002 the fate of the less fortunate in our society did not progress? Another type of explanation could, nevertheless, conciliate the two stories.

The structure of representation during the period analyzed clearly demonstrates that a péquiste government was quite open to social claims. From this point of departure, it is clear that the "neo-liberal turn" in Quebec was less severe than in almost all other provinces. As François Saillant concluded: "jusque-là on s'en est relativement bien sorti (de la vague néolibérale)" (Interview 2002). But this relative moderation in neo-liberal policy implementation does not mean that the balance of power was not challenged. The first story corresponds to the progressive entry of a social problematic (the need to act against poverty), inside the state. Here the movement is "bottom up." This problematic contains a very low potential for subversion and was initiated by numerous actors who chose to build a non-conflictual relationship with the state. They chose to cooperate with state representatives in order to create a law (Interviews Labrie, Lamarche, Bellemare 2002; Noël 2003). This strategy allowed the progressive inclusion of (past) marginal social actors into the decision-making process. At the same time, however (and this corresponds to the second story), as the anti-poverty project (and the groups behind it) succeeded in penetrating the state, it diminished the capacity of actors to create or to maintain a balance of power. This is one reason why some of the actors (FRAPRU, FFQ, Au-bas de l'échelle) involved in the Collectif pour l'élimination de la pauvreté, were less involved at the end of the period when the distance between the state apparatus and others had diminished.[12] These actors were instead attempting to occupy a new field of action – globalization – within which the balance of power could be restored.

This interpretation of the two stories raises a central question: Does the institutionalization of social actors and their progressive inclusion in state structures – as "partner," "manager" of decentralized social services, or "experts" of social policies – lead to the diminution of their advocacy capacity (Shragge 1999; White 1997), even if concrete gains are made? Or, on the contrary, does it contribute to the renewal of their capacity to act (Hamel et al 2000, 14), for example, through the adoption of a law which they can participate in drafting? Without proposing a final answer to these questions (history will do this), I conclude that the advocacy mandate of some of social actors involved in the fight against poverty did not disappear but instead shifted towards a new field of protest. In summary, the second story is the story of the radicalization of social actors who were confronting a pro-globalization state.

THE STATE IN THE GLOBALIZATION SPACE

The Quebec state (and also Quebec political elites) was an ardent defender of free trade during the first free-trade campaign at the end of the 1980s, and continued to be so throughout the 1990s (Duschatel 2003). From 1993 to 2001, the péquiste government adopted two positions with regard to the globalization problematic: first, in continuity with its traditional position toward free trade, it supported the idea that Quebec would gain from the globalization of economies and from the openness of markets. More wealth would be created in Quebec (Bouchard 1997), increased economic autonomy would serve as a tool for independence from the rest of Canada (Parizeau 2001), and Quebec would gain politically from this due to the recognition by international organizations (for example, UNESCO) of the distinctive character of its society (Vastel 1999). Second, the government argued that if people wanted Quebec to have a voice at the global level (and here globalization is portrayed as more a constraint than an opportunity), it is absolutely necessary that Quebec reach the status of an independent country (PQ 2000; Radio-Canada 2001a and 2001b). As such, Quebec could be the voice of "another globalization," Canada's leader in the promotion of a politically regulated and human and environmentally friendly globalization (PQ 2000; Salvet 2001; Rouillard and Bethiaume 2003; Lévesque 2001). This last argument was used by the péquiste government at the end of the period considered (not before 2001) and marked the growing sensibility of the government (and the PQ) to the emerging "new left."

From a more strategic point of view, the péquiste government used globalization as an external constraint to explain a large part of the severe restructuring implemented inside, and also as a constraint that prevented the government from responding to social claims. As we have seen, the progressive globalization of protest accompanied a partial diminution of the national state's capacity to respond effectively to the problems encountered by their national citizens. As noted earlier, during the World March of Women in 2000, the Quebec state clearly used this "global economic constraint" argument to explain its conservative position, an argument that was also made by women themselves.

The pro-globalization position of progressive governments is a characteristic of English-speaking countries (Hay and Rosamond 2002, 155). As in Quebec, globalization is presented as a "good thing" for the nation but also as an external challenge that everyone must deal with. The appropriate response to this challenge is further openness and liberalization, not resistance to it. The position of Quebec with regard to globalization, however, has one particularity: the pro-free-trade position of Quebec leaders is embedded in a battle against the rest of Canada. When it became clear to social actors that supporting the national project of the péquiste government also meant supporting its pro-globalization position, a slow disjuncture appeared in the discourses of social actors between the political project for Quebec and the social project they wanted to fight for, opening a new space for the development of a left/ right problematic.

THE RIGHT–LEFT LINE OF DEBATE

Although in English Canada large protests against globalization appeared as early as the beginning of the 1980s, in Quebec it was only after 1995 that we witnessed such phenomena. One of the main reasons for this disparity is that in Quebec society, since the middle of the 1990s, the political project of sovereignty and social protest were closely linked. As Diane Lamoureux has pointed out:

> L'acharnement actuel du Parti Québécois à sacrifier L'État providence sur l'autel de la mondialisation et du "déficit zéro" ne doit pas nous faire oublier que la construction de cet état providence a été un point de convergence entre nationalistes et féministes dès les années 60 et 70 (Lamoureux 2001, 145)

In 1995, while the PQ was one of the most active defenders of free trade, it was also supported by all unions (with the exception of the Centrale des Syndicats Démocratiques) and major social groups. Nevertheless, some cracks were evident in this alliance. During the campaign, several social actors accused the PQ of presenting the sovereignty project as an end in itself, instead of a means to achieving a social project (see the final Report of the Commission nationale sur l'avenir du Québec 1995). From this moment on, in a context of welfare state retrenchment, social groups increasingly charged the government with forgetting about the social project that was the basis of their adhesion to sovereignty.

Although in the middle of the 1990s social actors in Quebec regretted the progressive disjunction of these two projects, a few years later they would work towards deepening it. At the very moment the social question became disconnected from the national question in government discourse, it recovered a certain degree of autonomy and gradually took on another dimension, for social actors as well. Today, social actors who are opposed to free trade speak only of the threat that globalization presents for the social project of Quebec. The political question is, de facto, solved by the mention of the right of Quebec to self-determination.[13] On this side, the debate seems to be closed, with discussion limited to social problems. By comparison, in the rest of Canada, the fight against free trade was initially pitched from a nationalist perspective, to defend the political project of a Canada distinct from domination by the United States (Gabriel and MacDonald 2003; Watkins 2003). It is only recently that mobilization against globalization has taken on a more "social" tendency. It is as if in the globalization space, national considerations lose their priority to the benefit of social debates. In this new space of protest, alliances between pan-Canadian actors are possible, even between left political parties, a situation unthinkable a few years earlier (Penner 2003). As Salée indicates:

> The whole Quebec–Canada question is totally surreal and disconnected from activists' experiences on the ground (...). Their criticisms of the Quebec state therefore cannot be appreciated in terms of anti-Quebec, or anti-sovereignty, and pro-Canada sentiments; it operates at a broader and more general level. (Salée 2003, 42)

The question today is less to defend the Canadian nation against US hegemony or to promote the Quebec nation against Canadian hegemony but more to defend social and human rights of citizens here and abroad.

Sovereignty is no longer a "hot" subject (Hudon 2001, 327), even for groups who were very engaged in the debate in 1995. Today, they are reasoning in terms of social justice, redistribution of wealth, and for some, radical political change. The development of globalization as a political space in Quebec has influenced the reappearance of the division between left and right, and the delegitimization (at least partially) of the federalist/sovereignist debate. More than globalization in itself (as an external factor) it is the fact that, during the period considered, to fight against a pro-globalization state was to fight against a péquiste government. In other words, it was more and more difficult for sovereignist or past sovereignist groups to defend an alliance with the PQ as long as the PQ was clearly in favor of globalization. Since 2001, the PQ has made several attempts to define an alternative position on globalization and the articulation between sovereignty and globalization, but the issue is still very vague. In the same period, more and more political actors have developed political agendas that appear to escape the sovereignty/federalism dichotomy. For example, for the Union des forces Progressistes and for the movement Option Citoyenne, the question of the political status of Quebec is at best a secondary objective to the project of forging a more just and progressive society. This explains why today the PQ's sovereignty platform looks like a political project with a very low probability of success.

CONCLUSION

The question of the status of Quebec has not disappeared because of globalization. Those political parties who have attempted to put it in the cupboard, such as the ADQ during the last election, have probably paid for it, as the ADQ was not able to capture much of the francophone nationalist vote (Drouilly, Guay, Talin, 2003, A7). However, the globalization problematic, as a new political space, has undoubtedly contributed to the reshaping of the Quebec question. Today, social actors who had long been the main and most faithful defenders of sovereignty are investing their time and energy elsewhere. Their goal is to "save the furniture" that the péquiste government has not yet destroyed. In this fight, they are increasingly connected with other societies, including the rest of Canada, and decreasingly with a specific position vis-à-vis sovereignty. Increasingly, social actors in Quebec seem to agree that any defence of the "Quebec model" should be built on the will of local community actors to promote a certain kind of collective solidarity, highly interconnected with global solidarity, and tied less to the question of Quebec's future within Canada. The enemies are not the "Rest of Canada" but all neo-liberal agents, regardless of geographical locale.

The question of the political status of Quebec within the Canadian federation is less and less a terrain of dispute for social actors. In particular, new social groups fighting against globalization prefer to recognize Quebec's absolute right to self-determination than to spend their time arguing about the specificities of this right in a federal context. In other words, in the globalization space, the Quebec question is not a central point of debate among actors. At the same time, in relation to the new conservative vision of Quebec, the situation of Quebec within the federation has never before been faced with such a threat (Laycock 2002, 154). What is the probability that the Quebec ideal will survive? Instead of arguing about the probable death of the national question in Quebec (Hudon 2001, 330), we should work instead to understand its transformation. With globalization, the national question is never posed in fixed terms, but is an open question. What is at stake is less the survival of a past model (the reproduction of the Quebec nation) than the building of a diverse society grounded in a global context. For the moment, three avenues seem to have opened: the first, and perhaps the most promising, is being created by left parties and social forces attempting to articulate a project of "common goods"[14] (for Quebec citizens but also for citizens abroad) in a society where the question of the nation has for a long time been the main political cleavage; the second avenue could be opened by the PQ itself even if the post-2003 election period looks more like a crisis of the organization than a period of creative proposals for the articulation of global and national dimensions; and the third one is in the hands of the non-sovereignty forces, including the national federalists of the PLQ but also the partisans of the ADQ (which recently announced a return to the nationalist question) (Chouinard 2003, A1). The PQ seems to be wavering between a return to the classic agenda of sovereignty and a mixed agenda of social and national proposals (the final decision will be taken during the next PQ Congress in June 2005). In the federalist camp, no clear lines of demarcation have emerged, with the Charest government both promoting renewed federalism (through, for example, the experience of the council of the federation) and confronting, as usual, the federal government on fiscal questions (for example with respect to the Quebec parental leave proposal). Of course, these avenues are very dependent on the political context, and it would be presumptuous to predict how the Quebec–Quebec debate will look in ten years. Nevertheless, the form and the content of political debate is changing in Quebec society, and globalization, as a space for discourse and action, has contributed to this shift.

NOTES

1 This paper is part of a more comprehensive research project that benefited from a SSRHC post-doctoral research grant.

2 The expressions "social forces" and "social actors" are used without any distinction. I am considering only progressive activists.

3 In this specific sense, globalization is not a scale of protest or actions, as in the "scale literature," but a space where actions take place. On the question of scale see Brenner (2001).

4 See, for example, the special issue of *Studies in Political Economy* 66 (Autumn), 2001.

5 The term "frame" is employed exactly in the sense given to it by the "framing approach" (Snow, Burke and Benford 1986).

6 This means that the belonging to the globalization space is neither predetermined nor fixed in time. The question of who is in and who is out is an empirical question that changes over time.

7 In 1978, James Tobin, a Nobel Prize-winning economist, first proposed the idea of a tax on foreign exchange transactions that would be applied uniformly by all major countries. A tiny amount (less than 0.5 percent) would be levied on all foreign currency exchange transactions to deter speculation on currency fluctuations.

8 Including unions such as Fédération des Travailleurs du Québec, environmental groups, and groups involved in the defense of human rights.

9 Most of the members of the network agreed with this position, although some internal debates existed within some groups, such as within the Canadian Labour Congress. The National Action Committee on the Status of Women was not present in Quebec and strongly disagrees with civil disobedience. (Interviews of both actors, Summer 2001).

10 This frame applies only to the Quebec situation. In English Canada, the lowest common denominator of actors fighting against globalization is different, including for example, more nationalist and protectionist considerations.

11 Françoise David, President of the FFQ, François Saillant, from the *Front d'action populaire en réaménagement urbain* (FRAPRU) and the *Solidarité Populaire Québec* (SPQ), and Thérèse Sainte-Marie, from the *Coalition nationale des femmes contre la pauvreté*.

12 The other reasons mentioned were the high quantity of time devolved to the Collectif, the need to return to their own mandate and the uncertainty of gains that might be achieved through legislation.

13 It is interesting to note that this method of "solving" the national question is also shared by English Canadian groups and new left parties, such as the Green Party of Canada or the New Left Initiative.

14 As indicated by the title of Françoise David's last book, *Bien commun recherché. Une option citoyenne,* Montreal: Écosociété, 2004.

REFERENCES

Ancelovici, M. 2002. "Organizing against Globalization: The Case of ATTAC in France." *Politics and Society* 30(3): 427–63.

Ayres, J. 2001. "Transnational Political Processes and Contention Against the Global Economy." *Mobilization* 6(1): 55–68.

Bouchard, L. 1997. "Vers les Amériques de 2005: Démocratie, développement et prosperité." Accessed online at http://www.copa.qc.ca/Francais/nos_activites_fr/Assgempreced/ Quebec1997/Bouchardalof.html

Brenner, N. 2001. "The Limits to Scale? Methodological Reflections on Scalar Structuration." *Progress in Human Geography* 54(4): 591–614.

Brunelle, D. and C. Deblock. 2000. "Les mouvements d'opposition au libre-échangisme dans les Amériques et la constitution d'une Alliance sociale continentale." *Nouvelles pratiques sociales* 13(2): 131–47.

Chouinard, T. 2003. "L'ADQ renoue avec la question nationale. Dumont entend proposer une sorte de rapport Allaire actualisé." *Le Devoir*, 3 November, A1.

CommenTerre, Bulletin of Opération Salami (previously Bulletin de Salami). Accessed online at www.alternatives.ca/salami/

Cornellier, M. 2001. "Sommet des Amériques: une contestation aux multiples visages." *Le Devoir*, 4 April, A1.

Drouilly, P., J.-H. Guay and K. Talin. 2003. "Quelques conclusions à tirer des élections – 2. Victoire libérale ou défaite péquiste?" *Le Devoir*, 23 April, A7.

Dufour, P. 2003. "Politiques et pratiques du hors-travail: le cas du Québec et de la France." In *Fédéralisme et mondialisation. L'avenir de la démocratie et de la citoyenneté*, ed. J. Duschatel. Montreal: Athéna.

Dupuis-Déri, F. 2003. *Les Blacks Bloc: La liberté et l'égalité se manifestent*. Montreal: Instinct de Liberté.

Duschatel, J. 2003. "De libre-échangistes, les Québécois sont-ils devenus antimondialistes?" In *L'annuaire du Québec 2004*. Montreal: Fides.

Fédération des travailleurs du Québec (FTQ). 1998. "Les syndicates. Artisans d'un monde meilleur." *List of Resolutions*, 25th Congress.

Gabriel, C. and L. MacDonald. 2003. "Beyond the Continentalist/Nationalist Divide: Politics in a North America 'Without Borders.'" In *Changing Canada: Political Economy as Transformation*, eds. W. Clement and L.F. Vosko. Montreal and Kingston: McGill-Queen's University Press.

Gagnon, M.-J. 2000. "Les intellectuels critiques et le mouvement ouvrier au Québec: fractures et destin parallèle." *Cahiers de recherche sociologique* 34: 145–76.

Giraud, I. 2001. "La transnationalisation des solidarités: l'exemple de la marche mondiale des femmes." *Lien social et politiques – RIAC* 45(Spring): 145–62.

Graefe, P. 2002. "The Social Economy and the State: Linking Ambitions with Institutions in Québec, Canada." *Policy and Politics* 31(2): 247–62.

– 2003. *Broadening the Options: Inflecting Quebec's Post-Industrial Trajectory*. Canadian Association of Political Science.

Graveline, P. 1995. "Du pain et des roses." *Le Devoir*, 9 March, A6.

Guidry, J.A., M.D. Kennedy and M.N. Zald. 2000. *Globalization and Social Movements. Culture, Power and the Transnational Public Sphere*. Michigan: University of Michigan Press.

Hamel, P., L. Maheu and J.-G. Vaillancourt. 2000. "Repenser les défis institutionnels de l'action collective." *Politique et Sociétés* 19(1): 3–25.

Harvey, C. 1998. "Le Conseil du statut de la femme à l'heure des bilans." *Le Devoir,* 23 May, E1.

Harvey, R. 2001. "Québec 2001, ce n'était pas une fin de soi: Henri Massé de la FTQ, affirme la nécessité de la solidarité." *Le Devoir*, 28 April, E3.

– 2000. "Une entrevue avec Henri Massé: Le langage de la démocratie. les activités de la FTQ débordent sur le monde." *Le Devoir*, 29 May, F5.

Hay, C. and B. Rosamond. 2002. "Globalization, European Integration and the Discursive Construction of Economic Imperatives." *Journal of European Public Policy* 9(2): 147–67.

Hudon, R. 2001. "Back to the Start! Fin de siècle or Fin de rêves Politics in Québec." In *Party Politics in Canada*, eds., H.G. Thorburn and A. Whitehorn. Toronto: Prentice Hall.

Jenson, J. 1998. "Les réformes des services de garde pour jeunes enfants en France et au Québec: une analyse historico-institutionaliste." *Politique et Sociétés* 17: 1–2.

Labrie, V. 1996. "La clause d'appauvrissement zéro: Une jeune idée qui demande à mûrir." *Le Devoir,* 11 November, A7.

Lamoureux, D. 2001. *L'amère patrie. Féminisme et nationalisme dans le Québec contemporain*. Montreal: Les éditions du remue-ménage.

Laycock, D. 2002. *The New Right and Democracy in Canada. Understanding Reform and the Canadian Alliance*. Toronto: Oxford University Press.

Leduc, L. 2000. "Françoise David au Devoir: les femmes se radicalisent." *Le Devoir*, 21 October, A5.

Lemire, M. 2000. "Mouvements sociaux et mondialisation économique: de l'AMI au cycle du millénaire de l'OMC." *Politique et Sociétés* 19(1): 49–78.

– 2003. "Les mouvements sociaux face à la globalisation des marches." In *Québec: État et Société*, ed. A.-G. Gagnon. Montreal: Québec-Amérique.

Lévesque, B. 1993. "Les coopératives au Québec: deux projets distincts pour une société." *Coopération: Défis pour une démocratie économique*. Brussels: Éditions Vie Ouvrière.

Lévesque, B. et M. Mendell. 1999. "L'économie sociale au Québec: éléments théoriques et empiriques pour le débat et la recherche." *Lien social et politiques – RIAC* 41(Spring): 105–118.

Lévesque, K. 2001. "Le PQ manifestera contre le processus de mise en œuvre." *Le Devoir*, 13 April, A2.

Mahon, R. 1977. "Canadian Public Policy: The Unequal Structure of Representation." In *The Canadian State: Political Economy and Political Power*, ed. L. Panitch. Toronto: University of Toronto Press.

– 1984. *The Politics of Industrial Restructuring: Canadian Textiles*. Toronto: University of Toronto Press.

Maillé, C. 2003. "Le mouvement des femmes au Québec: histoire et actualité." In *Québec: État et Société*, ed. A.-G. Gagnon. Montreal: Québec-Amérique.

Multilateral Agreement on Investment (MAI). Accessed online at http://www.finances.gouv.fr/pole_ecofin/international/ami_ocde97/ami.htm

Noël, A. 2003. "Une loi contre la pauvreté: la nouvelle approche québécoise de lutte contre la pauvreté et l'exclusion sociale." *Lien Social et Politiques – RIAC* 48(Autumn): 103–14.

Offerlé, M. 1994. *Sociologie des groupes d'intérêts*. Paris: Montchrestien.

Parizeau, J. 2001. "Le libre-échange, les droits des multinationales et le dilemme de l'État." *Le Devoir*, 5 May, A11.

Parti Québecois. 2000. "Chapitre 3: Le développement durable des richesses collectives." *Programme*. Accessed online at http://www.partiquebecois.org/temp/progr_chapitre3.pdf

Piotte, J.-M. 1998. *Du combat au partenariat*. Montreal: Les presses de l'Université du Québec.

Pedretti, M. 2001. *La figure du désobéissant en politique. Études de pratiques de désobéissance civile en démocratie*. Paris: L'Harmattan.

Penner, N. 2003. "The Past, Present and Uneasy Future of the New Democratic Party." In *Canadian Parties in Transition*, eds. A.B. Tanguay and A.-G. Gagnon. Scarborough, Ontario: Nelson Canada.

Radio-Canada. 2001a. "ZLEA: Bernard Landry condamne les gouvernements." Radio-Canada Website. Accessed online at http://radio-canada.ca/nouvelles/Index/nouvelles/200104/19/006-landry-libre-echange.asp

– 2001b. "Bernard Landry dresse un bilan positif du Sommet." Radio-Canada Website. Accessed online at http://radio-canada.ca/nouvelles/Index/nouvelles/200104/23/003-LANDRYSOMMET.asp

Rapport de la Commission nationale sur l'avenir du Québec. 1995. *Le Devoir*, 20 April, A9.

Rouillard L., L.-E. and M.-P. Berthiaume. 2003. "Entre guerre et élections, que devient le libre-échange?" *Alternatives*. Accessed online at http://www.alternatives.ca/article538.html

Salée, D. 2003. "Transformative Politics, the State and the Politics of Social Change in Québec." In *Changing Canada: Political Economy as Transformation*, eds.W. Clement and L.F. Vosko. Montreal and Kingston: McGill-Queen's University Press.

Salvet, J.-M. 2001. "La Une." *Le Devoir*, 4 June, A1.

Shragge, É. 1999. "Looking Backwards to go Forward: The Quebec Community Movement 30 Years Later." *Intervention* 110 (October): 53–60.

Snow, D.A., E.B. Rochford, S.K. Worden and R.D. Benford. 1986. "Frame Alignment Processes, Micromobilization and Movement Participation." *American Sociological Review* 51: 464–81.

Sommier, I. 2001. *Les nouveaux mouvements contestataires*. Paris: Flammarion.

Tarrow, S. 2000. "La contestation transnationale." *Cultures et conflits* 38–39 (Summer–Fall): 187–219.

Tilly, C. 1986. *La France conteste de 1600 à nos jours*. Paris: Fayard.

Vaillancourt, Y., F. Aubry, M. Jetté, C. Thériault and L. Tremblay. 2000. *Économie sociale, santé et bien-être: la spécificité du modèle québécois au Canada*, Cahiers du LAREPPS No. 00-01, Montréal: Laboratoire de recherché sur les pratiques et les politiques sociales, April.

Vastel, M. 1999. "La mondialisation marginalise l'État fédéral." *Le Droit*, 30 April. Accessed online at http://www.vigile.net/economie/mondialisation/vastelmarginalise.html

Waterman, P. 2001. *Globalization, Social Movements and the New Internationalism.* London and NewYork: Continuum.

Watkins, M. 2002. "Politics in the Time and Space of Globalization." In *Changing Canada: Political Economy as Transformation*, eds. W. Clement and L.F. Vosko, Montreal and Kingston: McGill-Queen's University Press.

White, D. 1997. "Contradictory Participation: Reflections on Community Action in Quebec." In *Community Organizing: Canadian Experiences,* eds. B. Wharf and M. Clague. Toronto: Oxford University Press.

ZLEA: Louise Beaudoin en accord avec Parizeau. 2001. *Le Devoir,* 8 May, A2.

INTERVIEWS

Bellemare, Marc. Fédération des travailleurs du Québec, October 2002.

Barbot, Vivian. Fédération des femmes du Québec, October 2002.

Convergence de Luttes Anti-Capitalistes (CLAC), November 2002.

Desgagné, Jean-Yves. Front commun des personnes assistées sociales du Québec, October 2002.

Jasmin, Robert. Association for the Taxation of Financial Transactions for the Aid of Citizens (ATTAC) – Quebec, September 2002.

Labrie, Vivian. Collectif pour l'élimination de la pauvreté, October 2002.

Lamarche, François. Confédération des syndicats nationaux, October 2002.

Molly, Alexander, Union des forces progressistes. November 2002.

Mouvement autonome et solidaire des sans-emploi, October 2002.

Paquette, Esther. Au-bas de l'échelle, January 2003.

Saillant, François. Front d'action populaire en réamnénagement urbain, October 2002.

CONFERENCE

Rebick, Judy. Conference on "Mouvements sociaux et gauche politique." Université du Québec à Montréal, October 2002.

7

State Restructuring and the Failure of Competitive Nationalism: Trying Times for Quebec Labour

Peter Graefe

Ce chapitre décrit les stratégies adoptées par les plus grandes centrales syndicales au Québec dans les années 1990.Ces stratégies cherchaient à renouveler l'intervention syndicale dans différents domaines de gouvernance économique et sociale, des lieux de travail jusqu'aux grands sommets concertationnels. Le chapitre avance que les centrales ont adopté les stratégies de compétitivité progressiste associées au discours social démocratique de l'époque, tout en y intégrant une dimension nationaliste. Suivant cette approche, le nationalisme contribuerait à la compétitivité internationale de l'économie québécoise. En retour, cette compétitivité alimenterait le nationalisme québécois. Cette approche a permis aux syndicats de faire des gains, mais a aussi limité leur marge de manoeuvre dans certains cas, et a miné leur capacité de définir l'ordre du jour pour la gauche. C'est ainsi que les mouvements de femmes et communautaires commencent à jouer un rôle plus important dans la définition d'une économie politique alternative pour le Québec, avec pour résultat une baisse d'appui temporaire envers le mouvement souverainiste. Toutefois, cette tendance n'a pas augmenté la légitimité ou la crédibilité du fédéralisme canadien dans ce milieu.

INTRODUCTION

The 1990s were difficult years for North American labour movements, as the secular labour market trend to employment growth in difficult to organize sectors (especially the private service sector) and employment statuses (part-time, dependent contractor, temporary) combined with stubbornly high unemployment rates that limited collective bargaining gains. It was a decade that demanded union renewal on all fronts, from organizing and negotiating strategies, through rethinking modes of political and social intervention, to reconceiving mechanisms of international solidarity (Peters 2002; Charest 2003). This challenge was particularly acute for the Quebec labour federations, since their response to earlier rounds of economic restructuring was dominated by what Carla Lipsig-Mummé (1993, 404) terms a "strategic paralysis" of "doing what they had always done, regardless of the fact that it no longer worked."

Paying particular attention to Quebec's two largest labour federations – the Fédération des travailleurs et travailleuses du Québec (FTQ) and the Confédération des syndicats nationaux (CSN)[1] – this essay will argue that they did manage to articulate a new strategic agenda in the late 1980s and early 1990s, which provided a means of renewing their intervention in a variety of spaces of economic and political governance, including the national question. The unions adopted a "progressive-competitive" political economy that argued for social partnerships or forms of "conflictual concertation" in the workplace and in forums of economic and social governance, on the grounds that this could lead to positive-sum class compromises. This led into an embrace of "competitive nationalism," wherein the nation could provide additional cultural resources and social solidarity to ease and reinforce such positive-sum compromises. The first section of the essay will sketch out the strategic paralysis of Quebec labour underlined by Lipsig-Mummé, and the response of "competitive nationalism."

While the competitive nationalist strategy has had some success in legitimizing union participation in a number of decision-making locales, it has also imposed significant costs on the labour federations both in terms of protecting their members' interests in the face of economic and state restructuring and in terms of articulating a project of social change for the broader left in Quebec. In the second section, the argument will highlight how competitive nationalism has handcuffed the labour federations, as the national imperative of competitiveness is taken up by firms and by the state to justify one-sided deals or inaction that hobble the transformative potential of the unions' project. In this context, the women's and community movements have started to take on the mantle of articulating an alternative left-wing project. It remains unclear whether the projects they brandish will lead to a new articulation of the national question, as they remain in tension with the mainstream sovereignist *rapprochement* with the United States, yet lack an alternative.

RENEWING THE LABOUR AGENDA AT THE TURN OF THE 1990S

STRATEGIC PARALYSIS

A decade ago, Carla Lipsig-Mummé (1991) described a Quebec union movement in a state of strategic paralysis. Faced with economic and labour market restructuring that undermined its ability to successfully represent the working class, the movement seemed unable to develop tactical and strategic positions that might lead to its renewal. The militant unionism of the 1970s lacked the tools to deal with the hollowing out of industries facing international competition (particularly in the soft industrial and primary processing sectors), and could not make sense of demands for quality work and services (also Piotte 1998, 193–94). Among the stumbling points that Lipsig-Mummé emphasized were the difficulties of elaborating a useful political strategy, and of defending an autonomous position on the national question. In terms of politics, the largest problem was the tradition of non-involvement by the CSN and the CEQ (now CSQ) – a tradition inherited from their confessional origins and reproduced through their Marxist-syndicalist phase in the 1970s and early 1980s (also Denis 1998, 145–48). Nevertheless, the FTQ's decision to throw its lot in with the Parti Québécois (PQ) without transforming it into some variant of social democratic or labour party was also noted, since it aided the PQ in securing a base on the left without developing institutions or mechanisms of accountability to that base.

In terms of the national question, in turn, the various union federations had generally acted as what I would term "nationalism takers," supporting the dominant nationalist project without articulating a specifically working class nationalist agenda.[2] Indeed, through the late 1960s and 1970s, the union federations followed, rather than led, their members towards the PQ. The FTQ endorsed the PQ in 1976, 1981, 1989 and 1994, and the BQ in 1993, but it never sought to find a way to institutionalize a role inside these parties so as to create some form of accountability (Guentzel 2000). Again, in 1990, the wave of support for Quebec sovereignty among the membership took the leadership by surprise. However, when the chance came to lead the wave by running Gilles Duceppe on a left-sovereignist platform in the 1990 Laurier-Ste-Marie by-election, the union leadership again backed off and let the Bloc Québécois define the nationalist project offered to Quebecers (Lipsig-Mummé 1991, 103–04).

The labour movement is also nationalist in the second sense that it targets most of its political action at the Quebec government. There is a reflex response of seeing Quebec as the frame within which policy problems are to be solved, regardless of the actual constitutional division of powers. The FTQ retains an indirect presence on the federal stage through its affiliation with the Canadian Labour Congress, but this arrangement further turns the FTQ's attention towards the National Assembly rather than Parliament. This point should not be exaggerated, however, as the Quebec federations do act on the federal scene when their interests are at stake, such as in budget making, or more visibly in recent scuffles over the Employment Insurance fund.[3]

Despite Lipsig-Mummé's sombre portrait, the union movement has maintained its membership above 40 percent of the non-agricultural labour force through the last two decades. Quebec remains Canada's most unionized province and has a high rate of density in international comparisons. Quebec's unions have also had some high-profile successes in organizing the service sector (McDonald's, Walmart), although Charest (2003, 310) underlines that density in dynamic private sector services is only about 14 percent. This relative health leads us to nuance Lipsig-Mummé's claims of paralysis, but also to share her questioning of why this high level of organization has not translated into the political capacity to transform Quebec's largely liberal political economy.

PROGRESSIVE COMPETITIVENESS AND COMPETITIVE NATIONALISM

In the early 1990s, the labour movement started to develop a new strategic project, although, as we will see, the relationship to politics and the national question remained problematic. An important step in this direction came from the CSN, as it cast off a militant, conflict-based unionism in search of positive-sum partnerships with employers. The idea was to "take the lead" in work re-organization by proposing plant-level cooperation that increased the productivity and competitiveness of the plant, even while enhancing union goals such as increased workplace health and safety, job enrichment, reduced work time and training. Rather than maintaining a militant unionism that risked pricing private sector workers out of their jobs and that maintained inflexible internal labour markets, the new strategy sought out plant-level social contracts whereby employers agreed to enhance the voice of workers in the organization of work in return for more flexible work rules and a more cooperative industrial relations climate (CSN 1991; Doré 1989).

This outlook of "partnership," in turn, looked beyond the workplace. Local and regional development, for instance, was recast in terms of potential cross-class projects promoting a combination of employment creation, enhanced social provision and private accumulation. Industrial policy, in turn, should aim to link up sectoral and local/regional development bodies for concerted effort in developing particular clusters (Paquette 1996; 1997). Concertation was embraced in this context not only for its ability to unleash positive-sum compromises, but also for bringing disparate development policies into a more coherent whole. The CSN's position was by no means unique, as schemes to develop positive-sum class compromises were developed elsewhere in the same time frame, including in the United States. A notable difference with non-American examples, however, was the lack of a labour party to enact the necessary macroeconomic framework and microeconomic adjustment policies, as, for instance, with the *Australian Accord* of the mid-1980s.

This initiative also had some resonance with the FTQ. In particular, the latter federation could deploy to its labour-sponsored investment fund, created originally as a response to the early 1980s recession, as a strategic resource in negotiating workplace agreements on new forms of work organization, or in addressing local economic development projects. The FTQ was more cautious and nuanced than the CSN in its analysis of the potential for democratization and participation, as well as in the challenges to union structures and processes such participation entailed, but nevertheless argued that workplace cooperation offered strategic possibilities to advance union objectives (FTQ 1993; Bergeron and Bourque 1996, 11).

The strategy adopted by the CSN and the FTQ can be classified as a form of "progressive competitiveness," a post-Keynesian development strategy adopted by social democratic parties and labour unions in many countries and contexts in the 1980s and 1990s. It is based on the idea that the survival of firms faced with intense international competition increasingly relies on flexibility and continuous innovation so as to create high productivity and/or niche product differentiation. By constantly staying ahead of other competitors, and particularly those in low-wage countries, firms can continue to afford a higher wage and tax burden. Continuous innovation is nevertheless not a simple technical question of research and technological adoption, but instead increasingly relies on tapping the know-how and ingenuity of the workforce, and on the ability of the workforce to adapt flexibly to change. In this context, labour can offer capital a deal it cannot refuse: it can agree to cooperate in enhancing productivity in return for employment guarantees, workplace democratization, and the maintenance of high wages and working conditions. This strategy in turn emphasizes the role of a strong labour movement in bringing positive-sum results, because labour unions and federations play important roles in resolving collective action problems related to skill upgrading and training, macroeconomic coordination, and acceptance of technological change (Wright 2000, 959–60; Rogers and Streeck 1994, 134–38). The broader emphasis on creating forums of concertation at different scales of governance also draws inspiration from these sources, in addition to a broader literature on the role of associations and of institutionalized relationships in spurring successful local and regional development policies. Here again, the emphasis is on the capacity of localities to provide a "thick" institutional and associative milieu that can provide the extra-economic inputs required for innovation and high-end production. The wager here is that firms become embedded in the milieu through their reliance on these institutions and associations, and will thus continue to invest, pay taxes, and employ workers in higher-wage, higher-tax jurisdictions (cf. Amin 1999).

This strategy had several benefits. First, it enabled a partial representation of the unions within the field of economic development. Earlier development strategies had given lip service to forums of labour-management coordination, such as the Economic and Social Council proposed in the 1979 industrial policy statement, *Bâtir le Québec*. The PQ had also experimented with sectoral concertation tables and a *Table nationale de l'emploi* at the end of its second term in office (Bourque 2000, 56). The Quebec Liberal government's new industrial policy, announced in December 1991, nevertheless gave a much greater place to coordination and partnership. Indeed, its choice of the language of "clusters" was motivated by the desire to find a means of harnessing all of Quebec's major economic actors behind a common development strategy (Brin d'Amour 1992, 82–83). The cluster strategy, influenced by the work of the likes of Michael Porter and Lester Thurow, was less interested in labour/management partnerships than in creating synergies and networks between firms in the same sector (including between firms and their suppliers and clients). Nevertheless, the similar partnership and productivity orientation of the union strategy enabled union participation on many of the sectoral tables set up by the policy, and encouraged plant-level concertation to increase the competitiveness of Quebec industry (Gagné and Lefèvre 1993, 85, 88–90).

This partnership strategy also created a space for political action outside the partisan realm. The logic of partnership gestured towards corporatist or associative forms of governance in many realms of social activity, ranging from the level of the plant, to local and regional development and training bodies, to sectoral industry and training bodies, to national level forums. These could take the form of multi-stakeholder institutions such as the regional health boards and regional and local development councils created in the 1990s. The prototypical example was the Société québécoise de développement de la main-d'oeuvre (SQDM), a body dominated by union and business representatives (albeit with some representation from the educational community) with the ambition of exercising significant control over the province's labour market programs. The SQDM was launched by Bourassa's Liberal government with the express goal of ensuring pro-active labour force adjustment to competitive pressures in local, regional, national and sectoral arenas (MMSRFP 1991) and promised the unions an opening to ensure that adjustment favoured high-end reskilling, increased training of the existing workforce, and the pursuit of full employment. Ironically, it was the PQ government that wound down the SQDM into a less powerful Table des partenaires.

Finally, this strategy enabled a certain rapprochement with the Parti Québécois on the national question. In its "action plan for sovereignty" released before its election in 1994, the PQ laid out a rationale for sovereignty that fit reasonably well with the labour centrals' progressive competitiveness. The action plan argued that globalization demanded more state intervention rather than less. However, this intervention did not involve challenging the rights and prerogatives of capital so much as resolving collective action problems and market failures that reduced the economy's productive potential. In this view, the nation became a key site for managing adjustment, since it provided the social solidarity that enabled coherent adjustment strategies at all levels from the workplace to society as a whole. As with the union strategy, the PQ's "competitive nationalism" set out the possibility of a virtuous circle of growth: the coordination and adjustment promoted by the nation would enhance the competitiveness of its firms; this competitiveness, in turn, would provide employment and redistribute income (through taxation), thus reinforcing social cohesion and ensuring resources for further adjustment and coordination. This program could be seen as a form of "supply-side socialism" that reconciled social rights with private accumulation on the basis that "fair is efficient" (Thompson 1996, 49–50).

This program justified sovereignty on two grounds. First, given the importance of coordinated adjustment strategies for ensuring that the "losers" of restructuring were not left behind, the division of authority and competing programs arising from the federal system could no longer be tolerated. Second, both competitive success and adjustment strategies required a common culture and horizon of solidarity that could be provided by the Quebec nation, but not the Canadian political community (PQ 1994, 1–4, 11, 25; Latouche 1993). The unions' progressive competitiveness thus connected closely to the PQ's competitive nationalism, since nationalism could support a positive-sum class compromise by providing additional cultural resources necessary for high-end innovation and economic coordination (Graefe 2003). This was nevertheless a risky strategy since it tied the union's agenda, not to mention the fate of the nation, to the competitive success of firms. While invoking the economic survival of the nation can be used to compel business participation in multi-stakeholder consultations and compromises, it has the potential to boomerang and to compel unions to agree to one-sided "compromises" also in the name of the nation. Given the logic of capitalist competition, and the persuasiveness of claims about intense global economic competition, this provides business with a powerful voice concerning what policies enable their survival (and thus that of the nation) and a significant trump when policies challenge their decision-making prerogatives or attempt to address social inequality (Keating 1998, 157; Coates 2000, 254, 259–60; Uitermark 2002, 753–54).

The competitive nationalist project spared the union federations the effort of elaborating a sovereignist project to the left of the PQ, because sovereignty itself could now be seen as an essential step in the achievement of a social democratic Quebec. The 1995 referendum campaign indeed saw the federalist/ sovereignist split map relatively closely onto a right/left split, with sovereignty promising a more inclusive form of restructuring than that being pursued in Canada at both the federal and provincial levels (Gagnon and Lachapelle 1996, 182–85, 191). As such, it was easy for the union federations to once again be "nationalism takers" and stand uncritically behind the PQ's "Yes."

Serge Denis (1998) nevertheless underlines that the early 1990s mark the first time that the CSN truly made the national question a dynamic part of its political project, for instance, by coming out in favour of independence in May 1990, and supporting the sovereignist option in the Bélanger-Campeau Commission. The CSN also attempted to knit a progressive coalition to ensure sovereignty and social progress remained linked (e.g. via the creation of the Partenaires pour la souveraineté). In this sense, it may have pulled the sovereignist project leftwards. Yet, if it did manage this feat, it did so silently, without making demands on the PQ project. For instance, in the Bélanger-Campeau Commission, the CSN's stand in favour of sovereignty came out far more clearly than any coherent project for changing the political economy of an independent Quebec (Lipsig-Mummé 1991, 104). Likewise, in the lead-up to the 1995 referendum, the CSN stated its support was without pre-conditions on the grounds that sovereignty provides the political framework most favourable to attaining its societal project (CSN 1995, 9–10). While the CSN foresaw additional possibilities for realizing its goals in a context of sovereignty, it was largely willing to trust the PQ and its closely allied organizations to set the parameters of the project. Indeed, even the Partenaires pour la souveraineté managed to fall under the sway of mainstream nationalist organizations (such as the Société Saint-Jean Baptiste) in certain regions (such as Montréal), leading to a significant bleeding away of progressive organizations (CCMM 1998, 2).

STATE RESTRUCTURING: LABOUR'S RENEWED PARALYSIS?

While the political economy of competitive nationalism provided the labour federations with strategic openings in the early and mid-1990s, it in time proved less capable of meeting their ambitions. Progressive competitiveness failed to deliver on its promise of inclusion, which in turn begged the question of whether the nationalism of concertation and partnership it supported was, in fact, a nationalism that excluded the projects and aspirations of the social democratic left. In the process, new organizations came to supplant the labour movement as the "leaders" of the left project within Quebec in terms of defining strategic directions, and they brought with them a vision of nationalism and a nationalist project that could not be so easily metabolized by the PQ. The Quebec left nevertheless finds itself in a difficult predicament: it remains committed to a project of independence, yet increasingly rejects the rapprochement with the United States that the mainstream sovereignist project implies; it might look to work with the left in the rest of Canada, but it lacks the institutions for dialogue; or it could advance an autonomous left nationalist project, but it has to date proved incapable of building institutions and movements to carry this forward.

HANDCUFFED BY COMPETITIVENESS

The plan for a progressive competitive strategy building labour's voice and concerns into decision-making ran into important snags at all levels, most of them involving a lack of business buy-in. At the workplace level, the idea of a new social contract did not catch the fancy of employers, except in cases where firms were already in financial difficulties. A government study of nineteen cases that adopted new forms of work organization revealed that three cases in five involved firms with a high risk of failure. Furthermore, despite the call to "take the lead" on work organization, none of the cases resulted from the union's initiative (although six came from joint initiative), and the primary motivation for union participation was avoiding job loss (Lapointe and Paquet 1994, 294). This led to an increase in workload and work intensity, but little visible improvement in work conditions or wages (Ministère du travail 1996). This result is not particularly surprising, given that the determinants of social relations lie mostly outside the bounds of individual workplaces, and are crucially affected by the broader macroeconomic context (Denis 1998, 154; Gagnon 1994, 90). Nor is it surprising given similar results for these types of initiatives in other liberal polities (Lambert 2000, 100–101; Wells 1987). Employers may take up offers of partnership in situations where their weak competitive situation limits the concessions they must make, but otherwise they remain allergic to surrendering their managerial power. Attempts at renewing work organization in the public sector were no more successful. The main unions in the provincial public sector adopted the CSN's work organization agenda with skepticism – a skepticism that proved well-justified given public sector management strategies focused single-mindedly on cost reduction and bypassing union structures (Jetté 1997; Charest 1998).

As one moves up from the plant level to the broader economic strategy of partnerships and clusters, the results are scarcely more encouraging. The development of competitive clusters has had few net employment effects, with job gains in certain industries such as plastics, printing and publishing, and transportation equipment being cancelled out by losses in others such as textiles and clothing, and the forest and wood products industry (Statistics Canada 1996). There is further evidence that success in the export sector has come significantly uncoupled from employment growth. While exports increased 36 percent in volume and 56 percent in value over the 1990–1997 period, direct and indirect employment gains were only 6.7 percent. Success in competitive export markets has put the emphasis on productivity over employment growth. The number of direct and indirect jobs per million dollars in international exports decreased from 10.9 to 7.3 over the same period. The Institut de la statistique du Québec explains the disjuncture between export growth and employment stagnation as a result of increased labour productivity (explaining 60 percent of the gap), coupled with changes in the sectoral and geographic composition of exports and changes in technical coefficients used in modelling.[4] While the employment situation may well have been worse without these industrial policies, these figures suggest that the competitive success of firms did not translate into the anticipated welfare gains (increased employment, income for redistribution) promised by a progressive competitive nationalism.

At the level of stakeholder institutions, the results are less one-sided. The goal of building institutions and structures of concertation appears well chosen, given international evidence that the negative social welfare effects of international capital mobility and international competition appear to be greatly attenuated in polities managing adjustment through forms of social corporatism rather than pluralism (Swank 2002, 279; Hall and Soskice 2001). The unions can point to their recognition as stakeholders in the varied concertational institutions created over the past few years as progress toward this goal. However, two questions remain unaddressed in this context. First, what is the real margin of action granted to these institutions? In all cases, these institutions must work within rules set by the government, both in terms of their constitution and mandate, but also concerning how they manage particular governmental programs. Second, and perhaps more fundamentally, within this margin of action, how successful have union representatives been in mobilizing the other social partners around their projects? It is quite possible that the unions' interest in these forums did not always match the commitment of employers and the state. The case of the SQDM is particularly illustrative of these points. As noted earlier, the SQDM held out the promise of significant labour movement input in labour market programming and can legitimately claim some significant successes in its brief six-year existence, including working through a compromise on the province's one percent training tax, reforming the apprenticeship system, creating regional boards, adopting a sectoral strategy, and backing up the Quebec government's "Quebec consensus" on labour market powers. These successes nevertheless must be balanced against the opposition of politicians and bureaucrats who dogged the legitimacy and effectiveness of the SQDM through its whole existence, along with the inability to bridge differences between unions and employers concerning the goals, content and funding of training (Haddow 1998, 347, 360–61). Given the importance of managing labour force adjustment to progressive competitive and competitive nationalist strategies, the failure of the SQDM suggests that the hold of these projects outside the labour movement was more rhetorical than substantive.

In light of the comparative literature on "varieties of capitalism," the case of the SQDM and the plant-level results are not particularly surprising: in liberal political economies like Quebec, employers lack the necessary incentives to participate in mechanisms of co-decision and concertation that impose binding decisions. Indeed, even in what are deemed coordinated market economies, significant power must be exercised by labour unions to continue to enforce employer compliance and participation (Thelen 2001, 100–101). If there is a surprise, it is that there was so much experimentation with concertation and associational governance – an indication of the power of nationalism to destabilize the incentive structures of liberal political economies and to broaden possibilities for labour.

Moving to the peak level, the emphasis on competitiveness handcuffed the labour federations and limited their bargaining power more than it provided a lever for achieving their agenda. An important example involves the social and economic summits in March and October 1996. The government called upon its socio-economic partners to help it renew and reform a national consensus around a strategy of deficit reduction and employment creation. This was booby-trapped ground for the unions, since the employers' organizations made it clear from the start that their bottom line was deficit reduction without tax increases. A lack of fiscal rectitude or increased taxes would hurt their already fragile competitive position. Moreover, the background documents for both summits emphasized deregulation as the main motor of private sector job creation, and opposed even relatively minor measures for reducing working time on the basis that they would hurt the competitiveness of Quebec firms (Conférence 1996, 5–7, 43; Chantier 1996, 15–18, 76–78, 89). The CSN and the FTQ nevertheless agreed to participate and indeed accepted the plan to balance the budget without raising corporate or personal income taxes on the grounds that it would hurt Quebec's competitiveness. They did extract the concession of pushing the time frame for balancing the budget from two years to four years, but on a larger deficit (including the capital budget) than originally proposed by the government (Piotte 2001, 30–31). Having accepted these two premises, they were therefore led over the course of the summits to the counterintuitive conclusion that, short of massive economic growth, competitiveness (and hence prosperity and well-being) required a significant reduction in public spending and hence in public services. Competitiveness went from a shared objective that allowed for a renewal of the labour agenda around themes of democratization and participation, to a binding and overriding constraint that had the federations signing off on a national consensus that attacked the interests of their members. Some restructuring of the state was inevitable in the political context, but the federations' actions had the effect of turning necessity into a virtue and of reducing their bargaining power in negotiating change.

The summit process was not entirely one sided. In their evaluation of the summit, the CEQ, CSN and FTQ underlined that the declarations signed at the October 1996 Summit committed the government and private sector actors to seek to create employment, and set the objective of bringing the unemployment rate down to eight percent in 2002. The summit also included elements of a national employment policy, along with measures or promises in the fields of regional development, the social economy, income security policy and vocational training (CEQ, CSN and FTQ 1996). Compared to the immediate impact in terms of budgetary reduction and state restructuring, however, these promises were thin gruel, and they could be countered by other measures or promises, including the tacit acceptance of the business community's push to make Montreal's economy more bilingual (i.e. less francophone)

(Piotte 2001, 10). As the "Declaration for Employment" that labour federations touted as their biggest gain rapidly disappeared from the public stage to be replaced by the departure of 30,000 public servants, the unions renounced their support for the summit's deficit commitments. Nevertheless, they could not shake the fact that they had been largely willing participants in elaborating this program. The federations' loss of credibility meant that the biggest downsizing of the Quebec state since the Quiet Revolution took place without a crisis in labour relations (Charest 1998; Gagnon 1997).

The labour federations' emphasis on competitiveness also proved an obstacle in opposing changes to labour legislation in the late 1990s. As with the summits, employers could take up the language of competitiveness and partnership to argue for their agenda of labour market deregulation. In their study of the 1996 amendment to the collective bargaining decree system (covering between 5–10 percent of the workforce), Guylaine Vallée and Jean Charest (2001) underline how increased international competition and the need to preserve jobs by decreasing the costs of labour market deregulation became core considerations of whether collective agreements should be extended by decree. In the process, the Ministry of Labour was bypassed by the Secretariat to Decrease the Regulatory Burden, which paid greater attention to price, competition, profit margin and changes in employment. By June 2000, only 20 of the 29 decrees in effect in 1996 still existed, reflecting in particular the abrogation of eight of the twelve decrees in manufacturing.

This pattern repeated itself with the amendments to the Labour Code in 2000–2001. The government's proposal to amend the code reflected long-term pressures from the labour movement, which sought changes to make it easier to organize small employers and to counter union-avoidance strategies (such as the widespread use of dependent contractors) (CEQ et al. 1999). The government's options paper nevertheless circumscribed the reform both by noting that any changes had to account for the "North American context" (read: the need to remain competitive with the deregulated labour markets of Ontario and the United States), and that no changes would be made without broad consensus. The employer federations thus had little trouble arguing against major changes by appealing both to their need to compete and the veto of national consensus. Combined with weak labour mobilization behind their program of changes, "competitive nationalism" seems to have worked against the union federations even on a key issue that puts a seeming prerequisite for progressive competitiveness (i.e. union strength) into question over the long run (Ministère du Travail 2000; Charest and Morrisette 2003).

Having prized a progressive competitive strategy and embraced a form of competitive nationalism, the labour federations found themselves in a particularly tight spot with the election of the Parti libéral du Québec (PLQ) in the April 2003 provincial election. The program of the PLQ, and the public statements of Premier Charest and his top ministers, placed state restructuring far more clearly on the neo-liberal track, with little interest in involving "social partners," even in a symbolic sense. Indeed, in an open letter to citizens, Jean Charest (Charest, "Lettre ouverte," 2003) argued on the need to review the institutions inherited from the Quiet Revolution, and especially the "corporatist interests" invested in them. This was a two-pronged attack on the unions: it challenged existing forms of union recognition, particularly in the public sector, as well as the stakeholder institutions that provided some political leverage under the competitive nationalism strategy. Important changes passed in late 2003 included changes to the labour code facilitating contracting out, a partial reduction of the scope of the training tax (covering firms with payrolls over $1 million rather than $250,000), and the reduction in the number of bargaining units in the health sector. More generally, the government has studiously bypassed existing mechanisms of shared governance and consultation (Boismenu et al. 2004; Rouillard et al. 2004).

For the new government, the strength of the nation will come from a leaner and more agile state, and no doubt also from invigorating private enterprise through the opening of public markets to public/private partnerships. With the loss of stakeholder institutions, the union federations are left with blunt instruments of political intervention. The CSN, in part due to a strong public sector membership that felt the full brunt of the PQ's state restructuring strategy, has recently devoted some consideration to how it can renew its political intervention. Nevertheless, it appears unwilling to challenge its founding opposition to partisan intervention. Its favoured solution involves increasing political education or education in citizenship, coupled with institutional changes that increase citizen access (decentralization, consultation) or that democratize representative institutions (especially voting system reform) (CSN 2002a, 43–45; 2002b, 2001). In the face of Charest's program, leverage and influence is more or less limited to mobilizations in the street, bringing the unions full circle to the early 1970s, albeit with much less optimism about the likely outcome.

WANING UNION INFLUENCE OVER THE LEFT

The strategy of supporting a competitive nationalism has therefore imposed significant costs on the union movement, in the sense that it comes to be associated with a series of restructuring policies that do not seem to be in its interests. In the process, the labour federations have also come to lose some of their dominance in setting the program for the Quebec left. I purposefully say "some," because the unions remain important partners in terms of money, organization and participation in Quebec's social movement left. However, at least through the late 1990s, the women's movement and the community movement overtook them as the leaders in articulating ideological alternatives to the government's restructuring policies.

With the 1995 Women's March Against Poverty and the inclusion of representatives from the women's and community movements at the 1996 summits, the unions ceased being the most visible standard bearers of an alternative project. The Women's March put forth a series of demands seeking to fight poverty and violence against women, including an aggressive reregulation of labour markets (minimum wages, pay equity, access to training) and a significant investment in social infrastructure, particularly to regularize insecure and unpaid or underpaid work in the public, para-public and community sectors (David and Marcoux 1995). The degree of support garnered by the march propelled the Fédération des femmes du Québec to a much more prominent place on the public stage, a place that meant that it was seen as the leader of the opposition to the 1996–1998 social assistance reform (FFQ 1998). Its anti-poverty program has also been taken up by other relays that pushed the PQ government to adopt an anti-poverty strategy, a framework law against poverty, and some improvements to minimum labour standards in 2002 (Noël 2002).

Parts of the community movement likewise used their participation in the 1996 summits to advance the social economy as a new motor for developing employment and community solidarities. The social economy project involved meeting unmet needs through the creative mixture of public and private funds and community entrepreneurship. It also involved a broad conception of the economic that embraced potential employment and welfare gains entailed in meeting the basic needs of citizens. This movement has since fragmented along the lines of different definitions of what the social economy involves, and has grown increasingly critical of how public policies have attempted to re-separate the economic (development of community enterprises) and the social (autonomous community action) and marginalize the women's movement's project of social infrastructures (Côté 2005; D'Amours 2001). Nevertheless, the idea of social and community entrepreneurship likewise presented an interesting alternative to the unions' failing progressive competitiveness and gave rise to some partial gains, including a policy for funding autonomous community action groups, as well as spaces in local development planning for the articulation of a "quality of life" agenda (Vaillancourt 2002, 20–22; Masson 2003). As one of the reviewers of this essay noted, the possibilities of the social economy should not be overstated as it represents less than five percent of GDP, is made up of organizations that depend on state financing and replace services that the state has offloaded, and whose workers hold precarious jobs. That the social economy gained so much attention and raised so many hopes among progressives despite these characteristics is a further sign of the unions' problems in defining an alternative project for Quebec.

Indeed, these initiatives made the union federations' projects look old and tired. Their workplace-level social contracts increasingly looked like means of protecting insiders. The signing of two-tier contracts (clauses orphelins) as a means of saving jobs earned a lot of negative publicity, even if the practice was never widespread. They made prime targets for a populist "insiders versus outsiders" politics, and indeed acted as whipping boys for the ADQ throughout the 2003 election (Collombat and Gagnon 2003). In addition, the decision to sign onto the agreements of the 1996 Summit further cemented the impression that labour leaders were more at ease with business leaders than with representing the interests of their members, particularly those in the public sector hard hit by subsequent state restructuring. Finally, the emphasis on competitiveness clashed with any vision of international solidarity, since, in a fundamental sense, it was based on the idea of exporting unemployment to those parts of the world less able to compete (De Martino and Cullenberg 1994, 12, 15). Competitiveness thus masked the federations' increased emphasis on developing links with union movements in other countries, both through membership in the Confederation of International Free Trade Unions and on a bilateral basis.

It is only with the 2001 protests against the Summit of the Americas, again initiated in networks bringing together antiglobalization and labour activists, that labour leadership was shaken out of its political torpor. Its leadership is in the process of being rebuilt, first by mobilizing opposition against the ADQ in the 2003 election, and then in leading opposition to the Liberal government (Boismenu et al. 2004, 79–85). It nevertheless remains a largely reactive leadership in terms of fighting neo-liberalism, as compared to the contribution of the women's movement in the 1990s in tracing out alternative political economies for Quebec.

The women's and community movements are pro-sovereignty, but fit more difficultly than the unions under the PQ's umbrella. Without a social project, the national question is not the priority (e.g. Solidarité populaire Québec 1992). However, as the founding debates of the Union des forces progressistes demonstrate, a firm stand in favour of independence (or at least a stronger form of sovereignty than offered by the PQ) remains a *sine qua non* for those proposing social projects to the left of the PQ, even if this stand may increasingly be challenged for being more divisive than unifying (Shragge and Levy 2003). As such, without renouncing the national question, the movements are not easily interpellated by a mainstream sovereignist project that they see as more interested in fighting sterile battles with Ottawa and in looking after private enterprise than in pursuing a transformative project (Salée 2002, 185–86).

HEMMED IN: DEFINING A NATIONALIST PROJECT TO THE LEFT OF THE PQ

Attempts to define a left sovereignist project remain more at the level of slogan than of a credible plan. In the PQ's vision of sovereignty, the close relationship of Quebec with the United States, cemented among other things through close trading ties, international trade agreements and the potential adoption of a common currency, will ensure a relatively seamless transition to sovereignty. Even short of sovereignty, a closer relationship with the United

States breaks Quebec's dependence on the rest of Canada, and thus expands its autonomy (Martin 1997). The rapprochement with the United States becomes a hard sell for the mainstream sovereignist project when it appeals to the left. One notes, for instance, the tension in the Bloc Québécois' (1999, 12) discussion paper on globalization between the hymn it sings to the bilateral and multilateral institutions of trade liberalization up to and including the World Trade Organization, and its portrayals of SalAMI's protests against the Multilateral Agreement on Investment as grand heroism. As the Quebec social movement left looks south to Porto Alegre rather than Washington and New York, the idea of the free trade project as a means of strengthening Quebec's autonomy and potential for sovereignty becomes difficult to sustain. The unions themselves have been pushed by the mobilization around the April 2001 Summit of the Americas to adopt a far more critical and radical language on existing and future free trade agreements than they had used before a committee of the National Assembly in the fall of 2000 (Gagnon 2002, 63; Rocher 2003, 474).

More provocatively, the idea of moving closer to the United States to move away from Canada is also open to question in light of the limits to the sovereignty of an independent Quebec that an increasingly imperial United States is likely to demand. Charles Doran's recent book on Canadian unity and Quebec sovereignty, written before the post-September 11 emphasis on security, lays out a number of American strategic defence goals that would entail the cession of important aspects of sovereignty by a post break-up Canada and Quebec (Doran 2001, 55–64). Given the significant pressures recently brought to bear on the Canadian government to support the war in Iraq and to follow the narcotics laws of the United States,[5] it is not unreasonable to assume that an independent Quebec will face significant pressures to use its sovereignty to back the United States' international projects, particularly given the asymmetry involved in its fast-growing trade with the United States (Rocher 2003). As Quebec's social movements mobilize against the project of continental free trade and against Washington's wars, it becomes increasingly difficult for them to sustain a strategy for autonomy and sovereignty that looks to the United States as a springboard out of Canada.

This is where the left nationalist project finds itself hemmed in. If the mainstream sovereignist project of national recognition with limited social transformation is not enticing, one alternative would be to look to the labour movement and social movement present in the rest of Canada in the hope of creating a common project based on a multinational and asymmetric federalism. If there is some openness on the left in the rest of Canada to a tepid version of this project, as seen for instance in the New Democratic Party's Social Democratic Forum document, it is by no means a hegemonic position. It continues to fight with the hold of Trudeau's "One Canada" nationalism on the Canadian left. More to the point, the division of the Canadian political community into two linguistically defined "global societies" is pronounced in the institutions of the left. While some ties are maintained in the labour movement through the internal structures of Canadian and American unions, and through the peak level collaboration of the CLC and FTQ, spaces of interaction within the labour movement and in the other social movements are sparse (McIntosh 1999, 149, 153, 163). For instance, the experience of collaboration between Quebec and English Canadian feminists that occurred in the late 1980s is unlikely to be repeated given the near-disappearance of the National Action Committee on the Status of Women. Nevertheless, the creation of a Canada/Quebec/First Nations social forum, and the very slight increase in the NDP's vote share in Quebec, suggest that this route has not been entirely written off.[6]

A more likely alternative would be to take up the project of building a genuinely left-nationalist alternative (c.f. Dubuc 2003). This course is fraught with difficulties, as the wreckage of numerous attempts to create such an alternative (Mouvement socialiste; Rassemblement pour une alternative politique; Parti de la démocratie socialiste) litters the landscape, and the labour federations' traditions of political involvement reduce the life expectancy of new attempts. Some hopes have been placed in the Union des forces progressistes (UFP), created by the fusion of three small vanguardist parties, and they are attracting some interest from the social movement left. The UFP nevertheless appears similar to earlier efforts in its impatience in taking on the form of a political party, rather than emerging somewhat more organically from heightened dialogue and organization between the women's and community movements. As this essay has argued, these movements have projects that have gained a broader cultural relevance and political credibility, for instance through the 1995 and 2000 women's marches, and that could serve as the basis for creating a broad "structured movement" along the lines proposed by Sam Gindin (1998). However, the UFP has instead given free reign to its radical manifesto writers, with the result of consolidating its hold over the one to two percent of the electorate on the far left in the 2003 election but of forfeiting credibility with potential constituencies in the social movements and labour federations. If the UFP is to provide a viable vehicle, it has to grow out of the organizations and political education of existing left institutions and movements, rather than expecting to rally them once it gets its manifesto "just right."

As such, the labour movement's partial loss of influence as the key site for elaborating an alternative political economy is unlikely to have a significant effect on the relationship of Quebec society, and particularly its progressive movements, with the rest of Canada. This partial loss of influence weakens the mainstream sovereignist project, since it no longer can rely on the unions to consolidate its left flank, and is thus less able to claim to speak for the whole nation. The greater influence, at least temporarily, of actors in the women's movement and the community sector is likely also to bring the sovereignist project's acceptance of trade agreements and close relations with the United States into question. However, given the weakness of left alternatives, be it the construction of a credible left nationalist movement or the less probable development of coalitions with the left in the rest of Canada, the likely result is simply to have the question of sovereignty downplayed for a period within a context where political energies remain focussed on the Quebec polity and society.

CONCLUSION

This essay has provided an overview of labour/state relations in Quebec over the past decade, paying particular attention to the articulation of a new union strategy of progressive competitiveness, which, in the context of the national question, became a "competitive nationalism." Even while recognizing the gains made by adopting this strategic repositioning, the argument noted how this strategy was quickly exhausted in light of limited government and employer buy-in. Indeed, the emphasis on nationalism as a means of forcing business to the table quickly came to be turned to the benefit of business who could claim that their competitive success (and by extension that of the nation) depended on giving priority to their interests. Faced with a series of setbacks, the union federations came to find that their leadership over the broader left was also less secure than it once had been.

The election of the Charest Liberal government in April 2003 presents a new challenge for Quebec's labour federations and for the broader left. The competitive nationalism that won labour some representation in Liberal economic development and labour market training policies in the early 1990s finds no echo in a government seeking to render the Quebec state less porous to non-business interests. The change in government, coupled with the partial loss of leadership over the broader left, demand that the labour movement once again be innovative if it is not to sink back into strategic paralysis. Without a coherent program of social change and national affirmation, it risks once again becoming a reactive "nationalism taker" as the PQ attempts to rebuild the hegemony of its project over the left at the same time as key figures in the party embrace a "recentrage" of the party somewhat to the right of where it currently sits (e.g. Facal 2003).

In terms of Canada/Quebec relations, the preceding discussion provides few indications of fundamental change. The Quebec left is likely to remain nationalist both in its political goals and in directing its activities largely at the Assemblée Nationale. The short-term emphasis on confronting the provincial government and the medium-term issue of redefining the articulation of the mainstream nationalist project with progressive demands may nevertheless reduce conflict along the Quebec/Canada cleavage by reducing the salience of the sovereignty issue. The hesitancy of Option Citoyenne (a new party formation drawing on the women's and community movements) on the national question reflects this issue of salience and prioritization as compared to a rereading of Quebec's destiny in the Canadian federation. This momentary cooling of sovereignist ardour on the left should not be confused, however, with a fundamental change in outlook or alliances. While the spectre of American imperialism renders the PQ's project increasingly problematic, it may also make the assertion of national sovereignty a pressing priority.

NOTES

1 The FTQ represents roughly 37 percent of unionized workers in Quebec, and the CSN roughly 24 percent.
2 A partial exception would be the FTQ's relatively early leadership on the question of making French the ordinary language of work in Quebec, where its positions in 1969 reflected much of the content of Bill 101 (Piotte 2001).
3 As anecdotal evidence of this nationalism, the author remembers seeing a copy of the FTQ newsletter circa 1996, which included a photo of a news conference on Employment Insurance featuring the leaders of the FTQ, CSN and CEQ, along with the leader of the CLC, with a caption that only recognized the three Quebec leaders.
4 The export and employment numbers concern both international and interprovincial exports, given the significant replacement of interprovincial with international trade over this period. The figure for jobs per million dollars for the aggregate of international and interprovincial trade fell from 11.7 in 1990 to 8.0 in 1997 (see ISQ 1999, 11, 16).
5 While it is the Canadian nationalist left that has made this case most forcefully, for instance in the recent debates over sovereignty in *Canadian Dimension*, the growing US pressures on the exercise of Canadian sovereignty are also recognized in mainstream accounts, such as Helliwell (2002, 90).
6 Piotte (2001, 28) hypothesizes that the ability of the CLC and the FTQ to strike a form of sovereignty/partnership came from the presence of a common enemy (the CSN), much like the Canadian and Quebec nationalist lefts had some success cooperating in the 1970s against the common foe of American imperialism. If he is correct, the renewal of American ambitions might bridge existing tensions.

REFERENCES

Amin, A. 1999. "An Institutionalist Perspective on Regional Economic Development." *International Journal of Urban and Regional Research* 23(2): 365–78.
Bergeron, J.-G. and R. Bourque. 1996. *Workplace Change in Quebec: Public Policy and the Union Response.* Kingston: Queen's University Industrial Relations Centre.

Bloc Québécois. 1999. *Faire notre place dans le monde: chantier de réflexion sur la mondialisation.* Montreal: Bloc Québécois.

Boismenu, G., P. Dufour and D. Saint-Martin. 2004. *Ambitions libérales et écueils politiques: Réalisations et promesses du gouvernement Charest.* Outremont: Athéna Éditions.

Bourque, G.L. 2000. *Le modèle québécois de développement: de l'émergence au renouvellement.* Sainte-Foy: Presses de l'Université du Québec.

Brin d'Amour, J. 1992. "La stratégie industrielle du gouvernement du Québec: rétrospectives et perspectives." In *Pour une gestion efficace de l'économie*, ed. C. Carrier. Montreal: Association des économistes québécois.

CEQ, CSD, CSN, FTQ. 1999. *Réforme du Code du Travail: Demandes de la partie syndicale.* Montreal: Conseil consultatif du travail et de la main-d'oeuvre.

CEQ, CSN and FTQ 1996. "Sommet sur l'économie et l'emploi: bilan intercentrales," Montréal, 25 novembre.

Chantier sur l'économie et l'emploi. 1996. *La relance de l'emploi au Québec: Agir dans la compétivité et la solidarité.* Quebec: Sommet sur l'économie et l'emploi.

Charest, J. 1998. "Le mouvement syndical." In *L'année politique au Québec 1997–1998*, ed. R. Boily. Montreal: Presses de l'Université de Montréal.

– 2003. "Transformations du marché du travail et lois du travail: le mouvement ouvrier à la recherche d'un nouveau souffle." In *Québec: État et société, Tome II*, ed. A.-G. Gagnon. Montreal: Québec/Amérique.

Charest, J. and L. Morrisette 2003. "L'État et les enseignements du Code du Travail." Paper presented at the Programme d'études sur le Québec, April, at McGill University, Montreal.

Charest, Jean. 2003. "Lettre ouverte aux Québécois – 'Le Québec a fait un pas en avant depuis six mois' – Jean Charest." *Le Devoir,* 14 October.

Coates, D. 2000. *Models of Capitalism: Growth and Stagnation in the Modern Era.* Cambridge: Polity Press.

Collombat, T. and M.-J. Gagnon. 2003. "Le syndicalisme québécois face à la résurgence d'une droite antisyndicale." *Chronique internationale de l'IRES* 83: 1–13.

Confédération des syndicats nationaux (CSN). 1991. *Prendre les devants dans l'organisation du travail.* Montreal: CSN.

CSN. 1995. *Nos choix stratégiques dans la conjoncture actuelle.* Montreal: CSN.

– 2001. *L'action politique à la CSN et les rapports avec les partis: document de réflexion.* Montreal: CSN.

– 2002a. *Agir pour un monde solidaire: Rapport du comité exécutif.* Montreal: CSN.

– 2002b. *Faire progresser la démocratie: document de réflexion.* Montreal: CSN.

Conférence sur le devenir social et économique du Québec. 1996. *Un Québec de responsabilité et de solidarité: Oser choisir ensemble.* Quebec: La Conférence.

Conseil central du Montréal métropolitain – CSN (CCMM). 1998. "Question nationale et stratégie syndicale." Position paper. Montreal: CCMM.

Côté, D. 2005. "Le débat québécois sur l'économie sociale: mais que sont nos politiques devenues?" In *Femmes et politiques: l'État en mutation*, ed. D. Masson. Ottawa: Presses de l'Université d'Ottawa.

D'Amours, M. 2001. "Économie sociale au Québec: Vers un clivage entre entreprise collective et action communautaire." Accessed online at http://www.unites.uqam.ca/econos/Chercheurs-D'Amours.pdf

David, F. and L. Marcoux. 1995. *Du pain et des roses: cahier de revendications et guide d'animation.* Montreal: Marche des femmes contre la pauvreté.

De Martino, G. and S. Cullenberg. 1994. "Beyond the Competitiveness Debate: An Internationalist Agenda." *Social Text* 41: 11–39.

Denis, S. 1998. "'De l'apolitisme à la souveraineté': l'action politique de la CSN, essai de synthèse." In *La CSN: 75 ans d'action syndicale et sociale*, eds. Y. Bélanger and R. Comeau. Sainte-Foy: Presses de l'Université du Québec.

Doran, C.F. 2001. *Why Canadian Unity Matters and Why Americans Care.* Toronto: University of Toronto Press.

Doré, M. 1989. *Mieux comprendre, mieux agir sur l'organisation du travail.* Montreal: CSN.

Dubuc, P. 2003. *L'autre histoire de l'indépendance. De Pierre Vallières à Charles Gagnon, De Claude Morin à Paul Desmarais.* Montreal: Éditions du Renouveau québécois.

Facal, J. 2003. "Le Parti québécois fera-t-il le choix de l'examen de conscience sincère ou celui de l'orthodoxie intransigeante et nostalgique." Accessed online at http://www.partiquebecois.org/nv/micro/sdi/textes.php?txt=15

Fédération des femmes du Québec. 1998. *La bataille de l'aide sociale: un bilan provisoire*, document adopted by the Conseil d'administration of the FFQ, 22 August.

Fédération des travailleurs et travailleuses du Québec. 1993. *Face aux changements, de nouvelles solidarités.* Montreal: FTQ.

Gagné, P. and M. Lefèvre. 1993. *L'entreprise à valeur ajoutée: Le modèle québécois.* Montreal: Publi-Relais.

Gagnon, A-G. and G. Lachapelle. 1996. "Quebec Confronts Canada: Two Competing Societal Projects Searching for Legitimacy." *Publius* 26(3): 177–91.

Gagnon, M.-J. 1994. *Le syndicalisme: état des lieux et enjeux.* Quebec: Institut québécois de recherche sur la culture.

– 1997. "Le mouvement syndical." In *L'année politique au Québec 1996–1997*, ed. R. Boily. Montreal: Fides.

– 2002. "The Labour Movement and Civil Society: Reflections on the People's Summit From Quebec." *Just Labour* 1: 58–67.

Gindin, S. 1998. "The Party's Over." *This Magazine* 32(3): 13–15.

Graefe, P. 2003. "Trade Unions and Competitive Nationalism: A House of Mirrors." In *Global Turbulence: Social activists' and state responses to globalization*, eds. M.G. Cohen and S. McBride. Aldershot: Ashgate.

Guentzel, R. 2000. "Rapprocher les lieux du pouvoir: The Quebec Labour Movement and Quebec Sovereigntism, 1960–2000." *Labour/Le Travail* 46: 369–95.

Haddow, R. 1998. "Reforming Labour-Market Policy Governance: The Quebec Experience." *Canadian Public Administration* 41(3): 343–68.

Hall, P. and D. Soskice 2001. "An Introduction to Varieties of Capitalism." In *Varieties of Capitalism: The Institutional Foundations of Comparative Advantage*, eds. P. Hall and D. Soskice. Oxford: Oxford University Press.

Helliwell, J. 2002. *Globalization and Well-being*. Vancouver: UBC Press.

Institut de la statistique du Québec (ISQ). 1999. *Impact économique des exportations québécoises, années 1990, 1995 et 1997*. Sainte-Foy: ISQ.

Jetté, C. 1997. *Analyse des positions de la Fédération des affaires sociales en rapport avec les nouvelles formes d'organisation du travail (1970–1994)*. Masters' Thesis, Department of Sociology, UQAM.

Keating, M. 1998. *The New Regionalism in Western Europe: Territorial Restructuring and Political Change*. Cheltenham: Edward Elgar.

Lambert, R. 2000. "Globalization and the Erosion of Class Compromise in Contemporary Australia." *Politics & Society* 28(1): 93–118.

Lapointe, P.-A. and R. Paquet. 1994. "Les syndicats et les nouvelles formes d'organisation du travail." *Relations industrielles* 49(2): 281–302.

Latouche, D. 1993. "'Quebec, see under Canada,' Quebec Nationalism in the New Global Age." In *Quebec: State and Society*, 2nd Ed., ed. A.-G. Gagnon. Scarborough: Nelson.

Lipsig-Mummé, C. 1991. "Future Conditional: Wars of Position in the Quebec Labour Movement." *Studies in Political Economy* 36: 73–107.

– 1993. "Quebec Labour, Politics, and the Economic Crisis: Defensive Accommodation Faces the Future." In *The Challenge of Restructuring: North American Labor Movements Respond*, eds. J. Jenson and R. Mahon. Philadelphia: Temple University Press.

Martin, P. 1997. "When Nationalism Meets Continentalism: The Politics of Free Trade in Quebec." In *The Political Economy of Regionalism*, eds. M. Keating and J. Loughlin. London: Frank Cass.

Masson, D. 2003. "Engendering Regional Development Policy-Making in Québec (Canada)." Mimeo, Institute of Women's Studies, Université d'Ottawa.

McIntosh, T. 1999. "Organized Labour in a Federal Society: Solidarity, Coalition Building and Canadian Unions." In *Canada: The State of the Federation 1998– 1999 – How Canadians Connect*, eds. H. Lazar and T. McIntosh. Kingston: Institute of Intergovernmental Relations.

Ministère de la Main-d'oeuvre, de la Sécurité du revenu et de la Formation professionnelle (MMSRFP). 1991. *Partners for a Skilled and Competitive Québec: Policy Statement on Labour Force Development*. Quebec: MMSRFP.

Ministère du travail. 1996. *Les nouvelles pratiques en milieu de travail au Québec: Regard sur les démarches dans le secteur manufacturier*. Sainte-Foy: Publications du Québec.

– 2000. *Pour un code de travail renouvelé: Orientations ministérielles*. Quebec: Minstère du travail.

Noël, A. 2002. "A Law Against Poverty: Quebec's New Approach to Combating Poverty and Social Exclusion." Background Paper. Ottawa: Canadian Policy Research Networks.

Paquette, P. 1996. "Manque de capital ou pénurie d'idées." *Action Nationale* 86(6): 18–21.

– 1997. "La stratégie pour l'emploi proposée par la CSN." In *La Crise de l'emploi: de nouveaux partages s'imposent*, eds. G. Laflamme *et al.* Sainte-Foy: Presses de l'Université Laval.

Parti Québécois (PQ). 1994. *Québec in a New World: The PQ's Plan for Sovereignty.* Toronto: Lorimer.

Peters, J. 2002. *A Fine Balance: Canadian Unions Confront Globalization.* Ottawa: Canadian Centre for Policy Alternatives.

Piotte, J.-M. 1998. "Du combat au partenariat." In *La CSN: 75 ans d'action syndicale et sociale*, eds. Y. Bélanger and R. Comeau. Sainte-Foy: Presses de l'Université du Québec.

– 2001. "La FTQ: un microcosme du Québec." Paper presented at "La FTQ, ses syndicats et la société québécoise," conference, 23 March, at UQAM, Montreal.

Rocher, F. 2003. "Le Québec dans les Amériques: de l'ALE à la ZLEA." In *Québec: État et société, Tome II*, ed. A.-G. Gagnon. Montreal: Québec/Amérique.

Rogers, J. and W. Streeck. 1994. "Productive Solidarities: Economic Strategy and Left Politics." In *Reinventing the Left*, ed. D. Miliband. Cambridge: Policy Press.

Rouillard, C., É. Montpetit, I. Fortier and A.-G. Gagnon. 2004. *La réingénierie de l'État: Vers un appauvrissement de la gouvernance québécoise.* Quebec: Presses de l'Université Laval.

Salée, D. 2002. "Quebec's Changing Political Culture and the Future of Federal-Provincial Relations in Canada." In *Canada: The State of the Federation 2001 – Canadian Political Culture(s) in Transition*, eds. H. Telford and H. Lazar. Kingston: Institute of Intergovernmental Relations.

Shragge, E. and A. Levy. 2003. "The Union des forces progressistes in Québec: Prospects and Pitfalls." *Canadian Dimension* 37(2): 13–14.

Solidarité populaire Québec. 1992. *Le Québec qu'on veut bâtir: Rapport de la Commission populaire itinérante.* Montreal: Solidarité populaire Québec.

Statistics Canada. 1996. *Employment Trends in Selected Industries.* Ottawa: Statistics Canada, cat. no. 93F0027XDB96008.

Swank, D. 2002. *Global Capital, Political Institutions and Policy Change in Developed Welfare States.* Cambridge: Cambridge University Press.

Thelen, K. 2001. "Varieties of Labor Politics in the Developed Democracies." In *Varieties of Capitalism: The Institutional Foundations of Comparative Advantage*, eds. P. Hall and D. Soskice. Oxford: Oxford University Press.

Thompson, N. 1996. "Supply-Side Socialism: The Political Economy of New Labour." *New Left Review* 216: 37–54.

Uitermark, J. 2002. "Re-scaling, 'Scale Fragmentation' and the Regulation of Antagonistic Relationships." *Progress in Human Geography* 26(6): 743–65.

Vaillancourt, Y. 2002. "Le modèle québécois de politiques sociales et ses interfaces avec l'union sociale canadienne." *Policy Matters* 3(2): 52.

Vallée, G. and J. Charest 2001. "Globalization and the Transformation of State Regulation of Labour: The Case of Recent Amendments to the Quebec *Collective Agreement Decrees Act*." *International Journal of Comparative Labour Law and Industrial Relations* 17(1): 79–91.

Wells, D.M. 1987. *Empty Promises: Quality of Working Life Programs and the Labor Movement*. New York: Monthly Review Press.

Wright, E.O. 2000. "Working-Class Power, Capitalist-Class Interests, and Class Compromise." *American Journal of Sociology* 105(4): 957–1002.

8

The Politics of State/Civil Society Relations in Quebec

Rachel Laforest

Ce chapitre offre une analyse du discours politique et des réformes mises en place par le gouvernement libéral du Québec depuis son arrivée au pouvoir en 2003. Après avoir dressé le portrait de l'histoire des relations entre l'État et la société civile au Québec, il suggère que les réformes adoptées marquent une importante rupture avec le modèle traditionnel de représentation des intérêts québécois. En refusant de reconnaître le rôle de premier plan des acteurs de la société civile dans le processus politique québécois et en limitant leur accès à de nombreux espaces institutionnels, le gouvernement libéral du Québec cherche à minimiser leur influence. De plus, ces réformes sont accompagnées d'un important mouvement discursif qui remet en question la légitimité et la crédibilité même des organisations de la société civile. Ces changements ont été accueillis par de nombreuses vagues d'opposition et ont donné naissance à d'importantes crises sociales. Alors que le mouvement souverainiste gagne en popularité et devant le constat que le Parti libéral du Québec ne réussit pas à soulever la ferveur populaire à son endroit, il y a lieu de croire que ces transformations auront un impact important sur l'interface entre le Québec et le reste du Canada.

INTRODUCTION

On 14 April 2003, the Quebec Liberal Party (QLP) came to power and set out to re-engineer and modernize the Quebec state. It launched a series of reforms that were greeted with skepticism and much resistance. Only nine months after winning the election, the QLP faced a major credibility crisis, as 63 percent of Quebecers felt that they did not give the Liberal government the mandate to pursue its cost cutting agenda.[1] This important reversal of fortune reveals profound dissatisfaction not only with the content of the policies, but with how they have been implemented. In this essay, I argue that these waves of protest – which show no sign of abating – indicate that something profound is at play in Quebec politics, the outcome of which could fundamentally transform both the internal political dynamics between the state and civil society and the very distinct character of Quebec politics.

Since coming to power, the Liberal government has challenged the structure of popular political representation, particularly the privileged position of interest groups. It has proceeded with a series of major reforms without consulting either the general population or the major stakeholders involved. By changing the labour code to allow increased subcontracting by government departments to non-union shops, the QLP has implemented a series of major reforms which eliminate institutionalized access to the state for certain social groups and undermine their power in the policy process. In effect, the QLP is questioning the central role that a traditional partner – civil society – has played in the making of policy. This represents an important rupture in the Quebec model of interest representation, and it signals that the locus of decision-making is shifting in profound ways. The new patterns of governance the Liberal government is proposing are not compatible with the earlier forms of engagement overseen by the state. By moving to reduce the influence of the province's labour movement – which has been an integral component of Quebec society over the past decades – and undermining the autonomy of community organizations through a move towards greater sub-contracting, Charest is trying to erase history. This history has in the past been characterized by a partnership between the state and civil society around a common *projet de société,* and is one that views non-state actors as a vital part of the collective project.

Although it may be too early to tell, and the direction Liberal reforms may take is not foretold, it appears that the parameters of access to the state and the representation of interests are shifting. This essay examines this transformation with particular attention to how forms of representation and access are being rethought. The concept of structure of representation forms the core of the analysis. As well, the processes of representation and legitimacy of organizations as institutional actors in society are examined.

This essay proceeds in three parts. First, I will examine how the concept of structure of representation is relevant to understanding shifting relationships between the state and civil society. This provides the basis for understanding the dynamics that are shaping current transformations. The essay then examines the principles that underpinned the structure of representation leading up to the election of the QLP and the impact this structure had on the distinct character of Quebec politics in the 1990s. The third part explores the direction of change proposed by the QLP and how this new discourse may give rise to a particular vision of representation, access, and belonging.

STRUCTURE OF REPRESENTATION

The concept of structure of representation was first introduced by Rianne Mahon in 1977. It reflects the structure of power relations and the articulation of interests, as well as the processes of representation and legitimization. The concept is useful, for it allows us to focus on the bigger picture of how power relations and the power structure are constructed and perpetuated. By emphasizing the unequal nature of the structure of representation, Mahon sheds light on important power relations that permeate the structure. Embedded in the structure of representation is a particular idea of *who* are credible and legitimate actors, and *what* is an acceptable and legitimate activity for actors of civil society at a particular point in time. The overall structure of representation affects which issues will be taken up and pushed forward by these very actors, and shapes the range of potential options available to them by influencing the distribution of resources and opportunities upon which power is based. The structure of representation, while it remains relatively stable, is not fixed in time and it evolves as a reflection of the articulation of social forces in society (Mahon 1977, 165). New actors, new ideas and new interests can emerge, gain momentum and bring about change; at this time, the forms of access to the state and the articulation of interests are opened up for negotiation.

This essay argues that Quebec now stands at a critical juncture in which the state is questioning the historical nature of its relationship to actors of civil society and rethinking terms of access. Plans to re-engineer and modernize the Quebec government announced by the Liberal government call for a reconfiguration of the prevailing structure of representation and, in the process, affect the patterns of representation. These are not mere procedural issues about how we consult, participate and negotiate policy; they involve broader normative questions about the role of civil society actors in society and in policy. The answers to these questions reveal different ways of conceptualizing and explaining different patterns and structures of representation. Embedded in them are implicit assessments of what constitutes a legitimate activity, which organizations can do advocacy and which cannot, who takes part, on what basis and in what capacity. It signals an important shift in the organization of interests in society.

Such change, however, does not occur without a struggle, because the structure of representation is a crucial component of the mode of governing. Dismantling the structure of representation may profoundly alter the nature of Quebec politics and the capacity of actors in civil society to be progressive social forces. This essay attempts to contribute to the discussion of the role and place of the structure of representation by focusing on the example of the case of Quebec.

Already many studies have acknowledged the importance of the role of civil society actors in the policy making process (Noël 2003, Maillé 2003, Dufour 2003, Vaillancourt et al. 2002). Debates around the Quebec model of development, however, while providing valuable insight either on a particular policy field such as economic development and social economy or on specific actors such as labour unions and the women's movement, have neglected to situate these actors in relation to the broader structure of representation and to prevailing forms of interest representation. I believe that in order to understand the evolving balance between political forces in Quebec, we need to focus on the significance of these processes, linkages and relationships across sectors and within them. This is important for understanding the particular dynamics and undercurrents that fundamentally shape the multiple facets of political struggle and the responses of actors to new political opportunities. It provides an important lens for understanding the state/society interface. Moreover, the concept of structure of representation extends the analysis to areas and actions not previously defined as political. It includes not just deliberate activity within institutional channels but also activities external to these.

STRUCTURE OF REPRESENTATION: ACCESS, POWER AND LEGITIMACY

The articulation of the structure of representation is not without consequence. It directly affects the terms of access to policy making, the routes of political representation, the forms of political expression through which claims are made, and perhaps more importantly, it affects the legitimacy and credibility of the actors involved in the policy process. The state, of course, has a big role to play in determining the direction of change. It creates opportunities for actors of civil society to work in partnership and to play a greater role in policy and in service delivery. It can create new risks, too. For example, it can create challenges for organizations by reinforcing the unequal structure of representation through the uneven distribution of opportunities and resources (Gualini 2002, Painter and Goodwin 1995, Mayer 1995). In altering the terms of access, the availability of resources and the opportunities for participation, the state may have an impact on the lines of inclusion and exclusion. Some organizations may be insiders to the process while others may remain outsiders.

The process of delimiting insiders and outsiders is not without significance. The growing recognition and legitimacy conferred onto certain organizations can reconfigure the overall structure of representation. Expectations about who should be involved in policy making – and how they are involved – also play into this dynamic. Whether the skills, knowledge and experience of organizations are valued or whether organizations are valued because they represent a wider constituency will affect how they choose to represent themselves and on which basis their claims will be made. A shift in the structure of representation can enable or constrain the ability of organizations to mobilize, make claims and successfully influence policy. It can also make some political strategies, tactics, ideas and discourses more attractive and others less so. While the state plays a central role in delimiting spaces for political action and determining who has access to these spaces – ultimately privileging certain actors at the expense of others – the question of whether these opportunities have been exploited, and if so, how and by whom, is nevertheless important (Burstein 1999, McAdam 1982, Staggenborg 1991, Walker 1991).

In order to address these issues we must examine the discourses through which competing claims define potential actions and responsibilities for different players. The next section focuses on how the articulation of the system of representation has shaped both the legacy of the community movement in Quebec politics and the unique partnership between the state and civil society around a common *projet de société*.

ORGANIZING INTERESTS IN QUEBEC

STATE-SOCIETY RELATIONS

The community movement in Quebec has long been an important political force and a major engine of social change. Since the Quiet Revolution, the rise of nationalism has had a profound influence on the patterns of collective action and the structure of representation. For more than 30 years, politics in Quebec have revolved around the issue of independence, and to a large extent, nationalism has shaped the responses of community organizations to political opportunities. From its inception, the community movement has championed a vision of society that recognized community participation as a fundamental exercise in citizenship and democracy and as a means for empowering citizens (Noël 1996, Vaillancourt and Laville 1998, Bélanger and Lévesque 1992). Principles of social justice and democracy have inspired its actions. In fact, at various times the movement has been able to shape the political landscape in Quebec and influence policy making in a distinctive manner (Vaillancourt and Laville 1998, White 2001). As such, it has contributed in a very real way to the development of innovative social policy initiatives (Salée 2003). The establishment of a network of local community services centres, social economy initiatives (Vaillancourt et al. 2002, Vaillancourt 2003, Mendell 2003), the anti-poverty law (Noël 2003), and the policy of recognition and support of autonomous community action (Laforest and Phillips 2001, White 2001) are all examples of the distinctive contributions made by the progressive social forces to policy in Quebec.

The community movement also plays a valuable role in the construction of collective identity. It promotes a sense of shared solidarity and plays a unifying role by representing important symbols of the Québécois collectivity. Organizations embrace a vision of Quebec society where democracy, the exercise of citizenship and social participation should be enhanced, where citizens should have a say in their daily lives. This discourse ties organizations of civil society together around a common *projet de société* and a series of shared goals which permeate their struggle. The movement's active participation in policy therefore forms an important aspect of its role as organizer of the interests of collectivities. The Quebec state has in fact formally recognized and supported through core funding the valuable role of advocacy and of civil society actors in societal debates.[2]

Because of these two dimensions, the community movement has historically had a complex relationship with the Quebec state (White 2002). Dubbed alternately as "cooperative conflict," "contradictory participation" and "critical cooperation," the relationship between the government of Quebec and the community movement can be characterized as an ongoing struggle for recognition of autonomy with the state. On one hand, the state recognizes the value of their contribution to the political community, but on the other, tries to appropriate it to pursue its nation building project (Laforest and Phillips 2001, White 1997, Panet-Raymond and Mayer 1997). Moreover, the state has assumed a very active role in fostering and supporting the activities of the community movement. In fact, more than half of the funding of community organizations in Quebec is provided by the provincial government.[3] This funding dependency potentially places the community organizations in a particularly vulnerable position. Not surprisingly then, the community movement continually seeks to reassert its autonomy and distance itself from the Quebec state, and many organizations have lobbied for the recognition of autonomous community action for over a decade.

The tension between state and civil society lies in the long history of the Quebec state institutionalizing parts of the sector.[4] By altering the balance of power between state and society to achieve a balanced opposition, the community movement wants to ensure that it can maintain its critical capacity and its influence. Hence, mobilization and forms of representation that reassert the strength in numbers tend to be privileged alongside more institutionalized routes to participation. The drive for autonomy is often strongest during periods of increased state/society collaboration because the community movement does not want to be at the service of the state. This dynamic has allowed community organizations to play a vibrant role in policy debates, and has taken on many forms, from collaboration to conflict and confrontation (Coston 1998, White 2001, 1997).

The strong history of collaborative conflict emphasizes the need for unity within the community movement and for coordination around issues if it is to continue and assert itself as a pillar in policy making. However, the process of internal collaboration does not unfold without tensions, given the diversity of ideological stands that exist within the movement. In the next section, I will explore in more detail the internal dynamics that underpin the structure of representation. For the moment, however, it is important to note that the strength of the community movement in Quebec comes from its ability to mobilize and mount a common front despite internal differences. Forms of dissent have played an important part in shaping both civil society and the nationalist tradition. Community organizations have put contentious issues on the public agenda and have shaped the institutions and the development of Quebec. They have been at the heart of major social policy innovations and have left their mark on Quebec's distinct policy environment. In this sense, internal political dynamics are also important for understanding the face of Quebec politics and its distinct position with respect to the rest of Canada.

STRUCTURE OF REPRESENTATION IN QUEBEC

ROUTES AND FORMS OF REPRESENTATION IN QUEBEC

The structure of representation in Quebec presents a complicated picture. Far from revealing sharp new political cleavages, it has remained relatively stable over the past decade. In the early 1990s, while federal and provincial funding for organizations was being cut and the community movement in English Canada was undergoing a crisis of capacity (Jenson and Phillips 1996, Scott 2003), networking between community organizations in Quebec had intensified to the point where the community movement had developed an elaborate and intricate system of networks which brought together actors across all fields of activities.[5] These networks have an important function in the structure of representation, which is further cemented by their multiple links to organizations – local, regional and provincial in scope – via alliances and coalitions. Through provincial umbrella organizations, local and regional networks tap into information, support, and resources that can help them fight poverty and inequality. Moreover, the overlap in participation across sectoral and intersectoral tables allows the community movement to pursue multiple strategies fighting on multiple fronts. These networks also play a very important integrative function in Quebec politics. They are a powerful force for generating solidarity among diverse organizations. They connect organizations across policy fields and across policy issues and provide a space where issues can be debated and strategies deployed.

This is consistent with the forms of representation that actors of civil society have used since the 1980s. Organizations of civil society have traditionally encouraged and supported each other's efforts towards mobilization, as demonstrated in the collaboration of women's groups, unions, poverty organizations and student unions around the March for Bread and Roses. Similarly, in the fight against poverty, these organizations backed the idea of an anti-poverty law and became active members of the The Collective for a Poverty-Free Quebec, a coalition that pursues the goal of eliminating poverty and promoting social justice in Quebec. By empowering citizens on a variety of levels, these initiatives reassert the power of the community movement as a whole.

Organizations of civil society share the belief that in order to establish their balance of power, a certain level of cohesion and unity is necessary to mobilize under a common front. The recent mobilization efforts to oppose the policy reforms of the Quebec Liberal government in the fall of 2003 are a case in point. Social groups, anti-poverty groups, alter-mondialists, the women's movement, unions, and many more actors launched a series of protests in December 2003 to show their opposition. By looking beyond their sectoral claims and converging their struggles to exert pressure on the state, community organizations can be quite successful in positioning themselves as indispensable contributors to policy making.

However, such collaboration does not come without tensions. Collaboration is the product of a collective process and a coming together of a broad array of webs of relationships. As a result, it is subject to multiple influences. In fact, one of the particularities of the community movement networks in Quebec is that it groups actors from a wide range of the political spectrum. Accordingly, mainstream organizations work to collaborate with radical organizations which may have a very different view of effective strategy. In order to overcome these differences, organizations generally do not enforce a common approach, but rather privilege multiple routes of representation, ensuring that pressure is exercised on many fronts and that the message is conveyed through many frames. When tensions are high, networks are fragmented into parallel coalitions which work towards a common purpose of pressuring the state, while allowing organizations more liberty to frame the issues and make claims that reflect their ideological stance. Provincial umbrella organizations, then, will tend to overlap in membership across these coalitions in order to ensure a certain level of coherence. For example, in the case of the social security reform of 1994 (enacted in 1997), there was an important schism within the community movement between those who were opposed to the proposed social security review and who couched their opposition in a nationalist discourse, and those who did not want to frame their opposition as a nationalism issue. In order to resolve this difference and maintain a common front, two major coalitions worked in parallel: one in which claims emphasized the federal principle and the need to recognize social policy as a provincial jurisdiction and which promoted the independence of Quebec, and the other, which focused more specifically on the proposed reform and in which claims were put forward in the name of social justice and equity. Both participated and mobilized in common public protests, both received resources and support from the unions, the women's movement, and Solidarité Populaire du Québec (SPQ), yet each had a distinct policy discourse (Laforest 2000). The ability of the community movement to come together across such diverse ideological stances in effect cements its power position.

Another distinct characteristic of these networks is their openness to new actors. For example, Dufour observes how alter-mondialists and the anti-globalization movement – which tend to adopt more radical forms of representation – have successfully joined forces with some of the traditional actors on the Quebec scene, such as the unions and the women's movement (Dufour 2003).

The presence of a wide range of actors working together from different perspectives reveals an important characteristic of the structure of representation: forms of representation often involve action centered on the state as the institutional terrain as well as mobilization at the margin of it. In other words, the movement's actions are not aimed solely at the state, but at civil society as well, as organizations aim to develop a *projet de société* to shape values, to develop a vision for society and to bring about social change. Because of the diversity of interests and preferred strategies, the actions of community organizations manifest themselves at various levels and in various forms. Organizations will not hesitate to adopt multiple routes of representation, choosing to work both inside and outside of established, institutionalized channels of interest representation.

What is distinct about this structure of representation is that it is not dominated by peak umbrella associations with a representation monopoly. Moreover, representation is not ensured through functionally differentiated categories. Rather, organizations come together and collaborate around sectoral and intersectoral tables. As a result, organizations – even those from varied fields – frequently work together in order to pool their technical, financial or physical resources.[6] Organizations seek access to the resources, opportunities, and incentives offered by these dense webs of civic networks. First and foremost, organizations will draw on the resources and existing linkages as leverage in order to strengthen their position. Ultimately, because these opportunities are available through provincial, regional and local networks, organizations tend to maintain a strong focus on domestic social movement contention rather than shifting their focus onto other arenas of political contention, and they continue to do so, despite the pressures of globalization.[7]

To say that there is collaboration, however, is not to say that all actors share the same power and influence in policy making. In fact, an important feature of the system of representation in Quebec is the key role of labour unions and the women's movement in providing support to mobilizing activities (Harrisson and Laplante 2002, Laforest 2000). These actors are generally present when major reforms are discussed, and they have a long history of involvement in a variety of critical policy areas, such as health reform, economic development and social services. They are important allies in a wide range of policy areas, including the struggles around economic development (Bélanger, Boucher and Lévesque 2000, Favreau and Lévesque 1996), the creation of a law to eliminate poverty (D'Amours 2002), anti-globalization (Dufour 2003) and even the recognition of same-sex marriage (Smith 1998).

These key actors play an important supporting role within the structure of representation. They provide both financial and human resources, which help in the elaboration of analysis and argument. They also play a role in training. Through these networks, less experienced groups benefit from the support of those who are more experienced and who can assist them in their work towards social justice and democracy.

Another important feature of the structure of representation is found in collective action, which has mainly targeted the Quebec state as the vector of change and locus of democratic practice. In fact, the state has been a focus for collective action endeavours for the past thirty years because, historically, it has been a strong financial and institutional supporter of voluntary sector organizations and of advocacy in particular. Moreover, the Quebec state has traditionally assumed a very active role in both defining the political community and constructing a *projet de société,* for it retains exclusive jurisdiction over key social and economic policies within its territory. For these reasons, the strategies of social movements and community groups remain primarily embedded in "national politics" (Gagnon 2001). Their relationship with the federal government seems largely irrelevant. Although there have been some efforts in recent years to build bridges across respective community sectors, these have remained to a great extent unsuccessful (Laforest and Phillips 2001).

These distinct features of the structure of representation in Quebec shape the opportunities, resources and frames of political action. By drawing on their networks, through strategizing and information sharing, community organizations are able to assert themselves as agents of civil renewal and active citizenship.

RECOGNITION AND ACCESS

The structure of representation in Quebec has evolved out of this particular legacy of the state/society relationship. By 1990, community organizations had gained recognition as legitimate participants in the representation of interests and as valuable partners in economic and social development (White 1997, Laforest and Phillips 2001). This recognition took on many forms. First, the government of Quebec, under the Parti Québécois, began to consult more widely on issues pertaining to major policy reform. It also increased their institutional points of access to the state through the creation of a number of coordinating, governing and advisory bodies at the local, regional and provincial levels, thus acknowledging their legitimacy. As a result, community organizations were invited to sit on a number of intermediary para-public structures (such as the régies régionales de la santé et des services sociaux in 1992, conseils régionaux de développement in 1997, conseils locaux de développement in 1997, etc.) (White 1997, Panet-Raymond 1992). The state apparatus was constructed to represent the desire for greater public participation in various access points and to reflect regional preoccupations more accurately. Moreover, in order to create opportunities for the continued participation of community organizations in these bodies, representation was guaranteed ex-officio. With an invitation to participate in the 1996 Conference on the Economic and Social Future of Quebec alongside business and union leaders, the community movement also successfully positioned itself as a legitimate participant and as a valuable partner in economic and social development.

With such access to policy forums, the community movement was able to shape, in a distinct and innovative way, the social policy field (Lévesque and Vaillancourt 1998). Through the work of the Chantier sur l'économie sociale, for example, which came out of the socio-economic summit of 1996, over 30,000 new jobs and new services in areas such as home care, recycling, social housing and tourism were created and it continues to be a space for innovation in bringing together a variety of actors from the community movement.[8] Thanks to their successes, the concept of social economy is now generating attention in policy circles at the federal level as well.

Not only did community organizations become increasingly politicized through these institutionalized contacts, but by the end of the 1990s, they had won official recognition of their autonomy and efforts were launched to develop an official policy of recognition and support of autonomous community action (la politique de reconnaissance et de soutien de l'action communautaire autonome) in 2001. In order to support the elaboration of a policy of recognition and support of autonomous community action and to foster a community sector that is actively engaged in public policy and in the construction of a collective *projet de société*, the Quebec government announced in April 1995 the creation of the Secretariat for Autonomous Community Action (SACA). At a time when the federal government and its provincial counterparts were abolishing core funding programs for community organizations, the Quebec government was reasserting their relevance.

The creation of the Secretariat for Autonomous Community Action and its activities reaffirms the importance of protecting the autonomy of the community movement. The role of the secretariat is to help community organizations access governmental resources and to advise the government in its relationship to the sector. The Secretariat administers the Autonomous Community Action Fund (Fond d'aide à l'action communautaire autonome) through three programs: support to advocacy and the defence of collective rights, support to organizations which help the most vulnerable members of society, and support for special projects of community development.[9] Moreover, through

SACA, an ongoing dialogue between the autonomous community movement and the state was initiated concerning the content, design and implementation of such a policy. An advisory committee composed of 20 representatives was selected by a general assembly of community organizations on the basis of provincial and sectoral representation and worked in collaboration with SACA in order to help design the policy.[10]

Under this policy, government undertakings include formal recognition of the contribution of community action, funding to support the original mission of organizations, and recognition of the legitimacy of the movement's diverse roles, including public policy advocacy and representation. While the government pledged that the larger part of funding to organizations will be dedicated to providing core funding in support of their mission, it also reasserted the importance of diversification of their funding sources through project funding and contracting relationships. What is distinct about this policy, however, is that it recognizes the value of organizing and mobilizing interests around social action and the defense of collective rights. The Quebec state is open to collective action and recognizes the role of community organizations in the process of intermediation between citizens and the state.

As it stands, the policy of recognition and support of autonomous community action allows for three kinds of funding. First, organizations are assured of core funding to support their original mission, to cover their basic infrastructure needs (rent, staff and equipment), and to cover the expenses for activities of consultation, representation, education and advocacy. Given that organizations often take on both the role of service provision and of advocacy, the policy makes the provision that expenses relating to advocacy are covered under funding to their original mission. Secondly, the policy allows for project-based funding or contract funding from different ministries for organizations that deliver complementary or supplementary services to that of the ministry in question. Finally, under the policy, the Fund for Autonomous Community Organizations, administered by SACA, is recast to support mainly advocacy and representation via umbrella groups – essential characteristics of autonomous community action. In other words, advocacy organizations will not have to rely on the ministry in their policy field – with whom they may be in opposition – in order to receive funding. Further, they will be able to act in their role as social critic. The autonomy of the sector is protected by this distance between organizations and their lead departments.

In summary, over the past decade the community movement in Quebec and its contribution to policy not only gained official recognition, but the organizations were also successful in securing privileged access to policy makers via institutions such as SACA and a variety of other forums at the local, regional and provincial level. Under the leadership of the Quebec Liberal Party, however, both access and legitimacy have been undermined by a number of reforms.

THE LIBERAL GOVERNMENT: THE DAWN OF A NEW ERA

RE-ENGINEERING THE STATE, REENGINEERING THE RELATIONSHIPS

The arrival of the Quebec Liberal Party (QLP) to power marks important departures with past patterns of governing. Since becoming premier, Jean Charest has publicly called into question the Quebec model of interest representation and consensus building which has come to symbolize the distinctive character of Quebec politics. Plans announced by QLP to re-engineer and modernize Quebec government call for a reconfiguration of the prevailing structure of representation and a reformulation of the forms of legitimate representation. These reforms have the potential to profoundly transform the internal political dynamic in Quebec by closing off access to the political arena for community organizations, by undermining their credibility and legitimacy, and by rendering them more dependent on contracting and partnership. These are real and significant changes, which may affect the very nature of the relationship between state and society that has contributed to Quebec's distinct social and economic development.

CLOSING THE SPACES FOR POLITICAL PARTICIPATION

Already, the reforms enacted in December 2003 by the Liberal government have closed important points of access to the community movement. Traditionally, under the Quebec model of interest representation, the labour movement, the women's movement and various community organizations were generally invited to participate in discussions on the future of Quebec. By eliminating institutionalized access to the state for certain groups, the QLP is in effect shifting the locus of decision making away from society.

First, on 18 December 2003, the Quebec National Assembly approved Bill 25, *an Act respecting local health and social services network*. This bill is part of the Liberal government's plan to restructure and reduce costs in the health care sector, and is a clear example of how the QLP is moving to reduce the space for political participation. This reform merges local community services centres and hospitals under the administration of a new transitory body, thereby abolishing the structure of *régies régionales*. The effects of this reform are important in two respects. First, it confers greater power to the hospitals and undermines the philosophy of health grounded in local communities. Initially, the CLSC structure was created in order to support local community initiatives, bringing together state and community actors. It was inspired by the values and methods inherent to the community movement. CLSCs were to be spaces where democracy, the exercise of citizenship and social participation could be enhanced, where citizens could have a say in their daily lives (Panet-Raymond 1992, White 1997). With this move towards a hospitalo-centric vision of health care there is the danger that community health programs may be undermined. Secondly, this reform eliminates a governing body where community representation was guaranteed. In fact, the régies régionales were first created to improve the democratic character of regional governance. Although the Liberal government has been vague on the structure of the new governing bodies replacing the régies régionales, given the direction of the QLP, one can be skeptical about whether groups will retain similar representation on these boards. How this issue is resolved may ultimately lead to a long term change regarding the importance of these organizations in the policy process.

Bill 34, *an Act respecting the Ministère du Développement économique et regional,* further shifts power away from the regions and towards municipal governments by eliminating the Centres Locaux de développement (CLD) and the Conseils régionaux de développement (CRD). As a result, the Liberal government again closes access to important institutional spaces for dialogue and partnership where community organizations were traditionally represented. Together, Bills 25 and 34 effectively close the political spaces where community organizations could formerly participate.

Finally, another important step in reducing these groups' access and participation would be the dismantling of SACA, which has served as a promoter of autonomous community action. No official announcement has been made in this respect. Nevertheless, with the re-engineering of the state, the general feeling within the sector is that the Liberal government might move to dismantle SACA, but continue to consult on a regular basis with its advisory committee which is composed of representatives across a variety of sectors from the community movement.

What is clear from these three examples is that the discourse on access is changing in a profound way. The Liberal government is less interested in providing and guaranteeing access to the actors of civil society. The implication is that by closing off access, it may be harder for the community movement to continue to exercise the same level of influence in policy debate and infuse discussions with its unique perspectives and practices. The two reforms already put forward have profound implications both for the capacity of organizations to influence policy and for the capacity of regional interests to be heard within the system. Moreover, the swift move to enact these laws without prior consultation and without drawing attention to them is itself indicative of a profound shift in the way the Quebec government enacts policies. While the Liberal government may explain these reforms as part of its modernization agenda, they represent a clear attempt to deconstruct the Quebec model by negating the important contribution of civil society organizations in defining general policy orientations for Quebec.

QUESTIONING CREDIBILITY

Facing strong public resistance to the proposed reforms and an all-time low rating in the polls, Jean Charest launched a series of regional forums across Quebec in February 2004 in a bid to sell his re-engineering project to "ordinary citizens." These regional consultations led up to a National Forum held on the 13th and 14th of October 2004. They marked an important departure from traditional consultative practices in Quebec, for the Liberal government explicitly sought to extend participation beyond the traditional actors. The forums were conceived to allow individual citizens, not organizations, to present their views on the proposed re-engineering plans. In the end, however, they were not arenas where public interaction and communication were encouraged. Rather, they turned out to be platforms where the Liberal government disseminated information and tried to build public support for its reform project. Nonetheless, what is significant in these consultative efforts is that by targeting the engagement of ordinary citizens, the Liberal government has, in effect, bypassed established routes of political representation and ignored organized interests. Finally, it appears that this government is trying to redesign the democratic process in some fundamental ways.

This trend has been further reinforced by a discursive shift discrediting the role and place of community organizations in the making of policy. In fact, since coming to power, Charest has repeatedly called into question of the credibility of interest groups and discredited their advocacy role. In an open letter, he openly criticized the role of intermediary organizations alleging that "interest groups benefit from the status quo" and that they are motivated by their "corporate bias or exclusive self-interest."[11] Furthermore, he has also criticized the women's movement, anti-poverty groups and the labour movement. It is not that the government dismisses the value of the labour movement or of the women's movement in the policy process. Rather, it sees their roles as one actor among many, thereby ignoring their established roles in Quebec politics. Rather than promoting a corporatist model focused on cross-sectoral concertation and consensus building, the Charest government has become a proponent of a free market of ideas and interests.

Not only might the labour movement lose out in this shift as the overall system of interest representation is rethought; the labour movement also directly affects a broad range of actors, and its changing role may therefore have profound implications for practices of networking and coalition building. As we have seen, the labour movement has long been an important resource and supporter of a wide range of community initiatives. By undermining its capacity, the Liberal government affects a wider scope of actors who may no longer be able to rely on its support and its resources, thereby sending shock waves through the sector.

The broader attack on the credibility of community organizations and the shift towards engaging "ordinary citizens" undermines the representational role of organizations and challenges their privileged access to the state. It questions who is a legitimate voice in the policy process and on what basis they can participate. This shift in discourse is insidious and deep, in that it questions the value and the role of intermediary organizations. It bears a resemblance to discursive shifts that occurred at the federal level in the early 1990s, when advocacy groups came under attack as they were branded "special interest groups" (Phillips 2001, Jenson and Phillips 1996, Dobrowolsky 1998). This discursive shift is not harmless. It depicts organizations as being preoccupied with a single issue or cause, thereby representing at best a limited spectrum of public opinion. The QLP now echoes this view.

Moreover, the Quebec Liberal government has announced plans to re-examine its funding relationship with the community sector and has made clear its intention to profoundly revise the policy of recognition and support of the autonomous community action which outlines the funding practices of government.[12] The plans emphasize the need to rationalize funding to avoid duplication which, if enacted, would have significant impact on the resources and capacity in the community movement.

This further marks a clear attempt by the Liberal government to undermine the power of the leaders behind the community movement, thereby lowering the visibility and clout of particular organizations. It ignores the fundamental role of the community movement in shaping collective interests and questions the established relationship between the state and actors of civil society that contributes to Quebec's distinct policy environment. Not only have organizations lost privileged access to the state via institutional access since the Liberal party's arrival to power, their resource base is being reduced and the role of intermediary organizations is being questioned.

PRIVATIZATION AND CONTRACTING OUT

The third, more pernicious shift, is the move towards a greater contracting relationship with the community movement that profoundly undermines the autonomy and independence of the sector. Already in June 2003, the auditor general reported that $1.9 million dollars were spent in funding of community groups. Yet accountability mechanisms were lacking, and the Quebec government had little knowledge of how the money was being spent (Delisle 2003). On that basis, she calls for a re-examination of funding practices and accountability mechanisms. Clearly, then, the Liberal government is moving towards placing greater emphasis on contractual and project-based funding, thereby focusing on the role of community organizations in service delivery. This move strikes an important blow to advocacy organizations and those involved in the defense of collective rights, which rely on core funding in order to maintain their autonomy.

Bill 31, an *Act to Amend the Labour Code*, was passed in December 2004 against strong opposition from the labour movement. Bill 31 makes it easier for the Liberal government to contract out work, and is another indication of a shift towards greater privatization. It reduces the power of unions by allowing employers to hire contract workers during a strike, and deals a further blow to the values that have shaped modern Quebec by opening the door to public-private partnerships (Saint-Martin 2004, Boismenu, Dufour and Saint-Martin 2004).

Taken together, these measures reflect important transformations underway in Quebec. They point to a reconsideration of the structure of representation and a move away from the Quebec model of consensus building. A similar shift in the structure of representation has occurred at the federal level in the early 1990s, the effects of which are still being felt (Jenson and Phillips 1996). If a lesson has been learned from that experience, it is that once the capacity and credibility of organizations of civil society have been undermined, it is difficult to go back. While it is clear that the Liberal government is moving to dismantle the system of representation that has made civil society a vital part of collective choices, it is less clear if it will be successful, given the strong resistance of social forces to the proposed plans for re-engineering.

CONCLUSION

It is particularly important to pay attention to how events unfold in Quebec over the next year, for these shifts in discourse and practices have the potential to radically transform the relationship between state and civil society and the very distinct character of Quebec politics. To date, reforms have gone against the traditional democratic values that have shaped Quebec's distinct policy environment. They have discredited and undermined the traditional role of the community movement by closing off access to forums and redirecting the linkages between government and citizens. Yet it is the participation of these very actors in important policy arenas that has cemented some of the most innovative social policy reforms – reforms that have distinguished the policy routes taken in Quebec from those in rest of Canada.

Resistance has been strong, given the ability of the movement to mobilize and counter-attack, and there is no indication it will abate in the near future. If the Liberal government continues to ignore the voices of discontent and forges ahead, there may be important unforeseen consequences. Without solidarity and support on the home front, Charest may ultimately undermine his capacity to secure gains at the federal level. Moreover, community organizations still have the potential to shape their relationship with the state and create opportunities for action. It may be that the direction taken by the Liberal government – rather than undermining the capacity of the community movement – will inflame and reignite nationalist sentiment and cause it to strike back, thereby doing precisely what the sovereignty movement has itself been unable to do for a long time. With polls showing a rise in support for the sovereignty option, placing it at its highest level since 1998,[13] and the historical link between the community movement and the nationalist movement, Charest may have taken on more than he had bargained for.

NOTES

The author would like to thank Daniel Salée, Peter Graefe, Michael Orsini and the anonymous reviewers for their comments and thoughtful insight. Any remaining errors or omissions are solely the responsibility of the author.

1 Leger Marketing/TVA, *Globe and Mail* and *Le Devoir* Quebec survey conducted between 14 January and 18 January among 1,000 respondents, www.legermarketing.com/documents/pol/020902eng.pdf
2 Policy on recognition and support for community action, 2001, Quebec, gouvernement du Québec.
3 For information on the funding situation in Quebec, see Secrétariat à l'Action communautaire autonome, http://www.mess.gouv.qc.ca/francais/saca/
4 Examples include increased bureaucratisation and professionalization of CLSC, the institutionalization of being "harnessed by the state" (see Panet-Raymond 1987, White 1997, Panet-Raymond and Mayer 1997). For a history of Social economy initiatives, see Mendell (2003).
5 I refer to these as civic networks in the hopes of distinguishing them from policy networks, and highlight distinct nature of Quebec politics. Civic networks encompass multiple, overlapping, permeable networks that bring together actors of civil society in a variety of ways. They are distinct from policy networks used to describe when actors converge around various policy problems or within a policy field (Coleman and Skogstad 1990, Howlett 2002). Civic networks envelop conjunctural and permanent links, across both sectoral and intersectoral issues. Indeed, the community movement is a dense web of overlapping networks.
6 This dynamic is quite distinct from the structure of representation at the federal government, where interests are organized hierarchically into local chapters of provincial and federal umbrella organizations, with very little contact across silos of activities, and few multisectoral tables. Notable are recent efforts at the federal level to cross these divides and build a coherent strategy for the sector as a whole. However, because of the top-down nature of these initiatives, they have failed to

resonate with local chapters who remain skeptical of the value of cross-sectoral collaboration.

7 Queen's University and Public Policy Forum, *Globalization and the Voluntary Sector in Canada,* 2003. Available at http://www.ppforum.ca/ow/ow_p_05_05_2003.pdf

8 For more information on these initatives, see http://www.chantier.qc.ca/

9 These monies are generated by 5 percent of the annual earnings from the Quebec Society of lotteries.

10 The advisory committee is composed of representatives from following sub-sectors: health and social services, public education, community development, volunteering, literacy, communications, consumption, defence of collective rights, international solidarity, environment, family, youth, sports and leisure, handicapped persons, cultural communities, housing, women and aboriginal groups, as well as a number of cross sectoral coalitions.

11 Premier Jean Charest said in an open letter published 14 October 2003 http://www.premier.gouv.qc.ca/general/lettres_ouvertes/lettre2003-10-13_en.htm

12 Claude Béchard, "Lancement du Plan d'action gouvernemental en matière d'action communautaire," 17 August 2004.

13 See www.cric.ca

REFERENCES

Bélanger, P.R., J. Boucher and B. Lévesque. 2000. "L'économie solidaire au Québec: la question du modèle de développement." In *L'économie solidaire. Une perspective internationale,* ed. J.-L. Laville. Paris: Desclée de Brouwer.

Bélanger, P.R. and B. Lévesque. 1992. "Le mouvement populaire et communautaire: de la revendication au partenariat (1963–1992)." In *Le Québec en jeu,* eds. G. Daigle and F. Rocher. Montreal: Presses de l'Université de Montréal.

Boismenu, G., P. Dufour and D. Saint-Martin. 2004. *Ambitions libérales et écueils politiques.* Montreal: Athéna Éditions.

Burstein, P. 1999. "Social Movements and Public Policy." In *How Social Movements Matter,* eds. M. Guigni, D. McAdam and C. Tilly. Minneapolis: University of Minnesota Press.

Coleman, W.D. and G. Skogstad, eds. 1990. *Policy Communities and Public Policy in Canada: A Structural Approach.* Mississauga: Copp Clark Pitman ltd.

Coston, J. 1998. "A Model and Typology of Government-NGO Relations." *Nonprofit and Voluntary Sector Quarterly* 27(3): 358–82.

D'Amours, M. 2002. "Processus d'institutionnalisation de l'économie sociale: la part des mouvements sociaux." *Économie et Solidarités* 33(2): 27–40.

Delisle, N. 2003. "Fouillis dans les organismes sans but lucratif." *La Presse,* 11 June.

Dobrowolsky, A. 1998. "Of 'Special Interest': Interest, Identity and Feminist Constitutional Activism in Canada." *Canadian Journal of Political Science* 31(4): 707–42.

Dufour, P. 2003. "Globalisation as a New Political Space: The End of the Quebec-Quebec Debate?" Paper presented to the Quebec and Canada in the New Century: New Dynamics, New Opportunities, October.

Favreau, L. and B. Lévesque. 1996. *Développement économique communautaire. Économie sociale et intervention.* Sainte-Foy: Presses de l'Université du Québec.

Gagnon, A.-G. 2001. "The Moral Foundations of Asymmetrical Federalism: A Normative Exploration of the Case of Québec and Canada." In *Multinational Democracies,* eds. A.-G. Gagnon and J. Tully. Cambridge: Cambridge.

Gualini, E. 2002. "Institutional Capacity Building as an Issue of Collective Action and Institutionalisation: Some Theoretical Remarks." In *Urban Governance, Institutional Capacity and Social Milieux,* eds. G. Cars, P. Healey, A. Madanipour and C. de Magalhaes. Ashgate: Aldershot.

Harrisson, D. and B. Laplante, eds. 2002. *La construction du partenariat patronal-syndical: contraintes du marché et négociations locales.* CRISES: Université du Québec à Montréal.

Howlett, M. 2002. "Do Networks Matter? Linking Policy Network Structure to Policy Outcomes: Evidence from Four Canadian Policy Sectors." *Canadian Journal of Political Science* 35: 235–68.

Jenson, J. and S. Phillips. 1996. "Regime Shift: New Citizenship Practices in Canada." *International Journal of Canadian Studies* 14(3): 111–36.

Laforest, R. 2000. "La consultation publique et l'action collective." *Politique et Sociétés* 19(1): 27–48.

Laforest, R and S. Phillips. 2001. "Repenser les relations entre gouvernement et secteur bénévole: À la croisée des chemins au Québec et au Canada." *Politique et Sociétés* 20(2–3): 37–68.

Lévesque, B. and Y. Vaillancourt. 1998. *Les services de proximité au Québec: de l'expérimentation à l'institutionnalisation.* Montreal: Cahiers de recherches du CRISES et du LAREPPS.

Maclure, J. and A.-G. Gagnon, eds. 2001. *Repères en mutation. Identité et citoyenneté dans le Québec contemporain.* Montreal: Éditions Québec Amérique.

Mahon, R. 1977. "Canadian Public Policy: The Unequal Structure of Representation." In *The Canadian State: Political Economy and Political Power,* ed. L. Panitch. Toronto: University of Toronto Press.

Maillé, C. 2003. "Le mouvement des femmes au Québec: histoire et actualité." In *Quebec: État et Société,* ed. A.-G. Gagnon. Montreal: Québec-Amérique.

Mayer, M. 1995, "Urban Governance in the Post-Fordist City." In *Managing Cities: The New Urban Context,* eds. P. Healey et al. New York: John Willey & Sons.

McAdam, D. 1982. *Political Process and the Development of Black Insurgency, 1930–70.* Chicago: University of Chicago Press.

Mendell, M. 2003. "The Social Economy in Quebec." Paper presented to the VIII Congreso Internacional del CLAD sobre la REforma del Estadoy de la Adminitracion publica, Panama, Oct. Accessed online at http://unpan1.un.org/intradoc/groups/public/documents/CLAD/clad0047506.pdf

Noël, A. 1996. "Vers un nouvel État-Providence? Enjeux démocratiques." *Politique et Sociétés* 30: 3–28.

– 2003. *Une loi contre la pauvreté: la nouvelle approche québécoise de lutte contre la pauvreté et l'Exclusion sociale,* available at: www.cpds.umontral.ca/356.htm

Painter, J. and M. Goodwin. 1995. "Local Governance and Concrete Research: Investigating the Uneven Development of Regulation." *Economy and Society* 24(3): 334–56.

Panet-Raymond, J. and R. Mayer. 1997. "The History of Community Development in Quebec." In *Community Organizing: Canadian Experiences,* eds. B. Wharf and M. Clague. Oxford: Oxford University Press.

Panet-Raymond, J. 1987. "Community Groups in Quebec: From Radical Action to Voluntarism for the State?" *Community Development Journal* 22(4): 281–86.

– 1992. "Partnership: Myth or Reality?" *Community Development Journal* 27(2): 156–65.

Phillips, S. 1991. "How Ottawa Blends: Shifting Government Relations with Interest Groups." In *How Ottawa Spends 1991–92: The Politics of Fragmentation,* ed. F. Abele. Ottawa: Carleton University Press.

– 2001. "More than Stakeholders: Reforming State-Voluntary Sector Relations." *Journal of Canadian Studies* 35(4): 182–202.

Saint-Martin, D. 2004. "Why So Much Opposition to Social Policy Change in Quebec?" Canadian Policy Research Networks, Ottawa.

Salée, D. 2003. "Transformative Politics, the State, and the Politics of Social Change in Quebec." In *Changing Canada: Political Economy as Transformation,* eds. W. Clement and L. Vosko. Kingston: McGill-Queen's Press.

Scott, K. 2003. *Funding Matters: The Impact of Canada's New Funding Regime on Nonprofit and Voluntary Organizations.* Ottawa: Canadian Council on Social Development.

Smith, M. 1998. "Nationalisme et politiques des mouvements sociaux: Les droits des gais et lesbiennes et l'incidence de la charte canadienne au Québec." *Politique et Sociétés* 17(3): 113–40.

Staggenborg, S. 1991. *The Pro-choice Movement: Organization and Activism in the Abortion Conflict.* Oxford: Oxford University Press.

Vaillancourt, Y. 2003. "The Quebec Model in Social Policy and Its Interface with Canada's Social Union." In *Forging the Canadian Social Union: SUFA and Beyond,* eds. S. Fortin, A. Noel and F. St-Hilaire. Montreal: Institute for Research on Public Policy.

Vaillancourt, Y. and L. Tremblay, eds. 2002. *Social Economy: Health and Welfare in Four Canadian Provinces.* Quebec: Fernwood Publishing and LAREPPS.

Vaillancourt, Y. and J.-L. Laville. 1998. "Les rapports entre associations et État: un enjeu politique." *Revue du MAUSS semestrielle* 11: 119–35.

Walker, J. 1991. *Mobilizing Interest Groups in America: Patrons, Professions and Social Movements.* Ann Arbor: University of Michigan Press.

White, D. 1997. "Contradictory Participation: Reflections on Community Action in Quebec." In *Community Organizing: Canadian Experiences,* eds. B. Wharf and M. Clague. Oxford: Oxford University Press.

– 2001. "Maîtriser un mouvement, dompter une idéologie – L'État et le secteur communautaire au Québec." *ISUMA* 2(2): 34–46.

– 2002. "Harnessing a Movement, Taming and Ideology on the State and the Third Sector in Québec." In *Improving Connections Between Governments and Nonprofit and Voluntary Organizations*, ed. K.L. Brock. Montreal and Kingston: McGill-Queen's University Press.

IV

Quebec-Canada Relations: New Dynamics, New Opportunities?

9

Quebec and the Canadian Federation: From the 1980 Referendum to the Summit of the Canadas

Thomas J. Courchene

Cet article retrace l'évolution des relations politiques et constitutionnelles d'une part entre le fédéral et les provinces et, d'autre part, entre le Québec et le reste du Canada, et ce, à compter du referendum de 1995 jusqu'à la déclaration en 2006 reconnaissant « que les Québécoises et les Québécois forment une nation au sein d'un Canada uni. » Sur le front fédéral-provincial, l'analyse traite des coupes effectuées dans les transferts fédéraux en matière de santé et de programmes sociaux à l'occasion du budget fédéral de 1995 de même que de l'apparition du déséquilibre fiscal et la multiplication des interventions fédérales dans des secteurs de compétence provinciale exclusive qui ont suivi. Cette revue se termine avec l'adoption du « fédéralisme d'ouverture » de Stephen Harper qui renverse plusieurs des initiatives mentionnées ci-dessus. En ce qui a trait plus spécifiquement au volet Québec-Canada, l'analyse post-référendaire contenue dans ce chapitre revient sur la Déclaration de Calgary, la Loi fédérale de Clarification, l'élection en 2003 du gouvernement libéral de Jean Charest et la création du Conseil de la Fédération. Le chapitre se penche ensuite sur ce qu'il est convenu d'appeler le sommet des Canadas en 2004 où Ottawa et les provinces ont formellement pris acte de la spécificité du Québec, le tout culminant avec la reconnaissance du Québec comme nation au sein d'un Canada uni.

INTRODUCTION

What a difference a few months can make for policy analysts! All appeared quiet on the Quebec front in the time frame of the fall 2003 Institute of Inter-governmental Relations Conference *Quebec and Canada in the New Century: New Dynamics – New Opportunities*. The Charest Liberals were at the helm and the forces of sovereignty seemed safely at bay. Not much more than a year later, however, the environment is markedly different. Charest's confrontation with the unions and civil society has not gone well. More importantly, the Bloc Québécois captured an astounding 54 seats and 49 percent of the popular vote in Quebec in the 28 June 2004 federal election. And this was in spite of the fact that, in the days running up to the vote, Pierre Pettigrew and Stephane Dion warned Quebecers that a vote for the BQ was, in effect, a vote for sovereignty. PQ leader Bernard Landry as much as confirmed this by suggesting the likelihood of a third referendum in 2009 (i.e., after the PQ is presumed to have regained power). Moreover, with the Paul Martin Liberals reduced to a minority position in the House of Commons, the Bloc Québécois holds the balance of power in the sense that under some realistic scenarios it could bring the government down and precipitate an election. Hence, here too, uncertainty is now the order of the day. As I concluded in an earlier assessment of Quebec/Canada relations (1990), the lights at Canada's constitutional crossroads are not flashing green, nor are they flashing red. Rather, they remain, as the title suggests, *Forever Amber*.

In order to reflect on the changing (current and longer-term) nature of Quebec/Canada relations in the 21st century, the analytical storyline on both the political and economic fronts must begin much earlier. Accordingly, the second section focuses selectively on Quebec/Canada political relations in the 1980–1995 (or inter-referenda) era, dealing in turn with Charter federalism, the Meech and Charlottetown Accords and the 1995 referendum. The third section presents a similar highlighting of political milestones under the Chrétien era, focusing on Quebec's relations with the provinces under the rubric of pan-Canadian provincialism and then on Quebec-Ottawa relations in terms of the *Clarity Act* and the sponsorship scandal. Attention then shifts in the fourth section to Quebec/Canada economic relations dealing in turn with the implications flowing from NAFTA, the knowledge-based economy (KBE), Global City Regions, and "hourglass federalism" (or the federal invasion of provincial jurisdiction). Next, (Quebec/Canada Dynamics in Century 21) pulls together some of the observations and implications that arise from integrating the political and economic strands of the analysis in order to briefly document and assess the evolving nature of Quebec's political, economic and constitutional relationship with the rest of Canada. The final substantive section of the paper proper, Quebec and the Summit of the Canadas, brings the foregoing analysis to bear on the First Ministers' Meetings on health care and equalization in the fall of 2004. Attention is directed in turn to the proposals for health care and equalization arising out of the July 2004 Council of the Federation (COF). This includes the offer to Ottawa to take over responsibility for pharmacare and the rather historic recognition of Quebec's specificity in the Canadian federation as part of the pharmacare proposal. The remainder of the section then focuses on the politics, process and policy leading up to what is labelled as the "Summit of the Canadas." Finally, the Postscript focuses on the First Ministers' Meetings – in September 2004 on health care and October 2004 on equalization – replete with a few concluding observations.

QUEBEC/CANADA POLITICAL RELATIONS IN THE INTER-REFERENDA PERIOD (1980–1995)

CHARTER FEDERALISM

In the wake of the 60–40 victory for the federalist forces in the 1980 Quebec referendum, Trudeau launched the 1980–82 constitutional round which culminated with the patriation of the *Constitution Act, 1867*, and the enactment of the *Constitution Act* 1982 replete with the enshrinement of the *Canadian Charter of Rights and Freedoms*. That flags flew at half-mast over l'Assemblée nationale was unfortunate, to be sure, but Quebec's non-signatory status was only to be expected from a sovereignist government, or so the storyline presumably went. In any event, the Charter took hold almost immediately with Canadians, even in Quebec, so much so that the cleavages in the federation shifted from being territorially-based to being rights-based – Charter interests vs. vested interests, as it were. Indeed, the traditional territorial interests/cleavages arguably shifted from the provinces to the First Nations (and Aboriginals more generally), with the Charter intriguingly serving as catalyst.

Roughly coincident (and obviously related) was the emergence, initially in Alberta, of a new philosophy of Canadian federalism, the so-called symmetric or triple-E federalism. At the most general level, this meant equal powers for all provinces, equal-per-capita representation in the House of Commons and equal provincial representation in the Senate. The related and more familiar version is the "triple-E Senate" – equal (by province), elected and effective. The argument for symmetrical federalism (or the notion that all provinces are equal and must be so treated) is a peculiar one coming from Alberta, since this province is the principal beneficiary of the most lucrative asymmetry in the federation, namely crown ownership of sub-surface resource rights. Admittedly, this arose because Ottawa initially withheld sub-surface rights from Alberta, but it is an asymmetry nonetheless. The larger puzzle is why the most fiscally powerful province would be the lead advocate for a Triple-E Senate, when the result would surely be to curtail the powers of the provinces and their premiers.

Meanwhile, the second coming of Robert Bourassa (1985) saw Quebec embrace *le virage vers les marchés*. Importantly, this shift toward markets reflected a societal realization that Quebec's future would and should ultimately lie in North American, rather than in Canadian, economic space. Some of this was no doubt a response to the symbolic alienation emanating from the constitutional patriation process. More was due to the realization that with the "economic capital" of Canada shifting west (in light of energy price hikes) it made far more sense for Quebecers to turn to the markets that were much closer and much bigger, namely the US northeast, rather than somehow leap-frogging Ontario to compete in western Canadian markets. The most tangible result of this societal shift was that Quebec in effect gave Canada the FTA in the 1988 federal election by delivering a "super majority" of its seats (63 of 75) to the Mulroney Tories. Had Mulroney won only a simple majority of Quebec seats, the FTA would have been lost.

THE MEECH LAKE AND CHARLOTTETOWN ACCORDS[1]

The next highlighted milestone en route to the 1995 Referendum is the 1987–1990 Meech Lake Accord and ratification process. Designed to bring Quebec back into the Canadian constitutional family, the Accord, among other meas-ures, explicitly recognized the "distinct society" nature of Quebec. The 1987 First Ministers' unanimous endorsement of Quebec's five principles for as-senting to the Constitution gradually eroded over the three-year ratification period. Part of this was the result of the election of new premiers (Wells in Newfoundland, McKenna in New Brunswick and Filmon in Manitoba) who were, by definition, not signatories of the Accord. And in the case of Wells and McKenna, they actively campaigned against Meech in their respective elections. Considerable responsibility for this erosion of support in the rest of Canada must also rest with Bourassa himself and his decision in 1989 to re-sort to the "notwithstanding clause" to promote French on commercial signs.[2] Arguably, this was one of the contributors to the larger reason for the underly-ing malaise on the part of non-Quebec Canada, namely that special status for Quebec was offside with "Charter federalism," as elaborated earlier. The ulti-mate irony here is that Meech Lake was effectively hoisted on its own petard. The essence of the Accord was asymmetric treatment for Quebec (the dis-tinct-society clause) embedded within a symmetric (i.e., unanimity) ratification formula. On the eve of La Fête de la St. Jean and presumably drawing inspira-tion from the Charter, some provinces simply exercised their equality or symmetrical right to effectively veto the asymmetrical Accord. While it was no doubt of enormous comfort to Canadians that the tumultuous St. Jean Baptiste parade took place under Robert Bourassa's watch, the demise of Meech not only triggered dramatic political changes but, as well, set the sovereignty clock ticking inevitably toward a second referendum.

By way of elaboration, in the month or so prior to the formal collapse of Meech, federal Environment Minister Lucien Bouchard, joined by five other Quebec Tory MPs, bolted from the Mulroney government to sit as independ-ents. Initially committed to not forming a formal party, all this changed after

La Fête: within two months none other than current BQ leader Gilles Duceppe became the first elected Bloc Québécois MP (winning a by-election in the Montreal riding of Laurier-Sainte-Marie), even though the BQ's formal founding convention was not held until June 1991. And in the 1993 federal election, Bouchard led his 54-seat Bloc Québécois to the status of Her Majesty's Loyal Opposition.

Premier Robert Bourassa's response to the collapse of Meech was to launch two commissions on the future of Quebec. One of these was an internal Quebec Liberal Party assessment that produced the Allaire Report (after its Chair, Jean Allaire) which, among other things, spelled out twenty-two powers that ought to be transferred to the provinces and, in particular, to Quebec. Ironically, the Allaire Report served as the vehicle for the rise of Mario Dumont, initially as the leader of the Liberal youth wing and, later, as the head of the Action démocratique du Québec (ADQ). The second and more important response was the bi-partisan Bélanger-Campeau Commission, charged with conducting cross-province hearings and research and then reporting on the future of Quebec. Beyond providing a legitimate venue for keeping sovereignty issues front and centre in Quebec, the Bélanger-Campeau Commission provided a valuable platform for commissioners Lucien Bouchard, and to a lesser degree Jacques Parizeau and Mario Dumont, to enhance their profile among Quebecers.

Post-Meech, the Mulroney Tories were also active on the constitutional file, striking both the Spicer Commission to take the pulse of ordinary Canadians on renewing federalism, and the more formal Beaudoin-Dobbie joint Senate-House Constitutional Committee. What finally resulted from all of this was the Charlottetown Accord – a cobbling together of a myriad of concessions designed to elicit support from Canadians in all walks of life for an omnibus package that included numerous measures that privileged Quebec (e.g. a commitment that Quebec would have a guarantee of 25 percent of the House of Commons seats and of three Supreme Court Justices), but that also included much of the content of Meech, several key concessions to First Nations, and a collection of other measures running the gamut from regional policy to the Bank of Canada. As a result, there were no enthusiastic supporters of Charlottetown, only those that on balance believed that it merited a "Yes" vote in the referendum. However, associated with each of the major concessions were passionate and often non-overlapping opponents. Complicating this already complex Charlottetown process was the fact that several provinces had, post-Meech, enacted legislation requiring a referendum on all future constitutional proposals. More complicating still, the Bélanger-Campeau Commission had essentially committed Quebec to another referendum on sovereignty by October of 1992. Ottawa reacted by calling a national referendum on the Charlottetown Accord for October 26, 1992. This was an important strategic initiative since it allowed Bourassa to substitute the national referendum on Charlottetown for the Bélanger-Campeau commitment to hold a Quebec referendum on sovereignty. In the event, fully 60 percent of Quebecers voted against the Charlottetown Accord. Thankfully, the Accord was also rejected in several other provinces (and even in Ontario, if one were to require the "Yes" votes to be a majority of total votes cast, including the spoiled ballots). While the defeat of Charlottetown did succeed in deferring the second sovereignty referendum, this deferral was not to be for long.

THE 1995 REFERENDUM

Post-Charlottetown, there was a wholesale changing of the guard on the political front. Charlottetown was Mulroney's last stand, and in 1993 the Tory convention elected Kim Campbell as leader and Prime Minister. Earlier (1990), Jean Chrétien had replaced John Turner as Liberal leader. In the November 1993 federal election, the 1984–1993 Mulroney coalition evaporated completely, with the Kim Campbell Tories losing all but two seats, including that of the leader. Chrétien's Liberals emerged as victorious, but faced over 100 opposition members from parties that had not won any seats in the 1988 election. Lucien Bouchard's Bloc Québécois became the official opposition on the basis of the 54 (of 75) seats it won in Quebec. Preston Manning's Reform Party converted its opposition to the Charlottetown Accord, *inter alia*, into 52 seats in Western Canada.

On the Quebec front, the PQ returned to power in the 1994 election. Although the popular vote was a virtual dead heat, Jacques Parizeau and the PQ won a comfortable majority of seats over Daniel Johnson and the PLQ (Liberals). In spite of the fact that the PQ share of the popular vote was considerably less than what was expected, Parizeau nonetheless committed the province to a second referendum on sovereignty (eventually scheduled for October 30, 1995).

Canada was again in play!

The pace of events then escalated dramatically. Already viewed as having eclipsed Parizeau as the champion of Quebec independence, Bouchard's status among Quebecers reached divine-like proportions in the wake of his miraculous recovery from necrotizing fasciitis in the fall of 1994, so much so that Parizeau invited him to be co-chair of the "Yes" side. Among Bouchard's first moves was to bring Mario Dumont on board, thereby uniting the PQ, BQ and ADQ under the sovereignist mantle. Their 12 June 1995 signed agreement endorsed the following approach to the Referendum question:

> The sovereignty question was to be put in conjunction with an offer of a political and economic partnership with Canada that would follow a Yes vote. Ottawa

would have a year to decide. If no agreement could be reached, Quebec would move to full independence (Martin, 1997, 280).

Even with this conciliatory question the Parizeau-Bouchard "Yes" forces were trailing badly a month prior to the referendum. Then came the master stroke: Parizeau stepped aside and handed over control of the "Yes" forces to Lucien Bouchard. As all Canadians recall, it was only the eleventh-hour, 100,000-strong Parc du Canada rally that, arguably, saved the day. The "Yes" (independence) side lost by the slimmest of margins – 49.4 percent to 50.6 percent. Following his "money and the ethnic vote" comment on the referendum results on the night of the vote, Parizeau immediately resigned as Premier. Lucien Bouchard resigned his seat in the House of Commons and was shortly thereafter acclaimed premier of Quebec. This was only half of what Bouchard had long desired. The other half – Quebec independence – was, for the immediate future, a spent force.

CANADA/QUEBEC POLITICAL RELATIONS IN THE CHRÉTIEN ERA

PAN-CANADIAN PROVINCIALISM

The combination of a) Paul Martin's massive cuts to provincial transfers in his 1995 budget and his accompanying request that the provinces help design Canada's social policy principles in the CHST era, b) the emergence post-NAFTA of a north-south trading axis, and c) the perception if not the reality that Ottawa had bungled the 1995 Referendum, interacted to spawn a very innovative and exciting period in Canadian federalism, namely pan-Canadian provincialism. The underlying reality, fully recognized by the provinces, was that Ottawa was both fiscally able and politically more than willing to invade provincial jurisdictions if the provinces did not adopt a pan-Canadian approach to their collective actions. This might not prevent federal intrusions, but it would at least make them politically more difficult. The instrument chosen by the provinces (at least the non-Quebec provinces) for addressing these pan-Canadian policy spillovers and for advancing provincial interests was the revitalization of the Annual Premiers' Conferences (APCs). Under the aegis of the APC (and in response to Paul Martin's request), the Ministerial Council on Social Policy Renewal and Reform released its Report to the Premiers which, inter alia, embodied 15 principles to underpin social Canada. This document was endorsed by the premiers at the 1996 Jasper APC along with a further request (perhaps influenced by my 1996 ACCESS paper) that the Ministerial Council design provincial and/or provincial/territorial mechanisms and processes in order to develop and promote adherence to national principles and standards. The resulting mechanisms (both provincial/territorial and provincial/territorial/federal) were presented at the 1997 St. Andrews APC and further honed for, and ratified by, the 1998 Saskatoon APC.

By this time it became clear that the initiative and momentum for social policy reform had shifted to the provinces. Indeed, a year earlier, the 1997 federal budget took a page out of the Report to the Premiers and introduced the Canada Child Tax Benefit (CCTB). The CCTB was an exercise in creative federal/provincial co-determination. Ottawa sharply increased refundable child tax benefits to low-income families via the federal income tax system. For their part the provinces were allowed to reduce their payments for children in welfare-receiving families by a similar amount, provided that these monies were re-directed to other programs relating to child support in low-income families. With this model in mind, shortly after the summer 1998 Saskatoon APC the federal government joined with the provinces to formalize this creative federal/provincial co-determination in the form of the 1999 Framework To Improve the Social Union for Canadians, generally referred to as SUFA (Social Union Framework Agreement). Among SUFA's provisions are the following:

- a set of social policy principles, most adapted from Report to the Premiers;
- mutual recognition of occupational qualifications across provinces;
- creative ways to allow the exercise of the federal spending power in areas of exclusive provincial jurisdiction provided that a majority of provinces were on side and that provinces would have a role in both policy design and implementation flexibility; and
- a dispute avoidance and resolution procedure that would allow for third-party fact-finding (which could apply to the *Canada Health Act*).

All in all, a flexible intergovernmental and co-determinational process designed to allow the federation to accommodate external and internal pressures for change.

Nonetheless, readers will have recognized that what is missing from this overview of SUFA and pan-Canadian provincialism more generally is that Quebec was *not* a formal party to any of this. One could argue that this would follow directly from the fact that the PQ was in power in Quebec. For example, just prior to his defeat at the hands of Jacques Parizeau, Premier Daniel Johnson *was* a signatory to the Agreement on Internal Trade (AIT) in 1994. However, there is more at play here than whether Quebec is governed by the PLQ or the PQ, since all Quebec parties lined up against SUFA. One obvious substantive reason for this was that SUFA formally recognized the existence of the federal spending power in areas of exclusive provincial jurisdiction (although it must be noted that Quebec's long-standing desire to curb or eliminate the federal spending power in provincial jurisdiction necessarily requires a recognition of its existence in the first place). The larger issue is that Quebec is not about to enter an agreement with Ottawa that would impinge upon those policy areas that Quebec deems to fall under its exclusive jurisdiction. The issues surrounding the AIT are quite different, relating as they do to reciprocal responsibilities among and between equal constitutional players. In any event, SUFA represents a valuable instrument in an era when federal/provincial policy externalities and spillovers are ubiquitous. And even though Quebec is not a signatory, it is the province most likely to take advantage of any flexibility in future SUFA-influenced accords. (More on this later.)

By way of a further aside with respect to SUFA, the view of the Canadian policy community is, as I interpret it, that SUFA has been ineffective and/or irrelevant. To a degree, this criticism rings true. Part of the reason for this is that, post-SUFA, Ottawa's fiscal position has improved dramatically, both in absolute terms and relative to the provinces. Hence, unlike the time frame when SUFA was signed, the federal government is now fiscally able to drive home agreements with the provinces without involving the constraints of the SUFA process. But there are attendant costs to this. For example, both the 2000 and 2003 federal/provincial health accords were viewed by Ottawa as "buying" new health-care programs (home care, etc.). However, because these accords were anything but SUFA-informed, the provinces viewed the additional funds as unconditional transfers. In my view, buying leverage with the provinces will henceforth require the flexibility of SUFA-informed accords, rather than top-down Ottawa-driven agreements.

Two remaining initiatives relating to pan-Canadian provincialism merit highlight. The first of these is the 1998 Calgary Declaration. Although only a page long, this is a remarkable document because it reveals the extent to which the provinces other than Quebec were anxious to back away from the earlier "symmetrical federalism" philosophy. It is especially fitting that the declaration was signed in Calgary, the hotbed of the erstwhile symmetry rhetoric. Two of the principles are especially significant:

- "In Canada's federal system, where respect for diversity and equality underlies unity, the unique character of Quebec society, including its French-speaking majority, its culture and its tradition of civil law, is fundamental to the wellbeing of Canada. Consequently, the legislature and Government of Quebec have a role to protect and develop the unique character of Quebec society within Canada."
- "If any future constitutional amendment confers powers on one province, these powers must be available to all provinces."

In tandem, these provisions not only formally recognize the specificity of Quebec but endorse future Ottawa/Quebec deals provided they are offered to other provinces as well. This is a recognition of *de facto* asymmetry and, to a degree, *de jure* asymmetry as well. Since the Calgary Declaration was about Quebec, only the nine other provinces were signatories. And to add to its significance, the Declaration was passed in all nine of these provincial legislatures, often with considerable fanfare.

The final and, arguably, the most important exercise in pan-Canadian provincialism is the recent all-province agreement to embrace Premier Charest's proposal for a *Council of the Federation* (henceforth COF). Cynics may claim that this is the other provinces' way of thanking Jean Charest for wresting power from the PQ. However, it should be clear from the above analysis that the COF represents the obvious final step in the process that began with the revitalization of the APCs. Not surprisingly, therefore, the other provinces eagerly embraced the Quebec proposal. As an aside, Quebec nationalists can embrace the Council of the Federation (since it is an interprovincial body that excludes Ottawa) and yet not be party to SUFA because SUFA includes the fiscally dominant national jurisdiction as a party to an agreement about policies in provincial jurisdictions). To be sure, the issue foremost in the minds of the premiers when they created the Council was to utilize it as a vehicle for pressing Ottawa on the fiscal imbalance issue, one of the driving forces of which was the report of Quebec's Séguin Commission (named after Yves Séguin, until recently Quebec's finance minister) on the vertical fiscal imbalance in the federation. Important as this issue is to the provinces, the Council will nonetheless also be drawn into many other coordination and monitoring roles across a wide range of provincial policy responsibilities, running the gamut from overseeing aspects of the *Canada Health Act* to monitoring the interprovincial economic and social unions.

Overall, therefore, the post-1995-referendum period has coincided with the recognition by the provinces that unless they get their collective act together and internalize some of the resulting externalities, Ottawa will step in and do this coordination for them, and in the process erode some of their powers. While this collective decision by the provinces makes eminent sense in its own right, it is also the case that this new pan-Canadian role for the provinces is not independent of the manner in which the new global order is providing incentives for Ottawa to intervene in areas of exclusive provincial jurisdiction. Prior to focusing on this emerging relationship between federalism and the new global order, the analysis turns to the manner in which the Chrétien Liberals approached the Quebec issue in the post-1995-referendum period.

THE CLARITY ACT AND SPONSORSHIP

While the provinces were practising pan-Canadianism (the APCs and the Council of the Federation) and even accommodating Quebec (the Calgary Declaration), Ottawa was engaged in "combative" federalism, as reflected for example in Stephane Dion's letter-writing campaign against Bouchard and the separatists in the editorial pages of *Le Devoir* and *La Presse*, (e.g., if Canada is divisible, so is Quebec), and culminating in June 2000, with the *Clarity Act*. As prelude to this legislation, Ottawa submitted a reference to the Supreme Court of Canada, the ruling on which can be paraphrased as follows – Quebec does not have the right to secede unilaterally from Canada, but the rest of Canada has an obligation to negotiate Quebec's separation if a clear majority of Quebecers have voted in favour of separation. Ottawa responded to this ruling by elaborating, *inter alia*, on the meaning of "unilaterally" and "clear majority" and incorporating all of this "clarification" into the appropriately named *Clarity Act*. As indicated, the focus in the Act is on whether the referendum question is clear and whether there is a clear majority, along with the manner in which the rest of Canada would go about negotiating with Quebec, should the occasion arise. Not only does Jean Chrétien view the *Clarity Act* as one of his proudest achievements (www.canadianlawsite.com/clarity-act.htm), but there is a widespread view that the fact that the passage of the *Clarity Act* provoked so little concern among Quebecers was an important part of the reason why Lucien Bouchard stepped down as premier. More generally, the tough position that the Liberals took toward Quebec has come to be viewed as largely responsible for the erosion of support for sovereignty and for the victory of Jean Charest over Bernard Landry in the 2003 Quebec election.

While the passing of the *Clarity Act* did indeed coincide with the decline in support for independence, correlation is not the same as causation. In particular, my admittedly not widely accepted view is that the underlying economic realities also played an important role. Toward this end, note that during the 1995 referendum, Lucien Bouchard and company were able to get away with the claim that there would be no economic cost to separation. Some of this had to do with the fact that, as of 1995, it was far from clear that Ottawa would be able to get its own fiscal house in order, and in any event if it did so it was only because it was transferring its deficit to Quebec and the other provinces via dramatic CHST cuts. Moreover, presumably out of concern that the referendum process was running off the rails, Paul Martin asserted that independence would cost Quebec one million jobs, a sufficiently outrageous claim which served to transfer the cost-of-separation issue from the realm of economics to the political or rhetorical realm. Post-referendum, however, the evidence was clear – Quebec's economy did plummet, especially in relation to Ontario. As the Quebec economy gradually recovered, and as Ottawa tidied up its fiscal house (and indeed became the fiscal virtuoso of the G7), it became progressively more difficult to make any sort of case to the effect that Quebec would be better off economically outside of Canada, at least for the critical transition period which could be quite lengthy. Arguably, this was also part of the underlying environment which contributed to ensuring that the *Clarity Act* would *not* precipitate an upsurge in support for sovereignty.

However, as will be elaborated, there were and are other and more fundamental factors at work – north–south integration and the advent of the
knowledge-based economy – both of which are serving to alter Quebec's economic and political role within Canada. Moreover, the *Clarity Act* may well
be viewed by the PQ and BQ as a convenient "blueprint" for the process of
separation. But this is getting way ahead of the analytical storyline.

The other Canada/Quebec political development selected for highlight is
the sponsorship program and the consequent resurgence of the Bloc Québécois
in the 2004 federal election. If the *Clarity Act* was the stick in Ottawa's post-
referendum approach to Quebec, the sponsorship program was intended to be
the proverbial carrot – currying Quebec favour by raising the flag and lowering the (accountability) standard, as it were. This would have been serious
enough on its own, but Paul Martin attempted to take the high road here, not
only accepting no responsibility for, let alone knowledge of, the affair but
also associating it with the Chrétien wing of the Liberal Party and inadvert-
ently or otherwise embarrassing the Québécois political class. Moreover, it
was somewhat ironic that, despite the sponsorship scandal, Chrétien was in
this time frame probably held in higher regard in Quebec than at any time in
his long career, due in large measure to his standing up to George Bush and
keeping Canadian troops out of Iraq. In any event, rather than making the
expected gains in Quebec in the 2004 election, the Martin Liberals fell to 21
seats, with Gilles Duceppe and the Bloc winning 54 seats and 49 percent of
the popular vote in Quebec. Arguably more importantly, the Bloc denied the
Liberal/NDP tandem a majority coalition and, in this sense, the Bloc held the
balance of power in the House of Commons.

While it is obviously the case that the Bloc garnered the protest votes of a
goodly number of federalist and nationalist voters, the fact remains that we
are once again, and surely unexpectedly, in uncharted political waters. The
Parti Québécois is already talking about retaking L'Assemblée nationale and
holding yet another referendum by decade's end.

As a companion to the above overview of Quebec/Canada *political* relations, the analysis now turns to a similar overview of Quebec/Canada *economic*
relations, thereby setting the stage for an overall political-economy assessment of Quebec/Canada relations in the 21st century.

QUEBEC/CANADA ECONOMIC RELATIONS

QUEBEC AND NAFTA

With the FTA and NAFTA serving as catalysts, all provinces' trade has shifted
sharply north–south, relative to east–west. In Quebec's case, in 1989 (the first
year of the FTA) exports to its sister provinces exceeded its exports to the US

– 21.2 percent of GDP for east–west exports (or exports to the rest of Canada) and 16.0 percent of GDP for north–south exports (or exports to the USA). By 2001, however, this had changed dramatically. Quebec's north–south exports increased to 33.6 percent of its GDP while its exports to the rest of Canada fell to 19.4 percent. Indeed, as of 2001, all provinces except Manitoba exported more to the US than they did to the rest of Canada.

In effect, Canada has become a series of north–south, cross-border economies rather than a single east–west national economy. And because Canada's provinces/regions tend to differ industrially more from each other than from their cross-border counterparts, the provinces' attempt to enhance their prospects in North America will tend to result rather naturally in an enhanced degree of policy decentralization and operational asymmetry. It was this reality that led Colin Telmer and me to signal the emergence of North American region states (1998).

Several important implications flow from this development. First, Quebec's economic future is clearly in NAFTA economic space, not Canadian economic space. Compared to the province's trade dependence on the rest of Canada in 1995, let alone 1980, the economic costs of further loosening economic ties with the rest of Canada are now much reduced. (By way of maintaining perspective, the later analysis will also argue that the benefits of independence are also reduced).

Second, as north–south trade integration heightens, all provinces will become increasingly tolerant of Quebec's nationalist vision of its role in the federation, since they too will want greater degrees of policy freedom. The best example here is that the "Alberta Advantage" slogan (which promises that this province will have the lowest tax rates in NAFTA, let alone in Canada) is giving way in some Alberta quarters to a "firewall" vision of Alberta/Canada relations. In a sense, therefore, the earlier noted, post-Charter focus on symmetry as a philosophical goal of Canadian federalism has been trumped by the provincial/regional realities of North American trade integration. Phrased differently, this may be the international (NAFTA) economic reality underpinning the domestic politics of the 1998 Calgary Declaration.

The third implication is more troublesome. The provinces have become so dependent on NAFTA trade they can effectively be held hostage to interruptions in their access to the US market. And because provincial policies can and do differ widely, these border interruptions may affect the individual provinces differently (e.g. the softwood lumber issue affects B.C. but not New Brunswick), which in turn severely complicates national policy. Arguably, the Council of the Federation (COF) could play a most useful role in aggregating provincial interests in such situations. Ottawa should welcome having this pan-provincial body make the initial attempt to wrestle with issues that frequently play very differently, if not in a zero-sum manner, across the various provinces.

Fourth, it would seem to follow from the above observations that many provinces would eagerly trade off some of their power in the Ottawa corridors for more influence in Washington. This is reflected in the several proposals for broadening and deepening NAFTA. Relatedly, most of the provinces participate in Canada/US associations of heads of government. Indeed, Quebec is a member of two of these – with New England Governors and Maritime Premiers and with Ontario and the Great Lakes Governors. Others have Memoranda of Understandings (MOUs) with their cross-border states – the Alberta-Montana MOU, for example. Arguably, along the lines of Wolfe (2003), Blank (2002) and my own work (2003b), these represent attempts to broaden and deepen NAFTA from the bottom up, as it were – to "democratize" North American integration by bringing the states and provinces more fully into the political economy of North America.

North American trade integration is only one of the forces that is forging new Quebec-Canada and Quebec-North America economic linkages. Attention now turns to two other forces – the advent of the KBE and the associated rise of global city regions.

QUEBEC AND THE KNOWLEDGE-BASED ECONOMY (KBE)

The advent of the knowledge/information revolution will privilege human capital in much the same way that the Industrial Revolution privileged physical capital. Indeed, knowledge and human capital are now at the forefront in terms of the core policy objectives – competitiveness and wealth creation; achieving acceptable income distribution; and enhancing living standards. In terms of the latter, Lester Thurow (1993) is eminently quotable: "If capital is borrowable, raw materials are buyable and technology is copyable, what are you left with if you want to run a high-wage economy? Only skills, there isn't anything else." While this is an exciting development in its own right since it puts citizens and their human capital development centre-stage in terms of both economic and social policy, it is also fundamental to the evolution of Quebec/Canada relations since the constitutional powers needed to pursue a citizen-first policy are largely provincial powers. Indeed, this was the core of my message (1991) to the Bélanger-Campeau Commission, namely that in light of the fact that many of the policy levers traditionally associated with national sovereignty are now being incorporated in trade agreements (tariffs, trade policy and aspects of regulatory policy) or driven by global best practice (monetary policy),

> ... citizens will increasingly view "sovereignty" as the ability to have some influence on how they live and work and play. One can argue whether or not the level of government to deliver this is the provincial government or the local

government but, under our federal system, it is clearly *not* the national government. Indeed, will there be much left of sovereignty in the millennium other than "distinct societies? (*The Community of the Canadas,* 1991, 11).

I then added that after a further decade of north–south integration, during which Canada's provinces/regions would intensify their north-south trading axes, the rest of Canada would become largely indifferent to Quebec's choice of policy instruments, an assertion that has resonance with the later Calgary Declaration and, more recently, with the "opting out" provision with respect to pharmacare in the July, 2004 Council of the Federation meeting (see below).

In more general terms, the central implication arising from the KBE in terms of achieving meaningful sovereignty in the information era is that the KBE significantly increases the role of those powers that lie in provincial jurisdiction. (Note that this is not the same as saying that the KBE enhances the powers of the provinces, as the subsequent analysis makes clear). While it would not be correct to say that Quebec is now indifferent about acquiring new powers (e.g. the province would obviously like greater room to manoeuvre in terms of negotiating trade and cultural agreements), the fact is that under the KBE sovereignty will be more about exercising *existing provincial powers* than acquiring further powers. Moreover, the interaction between language and culture on the one hand and human capital development on the other is sufficiently close that Quebec will be able to play a larger role in the human capital development of its citizens than will be the case for any other province. In other words, language provides an environment within which Quebec will have more room to "policy determine" its KBE future. Or in terms of sovereignty, the emergence of the KBE allows Quebec to move toward a fuller nationhood *within* the Canadian state.

From this follows an even more important corollary: the key to Quebec's future in the Canadian state lies in gaining access to revenues sufficient to make use of its existing powers. Hence, Quebec's rallying call has, appropriately, shifted from "acess to more powers" to "access to more revenues." Small wonder then that restoring fiscal balance in the federation is Quebec's foremost priority. And for somewhat similar reasons (see below), this is also the number one priority of the other nine provinces as well.

GLOBAL CITY REGIONS (GCRS)

Global city regions (Toronto, Montreal, Vancouver, Calgary/Edmonton) are emerging as the dynamic economic motors of the knowledge/information era (Courchene 2000). This is so in large part because these GCRs are home to dense concentrations of knowledge and human capital networks (health, biosciences, R and D, universities, corporate services, cultural, etc.). Following

Harris (2003), Canada's future in terms of productivity growth and living standards will depend on how well our GCRs will fare against US and international GCRs.

The complicating issue here is the following. On the one hand, cities are constitutionless – they are the creatures of the provinces. On the other hand, with their economic and political star in ascendancy the GCRs want to become more fully and more formally integrated into the system of intergovernmental relations and fiscal federalism. Intriguingly, the provinces, despite their constitutional supremacy over cities, find themselves in a dilemma of sorts. Either they cater to the demands of the cities for greater autonomy, financial flexibility and infrastructure (rights that many international GCRs already have) or the cities will band together and pressure the federal government to satisfy these demands. Actually, there is, in principle at least, a third option, namely that the GCRs can aspire to become "city provinces," like the city-Länder of Germany (Berlin, Bremen and Hamburg). The power of the GCRs is such that they *will* play a more important political, economic and even jurisdictional role in the Canadian federation, the only issue is *how* they will play this role and how this will impact on the various provinces.

Up to this point, the lens for viewing the implications of the KBE has been a provincial lens. But Ottawa is much more than a spectator in all of this. Indeed, it is actively engaged in finding ways that it, too, can get access to the policy levers that deal with cities and citizens. Enter "hourglass federalism."

KBE INTERGOVERNMENTAL RELATIONS: *HOURGLASS FEDERALISM*

It did not take the federal government long to realize that nation-building and electoral saleability in the KBE is not about old-style resource-intensive mega projects but, rather, has everything to do with citizens' issues – education, health, training and the like. Indeed, and as already noted, with knowledge at the cutting edge of competitiveness, investment in education/skills and human capital generally holds the key to competitiveness and cohesion alike, both of which are of obvious interest to central governments of all nation states, federal or unitary. And since the performance of Canada's cities, especially the GCRs, will determine productivity growth and living standards, this too comes into Ottawa's sights.

Cast in this light, it is clear that politically, economically and electorally these policy areas are far too important to be rendered off-limits to Ottawa by whatever the Constitution may or may not say. So the operational objective for Ottawa becomes one of finding convenient avenues and processes by which it can interact directly with cities and citizens. Not only did Ottawa find a way to do this, but it did so in such a manner that cities and citizens alike welcomed the federal intervention.

In a recent article (2004), I have called this "hourglass federalism," namely Ottawa's use of the spending power and other measures to privilege cities and citizens, leaving the provinces increasingly as the squeezed middle of the division-of-powers hourglass. Hourglass federalism evolved in the following manner. First, to make room for these new areas on the policy agenda, Ottawa transferred aspects of last-paradigm's nation building (forestry, mining, tourism, fishing and energy) to the provinces. Second, Ottawa got its fiscal house in order in large measure by downloading its deficit to the provinces. The key initiatives here were the massive CHST cuts contained in Paul Martin's 1995 budget. Third, while these cuts were viewed by most analysts as cuts to health transfers, they had precisely the opposite effect. Since health was at the very top of all the provinces' priority list, it simply could not be cut. What happened in all provinces is that funds were directed from here, there and everywhere to sustain, indeed increase, health-care spending. Fourth, the result is that medicare is accounting for over 40 percent of program spending for many provinces and still rising, while spending on most other areas is declining. Fifth, this has opened the way for Ottawa to go around the provinces and to deal directly with these cash-starved areas, whether relating to citizens (millennium fellowships, Canada Research Chairs, the Canada Child Tax Benefit, early child development, etc.) or to cities (the GST exemption and the promise of a share of the federal sales tax). In passing, it is appropriate to note that Canadians may well be very happy with hourglass federalism, i.e., with the federal government playing a more active role in a variety of areas falling under provincial jurisdictions. While this is an important observation it is somewhat aside from the issue at hand.

Intriguingly, the provinces are well and truly trapped by hourglass federalism. As medicare budgets inexorably approach 50 percent of program spending, the provinces will have to dip deeper and more broadly into existing spending levels of other policy areas. There would appear to be only three ways for the provinces to extricate themselves from this dilemma. One way is to upload aspects of medicare to Ottawa. A second is to download medicare to citizens (via privatization/delisting or by imposing dedicated taxes/premiums, with Ontario doing both in its 2004 budget). The third is for Ottawa to address the vertical fiscal balance in the federation (i.e., to provide the provinces with funds sufficient to maintain medicare at sustainable levels, consistent with addressing their other expenditure responsibilities).

Enter the July 2004 Council of the Federation conference in Niagara-on-the-Lake. In a move described by Ralph Klein as a "brilliant strategy" and one that caught all Canadians by surprise, the premiers unanimously proposed to upload (i.e., to turn over responsibility for) pharmacare to the federal government. At one level this makes eminent sense since Ottawa controls drug patent laws (e.g., the length of time before a generic version of a drug can come on the market) and it is Ottawa that oversees drug testing/drug approvals, all of which have a major influence on the cost of drugs and, therefore, complicate provincial responsibility for prescription drugs. Moreover, Prime Minister Martin campaigned for a national pharmacare program as the next major step in the evolution of medicare so that at another level this provides a way for Martin to create such a national program. This COF proposal fed into the first ministers' meeting (FMM) on health care scheduled for 13–15 September 2004, and will be elaborated on in more detail below.

However, this 2004 FMM was bound to have an impact well beyond the financial evolution of medicare because many of the economic, political and jurisdictional issues highlighted in the above analysis would inevitably feed into this health care summit. Indeed, so much was at stake here that the FMM holds the promise of being one of the signal societal events in terms of determining the evolution of Quebec/Canada relations. As such, assessment of the role of the FMM in the context of the above analysis will constitute the concluding (Postscript) section of the paper. As prelude to this exercise in societal R*ealpolitik*, the following section draws out some analytical observations arising from marrying the foregoing Quebec/Canada economic and political assessments with an eye toward suggesting new opportunities or dynamics for Quebec/Canada relations.

QUEBEC-CANADA DYNAMICS IN CENTURY 21

The quarter century following the first Quebec referendum has been both politically tumultuous and societally transformative for Canada and Quebec alike. In terms of the most fundamental issue, namely Quebec sovereignty, the associated political tumult has been indelibly etched into the consciousness of all Canadians. But the transformation of the sovereignty issue over time has been far-reaching. At the level of *vox populi* the following oversimplification nonetheless carries much truth. In the 1980 Referendum, Quebecers may have had the political will to assume nation-state status but the underlying economics were not on side. In the current time frame, the economics of an independent Quebec within NAFTA economic space are clearly more feasible but the benefits associated with statehood are now deemed to have diminished. Phrased differently, under the former paradigm states created nations, as it were. In the knowledge/human-capital era nations can thrive within states – Catalonia is probably the best example of such a "stateless nation." Facilitating this transformation in Quebec's case is the two-fold reality: a) Canada is a very decentralized federation in terms of the constitutional powers of sub-national governments[3] and b) these are more or less the powers that are linked to "nationhood" in the information era. Arguably, therefore, the essence of the "Quebec issue" in the 21st century has become one of enabling the province to become a full nation within the framework of the Canadian state.

However, allowing Quebec to become a full nation within Canada was a non-starter in the inter-referenda (1980–1995) era. The key difference today is that the rest of Canada has also undergone complex transformative change. Fundamental to this transformation has been the dramatic relative shift from a domestic, east–west trading axis to a cross-border, north–south trading axis, with the consequent policy decentralization and asymmetry across the provinces. And along the way this provincial policy asymmetry, best exemplified by the "Alberta Advantage," paved the way for the Calgary Declaration and SUFA and the associated increased tolerance and even formal recognition of the ability of Quebec (and other provinces) to tailor their powers to the needs/aspirations of their citizens.

This coming together of provincial interests led to the creation of the Council of the Federation (COF) as the overarching institution embodying pan-Canadian provincialism. Among its first initiatives, and certainly its first priority, was to forge a common front around the issue of vertical fiscal imbalance (VFI). That VFI should be the rallying cry for the 21st century Quebec is rather obvious, given the earlier assertion that the key to KBE nationhood rests, by and large, with Quebec's existing powers and given also the requisite corollary that Quebec needs to have access to adequate revenues in order to exercise these powers. For reasons of political and fiscal autonomy (as distinct from "nationhood"), the other provinces have also fully endorsed the VFI thrust.

Unfortunately for the provinces, Ottawa has undergone its own transformation. With many of its erstwhile nation-building policy levers circumscribed by international agreements (tariffs, trade policy and NAFTA) or by international best practice (inflation targeting by the Bank of Canada), it too has discovered that the key to electability and nation-building in the KBE is to become a player in the provincial-powers game. The form that this has taken has been referred to above as hourglass federalism – fiscally starving the provinces in the sense that they have to divert discretionary spending from everywhere to feed the voracious appetite of medicare, so much so that citizens and cities are welcoming of any and all federal spending initiatives directed toward them. Not only is hourglass federalism another name for VFI, but it is VFI with a purpose, as it were, so that Ottawa will not willingly unwind it. This is clear from Martin's initial medicare proposal, which admittedly does move Ottawa's share of medicare funding toward the provincial target of 25 percent, but does so in a manner that would commit the provinces to embark on several new and costly initiatives, i.e., in a manner that does *not* let the provinces escape from hourglass federalism.

What is clear from this brief résumé of the earlier analysis is that to an intriguing degree the political, ideological, fiscal, and jurisdictional/constitutional factors likely to play determining roles in the evolution of Quebec are being funnelled into the September FMM on health care. And other provinces are bringing some of their own issues to the bargaining table, e.g. regional/

equalization issues. While recognized as a defining moment for Paul Martin's minority government, the reality is that the FMM is about competing visions of Canada and as such may well turn out to be one of the defining moments for the evolution of Canada. Elaborating on just what is likely to be at stake in the FMM and how it may influence the future of Quebec/Canada relations is the subject of the final part of this essay.

QUEBEC AND THE SUMMIT OF THE CANADAS

THE INITIAL FEDERAL PROPOSAL

Drawing from St-Hilaire and Lazar (2004, 118), Prime Minister Martin's 2004 election proposal for the September FMM was to "fix medicare for a generation" to "buy changes" and to "deliver real, measurable progress" by

- Ensuring stable, predictable long-term funding ($3 billion over the next 2 years plus automatic increases in the future);
- Implementing a National Waiting Times Reduction Strategy – the "Five in Five" plan ($4 billion);
- Reforming primary care;
- Creating a National Home Care Program ($2 billion over 5 years);
- Developing a national strategy for prescription drug care by 2006; and
- Respecting the *Canada Health Act.*

By way of elaboration, the "five in five" plan is to reduce waiting times based on national targets over the next five years in five key areas – cancer, heart, diagnostic imaging, joint replacement and sight restoration. Since all of these five areas are under the provinces' jurisdiction, the suggested $4 billion price tag is presumably the federal government's best guess as to what it will cost to induce the provinces to address these five waiting periods.

THE COUNCIL OF THE FEDERATION (COF) PROPOSALS

The COF agenda for the FMM includes pharmacare, opting out for Quebec, VFI, and equalization.

Pharmacare

The surprise proposal from the COF was, as already noted, the unanimous recommendation to transfer responsibility for pharmacare to the federal government, in part a response to Paul Martin's call for a "national strategy" for pharmacare. In the words of the COF press release (http://www.scics.gc.ca/cinfo04/850098004_e.html):

> The federal government already plays a significant role in the management of pharmaceutical drugs in Canada – it is responsible for the approval of drugs for use in Canada and for deciding which drugs are available by prescription and which over-the-counter. It is responsible for the *Patents Act* and for the drug plans for Aboriginal peoples, the military, and the RCMP.

Currently, the provinces are spending in the range of $7 billion while "full coverage" is estimated to be in the $12 billion range. Note that Martin's proposals did not include a price tag for his prescription drug care strategy for 2006. Indeed, the cost of pharmacare probably exceeds the total value of annual transfer increases contained in Martin initial proposals.

Quebec's Opting Out

Often overlooked in the press coverage of the COF meeting in Niagara-on-the-Lake, but central to the analysis in the present paper, is that the provinces have agreed that Quebec could and would opt out of the pharmacare plan with compensation. Again in the words of the press release: "It is understood that Quebec will maintain its own program and will receive a comparable compensation for the program put in place by the federal government." This is a remarkable concession, one that builds upon the spirit and the letter of the 1998 Calgary Declaration (and also resurrects one of the principles of the Meech Lake Accord). Indeed, it fits squarely in the venerable tradition (pre-Charter) of "opting out" serving to facilitate "win-win solutions" – Quebec is allowed to opt out and advance its "nationhood" agenda, while the rest of the provinces can work with Ottawa to design a mutually acceptable national program which would not have been possible without Quebec's opting out. Earlier examples are the CPP/QPP compromise and Quebec's opting for its own separate personal income tax (PIT) system thereby allowing Ottawa and the other provinces to develop a shared PIT which is decentralized yet harmonized.

VFI (Vertical Fiscal Imbalance) and Health Care

On the larger issue of funding medicare, the provincial position has remained unchanged for some time now:

1. Ottawa should increase its share of funding under the Canada Health transfer to 25 percent of total health care spending;
2. the 25 percent share should be maintained through time;

3. these funds are to be unconditional; and
4. the premiers added in the recent COF press release "that any new initiatives agreed to at the upcoming FMM will require *additional ongoing* federal dollars [i.e., additional to the 25 percent, TJC] to cover the costs associated with these initiatives" (Press Release, *op. cit.,* emphasis added).

This COF position on health care financing is in dramatic contrast with Paul Martin's electoral platform proposals outlined above. Martin *is* willing to increase cash transfers toward the 25 percent share, but this is tied to a series of additional requirements (decreasing waiting lists, reforming primary care) and new initiatives (home care, pharmacare). St-Hilaire and Lazar (2004,122) noted that the provinces will not likely be willing to take on the attendant cost risks and pressures with the federal proposal:

> The idea that provinces should embark on new national health care programs with the federal government only offering the equivalent of seed money and no guarantee of sharing uncertain future costs, as the federal plan proposes, is simply beyond reason. Quebec's recent experience with $5 day care and pharmacare certainly illustrates both the fiscal and political risks involved.

Equalization

While VFI has top priority for the provinces, the equalization-receiving provinces have rallied all provinces to also push for ameliorating horizontal fiscal imbalance (HFI) across the provinces. As the COF press release noted, equalization entitlements to the recipient provinces have been reduced by $3.7 billion over the last three years. The issue in the context of health care funding is that an infusion of additional federal transfers allocated on an equal per capita basis (as has characterized recent transfer increases) is deemed to be inadequate for the have-not provinces without some corresponding provision for offsetting the decline in formal equalization payments. Accordingly, the COF recommends that "as an immediate measure, total Equalization Program funding should be restored to the 2000–01 level." Because Quebec receives the lion's share of aggregate equalization payments, this can also be viewed as an issue near and dear to this province. However, linking HFI with VFI will obviously serve to further complicate the September First Ministers' Meeting, especially in light of the fact that the equalization program is already reeling under a series of long-standing issues (Courchene, 2004a), let alone the HFI challenges associated with the price of oil in the US$60 range.

Summary

All in all, this was an impressive package. The provinces would escape from the straightjacket of hourglass federalism by passing pharmacare upward and by receiving an unconditional 25 percent share of medicare costs. Moreover, they addressed their internal tensions by recognizing Quebec's right to self-determination in respect of its social envelope and they accommodated the poorer provinces by recommending a generous equalization component. The Postscript will deal with Ottawa's reaction to these COF proposals.

PRIVATE DELIVERY AND THE CANADA HEALTH ACT

All parties endorse the Canada Health Act, although they do not all embrace the same interpretation of its principles. One controversial issue has to do with interpreting the "public administration" tenet. The 2002 Senate Report's interpretation and that by Kirby and Keon (2004a, 2004b), which I carried into my own work (2003a), is that "public administration" has to do with *public funding*, but then the system ought to be agnostic as to whether the delivery of services is by the public or private or third sectors. Alberta goes at least this far and Quebec has been here for a while. Indeed, in a rare return to the policy limelight, former Premier Lucien Bouchard suggested recently that private clinics make *le gros bon sens* (plain common sense), which may put him beyond the Kirby/Keon camp and into a parallel private system in some delivery areas (Yakabuski, 2004). On the other hand, Martin will be under pressure from Jack Layton and the NDP to disallow the spread of private delivery of any sort. Martin could also argue that, given the importance of medicare in the campaign, Canadians gave the Liberals a mandate to ensure transformative change along the lines of his platform plank as elaborated above. However, the political reality is such that the only way to ensure that Alberta and Quebec, among others, would swear off all privatization would be for Ottawa to fully address the VFI issue with unconditional transfers, which is hardly Martin's position.

FURTHER QUEBEC ISSUES

No doubt there are a variety of other issues that will be raised by the provinces and Ottawa at the September summit. Since the focus in this essay is on Quebec, there are two further issues that this province will bring to the table. The first relates to the recommendations of Quebec's Séguin Commission, namely that Ottawa convert its cash transfers to tax point transfers and, in particular, that it transfer the GST to the provinces. This is unlikely to fly (although it might find support from other provinces), but it will nonetheless be part of the Quebec position. However, were pharmacare to be transferred to Ottawa, Quebec might have more success arguing that its opting out with compensation should take the form of tax transfers rather than cash transfers.

The second derives from Quebec's long-standing view that it will not allow the federal government to regulate, legislate or otherwise dictate in areas of

Quebec's constitutional jurisdiction. This is what Quebec nationhood within the Canadian state is all about.

ANALYSIS

While the politics, process and policy associated with the September 2004 FMM are probably in the nature of a seamless web, it seems appropriate to deal with each separately, at least initially.

Politics

The view of many in the chattering classes seems to be that none of the federal parties wants to face the voters for a while, so the Liberal minority government is unlikely to be brought down as a result of the outcome, or non-outcome as the case may be, of the FMM. This reasoning seems faulty on two fronts. First, a Parliamentary defeat of the Martin government in the immediate aftermath of the FMM, denying him confidence on the Throne Speech might not trigger an election. Rather, the Governor General could, arguably, invite Stephen Harper to try to form a government. In other words, while Canadians may well want minority government to work and may well be willing to punish those parties that pull the electoral plug, this is quite different from saying that Canadians want a *Liberal* minority government. Hence, Paul Martin will need to ensure that the outcome of the FMM finds some resonance with either or both the Conservatives or the BQ.

The second point is that the politics enveloping the FMM obviously transcends federal politics. Given the perspective of this essay, the politics of Canada/Quebec relations will also be in play. The combination of the sponsorship scandal (including the downplaying of the Chrétien wing of the Liberal Party) and the resurgence of the BQ (including its potential balance-of-power role in the Commons) has left the federalist forces in Quebec in a very weak position. In this environment, it would be foolhardy on Ottawa's part (i.e., on the part of the federalist parties in the House of Commons) to leave Charest high and dry in terms of the outcome of the FMM. His position in Quebec will be weakened considerably unless he emerges from the summit with meaningful progress on the VFI front and with minimal infringement on Quebec's ability to legislate on the medicare front.

What thus emerged (post-COF and in the run-up to the September 2004 FMM) was how the Liberals could meet their electoral commitment of buying new programs and commitments from the provinces with an increase in proposed transfers that would arguably be *less* than that required to address the 25 percent Romanow target. The NDP and a goodly number of Canadians would attempt not only to hold the Liberals to their campaign proposal but perhaps as well to embrace the COF proposal that Ottawa launch a national prescription-drug program. But Martin's initial proposal seemed to fall well short of what the provinces would settle for and what the Conservatives and BQ would support.

All in all, a daunting challenge.

Process

My comment on process is contained in a single word – SUFA. If Prime Minister Martin wants to play in areas of exclusive provincial jurisdiction, then SUFA or a SUFA-equivalent approach is the agreed-upon process. SUFA involves, *inter alia,* federal-provincial co-determination in terms of program design, provincial flexibility in terms of implementation, and combined federal-provincial monitoring and oversight. Moreover, SUFA is arguably flexible enough to accommodate the opting-out-with-compensation for Quebec (as embodied in the COF pharmacare proposal). As already noted, the 2000 and 2003 health accords were viewed by Ottawa as buying "change," whereas the provinces simply presumed the transfers to be unconditional independent of the "accord." This will happen in 2004 as well if the federal government does not work through a SUFA or SUFA-equivalent process.

Policy

While process and a flair for the political are necessary ingredients for a successful FMM, substance and policy must occupy centre stage. Beginning with policy, an appropriate launch point for an analysis of the range of choices facing the first ministers is to focus on that which is "new" to federal-provincial health care meetings, namely the COF proposal with respect to pharmacare. Earlier, this proposal was viewed as a master stroke on the part of the provinces since it allows them to escape from the hourglass-federalism straightjacket. Yet this proposal should, in principle, also be eagerly welcomed by Ottawa because it presents the federal government with the right to deal directly with Canadians in ways that heretofore it could not. Phrased differently, Ottawa would now be spending these dollars in its own jurisdiction, which would in turn alter the degree of VFI. It would also expand the scope of Canadian medicare in ways in which the Liberals themselves called for in their election platform, and it increases the degrees of freedom that Ottawa has in negotiating with the provinces.

Ottawa's initial reaction to the COF pharamacare proposal appears to be one of backing away from rather than embracing it. Even accepting that the cost side might pose problems for Ottawa, this decision summarily discards several creative options. Consider, initially, the following option:

- Ottawa accepts responsibility for pharmacare, commencing with a takeover of a standardized version of existing provincial programs;
- it maintains existing funding levels for the rest of the system; and
- it agrees to index the existing transfers (either to inflation or to the growth of medicare expenditures) in turn for a SUFA-type agreement to get joint input into standards, etc., where this joint input into standards would now include pharmacare.

While this would not address the letter of the Liberal proposal, it would none-theless score high points in an important number of key areas: first, it expands medicare into an important area; second, it takes a huge medicare cost-driver off the provinces' books; third, by maintaining the existing level of transfers (indexed), it satisfactorily addresses the VFI; and fourth, it offers scope for some mutually-agreeable commitments on issues like waiting lists, etc. It seems that Alberta and Quebec (and arguably the BQ and Conservatives respectively) would be on side, and most of the rest of the provinces could probably be finessed with an equalization commitment (which would be negotiated at a later date). Finally, the long-standing jurisdictional quagmire surrounding medicare would be rationalized by dividing up the policy area.

This specific example is not intended to serve as a preferred outcome. Rather it is meant to suggest that throwing pharmacare into the hopper substantially increases the degrees of policy freedom. Consider some other options:

- Ottawa takes over pharmacare for the elderly
- Ottawa takes over pharamacare for the elderly and children
- Ottawa takes over either one of the above but does so in the context of income-tested, catastrophic coverage, run through the federal personal in-come tax system
- Ottawa takes over pharmacare but only on a catastrophic basis

All of these options could be combined with the status quo in terms of exist-ing CHA transfers (as in the original example).The focus on the elderly and children is deliberate because Ottawa now plays the key role in terms of their income support (e.g., OAS/GIS for the elderly and the CCTB for children), so that responsibility for some version of pharmacare would not constitute a huge departure in terms of the federal mission.

If, however, Ottawa rejects the creative COF pharmacare proposal, then forging a package acceptable to the provinces becomes much more difficult, because the formal Liberal proposal would certainly not be acceptable to the four largest provinces and perhaps not to the remaining six either. The earlier quotation from Lazar and St-Hilaire indicates why this is so. From the prov-inces' vantage point, the minimum acceptable package (absent the pharmacare option) would seem to be a move to a 25 percent unconditional funding share. Buying new provincial programs/commitments would be possible only with additional transfers (i.e., beyond the 25 percent share), and again run through some SUFA-like process. One major disadvantage of this latter strategy is that it continues to increase the magnitude of federal transfers that are directed to areas of provincial jurisdiction. Even with a SUFA agreement in place it will become progressively easier for the provinces to harbour the view of a vertical fiscal balance, since one (not the only) definition of an increasing VFI is increasing federal spending/transfers directed to areas of exclusive provincial jurisdiction. The advantage of the various pharmacare options is that aspects of prescription drugs would in effect henceforth come under *federal jurisdiction*.

Two final observations are in order. The first is that Ottawa could stand its ground and drive home a take-it-or-leave-it deal, based on some version of its initial proposal. From a fiscal standpoint, the provinces would probably take the offer but, led by Alberta they would probably embark on a privatization process. The second focuses on the other extreme. If one adds up all of Martin's commitments, they may well overextend Ottawa's fiscal capacity. Since deficits are presumably out of the question, tax hikes are not beyond the pale as a way to finesse this fiscal dilemma.

By way of a few concluding comments it is appropriate to return to the theme of Quebec/Canada relations. The thesis of this essay is that Quebec's demands have shifted from acquiring greater powers to acquiring greater revenues (preferably taxes) so as to be able to exercise fully its existing powers. Far and away the most exciting recent development in this area has been the formal recognition of Quebec's "distinct society" priority in the context of the COF pharmacare proposal. (Presumably this same opting-out-with-compensation provision will apply to any provincial consensus relating to how Ottawa would transfer additional revenues to the cities.) The very existence of this provincial acceptance of Quebec's specificity makes it progressively more difficult for Ottawa not to follow suit. Yet the obvious complication here is that Paul Martin has already indicated that the three priorities in the fall Speech from the Throne will be medicare, early childhood development and cities. All are viewed by Quebec as under its jurisdiction and essential to its future in Canada.

These, then, are the opportunities and constraints that comprise the new dynamics in Quebec/Canada relations. The good news is that Quebec appears nearer than ever to assuming the mantle of a 21st century nation within the framework of the Canadian state. Yet, were this avenue for whatever reason to become blocked, Quebec may well revert back to seeking its future as its own nation-state. In this sense, and also because medicare, vertical and horizontal fiscal balance, and the division of powers are all in play, the September 2004 FMM is indeed a Summit of the Canadas.

POSTSCRIPT: THE SEPTEMBER AND OCTOBER 2004 SUMMITS

HEALTH CARE

While Ottawa took a pass on the COF pharmacare proposal, on the eve of the September FMM it tendered a fresh offer to the provinces that provided for $25 billion in new funding over the next 10 years. However, in the context of the FMM the provinces drove home a much more generous bargain – roughly $41 billion over these same 10 years. By Ottawa's calculation, this filled the "Romanow Gap" (i.e., 25 percent of health costs). In return for all this, Ottawa obtained commitments from the provinces to address waiting periods, including the acceptance of evidence-based benchmarks. In addition, the provinces agreed, among other things, to increase the supply of health professionals in general and for minority communities in particular, to increase short-term acute home care and end-of-life home care, to report on their progress relating to primary health care reform, and to establish a ministerial task force to develop and implement a national pharmaceuticals strategy, this latter with the understanding (drawing from COF agreement) that Quebec will maintain its own pharmacare program.

Two other features merit highlight. The first is that accountability pursuant to this agreement *will be to the citizens of the various provinces* (and *not* to the federal government). Relatedly, there are no designated penalties for non-compliance. In the words of the FMM news release: "All governments agree to report to their residents on health system performance including the elements set out in this communiqué." The second and the most relevant for present purposes is the asymmetrical federalism side agreement, which explicitly recognizes Quebec's specificity. In effect, this is the federal counterpart to the recognition of Quebec's distinctiveness in the Council of the Federation as well as in the Calgary Declaration. As noted above, while Quebec agrees to work in collaboration with Ottawa and the provinces in terms of the range of issues in the communiqué, Quebec's own policies will be determined "in accordance with the objectives, standards, and criteria established by the relevant *Quebec authorities*" (cited from the Canada-Quebec addendum to the FMM, entitled "Asymmetric Federalism that Respects Quebec's Jurisdiction"). Apparently, in the final countdown to the deal, Ottawa verbally agreed that Alberta and British Columbia (and by extension all the provinces) could have the same deal as that offered to Quebec. This brings the Canada/Quebec asymmetric rider into line with the relevant provision of the 1998 Calgary Declaration, as elaborated earlier.

Finally, it is instructive to note that the health care deal falls largely, if not wholly, within a SUFA-type framework, including mutually agreed upon benchmarks/indicators, flexible implementation, and information sharing but with accountability to one's own citizens. Although Quebec was not a SUFA signatory, the asymmetrical rider allowed Quebec to sign the communiqué. By way of a closing comment on both the communiqué and the thrust of the foregoing analysis, a case can be made that the treatment of Quebec is in line with the manner in which John A. Macdonald anticipated our federation might evolve. To see this, consider section 94 of the *Constitution Act, 1867*. Entitled "Uniformity of Laws in Ontario, Nova Scotia and New Brunswick," it reads as follows:

> Notwithstanding anything in this Act, the Parliament of Canada may make Provision for the Uniformity of all or any of the Laws relative to Property and Civil Rights in Ontario, Nova Scotia, and New Brunswick, and of the Procedure of all or any of the Courts in those three Provinces, and from and after the passing of any act in that Behalf the Power of the Parliament of Canada to make Laws in relation to any Matter comprised in any such Act shall, notwithstanding anything in this Act, be unrestricted; but any Act of the Parliament of Canada making Provision for such Uniformity shall not have effect in any Province unless and until it is adopted and enacted as Law by the Legislature thereof.

The late Frank Scott (1977) suggested that the Fathers of Confederation, unable to obtain a unitary state, included this clause so that an easy way would be available for the provinces other than Quebec to pursue a more uniform and unified future. Samuel LaSelva (1996, Chapter 3) suggests that one reason why section 94 has received so little attention both from the courts and from constitutional experts has to do with its misleading label: rather than "Uniformity of Laws" it should have been entitled "Transferring Constitutional Jurisdiction," to make it clear that it is in fact an amending procedure. In general, amending the division of powers requires unanimous consent of all the provinces (plus Ottawa). However, section 94 allows the non-Quebec provinces to transfer powers related to property and civil rights to Ottawa *without* the consent of Quebec. In an important sense, the recent health care deal can be viewed as a non-constitutional way to accomplish a similar goal. It allows the nine provinces to opt into a more uniform and unified approach to the CHA while at the same time allowing Quebec to cooperate and collaborate in most respects but to retain *de jure* control over health care. Actually, the SUFA-like process with opting out for Quebec has several advantages for the provinces over a section 94 process, the most important of which is that it avoids the s.94 consequence that, once powers are transferred to the federal government, Ottawa can legislate at will and without consulting the provinces.

EQUALIZATION

One final point on the subject of equalization. In the October 2004 FMM on equalization, Ottawa agreed to restore equalization and territorial formula financing (TFF) to their 2000–01 levels and then to index this by 3.5 percent. Finance Canada estimates that over the next ten years this will equal $28.8 billion of new spending on equalization and $4.6 billion on the Territorial Funding Formula. (Note that these estimates assume that in the absence of this agreement the levels of equalization and TFF would have remained at 2004–05 levels). The FMM also struck a blue-ribbon committee whose role will be to decide on a new allocation formula. Early in 2005, Ottawa agreed to a generous energy equalization deal with Nova Scotia and Newfoundland and Labrador that will effectively exempt their off-shore energy royalties from equalization clawbacks. In tandem these equalization agreements not only run afoul of the constitutional underpinnings of equalization but have left the horizontal fiscal balance of the federation in shambles. But this is a story for another time.

Given the thrust of this paper the last words have to be about Quebec. By making substantive inroads into Quebec's concerns about distinctiveness, powers and vertical balance, we are also making it easier for Quebec to become its own nation within the Canadian state and to become more fully and more formally part of the Canadian constitutional family. The 15 September 2004 First Ministers' Meeting is indeed a defining moment in the evolution of our federation.[4]

NOTES

An earlier version of this paper appears as "The Changing Nature of Quebec-Canada Relations: From the 1980 Referendum to the Summit of the Canadas" (Courchene 2004a). The present paper reworks aspects of this Working Paper and then adds a Postscript which briefly details the results of the 2004 First Ministers Meeting on health care and equalization. It is a pleasure to thank John Richards for valuable comments and insights.

1 Aspects of this section draw from Lawrence Martin (1997).
2 In private correspondence, John Richards suggests that Premier Bourassa and his lieutenants (such as Claude Ryan) understood full well the danger of using the notwithstanding clause in response to the Supreme Court's ruling on the language of commercial signs. They used it nonetheless because they felt, in Richards' view, that the Court's decision was profoundly misguided and to accept it would have been worse not only on political grounds but more importantly for the survival of the federation. Meech may have been lost as a result, but Canada remains intact. I accept this interpretation.
3 It is also the case that Canada probably ranks as the most *centralized* federation in terms of the influence of the provinces in the operations of the central governments. Indeed, it is the provinces' lack of any role in the institutions of the central

government that contributes to the need for regional/provincial interests to be exercised by the provinces and their premiers.

4 As the opening sentence of this paper notes, a few months can make an enormous difference in the march of policy fortunes. While the above analysis ends with the 2004 First Ministers' Meetings, the reality as this paper goes to press is that Stephen Harper is the Prime Minister of a Conservative minority government and fully intent on addressing the long-standing vertical fiscal imbalance issue as well as allowing Quebec to play a greater role on the global stage when the issues relate to its legitimate constitutional interests (e.g., UNESCO). In this sense, the evolution toward Quebec achieving nation status within the Canadian state marches onward.

REFERENCES

Blank, S. 2002. "The United States and Canada: The Emerging Architecture of North America." A submission to the Carnegie Endowment for International Peace for the National Commission on America and the New World. New York: Americas Society.

Courchene, T.J. 1990. *Forever Amber: The Legacy of the 1980s and the Ongoing Constitutional Impasse,* Reflections/Reflexions 6. Kingston: Institute of Intergovernmental Relations, Queen's University.

– 1991. "La communauté des Canadas." In *Les avis des spécialistes invités à répondre aux huit questions posées par la Commission,* background document number 4 to the Commission sur l'avenir politique et constitutionnel du Québec (Bélanger-Campeau Commission). Quebec: Government of Quebec. Also published as *The Community of the Canadas,* Reflections/Reflexions 8. Kingston: Institute of Intergovernmental Relations, Queens University.

– 1996. *ACCESS: A Convention on the Canadian Economics and Social Systems.* Toronto: Ministry of Intergovernmental Affairs, Government of Ontario. Reprinted by the Institute of Intergovernmental Relations as part of the *Council of the Federation* Series, 2003.

– 2000. "Responding to the NAFTA Challenge: Ontario as a North American Region State and Toronto as a Global City Region." In *Global City Regions: Trends, Theory, Policy,* ed. A. Scott. New York: Oxford University Press.

– 2003a. *Medicare As A Moral Enterprise: The Romanow and Kirby Perspectives. Policy Matters* 4(1). Montreal: Institute for Research on Public Policy.

– 2003b. "FTA at 15, NAFTA at 10: A Canadian Perspective on North American Integration." *North American Journal of Economics and Finance* 14: 263–85.

– 2004. "Hourglass Federalism. *Policy Options* (April): 12–17.

– 2004a. *Confiscatory Equalization: The Intriguing Case of Saskatchewan's Vanishing Energy Revenues. Choices* 10(2). Montreal: Institute for Research on Public Policy.

– 2004b. "Pan-Canadian Provincialism – The New Federalism and the Old Constitution." *Policy Options* (November): 20–28.

– 2004c. "The Changing Nature of Quebec-Canada Relations: From the 1980 Referendum to the Summit of the Canadas." IRPP Working Paper No. 2004-08. Montreal: Institute for Research on Public Policy.

Courchene, T.J. with C.R. Telmer. 1998. *From Heartland to North American Region State: The Social, Fiscal and Federal Evolution of Ontario.* Toronto: Centre for Public Management, Rotman School of Business, University of Toronto.

Harris, R.G. 2003. "Old Growth and New Economy Cycles: Rethinking Canadian Economic Paradigms." In *The Art of the State: Governance in a World Without Frontiers,* eds. T.J. Courchene and D.J. Savoie. Montreal: Institute for Research on Public Policy.

Kirby, M. and W. Keon. 2004a. *Why Competition is Essential in the Delivery of Publicly Funded Health Care Services. Policy Matters/Enjeux publics* 5(8). Montreal: Institute for Research on Public Policy.

– 2004b. "Why Competition is Essential in the Delivery of Publicly-Funded Health Care Services." *Policy Options/Options politiques* (September): 103–110.

LaSelva, S. 1996. *The Moral Foundations of Canadian Federalism: Paradoxes, Achievements, and Tragedies of Nationhood.* Montreal and Kingston: McGill-Queen's Press.

Martin, L. 1997. *The Antagonist: Lucien Bouchard and the Politics of Delusion.* Toronto: Penguin/Viking.

Scott, F. 1977. *Essays on the Constitution.* Toronto: University of Toronto Press.

Standing Senate Committee on Social Affairs, Science and Technology. 2002 *Recommendations for Reform 6: The Federal Role.* Ottawa: Queen's Printer for Canada.

St-Hilaire, F. and H. Lazar. 2004. "A Fix For a Generation?" *Policy Options/Options politiques* (September): 118–23.

Thurow, L. 1993. "Six Revolutions, Six Economic Challenges." *The Toronto Star,* 28 January, A21.

Wolfe, R. 2003. "See You in Washington? Institutions for North American Integration," *Choices* 9(4). Montreal: Institute for Research on Public Policy.

Yakabuski, K. 2004. "The Common Sense Question that Bouchard Dared to Ask." *Report on Business, The Globe and Mail,* 11 August, B2.

10

Breaking the "Vicious Cycle:"
A Retrospective and Prospective Examination
of Quebec/Canada Relations

John Richards

Cet article traite de la politique contemporaine au Québec. D'abord, il trace l'évolution de l'attitude des Québécois francophones face aux mesures qui ont été instaurées pour assurer la prédominance du français à Montréal. Pour les fédéralistes autant que pour les souverainistes, la Charte de la langue française (la Loi 101) est la clé de voûte de la politique linguistique. Tout essai de la déloger, pour quelque motif que ce soit, risque d'ébranler l'équilibre fédéral. L'article traite brièvement des tentatives qui ont été faites depuis 1995 pour faire réintégrer le Québec dans le giron fédéral. La dernière et la plus prometteuse est la création du Conseil de la fédération, quoique le Conseil reste à présent une organisation informelle. Finalement, l'article aborde les analyses d'Alain Dubuc et des signataires du manifeste 'Pour un Québec lucide' qui décrivent comment le blocage de la politique provinciale freine sérieusement la croissance économique du Québec.

After 40 years, Quebec's politics have reached a stalemate. Separatists are wed to a political option Quebecers don't want. Federalists continue to invent constitutional reconciliations in which the rest of the country has no interest. Elsewhere, the world is getting on with the 21st century. If Quebec is not to be left behind, Quebecers must turn the page on the national question. In fact, the crucial battle – that for survival – has been won. Quebecers should hold their own debate on whether they are a people, a nation or something in between, declare that question closed, and then turn to their next national project: success – in education, in culture, and in the new economy, all of which are within Quebec's constitutional competence.

Alain Dubuc, "We Must Break this Vicious Cycle"

INTRODUCTION

Tom Courchene has provided a good survey of the history of Quebec/Canada relations since the first sovereignty referendum of 1980 – with one important exception. Missing is the matter of language policy. Were a foreigner, someone with no knowledge of Canadian history, to read it, he would garner no idea of the extent to which Quebec/Canada relations over the last half-century have turned around the dilemmas posed by preservation intergenerationally of more than one lingua franca.

In this essay, I undertake several tasks. I introduce the linguistic dimension to the discussion, and make the case for explicit constitutional acknowledgment of a Quebec linguistic jurisdiction. Second, I offer some speculations on post-1995 intergovernmental diplomacy and the importance of Quebec's rejoining the debates. Finally, I build on Alain Dubuc's image of a "vicious cycle" and assess why the economic catch-up of the Quiet Revolution stalled.

THE LINGUISTIC DIMENSION

"What does Quebec want?" – the perennial question posed by those interested in Quebec/Canada relations. Among francophone Quebecers (henceforth Québécois), the lowest common denominator of their answers has been that French survive as the dominant public language spoken in Quebec, that it not succumb to folkloric status as has been the fate of all immigrant languages, other than English, Portuguese, and Spanish, brought to the western hemisphere. On this, Québécois have been consistent ever since late 18th century debates over language to be spoken in the legislative assembly of Lower Canada.

Celui qui perd la langue perd la foi. As this old maxim implies, in the 19th century language and faith were intimately intertwined in Canadian public life. In negotiating Confederation, francophone clerical and political leaders insisted upon section 93 of the *British North America Act*, the section assuring provincial control of education and a constitutional legitimacy for the Roman Catholic school system in the province of Quebec. Outside Quebec, conflicts over language and religion did not take long to arise. Manitoba, for example, entered Confederation in 1870 as an officially bilingual jurisdiction. Over the next two decades, English-speaking settlers shifted the province's linguistic distribution definitively in favour of English. And, in 1890, the provincial government enacted the *Official Languages Act,* whereby English became the province's sole official language.[1] Within Quebec, conflicts over language did not become significant until the 1960s, gaining in salience as an inevitable by-product of large-scale post-World War II immigration to Montreal.

For a language to flourish in an urban, technical society, more is at stake than its intergenerational transmission via schools. Montreal is among the metropolitan centres in this hemisphere producing works of high art and mass culture, sustaining major universities, and conducting business at a sophisticated level. It is the *only* one doing so in French. There are scale economies in such activities. For French to remain a useful language in contemporary North America, it has been crucial that at least one metropolitan centre be majority French speaking.

Since the 18th century, Montreal has been a bilingual city. At times in the 19th century, Montreal was majority English speaking. But the combination of high fertility among Québécois and rural-to-urban migration assured a francophone majority over the first half of the 20th century. With the arrival post-World War II of large numbers of allophone immigrants (those for whom neither French nor English was mother tongue), Montreal – like Toronto and Vancouver – became a multilingual city. These immigrants were neighbours to a small group of six million francophones but, quite reasonably, they identified as part of a continent of 300 million anglophones. They made a rational cost-benefit choice, and in a ratio approaching ten to one opted for English over French as the medium of instruction for their children. The linguistic implication was obvious; so was the solution. The great majority of Québécois favoured linguistic protection. A decade of political debate culminated in adoption of *La Charte de la langue française*. (The law is still known as Bill 101, the number attached to the draft legislation as Camille Laurin shepherded it through the National Assembly in 1977.) The preamble of Bill 101 states the intent of the newly elected Parti Québécois (PQ) government:

> Whereas the National Assembly of Quebec recognizes that Quebecers wish to see the quality and influence of the French language assured, and is resolved therefore to make of French the language of Government and the Law, as well as the normal and everyday language of work, instruction, communication, commerce and business ...

> Whereas the National Assembly intends to pursue this objective in a spirit of fairness and open-mindedness, respectful of the institutions of the English-speaking community of Quebec, and respectful of the ethnic minorities, whose valuable contribution to the development of Quebec it readily acknowledges ...

> Therefore, Her Majesty, with the advice and consent of the National Assembly of Quebec, enacts as follows ... (Quebec 1977)

The political compromise codified in Bill 101 has been modified since 1977, but its major features remain intact:

- French is the official language of Quebec, and the Quebec government will promote French as the *langue commune* for public use.
- Major workplaces must assure that it is feasible for employees to function in French.
- Provincially licensed professionals must, as a condition of licensure, demonstrate a working knowledge of French.
- Access to publicly funded English language K–12 education is restricted. Originally, Bill 101 restricted access to children of Canadian citizens who had themselves received their K–12 instruction in English in Quebec. Provisions of the *Charter of Rights* obliged Quebec to relax the constraint to allow instruction in English to children of Canadian citizens who had received K–12 education in English anywhere in Canada. Recently, some have suggested the restriction be extended beyond K–12 to include the CEGEPs (Lisée 2001).
- Originally, Bill 101 required that all commercial signs be unilingual French. As amended in 1993, in the wake of the *Ford* decision (see below), bilingual commercial signs are permissible in most instances, provided French predominates.

Bill 101 quickly assumed iconic status among Québécois. Ironically, it probably played a major role in undermining the sovereignist vote at the time of the 1980 referendum: If Canadian federal institutions were sufficiently flexible to accommodate Bill 101, why secede?

Following the 1976 PQ victory, Prime Minister Trudeau established the Task Force On Canadian Unity (Pepin-Roberts). It endorsed Bill 101 as a positive step toward Quebec/Canada reconciliation. Writing in 1979, the commissioners concluded: "We support the efforts of the Quebec provincial government ... to ensure the predominance of the French language and culture in that province .... There can be nothing more damaging, in our view, to the cause of Canadian unity than the rejection of these aspirations of francophone Québécois by English-speaking Canadians" (Canada 1979, 51). Whereas Bill 101 enjoyed iconic status among Québécois and approval of the Pepin-Roberts commissioners, it excited intense opposition from anglophone and allophone Quebecers. They perceived it as unwarranted discrimination by the francophone majority against linguistic minorities within Quebec. Their political champion turned out to be Trudeau.[2]

There is much truth to the old joke that Pierre Trudeau and Jacques Parizeau agreed on everything – with one small exception. Both were cosmopolitan, fluently bilingual intellectuals whose ambition and talent enabled them to reach the pinnacles of political power; they shared a centre-left political agenda; both favoured centralized political institutions able to act decisively on key dossiers; and both mistrusted the messy compromises that emerge from federal-provincial relations. Their only disagreement has been whether the territory that is now Canada needs one or two such states.

Beyond Trudeau and Parizeau, the class of politically engaged intellectuals of Quebec's Quiet Revolution agreed on a great deal. They took to heart the theme stressed throughout Courchene's survey: Widely diffused scientific and technical knowledge among a well educated labour force is the precondition for economic success. Quebec education levels were, at the time, well below the Canadian average; accordingly, the state had an obligation to wrest control of the education system from the Catholic church and to invest in its rapid expansion. The generation of Trudeau and Parizeau rejected the otherworldly stance of earlier Catholic leaders.[3] The secular world of science and business should not be the preserve of *les Anglais* in Westmount. Where this generation disagreed was whether the federal government in Ottawa or the provincial government in Quebec City should take the lead. The election of the self-consciously modernizing government of Premier Jean Lesage in 1960 allowed the first move to those advocating provincial initiatives. The election of Lester Pearson as Prime Minister in 1963, and his recruitment of major Quebec lieutenants to Ottawa, assured that both sides achieved positions of influence.

As an alternative to linguistic protection for French within Quebec, Trudeau proposed an idealistic agenda designed to create a coast-to-coast community of French-English bilingual Canadians, and to transform the federal public service into a genuinely bilingual institution. Over the course of his reign, 1968–84, the status of French in the federal public service improved markedly, but coast-to-coast French/English bilingualism was always a utopian goal. Relative to 1960, French/English bilingualism has increased somewhat outside Quebec, but only modestly.[4] Integral to Trudeau's strategy was the creation of justiciable language rights in the *Charter of Rights and Freedoms* (sections 16 to 23). By defining a legal equality among official language minorities – francophones outside Quebec and anglophones in Quebec – he attempted to transform language policy into a matter of civil liberties. The inadequacy of this strategy was that it ignored the importance of preserving francophone predominance in Montreal, and did so in a linguistic environment in which the overwhelming incentive among allophones was to make a linguistic transfer to English, and among anglophones to avoid investment in the cost of learning French.[5]

Predictably, the Charter encouraged challenges to Bill 101. The clash between the utilitarian ethic of Bill 101 and the civil liberties ethic underlying the Charter reached a crescendo in the furor surrounding the1988 *Ford* decision, a decision that struck down the unilingual French commercial signs provision of Bill 101 as an infringement of freedom of speech. In reaching its decision, the Supreme Court stretched the interpretation of the free speech provisions of both the federal and Quebec charters of rights, so as to include commercial use of language. Among anglophones and allophones across Canada, the decision was perceived as a worthy extension of civil liberties. The justices' paean to freedom of choice over language had a ring of nobility to it:

> The "freedom of expression" guaranteed by s. 2(b) of the Canadian *Charter* and s. 3 of the Quebec *Charter* [of Human Rights and Freedoms] includes the freedom to express oneself in the language of one's choice. Language is so intimately related to the form and content of expression that there cannot be true freedom of expression by means of language if one is prohibited from using the language of one's choice. Language is not merely a means or medium of expression; it colours the content and meaning of expression. It is a means by which a people may express its cultural identity. It is also the means by which one expresses one's personal identity and sense of individuality. (*Ford v. Quebec* 1988, 716)

Read literally, the decision did not change much of substance. As a precedent, it changed a great deal. It seemingly established the authority of the Supreme Court, an institution whose members are appointed by the Prime Minister, as final arbiter of Quebec language policy. As convinced a federalist as Stéphane Dion articulated anxiety about the Supreme Court's taking unto itself this role:

> A Supreme Court might decide someday that denying the right of a new immigrant or of a francophone to go to an English school, when English speakers have such a right, is contrary to the *Charter of Rights*; the Court could invoke ... Article 15 prescribing legal equality of all citizens. Such a judgment may seem unlikely today, but who knows for the next generation? (Dion 1992, 119–20)

Presumably because they realized its affront to Québécois sensibilities, the justices delayed the decision's release until after the hotly contested free trade election of that year. Indeed, it did offend sensibilities. The Supreme Court catalyzed Quebec nationalist opinion and revived political support for the Parti Québécois. Under intense public pressure to respond to the decision, the provincial government – at the time a Liberal administration led by Robert Bourassa – utilized the Charter's notwithstanding clause to impose a legislated compromise.

The *Ford* decision excited anger among Québécois; use of the notwithstanding clause in response did the same among non-francophones in Quebec and elsewhere in Canada. The most prominent victim of these conflicting passions was the Meech Lake Accord. Its key provision was to entrench an interpretive clause in the constitution requiring courts to assess Quebec laws subject to the concept of the province's being a "distinct society." If the Accord would enable Québécois to discriminate and suppress free speech, concluded non-francophones in and out of Quebec, it should be rejected. If the Supreme Court expected to decide matters pertaining to the survival of Quebec's francophone culture, argued Québécois, the Accord was the minimum constitutional guarantee required for Quebec to remain in Canada. At the time the *Ford* decision was released, in late 1988, the eleven first ministers had approved it, but the Accord had yet to satisfy the requirements for constitutional entrenchment. It never did.

As for Dion's anxieties, they ceased to be hypothetical when a challenge to Bill 101 was mounted to provide francophone Quebec students the right to send their children to publicly funded English-language schools in Quebec. Tactically astute, the appellants based their case on the equality provisions of the Quebec *Charter of Rights* as opposed to analogous provisions of the Canadian Charter. The challenge reached the Supreme Court, which gave its decision in early 2005:

Section 73 of the *Charter of the French Language* [Bill 101] provides access to English language schools in Quebec only to children who have received or are receiving English language instruction in Canada or whose parents studied in English in Canada at the primary level. The appellant parents, who do not qualify as rights holders under s. 73 or under s. 23 of the *Canadian Charter of Rights and Freedoms*, claim that s. 73 discriminates between children who qualify and the majority of French-speaking Quebec children who do not, and violates the right to equality guaranteed at ss. 10 and 12 of the Quebec *Charter of Human Rights and Freedoms*. Equality requires, the appellants argue, that all children in Quebec be given access to publicly funded English language education. ...

Since the appellants are members of the French language majority in Quebec, their objective in having their children educated in English simply does not fall within the purpose of s. 23 of the *Canadian Charter*. The appellants have no claim to publicly funded English language instruction in Quebec and, if adopted, the practical effect of their equality argument would be to read out of the Constitution the compromise contained in s. 23. (*Gosselin v. Quebec* 2005)

One conclusion from this brief survey of Canadian language conflicts is that the Supreme Court has finally "got it." With *Gosselin*, the justices did not indulge the judicial hubris of the *Ford* decision. They did not seek to expand equality rights into the school system. They accepted the core element of Bill 101, the National Assembly's ability to discriminate in determining access to English-language instruction within the province. Would the justices have reached the decision they did on *Gosselin* without the intervening 17 years of Quebec/Canada turmoil? Perhaps. But, following *Ford*, observers as sophisticated as Dion were far from certain.

From this selective history, I want to draw out three conclusions:

1. Any feasible language policy in Canada entails material tradeoffs. The "net-work externality" associated with language use is so important that treating choice of language as a civil liberty and requiring governments to afford equal linguistic services in all places to speakers of both official languages implies intergenerational disappearance of French as a viable language – a material loss to those for whom French is mother tongue. Fewer have suf-fered linguistic losses with Bill 101 than would have been the case without, but linguistic protection of French has created losses for non-francophones in the province, evidence of which is to be found in the extent of their out-migration. Ideally, a political compromise reigns, one that affords substantial protection to French, while providing some English language services.

2. Patriation of the constitution in 1982 with the minority language rights provisions of the Charter as drafted unnecessarily exacerbated Quebec/Canada relations. Bill 101, an innovation of iconic importance to contem-porary Quebec, received no constitutional sanction. The spirit – in the sense that Montesquieu used the term – of the Charter's language provisions is that any majoritarian promotion of its language is suspect.

3. Quebec enjoys de facto constitutional jurisdiction over matters pertaining to public use of language in the province. In legislating Bill 101, Quebec adopted a language regime similar to those prevailing in small European countries, such as those of northern Europe. All such regimes are compro-mises combining protection of the dominant local language with varying degrees of accommodation of other languages. Privately, if not publicly, most among the Canadian political elite acknowledge that any major re-versal of Quebec's language regime would precipitate Quebec secession.

These conclusions need to be supplemented with a few observations on the 1995 referendum. Opposition to Quebec language laws helps explain the over-whelming "No" vote among the one fifth of the population for whom French is not their mother tongue. Language policy was probably a major determi-nant of voting choices among Québécois. Polling evidence is unambiguous in finding that a majority of Québécois are, in varying degrees, anxious about survival of French as lingua franca in Quebec, and a plurality think Quebec sovereignty would improve the odds of linguistic survival.[6] There is also evi-dence that holding these opinions increased the probability of voting in favour of sovereignty in the 1995 referendum.[7] Approximately three in five Québécois voted "Yes." Without the overwhelming "No" majority among non-francophones, the sovereignists would have won their referendum – admittedly a referendum based on a convoluted question.

Prior to the referendum, the federal Liberal leadership in Ottawa was too complacent. The narrowness of the federalist victory induced Ottawa to pay far more attention to countering the appeal of secession among Québécois. Any evaluation of Ottawa's post-1995 strategy must also acknowledge the fiasco of the sponsorship program. The program implied Québécois identities could be shifted with something as trivial as an advertising campaign. In constructing the program, the Prime Minister's Office flagrantly ignored the distinction between spending on programs with a public purpose and, on the other hand, indulging political clientelism and corruption. The program revealed the underbelly of what has too often been Ottawa's approach to Quebec: "buy" support for the status quo. The sponsorship scandal has, within Quebec, decimated the credibility of the Liberal Party of Canada, the primary federalist party in the eyes of Québécois for the last half century.[8]

Chrétien's induction of Dion into the inner circle of those designing Ottawa's post-1995 strategy had the desirable effect of diluting the Trudeau tradition of justiciable language rights. The federal Liberal Party dissociated itself from the "angryphones" (those among the anglophone and allophone Quebec community who wish to pursue Charter-based challenges to Bill 101). Maybe Dion's reorientation of Ottawa's tactics and the newfound realism of the Supreme Court will suffice to remove language as a *casus belli*. On the other hand, non-francophone Canada has yet to acknowledge clearly that Trudeau was mistaken in his opposition to Bill 101. In other words, the strategy of "letting sleeping dogs lie" may not suffice. Language controversies have been central to our history for over two centuries, and with a high probability will re-emerge at some point in the future. Before the next conflict arises, I would like that we craft suitable constitutional language to reassure Québécois that neither legislation enacted by Parliament nor decisions of the Supreme Court will seek to undermine the francophone character of the province.

What I have in mind is that "English" Canada acknowledge Quebec's de facto jurisdiction over language in a manner analogous to acknowledgment in the *BNA Act* of the Roman Catholic authority over the 19th century Quebec school system. The *BNA Act* did not articulate grand principles; it was a pragmatic document addressing the sources of political conflict in mid-Victorian Canada. It afforded explicit, if qualified, constitutional powers to the interested parties. Admittedly, constitutional language may be ignored or reinterpreted over time, but creation of an explicit Quebec legislative power over public use of language would give a solid bargaining position to Québécois on this matter, and has the potential to lower Québécois anxieties over the evolution of Canadian legislative and judicial behaviour.

The Meech Lake Accord attempted to provide this sort of assurance by requiring courts to interpret the constitution through the filter of Quebec's being a "distinct society," but it did so in a less than explicit manner. It also contained the unfortunate implication that other Canadians were somehow less distinct than Québécois. Preferable would be an explicit constitutional amendment affording a legislative power to Quebec in this domain, as recommended a quarter century ago by Pepin-Robarts.[9]

POST-1995 INTERGOVERNMENTAL DIPLOMACY

This is an admittedly nebulous subject and I may well be wrong in my assessment – which is more pessimistic than Courchene's. On the other hand, he was an active participant in what he describes as "pan-Canadian provincialism" and may be guilty of some overly optimistic interpretations.[10]

First, the 1998 Calgary Declaration deserves scant mention. It was a diluted version of the Charlottetown Accord, which was a dilution of the Meech Lake Accord, which had in turn diluted the recommendations of Claude Ryan's "Beige Paper" and the Pepin-Robarts report. More interesting is the Report to the Premiers (Ministerial Council 1995). Despite its committee-driven prose style, the *Report* – endorsed by all provinces except Quebec – was an interesting manifesto. Based on this document, the provinces and Ottawa attempted to clarify federal and provincial responsibilities, and define a set of rules governing federal-provincial management of social policy. However, I share the conclusion of most analysts to the effect that what emerged, the Social Union Framework Agreement (SUFA), is a disappointment.[11] Neither Ottawa nor the provinces have substantively invoked it in subsequent intergovernmental negotiations.

Until a week before signing the final text in early 1999, the premiers proposed a SUFA draft that tackled more seriously both federal concerns (over matters such as interprovincial mobility) and provincial concerns (over Ottawa's unilateral use of its spending power in areas of provincial jurisdiction). The draft enjoyed support from all ten premiers, including Premier Bouchard.[12] Employing the stick (of an ideological battle against the Ontario Tories in the forthcoming provincial election) and the carrot (of a large discretionary increase to intergovernmental transfers), Chrétien broke apart the provincial consensus brokered at the 1998 Annual Premiers' Conference. In the end, Quebec was once again isolated, the only province still supporting what had been a united provincial position. My interpretation is that the federal negotiating team overreacted against provincial demands for a constraint on federal spending power. Ottawa got its way in the drafting of the final text, but created thereby unnecessary animosity in many provincial capitals, not only in Quebec City. Had the federal cabinet accommodated more of the Premiers' "provincial consensus," and been less sensitive about preserving unilateral federal freedom to use the spending power, they could have brought Quebec on side which, in turn, would have been an important diplomatic achievement.

Were I writing the history of post-1995 intergovernmental diplomacy with the intention of stressing the potential of the provinces collectively to address pan-Canadian aspects of policy, I would concentrate on the Council of the Federation. At a minimum, the Council will improve administrative support for the Annual Premiers' Conference. But it may do more. Unlike SUFA and the Calgary Declaration, this is an interprovincial venture crafted without federal officials breathing over provincial shoulders. Its origins lie with Quebec federalists. It figured prominently in the 2001 constitutional report issued by the Quebec Liberal Party (QLP 2001).[13] Given time, the Council may come to exercise a useful constraint on the impulse within the federal Liberal Party and the Ottawa mandarinate to take the initiative on all policy dossiers, regardless of constitutional convention and common sense. What Alain Dubuc (see below) describes as "the central government's irrepressible urge to intervene" is an unattractive feature of Canadian politics. An unconstrained exercise of the federal spending power will in time destroy the essence of fiscal federalism, namely that both orders of government inhabit a political culture in which they undertake the political calculus of balancing incremental benefits of spending against incremental costs of taxing.

Between 1975 and the early 1990s, the habits of sound fiscal federalism were sorely tested. Federal/provincial fiscal entanglement led provincial politicians to damn Ottawa for any cuts in transfers while avoiding the conflicts attendant upon provincial program redesign. The entanglement led Ottawa to blame the provinces for perverse utilization of transfers while avoiding analogous conflicts in redesign of its programs. For many years, neither order of government was willing to assume responsibility for the accumulating public debt. By the early 1990s, Canada was among the most indebted of OECD countries. Fortunately, politicians at both the provincial and federal levels ultimately broke with the non-cooperative game of mutual blame and disentangled their fiscal responsibilities. Beginning with Alberta and Saskatchewan in the early 1990s, both the provinces and Ottawa undertook independent decisions to curtail their spending and redesign programs.

A decade after Canada's painful exercise in fiscal redress, "pan-Canadian provincialism" and respect for fiscal disentanglement are not part of the prevailing political discourse. The strategy of Paul Martin, as Prime Minister leading a minority government, has been to make extensive use of conditional intergovernmental grants – on matters ranging from health care to child care. Furthermore, Martin has undertaken ad hoc bilateral deals with particular provinces on equalization, thereby undermining the credibility of this program as a rules-based instrument to assure reasonable equality of fiscal capacity across provinces.[14]

QUEBEC'S ECONOMIC PERFORMANCE: A CATCH-UP STALLED

Tracing per capita Gross Domestic Product (GDP) over the last half century is a useful introduction to this section. Since the 1960s, per capita GDP in

Quebec has remained in the range of 85–90 percent of the Canadian average (see figure 1). It is tempting to conclude, *plus ça change, plus c'est la même chose*. But the image of Lewis Carroll's red queen – who found it necessary to run hard to remain in the same place – seems appropriate here. The Canadian economy outside Quebec has evolved dramatically since 1960; hence, Quebec's not losing ground is an accomplishment worth acknowledging.

The regions of sustained economic prosperity in Canada have been the far West (Alberta and British Columbia) and southern Ontario. The economy in Ontario grew more slowly, in aggregate and on a per capita basis, than in the far West, and Ontario's per capita GDP converged on the national average. Since Quebec and Ontario are similar in their reliance on manufacturing, it is worth comparing one with the other. By this yardstick, Quebec has caught up by roughly 10 percentage points. Quebec per capita GDP was about 25 percent lower than Ontario's in the early 1960s, 15 percent lower in 2003. This catch-up took place in the two decades of the Quiet Revolution; subsequently, there is no evident trend.

Why did Quebec's catch-up stall post-1980? My explanation is primarily institutional. There are parallels between Quebec's Quiet Revolution and *les trente glorieuses*, as the French describe their successful state-led economic strategy in the three decades following World War II. Both entailed state-led initiatives that dramatically increased employment in the civil service – in the education and health sectors, and in state-owned enterprises. Initially, these

Figure 1: Quebec and Ontario Per Capita GDP, Selected Ratios

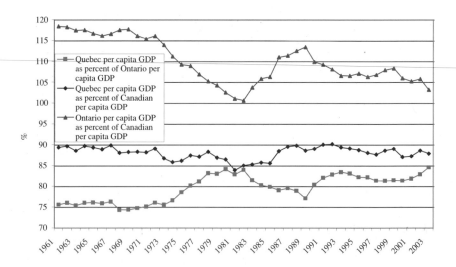

Source: CANSIM time series (V123698, V691901, V123710, V691924, C199226)

initiatives addressed evident weaknesses in the respective economies. However, in both Quebec and France, *dirigisme* became, by the 1980s, part of the problem, not the solution.

In writing an evaluation of Robert Bourassa's career, Pierre Fortin (2002) listed as one of his accomplishments that he succeeded in lowering by the 1990s the province's exceptionally high strike/lockout rate of the 1970s and 1980s.[15] While Fortin is right in this, Bourassa did so largely by continuing the PQ tradition of generous collective bargaining agreements that denied an adequate margin of manoeuvre to the provincial government in redesign of its programs, a tradition that also required high provincial tax rates and generated continuous deficits. The symbol of Bourassa's failure was the severity of the provincial debt he bequeathed upon his retirement in the early 1990s. Admittedly, Bourassa's failure here is a matter of degree, not of kind. Most provinces, and the federal government, incurred unsustainable deficits over much of the period 1975–95. Across the country, generous collective bargaining agreements with public sector employees were part of the fiscal problem.

In fall 2005, a group of prominent Quebecers – including former Premier Lucien Bouchard, his cabinet colleague, Joseph Facal, and the economist, Pierre Fortin – issued a manifesto *Pour un Québec lucide* (2005). The text acknowledges the accomplishments of the Quiet Revolution, which enabled Quebecers to realize education levels equal to those elsewhere in Canada, and to close much of the gap in per capita incomes. But this catch-up is now blocked, argue the signatories, by the very groups – they single out public sector unions – born of the Quiet Revolution. Quebec is again falling behind. Quebecers must embrace efficiency-enhancing changes to public policy, such as higher university fees combined with income-contingent loans the better to fund postsecondary education, reforms that shift taxation from income to consumption, and an end to cheap electricity so as to raise public revenue and lower the provincial debt.

This manifesto has generated widespread debate within Quebec, pro and con. A significant intellectual predecessor to the manifesto is Alain Dubuc's series of full-page editorials in *La Presse*. At the time editor-in-chief, he devoted a full page of his newspaper every day for a week in spring 2000 to a lengthy essay on the theme of political and economic renewal of the province.[16] Québécois had won the linguistic battle, he concluded, and were assured, thereby, "national survival." This was an important victory, but it was now time, he insisted, for Quebec politicians to set aside the national debate: set aside the pursuit of sovereignty, something about which Québécois are themselves divided and something non-francophone Quebecers overwhelmingly oppose; set aside the pursuit of a constitutional special status, something inherently ambiguous and which the other provinces will rebuff; and concentrate instead on detailed policy reforms to enhance the productivity of the provincial economy. Dubuc's underlying image – and I agree with him – is of

Quebec caught in a prisoner's dilemma game, a game played by sovereignists (both the Bloc Québécois in Ottawa and PQ in Quebec City), by Quebec Liberals and their federal namesakes.[17] All players have damaged Quebec's economic prospects by frequent, inefficient policy shifts designed to secure short-term support for their respective constitutional options.

Ottawa's manipulation of regionally variable employment insurance is one example. Quebec has disproportionately "benefited" from this feature of the EI program. While the short-term effect was to increase transfer income, its long-term effect was to retard the necessary productivity-enhancing investments in education levels among those experiencing seasonal unemployment in the affected regions, and also to lower regional employment rates.[18] A related example at the level of provincial policy is the tradition of offering generous access to passive income support via social assistance (see figure 2). Since the 1970s, the Quebec share of its population in receipt of social assistance has been usually well above the Canadian average. Except for the early 1990s recession, a time when Ontario ran the country's most generous welfare system, the Quebec share has also exceeded that in Ontario. At the end of

Figure 2: Social Assistance Beneficiaries, 1977–2001, Canada, Quebec, and Ontario (percent of jurisdiction's population)

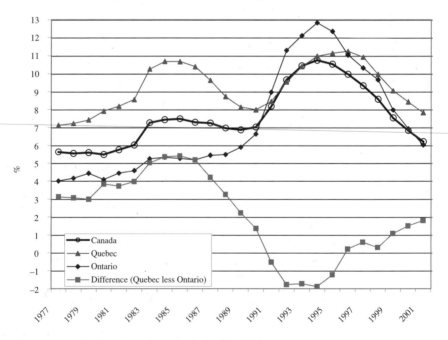

Source: Author's calculations from data in Canada 2004a

their first term in the mid-1980s, the PQ had allowed the interprovincial difference to reach five percentage points. One obvious reason for Quebec governments to sustain this tradition was the design of intergovernmental transfers. The Canada Assistance Plan (CAP) enabled Quebec to transfer half the cost of its social assistance budget to Ottawa.[19]

Canada can tolerate inefficient social programs in particular regions for lengthy periods, and not overtly suffer. The most serious adverse effect is loss of economic dynamism from the affected regions as the well educated emigrate. Other regions benefit, to the extent that the skills of their labour force are enhanced. With a relatively small population and its unique linguistic/cultural status relative to the rest of North America, Quebec cannot afford complacency. As late as the mid-20th century, religious and linguistic bonds have limited Québécois mobility. Relative to their grandparents, young Québécois are better educated, largely indifferent to the local parish, and much more bilingual. These trends increase the probability of well educated Québécois responding to inefficient Quebec social and taxation policy by emigrating. Post-Bill 101, few anglophone Canadians migrate into Quebec. Hence, interprovincial migration is largely one way.

While critical of many Quebec provincial policies, Dubuc does not see salvation via Ottawa:

> There are powerful arguments in favour of decentralization: to control the central government's irrepressible urge to intervene; to put an end to confrontational federalism; to increase efficiency; to bring services closer to the public; to better respond to the specificity of the different Canadian regions that are often poorly served by the central bureaucracy; and, of course, to give Quebec the tools warranted by its difference.

> ... However, we must be aware that a change in the current structure of the division of responsibilities [between Ottawa and the provinces], as desirable as it is, will have only limited effects. [Results] are mainly related to good management and the quality of services. (Dubuc 2000, 20)

In predicting future economic prospects, Courchene rightly focuses attention on all aspects of education – from K–12 schooling to the complex skills required for sophisticated knowledge-based industries. There is some good news for Quebec. Quebec performed well in the most recent international comparison of secondary school mathematics performance organized by the OECD: "At the provincial level, all provinces performed at or above the OECD average in mathematics. Furthermore, students from Alberta, British Columbia, and Quebec performed as well as those from the top performing countries" (Bussière et al. 2004, 63). On the other hand, Quebec suffers unduly high student drop-out rates.[20]

Add to this the importance of policy to nurture metropolitan centres. They are increasingly the locus of innovation and productivity growth. Courchene classifies four Canadian cities as "global city regions" – Vancouver, Calgary/Edmonton, Toronto, and Montreal. They are "the dynamic economic motors of the knowledge/information era." Dubuc makes a similar case:

> The first [policy] objective is education, which appears now to be the essential condition for global economic success. For it is through education that a society can develop a skilled labour force, encourage research and train people who will be able to think and adapt. Education, which is intimately tied to language and values, remains one of the building blocks of identity ...

> Montreal must be the crucible for this knowledge-based society. At present, the metropolis is the victim of a [provincial emphasis on] regionalism that is compromising its development. The future of Quebec will be jeopardized if Montreal's essential role is not recognized by all Quebecers. (Dubuc 2000, 26)

In pursuing their non-cooperative games, Quebec politicians – those in Parliament, in Montreal's Hôtel de ville, and in the National Assembly – repeatedly over the last quarter century ignored the cultivation of efficient networks of business, education, and government in Montreal.[21] As Jean Charest is discovering, undoing inefficient game playing is fraught with controversy. Beneficiaries of the status quo, led by public sector unions, have stymied the provincial government. Were a provincial election to be held at time of writing (December 2005), the PQ would almost certainly emerge as victors, and once again the Quebec government's primary goal would become the pursuit of sovereignty.[22]

CONCLUSION

Relative to most, Canada is a success story among the world's nation states. It has prospered economically, it has survived without major internal violence for nearly 150 years, and it has provided a model in the use of federalism to integrate more than one "founding people." I conclude, however, on a tentative note, sketching several scenarios whereby "the best country in the world" may yet come apart.

First, some random event, such as the sponsorship scandal, may undo the federation. Such random events serve as catalysts to trigger reactions among what are normally inactive ingredients. Among such ingredients are obviously Québécois and "English" Canadians' divergent expectations for language policy. It is a mistake, in my opinion, not to acknowledge explicitly in constitutional language the de facto linguistic jurisdiction Quebec exercises over public use of language within the province.

Another set of destabilizing ingredients are the interests allied to political game-playing – Dubuc's "vicious cycle." Federal strategies to "buy" Québécois acquiescence in the status quo have strengthened some of these interests and hence frustrated initiatives to enhance Quebec productivity. Not that Ottawa bears all the blame. Successive Quebec governments awarded interest groups, such as provincial and municipal public sector unions, with excessive legislative and fiscal benefits. The initiatives of recent Quebec premiers – from Lucien Bouchard to Jean Charest – to enhance productivity and reduce such benefits have engendered more political conflict than concrete results. To date, Quebecers have manifested their frustrations with provincial policies by alternating support between the Quebec Liberal Party and the Parti Québécois. The possibility exists that a majority of Quebecers – counting anglophones and allophones as well as francophones – will conclude at some point that Quebec sovereignty is required in order to end political game-playing and generate coherent Quebec public policy. In other words, a majority may conclude that Bouchard was right to argue that Quebec will become "un pays normal" only when it becomes "un pays souverain."

Widespread indifference in anglophone Canada – in western Canada in particular – to the requirements of linguistic/cultural accommodation is yet another danger. If not immediately under Stephen Harper, ultimately conservatives from the far West and Ontario may dominate a future federal government that is committed to reduction in all forms of interregional redistribution and is indifferent to the complexities of accommodation with Quebec. For reasons quite apart from those of Quebec sovereignists, such a government could endorse Quebec secession – or at least not strive unduly to keep the country together. The ending of the Czech/Slovak federation provides a recent precedent for the majority endorsing an obstreperous minority's wish for sovereignty.

In sum, any country comprising more than one linguistic community intent on intergenerational survival faces ongoing problems of national unity. Past success is not a guarantee for the future.

NOTES

I thank Doug Brown, Linda Cardinal, and Michael Murphy for comments on an earlier draft. Reviewing a manuscript does not imply agreement. I thank also Tom Courchene. He responded to my critique of his contribution to this volume by suggesting to the editors that they invite me to contribute to the volume.

1 Nearly a century later, in the 1970s, the Manitoba francophone community successfully challenged the constitutionality of the 1890 statute. By then, however, the victory was largely symbolic. In Manitoba, French had become a marginal language in terms of frequency of use.

2 Trudeau maintained his opposition to Bill 101 until his death. See, for example, the interview in *Cité libre* (Nemni & Nemni 1998).

3 Many of these intellectuals maintained a strong personal religious faith. This is true of Trudeau and, in particular, of Claude Ryan (2001, 2004).

4 Among Canadians who formerly did not speak French, by far the greatest progress has been made by those anglophones and allophones who remained in Quebec. Bill 101 provided strong inducement for them to learn French. In the 1960s, less than one third were French/English bilingual; the ratio is now roughly two thirds.

5 There is a large demo-linguistic literature on language use in Canada and, in particular, on French-English bilingualism. See Richards (1996) and Castonguay (1999) for surveys of evidence on distributions of mother tongue language, language of home use, intergenerational linguistic transfer and retention.

6 In their book, *Un combat inachevé*, Maurice Pinard and colleagues (1997) assembled an exhaustive survey of Quebec opinion on many political subjects, including language policy. One consistent result since the 1970s is that six in ten Québécois considered French to be "menacé" within the province. A more recent 2003 survey shows no diminution in Québécois anxiety (Mendelsohn et al. 2004). In 1977, the year of adoption of Bill 101, five in ten Québécois believed the situation of the French language in Quebec would improve were Quebec sovereign. This proportion declined somewhat, to about four in ten in polling conducted by the early 1980s. In subsequent polling of the 1990s, Pinard and colleagues found this ratio constant at four in ten (Pinard et al. 1997, 335).

7 André Blais and colleagues (1995a, 1995b) undertook a statistical exercise in explaining support for sovereignty among Québécois in the 1995 referendum. Not surprisingly, those who believed French would fare better in a sovereign Quebec were significantly more likely to endorse sovereignty. Mendelsohn's (2003) conclusion differs from Blais and colleagues. In his statistical assessment of variables underlying support for sovereignty among Québécois, he attributes much more importance to socio-psychological variables than to the rational choice variables stressed by Blais.

8 I make no claim to prescience here. In an article written in the last months of Chrétien's reign (Richards 2003), I concluded he had successfully contained the sovereignist movement for the foreseeable future. That future has proved far shorter than I imagined at the time. According to a poll conducted in May 2005, support for sovereignty (combined with an economic association with Canada) was 54 percent; among francophones support was 62 percent, among anglophones 13 percent, among allophones 31 percent. On the question of independence (with no necessary economic association), support was 46 percent; among francophones 52 percent, among anglophones 10 percent, among allophones 22 percent. These

are levels of support for sovereignty/independence not seen since the 1995 referendum campaign (Léger & Léger 2005).

9 For a discussion of Pepin-Robarts' case for an explicit provincial jurisdiction over public use of language, see my review essay (Richards 2002b).

10 On the subject of Quebec interpretation of intergovernmental relations, I invite readers to read the exchange of "letters" between André Burelle and Claude Ryan (2000).

11 From the provincial perspective, Ryan (1999) wrote the definitive critique of SUFA. I also have expressed scepticism (Richards 2002a). For a positive interpretation of SUFA, see the article by Greg Marchildon (2000) who, at the time, was Deputy Minister to Premier Romanow.

12 Joseph Facal (2005), Quebec Minister for Intergovernmental Affairs at the time of SUFA negotiations, has recently published his interpretation of relevant events.

13 The Council facilitated provincial preparations for the September 2004 federal-provincial negotiations over a health accord. The Council also served as a vehicle for the premiers to lay out a major health reform proposal. The Council proposed that Ottawa define a national pharmacare program. This is a component of health care with scale economies (it makes sense to establish a national formulary and to test new drugs once only). If Ottawa runs pharmacare, they also get "to touch Canadians directly," as opposed to simply writing checks. Obviously, the provinces like the idea of uploading pharmacare because it lowers the constraint of health care cost escalation on provincial fiscal initiatives (what Courchene has defined as "hour-glass federalism"). Unfortunately, the federal cabinet summarily rejected the proposal and it did not figure in the 2004 intergovernmental health accords.

14 Provincial dismay with ad hoc bilateral equalization arrangements has led to creation of an inquiry into the program (Canada 2005), chaired by Al O'Brien, a former deputy finance minister in Alberta.

15 Fortin documents the much higher ratio of days lost to strike/lockout per employee in Quebec relative to Ontario in most years of the 1970s and 1980s Admittedly, public sector unions aggressively opposed the fiscal redress imposed by the Harris Tories in the mid-1990s, and Ontario strike/lockout statistics briefly surpassed Quebec's. But the Ontario strike/lockout rates of the mid-1990s remained far below those of either province in earlier decades.

16 The series has been published, in translation, in *Policy Options* (Dubuc 2000).

17 Over the last decade, Reform/Conservative Party leaders have been very minor players in Quebec affairs. Their leaders have displayed a Trudeau-like hostility to Quebec's language regime (Grégoire 2005), which helps explain the party's derisory Quebec support.

18 Whereas Ontario's employment rate has been 1–4 percentage points above the Canadian average for the last quarter century, Quebec's employment rate has been 2–5 percentage points below the Canadian average. Admittedly, Quebec's employment rate has risen over the last decade and the gap between it and the Canadian average has declined (Canada 2004b).

19 The large discrepancy in per capita CAP transfers became, by the 1990s, a major irritant in intergovernmental negotiations. One element of the 1995 federal budget was abolition of CAP and substitution of a block grant to the provinces. The funding formula for the new transfer has evolved such that, counting cash plus tax transfer, each province receives an equal per capita amount.

20 One of the valuable means to maintaining public pressure on education quality is the survey of secondary schools in the province, published annually by *L'Actualité* (2004).

21 A relevant recent example is the PLQ's acceding to anglophone and suburban interests and legislating, post-2003, to weaken Montreal's metropolitan government. In a move to strengthen the quality of metropolitan Montreal administration, the PQ had in their last mandate merged municipalities into a metropolitan government ("une île une ville").

22 For trends in both federal (since 2000) and provincial (since 2002) voting intentions of Quebecers see the recent Léger and Léger (2005) survey.

REFERENCES

L'Actualité. 2004. "Le Bulletin des écoles secondaires du Québec." Report prepared by Fraser Institute and l'Institut économique de Montréal (15 November 2004).

Blais, A., P. Martin and R. Nadeau. 1995a. "Choosing a Nation: Risk, Uncertainty, and Political Choice." Paper presented to the annual conference of the American Political Science Association.

– 1995b. "Attentes économiques et linguistiques et appui à la souveraineté du Québec: une analyse prospective et comparative." *Canadian Journal of Political Science* 28: 637–59.

Bussière, P., F. Cartwright and T. Knighton. 2004. *Measuring up: Canadian Results of the OECD PISA Study – The Performance of Canada's Youth in Mathematics, Reading, Science and Problem Solving*. Ottawa: Human Resources and Skills Development Canada, Council of Ministers of Education, Canada and Statistics Canada.

Canada. 1979. *A Future Together: Observations and Recommendations*. Report of the Task Force on Canadian Unity. Chaired by Jean-Luc Pepin and John Robarts. Ottawa: Supply and Services.

– 2004a. *Social Security Statistics Canada and Provinces 1976–77 to 2000–01*. Tables 361, 435. Accessed online at http://www11.sdc.gc.ca/en/cs/sp/socpol/publications/statistics /9999-002455/page02.shtml

– 2004b. *The Canadian Labour Market at a Glance*. 71-222-XWE [online]. Ottawa: Statistics Canada. Accessed online at http://www.statcan.ca/english/freepub/71-222-XIE/2004000/chart-c11.htm

– 2005. *Key Issues for the Review of Equalization and Territorial Formula Financing*. Accessed online at http://www.eqtff-pfft.ca

Castonguay, C. 1999. "Getting the Facts Straight on French: Reflections following the 1996 Census" [online]. *Inroads* 8: 57–76. Accessed online at http://www.inroadsjournal.ca

Dion, S. 1992. "Explaining Quebec Nationalism." In *The Collapse of Canada?* ed. K. Weaver. Washington, DC: Brookings Institution.

Dubuc, A. 2000. "We Must Break this Vicious Cycle." *Policy Options* (June): 8–28. Accessed online at http://www.irpp.org

Facal, J. 2005. "Social Policy and Intergovernmental Relations in Canada: Understanding the Failure of SUFA from a Quebec Perspective." Public Policy Paper 32. Regina: Saskatchewan Institute of Public Policy. Accessed online at http://www.uregina.ca/sipp

Ford v. Quebec (Attorney General). 1988. *Supreme Court Reports* Vol. 2. Accessed on line at http://www.lexum.umontreal.ca/csc-scc/en/pub/1988/vol2/html/1988scr2_0712.html

Fortin, P. 2002. "Robert Bourassa et l'Economie du Québec." *Policy Options* (October): 32–36. Accessed online at http://www.irpp.org

Gosselin v. Quebec (Attorney General). 2005. SCC. Accessed on line at http://www.lexum.umontreal.ca/csc-scc/en/rec/html/2005scc015.wpd.html

Grégoire, I. 2005. "Y a-t-il une droite au Québec?" *L'Actualité,* 1 April, 20–29.

Léger & Léger. 2005. "Quebec Survey." Opinion poll commissioned by *Le Journal de Montréal* and *The Gazette*, 14 May.

Lisée, J.-F. 2001. "Invest in Quebec's Future." *Inroads* 10: 167–86. Accessed online at http://www.inroadsjournal.ca

Marchildon, G. 2000. "A Step in the Right Direction." *Inroads* 9: 124–33.

Mendelsohn, M. 2003. "Rational Choice and Socio-Psychological Explanation for Opinion on Quebec Sovereignty." *Canadian Journal of Political Science* 36: 511–37.

Mendelsohn, M., A. Parkin and M. Pinard. 2004. "A New Chapter or the Same Old Story? Quebec Public Opinion and the National Question from 1996–2003." Kingston: Institute of Intergovernmental Relations, Queen's University. Accessed online at http://www.iigr.ca/__site/iigr/__files/papers/PrsPaper.4032330ed4da0.pdf

Ministerial Council on Social Policy Reform and Renewal. 1995. *Report to the Premiers*. Ottawa.

Nemni, M. and M. Nemni. 1998. "Entretien avec Pierre Elliott Trudeau." *Cité libre* 26(1): 98–123.

Pinard, M., V. Lemieux and R. Bernier. 1997. *Un combat inachevé*. Sainte-Foy: Presses de l'Université du Québec.

Pour un Québec lucide. 2005. Manifesto launched by Lucien Bouchard. Accessed online in English and French at http://www.pourunquebeclucide.com

Quebec. 1977. *The Charter of the French Language*. Accessed online at http://www.oqlf.gouv.qc.ca/english/charter/preamble.html

Quebec Liberal Party. 2001. *A Project for Quebec: Affirmation, Autonomy and Leadership*. Benoît Pelletier, chair.

Richards, J. 1996. "Language Matters: Ensuring That the Sugar Not Dissolve in the Coffee." Monograph in Canadian Union Papers. *Commentary* 84. Toronto: C.D. Howe Institute. Reprinted in D. Cameron, ed. 1999. *The Referendum Papers.* Toronto: University of Toronto Press. Accessed online at http://www.cdhowe.org

– 2002a. "The Paradox of the Social Union Framework Agreement." *Backgrounder* 59. Toronto: C.D. Howe Institute. Accessed online at http://www.cdhowe.org

– 2002b. "La langue, toujours source de controverses." In *Le débat qui n'a pas eu lieu: La Commission Pepin-Robarts, quelque vingt ans après,* Collection Amérique française no. 9, ed. J.-P. Wallot. Ottawa: Centre de recherche en civilisation canadienne-française, University of Ottawa Press.

– 2003. "Le règne de Chrétien vu de ma cuisine" In *L'annuaire du Québec 2004*, ed. M. Venne. Montreal: Fides.

Ryan, C. 1999. " The agreement on the Canadian social union as seen by a Quebec federalist." *Inroads* 8: 25–49. Accessed online at http://www.inroadsjournal.ca

Ryan, C. and A. Burelle. 2000. "Letters." *Inroads* 9: 88–123. Accessed online at http://www.inroadsjournal.ca

– 2001. "Building the Temporal City." *Inroads* 10: 87–99. Accessed online at http://www.inroadsjournal.ca

– 2004. "I Leave this World with Regret …" *Inroads* 15: 10–11. Accessed online at http://www.inroadsjournal.ca

V

Chronology

11

Year in Review 2005

Aron Seal

Research assistance from Ying Feng, James Nicholson and Stephanie Quesnelle is gratefully acknowledged.

TABLE OF CONTENTS
(entries appear in chronological order within categories)

ABORIGINAL PEOPLES

28 April 2005
Business, Energy,
Northwest Territories

Imperial Oil Ltd., angered by costly demands by Aboriginal groups and delays in regulatory approvals, suspends all work on the proposed $7 billion Mackenzie Valley natural gas pipeline project. Four First Nations communities are claiming compensation for use of their territory; understaffed regulatory boards are further finding themselves unable to process the thousands of requests associated with the project. Government officials from both the federal and territorial governments remain confident that outstanding issues can be resolved.

10 May
Business, Energy,
Northwest Territories

Premier Joe Handley and Deputy Prime Minister Anne McClellan announce a funding agreement to strengthen Aboriginal social programs in the North. Aboriginal groups had demanded the funds in compensation for allowing the proposed Mackenzie Valley pipeline through their territory. Construction of the pipeline is currently on hold pending resolution of the Aboriginal claim and outstanding regulatory issues.

31 May
Aboriginal Peoples
and Federal
Relations

Prime Minister Paul Martin and leaders of five national Aboriginal organizations sign an agreement promising First Nations involvement in federal policy discussions. The pact outlines means through which Aboriginal organizations will be given direct influence over policies concerning their communities. Martin calls on provincial and municipal governments to offer similar influence to Aboriginal groups.

11 July
Business, Energy,
Northwest Territories

The federal government settles a lawsuit by the Deh Cho First Nation concerning the Mackenzie Valley pipeline project. In exchange for allowing the pipeline to pass through their territory, the Deh Cho receive a compensation package worth $21 million and guarantees regarding the environmental and economic spillovers associated with the development. Though the settlement does not resolve the outstanding project issues with the First Nations, it is seen as an important step.

20 July
Aboriginal Peoples,
New Brunswick,
Nova Scotia

The Supreme Court rules against Mi'kmaq loggers in Nova Scotia and New Brunswick claiming logging rights on Crown land. Although treaties accord native groups the right to trade "traditional items," the court rules that logging does not represent a "logical evolution" of historic Mi'kmaq trading practices. The decision is seen as a major setback for native rights. Government officials in both provinces pledge to negotiate an agreement to protect Mi'kmaq forestry activities.

25 October
Aboriginal Peoples,
Environment,
Ontario

The Ontario government declares a state of emergency on the Kashechewan native reserve as a result of the contamination of reserve drinking water. Water quality has been an issue on the reserve for several years; the Ontario Clean Water Agency described the situation as a "Walkerton-in-waiting" in 2003. The situation worsened when E. coli was found in the water on 18 October 2005. On 27 October 2005, the federal government commits to relocating the entire community to safer land.

23 November
Business, Energy,
Northwest Territories

Imperial Oil Ltd. announces plans to proceed to public hearings on development of the Mackenzie Valley pipeline. Planning of the pipeline has been stalled since April pending resolution of regulatory concerns and Aboriginal claims. Imperial is satisfied with progress on the issues, including a 17 November pledge of $2.8 billion in federal aid.

24–25 November
Aboriginal Peoples
and Federal
Relations: Kelowna
Accord

The First Ministers meet with Aboriginal leaders in Kelowna, British Columbia. $5 billion is committed by the federal government over five years towards improvement of Aboriginal quality of life, including health care, education, housing and employment opportunities.

7 December
Aboriginal Peoples

The Assembly of First Nations (AFN) Renewal Commission releases *A Treaty Among Ourselves,* a 300-page report containing 47 recommendations for improving the functioning of the Assembly. The committee had been formed in 2004 to re-examine the purpose and structure of the organization. Proposals include election of the National Chief of the Assembly through a universal vote of all First Nations citizens, greater AFN standing within Confederation, and an organizational focus on political advocacy.

AGRICULTURE

2 January *Alberta, BSE,* *Canada–U.S.* *Relations*	The Canadian Food Inspection Agency announces the detection of a BSE infected cow on an Alberta dairy farm. This is the second known case of mad cow disease in Canada. In reaction, Federal Agriculture Minister Andy Mitchell points to increased BSE protection and screening measures implemented since 2003 in order to try to reassure consumers of the continued safety of Canadian beef. American officials insist that the U.S. border will still be reopened to live cattle trade on 7 March as planned.
11 January *Alberta, BSE,* *Canada–U.S.* *Relations*	A third Canadian case of BSE, the second in less than two weeks, is detected by the Canadian Food Inspection Agency in Alberta. American agriculture officials send a delegation to Canada to investigate the case. Canadian officials again stress their confidence in the safety of the country's beef.
2 March *BSE, Canada–U.S.* *Relations*	A planned 7 March reopening of the U.S. border to Canadian beef exports is postponed indefinitely following an American federal court injunction. R-CALF USA, a lobby group representing cattle ranchers, is granted permission under the injunction to proceed with a lawsuit seeking indefinite border closure. The group claims Canadian beef puts U.S. consumers and cattle producers at risk.
29 March *Agriculture, Federal* *Government, BSE*	Federal Agriculture Minister Andy Mitchell announces a $1 billion aid package for Canadian farmers. The funds will be devoted primarily to grain farmers suffering from successive seasons of drought and cattle ranchers devastated by BSE-induced export market closures. Though the announcement is not tied to provincial matching, Mitchell calls on the provinces to provide supplementary aid.
21 November *Agriculture, Foreign* *Affairs*	Amid fears of avian flu, bans on imports of Canadian poultry are enacted in the United States, Taiwan, Japan and Hong Kong. 60 farms in the Fraser Valley have been quarantined for the disease following detection of an infected bird last week. Industry officials call the bans an overreaction.

BUDGETS

Federal Government

23 February

Finance Minister Ralph Goodale tables the first budget of Prime Minister Paul Martin's minority government. Highlights include five-year plans for $12.6 billion in tax cuts, $12.8 billion in military spending, $5 billion for child care and $5 billion for municipalities through sharing of fuel tax revenues. While Conservatives and New Democrats are satisfied with the budget, Bloc Québécois Leader Gilles Duceppe says his party will vote against it, citing a failure to address the fiscal imbalance with the provinces. Link to Federal Budget http://www.fin.gc.ca/budget05/bp/bptoce.htm

26 April
Federal Spending,
Federal Politics

Prime Minister Paul Martin, in exchange for New Democratic Party (NDP) support for the budget, agrees to replace $4.6 billion in planned corporate tax cuts with increases in education, housing and environmental spending. Layton stresses that although his party will support the budget, he is not promising unconditional future support to the government. The agreement does not guarantee the 155 votes needed for the passage of the budget, however, as the caucuses of the Liberals and the NDP total only 131 and 19 members respectively.

19 May
Federal Politics

The Liberal government narrowly survives a vote of confidence as House of Commons Speaker Peter Milliken votes in favour of the New Democratic Party (NDP) amendment to the budget to break a 152-152 tie. The Liberals were supported by the NDP and independents Chuck Cadman and Carolyn Parrish. The vote follows a week of high drama on Parliament Hill including the defection of Belinda Stronach from the Conservatives to the Liberals and uncertainty about Cadman's vote. Opposition leader Stephen Harper, though disappointed, notes that future opportunities will arise to defeat the government.

14 November
Federal Government,
Economic and Fiscal
Update

The government's Economic and Fiscal Update is interpreted as a pre-election "mini-budget" by the media given a multitude of new spending promises and policy initiatives. Buoyed by increases in forecasted surpluses, now

estimated at $54 billion over five years, Finance Minister Ralph Goodale announces a 1% tax rate cut for the lowest personal income tax bracket, a $500 increase in the basic personal tax exemption, as well as $230 million in corporate tax cuts and several new educational spending programs.
Link to Economic and Fiscal Update 2005
http://www.fin.gc.ca/budtoce/2005/ec05_e.html

Provincial and Territorial Governments

10 February *Northwest Territories*	Link to Northwest Territories Budget 2005 http://www.fin.gov.nt.ca/documents/2005budget.pdf
15 February *British Columbia*	The Liberal government tables a budget heavy on spending increases, tax cuts for low income earners and debt repayment. Highlights include an additional $1 billion for construction of schools, colleges, hospitals and transportation infrastructure, as well as an increase in the provincial basic personal tax exemption to $15,000. Finance Minister Colin Hansen calls the budget a blueprint for a "golden decade." He attributes booming growth to the deep tax cuts enacted during the government's first three years in office. Link to British Columbia Budget, 2005 http://www.bcbudget.gov.bc.ca/2005/summary/default.htm
24 February *Nunavut*	Link to Nunavut Budget 2005 http://www.gov.nu.ca/finance/mainbudgets/budget2005.pdf
8 March *Manitoba*	Link to Manitoba Budget 2005 http://www.gov.mb.ca/finance/budget05/papers/index.html
21 March *Newfoundland and Labrador*	Link to Newfoundland and Labrador Budget 2005 http://www.budget.gov.nl.ca/budget2005/pdf/BudgetSpeech05.pdf
24 March *Yukon Territories*	Link to Yukon Territories Budget 2005 http://www.finance.gov.yk.ca/pdf/2005_2006_speech.pdf

30 March *New Brunswick*	Link to New Brunswick Budget 2005 http://www.gnb.ca/0160/budget/buddoc2005/ budget_2005-e.pdf
31 March *Saskatchewan*	Link to Saskatchewan Budget 2005 http://www.gov.sk.ca/finance/budget/budget05/ budgetsummary.pdf
7 April *Prince Edward Island*	Link to Prince Edward Island Budget 2005 http://www.gov.pe.ca/budget/2005/address.pdf

13 April
Alberta

In a reversal of position from the deep cuts implemented during the early years of Ralph Klein's Conservative government, an abundance of natural resource revenues allows the government to boost spending across the board in the provincial budget. Critics, however, lament the decision to forgo significant tax relief; provincial treasurer Shirley McClellan responds by noting the tax cuts implemented by the government over the last six years and the fact that Albertans already face the lowest tax burden of all Canadians.
Link to Alberta Budget 2005
http://www.finance.gov.ab.ca/publications/budget/
budget2005/index.html

21 April
Quebec

A cautious budget with modest tax cuts and spending increases is tabled in the provincial legislature for 2005-06. For the third consecutive year, the Liberal government breaks its election promise to cut taxes by $1 billion per year. The government claims that significant change will only be possible once the federal government restores fiscal equity within the federation.
Link to Quebec Budget 2005
http://www.budget.finances.gouv.qc.ca/budget/2005-
2006/en/pdf/BudgetPlan.pdf

26 April 2005 *Nova Scotia*	Link to Nova Scotia Budget 2005 http://www.gov.ns.ca/fina/budget05/ budgetaddress2005_06.pdf
11 May *Ontario*	Link to Ontario Budget 2005 http://www.fin.gov.on.ca/english/budget/bud05/pdf/ papers_all.pdf

EDUCATION

2 April
Quebec

An agreement is reached between the federal government, the Quebec government and student government leaders to reinvest $482 million into post-secondary bursaries over five years, reversing a much maligned 2004 cut. Students at several CEGEPS and universities have been boycotting classes for several weeks to pressure governments on the issue.

7 October
British Columbia

British Columbia teachers undertake an illegal strike to protest the unilateral imposition of a labour contract extension by the provincial government. The province has unilaterally legislated an extension to the existing labour agreement through June 2006 without improvements to wages or working conditions. Teachers pledge to maintain their strike until a mutually acceptable agreement is reached regardless of possible fines or lost wages.

23 October
British Columbia

Teachers vote to accept a proposed agreement to end their illegal strike. The mediated settlement includes $40 million to harmonize teachers' salaries throughout the province and changes to the School Act to reduce class sizes. A $500,000 fine was levied on the union for contempt of court during the strike; teachers were denied strike pay for their two weeks off the job.

ENVIRONMENT

15 February
Federal Government,
Climate Change

The Kyoto Protocol comes into effect internationally. As yet Canada has no implementation plan for the protocol; Environment Minister Stéphane Dion says that one will be forthcoming "in the weeks following the budget" but does not offer a firm date.

13 April
Federal Government,
Climate Change

The federal government releases its Kyoto Protocol implementation plan. Estimated to cost $10 billion, the plan proposes advertising campaigns encouraging individuals and businesses to voluntarily take measures to reduce their emissions, funding for clean energy and conservation projects and possible purchases of emission credits from other countries. Critics deride the plan's reliance on voluntary initiatives and international credit purchases, claiming that few real emissions reductions will be achieved.

28 November–
9 December
Environment,
Climate Change

Montreal hosts the 11th Conference of the Parties to the United Nations Framework Convention on Climate Change. The conference is the largest on climate change to be held since the creation of the Kyoto Protocol in 1997. Discussions focus on implementation plans for environmental initiatives, including emissions trading, joint implementation mechanisms, and clean development measures.

EQUALITY RIGHTS

1 February
Federal Politics and
Same-Sex Rights

The Civil Marriage Act, a bill to extend marriage to same-sex couples, is tabled in the House of Commons. The legislation follows numerous provincial court rulings against the traditional definition of marriage as well as a Supreme Court reference affirming the authority of the federal government to define marriage. Prime Minister Paul Martin believes the bill contains sufficient assurances that religious institutions will be allowed to maintain their traditional marriage definitions.

6 June
Federal Politics and
Same-Sex Rights

Member of Parliament Pat O'Brien, displeased with the proposed same-sex marriage legislation, quits the Liberal party to sit as an independent. O'Brien, a supporter of the traditional definition of marriage, believes that "fair, full and meaningful" public hearings have not been held on the issue. While O'Brien intends to vote against the government on matters of confidence, Liberals remain positive that both their budget and the same-sex marriage bill will pass.

28 June
Federal Politics and
Same-Sex Rights

Bill C-38 passes final reading on a 158-133 House of Commons vote, making Canada the third country in the world to recognize same-sex marriage. Conservative leader Stephen Harper pledges to revisit the question should his party win the next election.

FEDERAL POLITICS

14 January *Federal Politics*	Judy Sgro resigns her cabinet post as Immigration Minister amid allegations of abuses of her authority. Sgro is alleged to have intervened to prevent the deportation of a pizza shop owner in exchange for contributions to her election campaign. The federal ethics commissioner is further investigating a temporary resident permit granted to a Romanian exotic dancer who had volunteered for Sgro during the campaign. Sgro denies all improprieties and vows to fight to clear her name.
6 March *Federal Politics*	Prime Minister Paul Martin receives 88 percent delegate support at the Liberal Party policy convention in Ottawa. Martin sees the result as a strong vote of confidence in his leadership and his government.
17–19 March *Federal Politics*	The newly created Conservative Party of Canada holds its founding policy convention in Montreal. Delegates hope to use the occasion to create a new image for the party, unite the former Canadian Alliance and Progressive Conservative factions and reduce the party's perceived social conservative focus and "hidden agenda." A Conservative government, delegates decide, would pursue significant personal and corporate tax cuts, a review of the Kyoto Protocol and increased assistance for parents. Delegates further pledge not to seek to regulate abortion.
10 May *Federal Politics*	A House of Commons motion calling on the government to resign passes by a 153–130 margin but is ignored by the Liberals. The motion, a request that the public accounts committee rewrite a report to call on the government to resign, is called "procedural" and not a matter of confidence. Prime Minister Paul Martin refuses a subsequent opposition call for an immediate confidence vote given that numerous opportunities will arise in the coming weeks for opposition members to defeat the government if they so choose.
17 May *Federal Politics*	MP Belinda Stronach crosses the floor to the Liberals, claiming discomfort with the policy direction of the new Conservative Party. Stronach is subsequently named Minister of Human Resources by her new party; she denies

that the promise of a cabinet appointment led to her defection. The move increases the likelihood of the Liberals surviving an upcoming confidence vote.

24 May
Federal Politics

Liberal candidate Todd Russell wins a by-election in the riding of Labrador, increasing the likelihood of the government surviving future votes of confidence. This is the first Liberal victory in the riding since 1968.

31 May
Federal Politics

Transcripts of taped conversations between Member of Parliament Gurmant Grewal and senior Liberal Party officials are made public by the Conservative Party. Conservatives interpret the content of the conversations as an offer of a cabinet appointment in exchange for Grewal's defection to the government. Opposition parties call on the RCMP and ethics commissioner Bernard Shapiro to investigate whether the conversations show breaches of the Criminal Code and/or conflicts of interest. Liberals claim that the tapes were edited prior to their release.

Ongoing controversy leads Grewal to take a "stress leave" from Parliament the following week.

21 June
Federal Politics

Ethics Commissioner Bernard Shapiro releases his final report into allegations that former immigration minister Judy Sgro handed out special visas to volunteers during her 2004 re-election campaign. While Shapiro places direct responsibility for the illegitimate visas on Sgro's chief of staff, he stops short of clearing the former minister, claiming that she could not have been unaware of the presence of the visa recipients on her campaign. Sgro continues to deny any wrongdoing.

10 July
Federal Politics

Independent Member of Parliament Chuck Cadman dies of cancer. Cadman was serving his third term as an MP; he will be best remembered for supporting the government in the 19 May 2005 confidence vote, as his vote represented the margin of victory for the government.

4 August
Federal Politics

Michaelle Jean is appointed Canada's 27th Governor General. Jean will replace the outgoing Adrienne Clarkson on 1 October. A Haitian-born Canadian, Jean is best known as an award winning CBC journalist.

17 August *Federal Politics*	Responding to allegations that she and her husband are Quebec sovereignists, Governor General Designate Michaelle Jean releases a statement affirming her commitment to Canadian federalism and its institutions. Controversy had emerged over a 1991 film made by her husband, Jean-Daniel Lafond, in which Jean joins in a toast among separatist intellectuals, although the cause being toasted is not clear. Jean's statement attests that neither she nor her husband have ever "belonged to a political party or the separatist movement."
29 August *Federal Politics*	Prime Minister Paul Martin announces the appointment of Francis Fox and Yoine Goldstein to the Senate. Fox is a former cabinet minister and corporate executive; Goldstein is a bankruptcy lawyer and Jewish community activist. Opposition parties criticize the appointees on their common Montreal background and their past involvements in the Liberal Party.
27 September *Federal Politics*	Michaelle Jean is sworn in as Canada's 27th Governor General. A Haitian-born journalist, Jean was announced as the successor to Adrienne Clarkson on 4 August. Jean uses her address at the swearing-in ceremony to call for an end to tensions between English- and French-speaking Canadians.
29 November *Federal Politics*	Following the defeat of the government in a vote of confidence the day previous, Prime Minister Paul Martin asks Governor General Michaelle Jean to dissolve Parliament. An election is called for 23 January 2006. Initial polls show the Liberals and Conservatives in a virtual dead heat. Martin announces that the Liberal Party will run on the strength of its record in government, including a consistently strong economy, balanced budgets and progress on social issues. He criticizes opposition parties for having forced the election, claiming that political ambition "has overwhelmed common sense." Opposition parties focus on the value of change. Conservative Leader Stephen Harper asks voters to allow his party to restore accountability to federal politics, while Bloc Québécois leader Gilles Duceppe argues that the Liberals have lost the moral authority to govern. New Democratic Party Jack Layton urges people to reject both

major parties, highlighting the successes it achieved during the tenure of Martin's minority government.

In the first major policy announcement of the campaign, Harper pledges to re-open the same-sex marriage debate and allow a full free vote on the issue if elected Prime Minister.

30 November *Federal Politics*	The Bloc Québécois is the first major party to release its election platform. Priorities include resolution of the ongoing fiscal imbalance, increasing Quebec's voice in international affairs and achieving the environmental targets outlined in the Kyoto protocol. Media reaction to the platform highlights a call for Quebec to field its own sports teams at international events.
1 December *Federal Politics*	Conservative Leader Stephen Harper announces plans to cut the Goods and Services Tax (GST) by two percentage points if elected Prime Minister. Harper would cut the tax by one percentage point immediately, with another one percentage point cut within five years. Liberals criticize the Conservatives' intention to reverse an announced income tax cut to fund the pledge. New Democratic Party leader Jack Layton claims tax cuts are not among the priorities of Canadians.
5 December *Federal Politics*	Conservative Leader Stephen Harper announces his party's child care plan, including an annual $1,200 per child payment to parents and a business tax credit designed to create 125,000 new daycare spaces over five years. The proposal contrasts with Liberal plans for a national daycare program which Harper calls a restrictive "child-care bureaucracy."
6 December *Federal Politics*	Prime Minister Paul Martin responds the following day by promising to boost the value of its child care plan to $10 billion over ten years.
8 December *Federal Politics*	The Liberal Party proposes a national handgun ban. The promise is primarily seen as a response to prominent gun crime in Ontario, particularly Toronto. Public Safety Minister Anne McClellan concedes, however, that the measure would have to be subject to provincial opt-out. Critics cite the ineffectiveness of the federal gun registry as evidence

of the shortcomings of bans as a means of preventing gun crime.

11 December
Federal Politics

Prime Minister Paul Martin's Director of Communications, Scott Reid, claims that the Conservatives $1,200 per year child care subsidy amounts to giving parents money to "blow on beer and popcorn." Reid later apologizes for the claim.

15 December
Federal Politics

The leaders of the three opposition parties mount a united attack on Prime Minister Paul Martin in the first French language election debate. Bloc Québécois Leader Gilles Duceppe leads the charge, claiming that the Liberals, having allegedly tried to buy the support of Quebecers through the sponsorship scandal, have lost the moral authority to govern. Martin points in his defence to his having appointed the commission of inquiry led by Justice John Gomery, an act he claims would only have been done by someone with nothing to hide. He tries to direct attention to the Bloc's ultimate goal of Quebec separation, arguing that Quebecers do not want to be forced into another referendum. Stephen Harper and Jack Layton, for their part, urge voters to punish the Liberals for their misdeeds without casting a vote that could be interpreted as support for Quebec sovereignty.

16 December
Federal Politics

Polls show no clear winner in the first English language election debate. Focus is initially placed on Conservative Leader Stephen Harper's positions on social issues such as same-sex marriage, with other leaders attacking Harper on his refusal to accept the decision of the last Parliament on the matter. On crime prevention, Prime Minister Martin touts the value of his promise to ban handguns, while Harper insists that crime prevention measures should not obscure the need for harsh penalties for offenders. Martin and Harper further clash over their contrasting child care proposals. New Democratic Party leader Jack Layton focuses his remarks on the importance of improvements to social spending. As was the case the night before, the opposition parties, led by Bloc Québécois leader Gilles Duceppe, all attack Martin on corruption within the Liberal Party, claiming that the Liberals have lost the moral authority to govern.

19 December
Federal Politics

Conservative Leader Stephen Harper makes his now famous "open federalism" pitch to Quebec voters, promising to give the province an increased international voice and improved fiscal arrangements if elected Prime Minister. He speaks specifically of giving the province a voice in international organizations such as UNESCO. Prime Minister Paul Martin responds by insisting that Canada must speak with a single, united voice on the international stage.

28 December
Federal Politics

The Royal Canadian Mounted Police announces an investigation into possible information leaks regarding the freeze on the creation of income trusts by the government on 23 November. The freeze announcement was preceded by a flurry of market trading during the day with the value of several trusts rising sharply. Finance Minister Ralph Goodale denies any improper disclosures in his department.

30 December
Federal Politics

Conservative Leader Stephen Harper promises a 16 percent tax credit for public transit users if his party is elected to government. The promise is the latest of a string of small, targeted tax breaks designed to appeal to targeted groups of voters. Opponents view the plan as ineffective in promoting public transit usage.

HEALTH

11 January
Alberta

In a highly anticipated speech to the Canadian Club of Calgary, Premier Ralph Klein outlines plans for health care reform in Alberta. Rejecting both the current Canadian system and the American private model, Klein proposes a "third way" that combines government and market provision. Proposals focus on increased flexibility in delivery options for regional health boards including partnerships with the private sector where deemed valuable. Klein stresses that his plan is a test of the boundaries of the Canada Health Act rather than an attack against it.

3 April
*Health and First
Ministers*

The Wait Time Alliance of Canada (WTA), an association of seven major Canadian medical associations, releases an interim report detailing acceptable wait times for a series of key medical services. The report builds towards the September 2004 First Ministers' commitment to establishing benchmarks for acceptable wait times by the end of 2005 as part of the "Ten-Year Plan to Strengthen Health Care." The final report is released in August 2005.

9 June
Supreme Court and Health

In a complex 4-3 decision on the case of *Chaoulli v. Quebec*, the Supreme Court rules that public prohibition of private health insurance violates the Quebec and Canadian Charters of Rights. The majority opinion contends that limiting access to private medical services is unjustifiable given life-threatening waiting lists for such services in the public sector. Reactions to the potential consequences of the ruling are widespread; federal officials call the ruling a "wake-up call" to improve the quality of public health care delivery, while others claim that the court has made the demise of universal public health care inevitable.

12 July
Alberta and Canada Health Act

Premier Ralph Klein announces the first of his "third way" health care reforms, including improved prescription drug coverage and provision of premium services such as luxury hotel rooms and specialized hip replacements. Though the reforms are seen by some critics as thinly veiled privatization, federal Health Minister Ujjal Dosanjh considers them consistent with the principles of the Canada Health Act.

17 August
Health and Private Insurance

Nearly two-thirds of delegates at the annual meeting of the Canadian Medical Association (CMA) vote to endorse a motion allowing patients to use private health insurance where publicly delivered services are inadequate. The motion, a response to the Chaoulli Supreme Court decision, serves as a CMA endorsement of a parallel private insurance system for Canadians.

12 December
Health

Provincial and territorial health ministers announce national benchmarks for acceptable wait times on ten major medical procedures. The "Ten-Year Plan to Strengthen Health Care" signed between the provincial and federal governments commits the provinces to establishing the benchmarks by the end of 2005. Critics note, however, that the non-binding benchmarks are significantly more generous than those proposed by the Wait Times Alliance in April and August 2005 reports.

INTERGOVERNMENTAL RELATIONS

28 January
Atlantic Canada and
Intergovernmental
Relations

The federal government reaches an agreement in principle with the governments of Nova Scotia and Newfoundland and Labrador concerning treatment of offshore natural resource royalties within the federal equalization formula. Provincial natural resource revenues will be exempted from equalization calculations for eight years; a further exemption will follow for the provinces should their revenues not reach the national average by 2012. Nearly 70 percent of resource royalties are at present lost to the provinces through reduced equalization payments. Saskatchewan Premier Lorne Calvert and Northwest Territories Premier Joe Handley respond to the agreements with calls for similar arrangements for their jurisdictions.

9 February
Ontario and
Intergovernmental
Relations

Premier Dalton McGuinty reacts to the equalization agreements signed last month between the federal government and the governments of Newfoundland and Nova Scotia, calling them "patently unfair" to taxpayers. Noting that Ontario contributes $23 billion more to the federal treasury than it receives back in services, McGuinty calls for increased federal fiscal support for his province. Following Saskatchewan Premier Lorne Calvert, McGuinty is the second provincial premier to criticize last month's agreement.

8 May
Ontario and
Intergovernmental
Relations

A day of negotiations between Premier Dalton McGuinty and Prime Minister Paul Martin results in a five-year, $5.75 billion funding agreement to offset the alleged $23 billion gap between federal revenues from and expenditures to the province. Although McGuinty recognizes the need for Ontario to contribute fiscally to the federation, he has called the current extent of the gap excessive. McGuinty had sought an immediate $5 billion payment; he pledges to continue pressuring the federal government for further funding.

INTERNATIONAL RELATIONS

24 February
Canada–U.S.
Relations

Prime Minister Paul Martin formally rejects Canadian involvement in the planned American ballistic missile defence system. The decision, following non-participation in the U.S.-led war in Iraq, is the second Canadian refusal of a major American military request in two years. U.S. Ambassador Paul Cellucci warns that the American government will not hesitate to breach Canadian airspace if necessary to intercept an oncoming missile.

27 April
International Relations

President George W. Bush nominates David Wilkins to be the next United States Ambassador to Canada. Wilkins, a close personal friend and Bush fundraiser, served as Speaker of the South Carolina legislature for 11 years. Critics of the appointment note his minimal experience with Canadian relations and his criticisms of Canadian softwood lumber practises.

15 June
International Relations

North Dakota agrees to delay the opening of the Devils Lake water diversion project pending resolution of pollution concerns. The Canadian federal, Manitoba and Minnesota governments fear that the project, designed to prevent flooding in Devils Lake, North Dakota, will pollute the Red River and Lake Winnipeg. Officials from North Dakota insist that the project will proceed but recognize the need for continuing pollution dialogue.

27 June
International Relations

The governments of Canada, Mexico and the United States announce plans for comprehensive continental security and economic integration. Proposals include improved screening of individuals and goods entering the continent, increased information sharing, and coordinated responses to threats. Critics decry the lack of public consultation prior to the agreements.

29 June
International Relations

David Wilkins formally becomes the United States' Ambassador to Canada. Wilkins was appointed by President George W. Bush on 27 April.

6–8 July
International Relations

The 31st meeting of the Group of Eight (G8) takes place in Scotland. Discussions focus primarily on world poverty and global warming. Prime Minister Paul Martin is criticized in some circles for refusing to commit to increasing Canadian foreign aid to an international target of 0.7 percent of GDP. The meeting is overshadowed by a bombing in the London, underground on 7 July.

20 July *International* *Relations*	Defence Minister Bill Graham travels to Hans Island as a symbolic assertion of Canada's claim of sovereignty over the territory, sparking Danish protest. A dispute with Denmark over claim to the island dates back to 1983.
6 August *International* *Relations*	Tensions over the proposed Devils Lake water diversion project are eased as North Dakota officials agree to comply with several Canadian recommendations, including construction of an advanced water filtration system and abandoning plans to transfer water into the Red River. Canadian officials had feared that the project as originally planned would cause increased pollution and harm wildlife. Though not all concerns are resolved, Manitoba Premier Gary Doer is satisfied with the improvements.
10 August *International* *Relations*	A dispute resolution panel under the North American Free Trade Agreement rules that the Canadian government does not unfairly subsidize its lumber producers. The ruling implicitly calls on the U.S. to eliminate countervailing duties on Canadian softwood exports. American officials indicate, however, that they will ignore the ruling.
19 September *International* *Relations*	Canadian and Danish officials call a truce in the ongoing dispute over Hans Island. The two countries agree to inform each other before any official visits to the island; discussions will further be held between representatives of the two countries to evaluate past treaties and documents in the hopes of resolving the sovereignty dispute. Neither country, however, renounces its claim to control of the island.
25 November *International* *Relations*	The federal government announces a $1.5 billion forestry aid package. More than half the money will assist exporters hurt by the ongoing softwood lumber dispute with the U.S., with the remainder devoted to industry development initiatives. American officials, calling it another subsidy, see the package as an example of ongoing unfair trade practises.
6 December *International* *Relations*	Following a review showing subsidies to be lower than originally estimated, the United States Commerce Department cuts duties on Canadian softwood lumber and promises a partial refund of duties previously collected. Countervailing duties are lowered to 8.7 percent from 16.4

percent, while anti-dumping duties are brought down to 2.1 percent from 3.8 percent. Though Trade Minister Jim Peterson views the cut as a positive step, he intends to continue to press for restoration of fully unobstructed access to the American market.

13 December
International
Relations

U.S. Ambassador David Wilkins criticizes Prime Minister Paul Martin's anti-American campaign rhetoric in a luncheon speech to the Canadian Club in Ottawa. Martin, Wilkins claims, has repeatedly disparaged the United States throughout the campaign, noting comments on issues including climate change and softwood lumber. Martin defends his comments and vows to protect Canadian interests against anyone who might threaten them. Liberals are hoping the anti-American sentiment will bolster their electoral hopes.

Continuing a string of daily policy announcements, Conservative Leader Stephen Harper promises $5.3 billion in new military spending if his party is elected.

MUNICIPALITIES

1 February
Municipalities

An allocation plan for $5 billion in fuel tax revenues promised to municipal governments is announced by Federal Infrastructure and Communities Minister John Godfrey. Allocations will be made on a per capita basis with a base amount set for small municipalities. Though concerns are raised regarding the speed of the transfer process, the plan is generally well received.

15 April
Municipalities

The federal government signs an agreement with the province of British Columbia and the Union of British Columbia Municipalities regarding federal gas tax revenue sharing. The deal is the first of a series of such agreements struck with provincial governments across the country.

5 June
Municipalities

Speaking at the annual meeting of the Federation of Canadian Municipalities, Prime Minister Paul Martin promises increased municipal involvement in federal policy discussions and permanent sources of new municipal funding. Although the address contains few specific policy initiatives, mayors interpret the remarks as evidence of a new partnership between the federal and municipal governments. Municipal initiatives already undertaken by Martin include pre-budget consultations and gas tax revenue sharing.

7 November
Municipalities

Elections are held in 780 municipalities across Quebec. In Montreal, Gérald Tremblay is re-elected mayor, defeating Pierre Bourque and Richard Bergeron. As with his first election, Tremblay received strong support from Montreal Island suburbs, many of which voted to de-merge from the amalgamated City of Montreal on 1 January 2006. Andrée Boucher, an independent candidate running with a $5,000 budget, is elected mayor of Quebec City.

14 November
Municipalities

The final report of the Joint Ontario–City of Toronto Task Force to Review the City of Toronto Acts and Other Legislation is released. Based on a belief that the city is "more like a province than a municipality," the report recommends that Toronto be given more independent authority with respect to taxation and legislative powers. The City of Toronto Act, implementing the recommendations of the report, is expected to be tabled in December.

19 November
Municipalities

Sam Sullivan is elected Mayor of Vancouver, defeating Jim Green by a margin of fewer than 4,000 votes. Sullivan, a paraplegic, becomes the first physically impaired mayor in Canadian history. His campaign focused on fiscal responsibility and crime prevention.

14 December
Municipalities

The City of Toronto Act, designed to give the city additional powers and responsibilities in recognition of its special status, is unveiled by the province. Measures covered under the Act include additional means of taxation, legislative jurisdiction over development, and the ability to negotiate agreements directly with the federal government.

POST-SECONDARY EDUCATION

7 February
Ontario and Post Secondary Education

Ontario: A Leader in Learning, a panel report on the state of post-secondary education in Ontario, is released. The report recommends that the province's tuition freeze be lifted alongside substantial increases to institutional funding and bursary programs. Reaction to the report is mixed; though many experts praise its findings, several groups fear the impact of tuition deregulation on low-income students.

PROVINCIAL POLITICS

5 May
Quebec, Provincial Politics

A study released by Parti Québécois (PQ) finance critic Francois Legault concludes that sovereignty would improve the finances of the province. An update of a report for the 1991 Bélanger-Campeau commission, the analysis forecasts budget surpluses for a sovereign Quebec of $17.1 billion over five years. The province is currently forecasted to run a total deficit of $3.3 billion through 2010. Critics dismiss the result, saying that the study underestimates the share of the federal debt that an independent Quebec would be forced to assume. They further argue that the fiscal gains claimed in the study could be achieved without sovereignty if the federal government were to address the fiscal imbalance.

18 May
British Columbia, Provincial Politics

Gordon Campbell's Liberal Party is re-elected to government, winning 46 of 79 seats in the provincial legislature. Though the Liberals suffer a substantial loss from the 77 seats they had won in the 2001 election, they maintain a comfortable majority over the 33 seat New Democratic Party opposition. Campbell is satisfied with the result, acknowledging the value of a strong opposition to keep government in check. The Premier's campaign focused on his government's record of tax cuts, fiscal restraint and economic stimulus.

In a parallel referendum, an electoral reform proposal based on a "single transferable vote" ballot obtains 57 percent support, just short of the 60 percent needed for its implementation. The proposal was drafted by the Citizen's Assembly on Electoral Reform, a committee of randomly selected citizens tasked with evaluation of alternative electoral systems for the province. Campbell calls the results indicative of support for electoral reform and pledges further action on the issue.

26 May
Quebec, Provincial Politics

The National Assembly unanimously rejects the establishment of Islamic tribunals. Quebec thus becomes the first province to explicitly ban sharia law. Some Islamic communities have called for such tribunals under Canadian guarantees of multiculturalism; critics of sharia law argue that it discriminates against women. Ontario is expected to make a decision on sharia law shortly.

4 June
Quebec, Provincial Politics

Bernard Landry, despite obtaining 76 percent support in a leadership confidence vote, steps down as leader of the Parti Québécois. Landry argues that the leader of the party must have unequivocal support if the sovereignty movement is to succeed. The resignation reflects a rift between the moderates and hard liners within the party.

10–12 August
Provincial Politics

The Council of the Federation meets in Banff, Alberta. The highlight of the three-day meeting is a call on the federal government to restore the Canada Social Transfer to its 1994–95 level; the call is quickly rebuffed by federal finance minister Ralph Goodale who notes that transfer cuts have been offset by increases in federal expenditures on social services through other means. Further issues discussed by the premiers include pharmaceutical strategy, the fiscal imbalance, and barriers to internal trade.

25 August
Ontario, Provincial Politics

The Ontario Chamber of Commerce releases Phase One of *Fairness in Confederation*, a report on the province's fiscal deficit in relation to the rest of the country. The report, an affirmation of the existence of a disproportionately large and growing gap between what the province contributes to the federal government and what it receives, bolsters Premier Dalton McGuinty's argument for restructuring Canadian fiscal federalism. Prime Minister Paul Martin continues to deny the existence of any sort of imbalance.

11 September
Ontario, Provincial Politics

Premier Dalton McGuinty announces that the province will outlaw all forms of religious arbitration including but not restricted to Islamic sharia law. Backlash against proposals for sharia law-based tribunals led the province to review the 1991 Arbitration Act, which allowed limited religious dispute settlements in the province. Opponents of sharia law argue that such tribunals discriminate against women. Following Quebec, Ontario becomes the second province to publicly consider and reject the practise of sharia law.

12 September *Alberta, Provincial Politics*	Following strong provincial surpluses resulting from high energy prices, Premier Ralph Klein announces plans to send each Alberta resident a tax-free "prosperity cheque." The amount of the cheques is later announced to be $400 per person. Critics view the cheques as irresponsible spending of temporary revenues. Klein says that the cheques will continue in future years if energy revenues remain at current levels.
12 September *British Columbia, Provincial Politics*	The provincial Speech From the Throne announces that a second referendum on electoral reform will be held in 2008. A first referendum on the implementation of a Single Transferable Vote system, originally proposed by the Citizen's Assembly on Electoral Reform, failed to achieve the required 60 percent support in May. Further issues discussed in the speech include Aboriginal poverty and measures to encourage innovation in government policy.
29 September *Nova Scotia, Provincial Politics*	Premier John Hamm announces plans to retire. Hamm served as Premier for three terms; he is remembered for balancing the budget in 2004 and for reaching an agreement with the federal government regarding offshore energy revenues in January 2005. He will officially step down following the election of a successor at a Progressive Conservative leadership convention next year.
11 October *Ontario, Provincial Politics*	Greg Sorbara resigns his position as Minister of Finance following allegations of fraud during his time as a director of Royal Group Technologies Ltd. Sorbara was named in a search warrant concerning an as-of-yet unnamed transaction; he claims neither knowledge of nor involvement in any alleged incidents. RCMP officials exercised search warrants at Sorbara Group offices earlier in the day.
12 October *Ontario, Provincial Politics*	The provincial Speech from the Throne focuses primarily on the achievements of the governments from its first two years in office, highlighting investments in education, health care and the environment. Planned initiatives include measures to reduce high school dropout rates, revamping of the province's automobile emissions program, and passage of the City of Toronto Act. The speech is overshadowed by the previous day's resignation of Greg Sorbara.

15 November
Quebec, Provincial
Politics

André Boisclair wins the leadership of the Parti Québécois, easily defeating all other contenders with 54 percent of first ballot support. Boisclair's victory is seen as a major directional change for the party. The new leader's acceptance speech pledges to bridge divides both within the party, between hard-line and moderate sovereignists, and across the province. Throughout the campaign Boisclair drew criticism over past cocaine use.

SENATE

24 March
Senate

Prime Minister Paul Martin announces nine new appointments to the Senate, including former federal defense minister Art Eggleton and former general Roméo Dallaire. The appointments do not include any of the Alberta senators-in-waiting elected on 22 November 2004.

SOCIAL POLICY

1 March
Quebec and Social
Programming

The federal government signs an agreement allowing Quebec to operate its own parental leave program. Following a Supreme Court ruling saying that parental leave is outside federal jurisdiction, the agreement will allow Quebec to opt out of the federal employment insurance-based parental leave program and receive $750 million in annual funding for its own program. Federal officials insist that similar agreements will be offered to any other interested provinces.

28 July
Ontario and Social
Programming

Ontario unveils its "Best Start" plan towards the development of affordable child care in the province. The project seeks to create 25,000 new child care spaces over the next three years using federal funds allocated in the February budget. Under a May agreement, Ontario will receive $1.9 billion over five years in federal child care funding. Critics of the proposals argue government monies should be allocated exclusively to not-for-profit daycare centers.

28 October
Quebec and Social
Programming

Quebec signs an agreement with the federal government to receive $1.125 billion over five years in child care funding under the federal Early Learning and Child Care Initiative. The province becomes the first to sign an agreement under the initiative. The unconditional transfer is cited as an example of effective asymmetrical federalism.

SPONSORSHIP/GOMERY INQUIRY

8 February
Sponsorship

Former Prime Minister Jean Chrétien testifies before the Gomery inquiry. Chrétien defends the sponsorship program, arguing that the value of national unity trumps any organizational failures associated with the program's delivery. He denies having had any knowledge of mistakes or misappropriated funds.

10 February
Sponsorship

Paul Martin appears before the Gomery commission. He claims that his involvement in the sponsorship program as Finance Minster was reserved to approving budgets; he says he had no discussions regarding the organization or operation of the program. It is the first time in 130 years that a sitting Prime Minister has testified before a public inquiry.

21 April
Sponsorship

Paul Martin, in a rare event for a Canadian Prime Minister, addresses the country on television. It is the first such televised Prime Ministerial address since 1995. Responding to ongoing sponsorship scandal revelations emerging from testimony before the John Gomery-led inquiry, Martin apologizes for having allowed the scandal to occur during his time as Prime Minister, saying that he "should have been more vigilant." He lists the measures taken by his government to repair the damage from the scandal, including appointing the Gomery commission, firing Alfonso Gagliano, and promising to repay any monies found to have been illegitimately gained by the Liberal Party. Responding to calls for the defeat of the government over the sponsorship issue, however, he promises to call an election within 30 days of the release of the final Gomery report, arguing that Canadians should judge the government only once all necessary information is unearthed.

Opposition leaders are subsequently granted airtime to respond to Martin. Although Conservative leader Stephen Harper and Bloc Québécois leader Gilles Duceppe commit to defeating the government at the first available opportunity, New Democratic Party leader Jack Layton offers to support the budget if corporate tax cuts are removed in favour of increased social spending.

30 May
Sponsorship

Former Prime Minister Jean Chrétien withdraws a Federal Court application calling for the removal of Justice John Gomery as head of the commission of inquiry into the sponsorship scandal. The application was based on allegations of bias given comments made by Gomery in interviews over his time at the head of the inquiry. Chrétien's lawyers intend to reconsider the application following the release of Gomery's final report.

12 September
Sponsorship

Justice John Gomery announces a delay for the release of his final report into the sponsorship scandal. Originally planned for 15 December 2005, the final report is now expected to be released on 1 February 2006. Gomery cites the volume of submissions to the inquiry as the reason for the delay. A preliminary report is still expected for 1 November 2005.

1 November
Sponsorship

The first report from the commission of inquiry into the sponsorship scandal is tabled in Parliament. Justice John Gomery is scathing in his attack on what he calls an elaborate kickback scheme designed to funnel hundreds of thousands of dollars into the Quebec wing of the Liberal Party of Canada. He places final responsibility for the program on former Prime Minster Jean Chrétien, exonerating current Prime Minster Paul Martin of personal blame.

Martin reacts to the report by banishing ten individuals from the Liberal Party for life. Chrétien vows to challenge the report's findings in Federal Court, claiming that Justice Gomery was biased against him.

30 November
Sponsorship

Former Prime Minister Jean Chrétien files a legal challenge in Federal Court against Justice John Gomery's first inquiry report into the sponsorship scandal. According to the claim, Gomery was biased against Chrétien and based his findings on unreliable evidence. Chrétien had announced his intention to file the challenge at the time of the report's release.

SUPREME COURT

30 March *Supreme Court*	The Supreme Court rules on three challenges to the education language provisions of Quebec's Charter of the French Language (Bill 101). Though restrictions on access to English language education are ruled to not violate the Charter of Rights and Freedoms, the court compels the provincial government to be more flexible when deciding eligibility for English language schooling. It is further ruled that children enrolled in French immersion schooling by choice should not lose future eligibility for English language schooling.
26 April *Supreme Court*	Chief Justice of the Quebec Court of Appeal Michel Robert incites controversy by suggesting that sovereignists should be disqualified from holding top positions in the federal government. In an interview with the Montreal Gazette, Robert suggests that those who do not support the Canadian constitution should not be allowed to occupy roles upholding it. Robert rejects subsequent calls for his resignation over the comments.
29 September *Supreme Court*	The Supreme Court rules that the British Columbia government can sue tobacco companies for five decades worth of health care costs associated with smoking. British Columbia passed the Tobacco Damages and Health Care Costs Recovery Act in 2001 towards recovery of such costs; the court rejected the claim that the law was outside the province's jurisdiction. The ruling paves the way for tobacco lawsuits by other provinces.

Queen's Policy Studies
Recent Publications

The Queen's Policy Studies Series is dedicated to the exploration of major public policy issues that confront governments and society in Canada and other nations.

Our books are available from good bookstores everywhere, including the Queen's University bookstore (http://www.campusbookstore.com/). McGill-Queen's University Press is the exclusive world representative and distributor of books in the series. A full catalogue and ordering information may be found on their web site (http://mqup.mcgill.ca/).

School of Policy Studies

Emerging Approaches to Chronic Disease Management in Primary Health Care,
John Dorland and Mary Ann McColl (eds.), 2007
Paper ISBN 978-1-55339-130-2 Cloth ISBN 978-1-55339-131-9

Fulfilling Potential, Creating Success: Perspectives on Human Capital Development,
Garnett Picot, Ron Saunders and Arthur Sweetman (eds.), 2007
Paper ISBN 978-1-55339-127-2   Cloth ISBN 978-1-55339-128-9

Reinventing Canadian Defence Procurement: A View from the Inside, Alan S. Williams, 2006
Paper ISBN 0-9781693-0-1 (Published in association with Breakout Educational Network)

SARS in Context: Memory, History, Policy, Jacalyn Duffin and Arthur Sweetman (eds.), 2006
Paper ISBN 978-0-7735-3194-9 Cloth ISBN 978-0-7735-3193-2 (Published in association with McGill-Queen's University Press)

Dreamland: How Canada's Pretend Foreign Policy has Undermined Sovereignty, Roy Rempel, 2006
Paper ISBN 1-55339-118-7 Cloth ISBN 1-55339-119-5 (Published in association with Breakout Educational Network)

Canadian and Mexican Security in the New North America: Challenges and Prospects,
Jordi Díez (ed.), 2006   Paper ISBN 978-1-55339-123-4 Cloth ISBN 978-1-55339-122-7

Global Networks and Local Linkages: The Paradox of Cluster Development in an Open Economy, David A. Wolfe and Matthew Lucas (eds.), 2005
Paper ISBN 1-55339-047-4 Cloth ISBN 1-55339-048-2

Choice of Force: Special Operations for Canada, David Last and Bernd Horn (eds.), 2005
Paper ISBN 1-55339-044-X Cloth ISBN 1-55339-045-8

Force of Choice: Perspectives on Special Operations, Bernd Horn, J. Paul de B. Taillon, and David Last (eds.), 2004   Paper ISBN 1-55339-042-3 Cloth 1-55339-043-1

New Missions, Old Problems, Douglas L. Bland, David Last, Franklin Pinch, and Alan Okros (eds.), 2004   Paper ISBN 1-55339-034-2 Cloth 1-55339-035-0

The North American Democratic Peace: Absence of War and Security Institution-Building in Canada-US Relations, 1867-1958, Stéphane Roussel, 2004
Paper ISBN 0-88911-937-6 Cloth 0-88911-932-2

Implementing Primary Care Reform: Barriers and Facilitators, Ruth Wilson, S.E.D. Shortt and John Dorland (eds.), 2004   Paper ISBN 1-55339-040-7 Cloth 1-55339-041-5

Social and Cultural Change, David Last, Franklin Pinch, Douglas L. Bland, and Alan Okros (eds.), 2004   Paper ISBN 1-55339-032-6 Cloth 1-55339-033-4

Clusters in a Cold Climate: Innovation Dynamics in a Diverse Economy, David A. Wolfe and Matthew Lucas (eds.), 2004   Paper ISBN 1-55339-038-5 Cloth 1 55339-039-3

John Deutsch Institute for the Study of Economic Policy

Health Services Restructuring in Canada: New Evidence and New Directions, Charles M. Beach, Richard P. Chaykowksi, Sam Shortt, France St-Hilaire and Arthur Sweetman (eds.), 2006
Paper ISBN 978-1-55339-076-3 Cloth ISBN 978-1-55339-075-6

A Challenge for Higher Education in Ontario, Charles M. Beach (ed.), 2005
Paper ISBN 1-55339-074-1 Cloth ISBN 1-55339-073-3

Current Directions in Financial Regulation, Frank Milne and Edwin H. Neave (eds.),
Policy Forum Series no. 40, 2005   Paper ISBN 1-55339-072-5 Cloth ISBN 1-55339-071-7

Higher Education in Canada, Charles M. Beach, Robin W. Boadway and R. Marvin McInnis (eds.), 2005   Paper ISBN 1-55339-070-9 Cloth ISBN 1-55339-069-5

Financial Services and Public Policy, Christopher Waddell (ed.), 2004
Paper ISBN 1-55339-068-7 Cloth ISBN 1-55339-067-9

The 2003 Federal Budget: Conflicting Tensions, Charles M. Beach and Thomas A. Wilson (eds.), Policy Forum Series no. 39, 2004
Paper ISBN 0-88911-958-9 Cloth ISBN 0-88911-956-2

Our publications may be purchased at leading bookstores, including the Queen's University Bookstore (http://www.campusbookstore.com/), or can be ordered directly from: McGill-Queen's University Press, c/o Georgetown Terminal Warehouses, 34 Armstrong Avenue, Georgetown, Ontario L7G 4R9; Tel: (877) 864-8477; Fax: (877) 864-4272; E-mail: orders@gtwcanada.com

For more information about new and backlist titles from Queen's Policy Studies, visit the McGill-Queen's University Press web site at:
http://mqup.mcgill.ca/ OR to place an order, go to:
http://mqup.mcgill.ca/ordering.php

Institute of Intergovernmental Relations
Recent Publications

First Nations and the Canadian State: In Search of Coexistence, Alan C. Cairns, 2002 Kenneth R. MacGregor Lecturer, 2005   ISBN 1-55339-014-8

Political Science and Federalism: Seven Decades of Scholarly Engagement, Richard Simeon, 2000 Kenneth R. MacGregor Lecturer, 2002   ISBN 1-55339-004-0

The Institute's working paper series can be downloaded from our website www.iigr.ca